Testing Teacher Candidates

THE ROLE OF LICENSURE TESTS IN IMPROVING TEACHER QUALITY

Karen J. Mitchell, David Z. Robinson, Barbara S. Plake,
and Kaeli T. Knowles, editors

Committee on Assessment and Teacher Quality

Center for Education
Board on Testing and Assessment
Division of Behavioral and Social Sciences and Education

National Research Council

NATIONAL ACADEMY PRESS
Washington, DC

NATIONAL ACADEMY PRESS • 2101 Constitution Ave., N.W. • Washington, DC 20418

NOTICE: The project that is the subject of this report was approved by the Governing Board of the National Research Council, whose members are drawn from the councils of the National Academy of Sciences, the National Academy of Engineering, and the Institute of Medicine. The members of the committee responsible for the report were chosen for their special competences and with regard for appropriate balance.

This study was supported by the U.S. Department of Education (award R215U990004). Any opinions, findings, conclusions, or recommendations expressed in this publication are those of the author(s) and do not necessarily reflect the views of the organizations or agencies that provided support for this project.

Library of Congress Cataloging-in-Publication Data

National Research Council (U.S.). Committee on Assessment and Teacher Quality.
    Testing teacher candidates : the role of licensure tests in improving teacher quality / Committee on Assessment and Teacher Quality, Center for Education, Board on Testing and Assessment, Division on Behavioral and Social Sciences and Education, National Research Council ; Karen J. Mitchell ... [et al.], editors.
        p. cm.
Includes bibliographical references and index.
    ISBN 0-309-07420-7 (hardcover)
    1. Teaching—United States—Examinations. 2. Teachers—Certification—United States. I. Mitchell, Karen Janice. II. Title.
    LB1762 .N37 2001
    371.12—dc21
                                               2001004490

Additional copies of this report are available from the National Academy Press, 2101 Constitution Avenue, NW, Washington, DC 20418.

Call (800) 624-6242 or (202) 334-3313 (in the Washington metropolitan area).

This report is also available online at http://www.nap.edu.

Suggested citation: National Research Council. 2001. *Testing teacher candidates: The role of licensure tests in improving teacher quality.* Committee on Assessment and Teacher Quality, Mitchell, K.J., Robinson, D.Z., Plake, B.S., and Knowles, K.T., editors. Board on Testing and Assessment, Center for Education, Division of Behavioral and Social Sciences and Education, Washington, DC: National Academy Press.

Printed in the United States of America

THE NATIONAL ACADEMIES

National Academy of Sciences
National Academy of Engineering
Institute of Medicine
National Research Council

The **National Academy of Sciences** is a private, nonprofit, self-perpetuating society of distinguished scholars engaged in scientific and engineering research, dedicated to the furtherance of science and technology and to their use for the general welfare. Upon the authority of the charter granted to it by the Congress in 1863, the Academy has a mandate that requires it to advise the federal government on scientific and technical matters. Dr. Bruce M. Alberts is president of the National Academy of Sciences.

The **National Academy of Engineering** was established in 1964, under the charter of the National Academy of Sciences, as a parallel organization of outstanding engineers. It is autonomous in its administration and in the selection of its members, sharing with the National Academy of Sciences the responsibility for advising the federal government. The National Academy of Engineering also sponsors engineering programs aimed at meeting national needs, encourages education and research, and recognizes the superior achievements of engineers. Dr. Wm. A. Wulf is president of the National Academy of Engineering.

The **Institute of Medicine** was established in 1970 by the National Academy of Sciences to secure the services of eminent members of appropriate professions in the examination of policy matters pertaining to the health of the public. The Institute acts under the responsibility given to the National Academy of Sciences by its congressional charter to be an adviser to the federal government and, upon its own initiative, to identify issues of medical care, research, and education. Dr. Kenneth I. Shine is president of the Institute of Medicine.

The **National Research Council** was organized by the National Academy of Sciences in 1916 to associate the broad community of science and technology with the Academy's purposes of furthering knowledge and advising the federal government. Functioning in accordance with general policies determined by the Academy, the Council has become the principal operating agency of both the National Academy of Sciences and the National Academy of Engineering in providing services to the government, the public, and the scientific and engineering communities. The Council is administered jointly by both Academies and the Institute of Medicine. Dr. Bruce M. Alberts and Dr. Wm. A. Wulf are chairman and vice chairman, respectively, of the National Research Council.

COMMITTEE ON ASSESSMENT AND TEACHER QUALITY

Acknowledgments

The work of the Committee on Assessment and Teacher Quality benefited from the contributions and support of many people. The committee is grateful for their help and wise counsel.

The Office of Educational Research and Improvement, U.S. Department of Education, was the sponsor of this study, and the staff members of that office were generous with both advice and assistance. Terry Dozier, senior advisor on teaching to former Secretary of Education Richard Riley, provided information and guidance to the committee and made the project an important priority at the department. Thelma Leenhouts, project monitor, administered the contract and kept the committee informed of events and publications relevant to its work. Pat O'Connel Ross provided general oversight to the project.

The committee was also greatly aided by individuals from four state education agencies who participated in its meetings and helped committee members understand the complex issues involved in teacher licensure. Carolyn Maiden of the North Carolina Department of Education, Maureen Carvan of the Ohio Department of Education, Patricia Glenn of the Illinois Department of Education, and Raymond Pecheone of the Connecticut State Department of Education shared important insights and provided full and clear information about their states' licensing systems.

Education officials from other states gave very useful assistance in answering the committee's questions about their licensure systems, providing documentation, and checking the accuracy of this report with respect to their programs. Committee members appreciated the contributions of Judith Entwife of the Alaska State Department of Education, Mark McLean and Robert Carlson of the California Commission on Teacher Credentialing, Alison Westfall of the Idaho State Department of Education, Virginia Pilato of the Maryland State Department of Education, Marge Harouff of the Nebraska State Department of Education, Adell VanPatten-Gorny of the Wyoming State Department of Education, and John Nicholson of the Ohio State Department of Education.

The committee is grateful to the staff of the Educational Testing Service (ETS), who provided publications, technical documentation, and data on the Praxis series of tests. Drew Gitomer, Mari Pearlman, and Richard Tannenbaum gave generously of their time and assistance. They provided voluminous materials, conducted analyses, and answered many questions about ETS's teacher licensure tests and testing results. The committee was impressed with their expertise and professionalism.

Jean Miller of the Interstate New Teacher Assessment and Support Consortium and Richard Allen of National Evaluation Systems (NES) helped committee members understand their tests and the role of their testing organizations in teacher licensure. Officials from a number of states using tests developed by NES also spoke to the committee about their programs.

Developers of several innovative teacher assessment systems provided very useful information about their work and helped stimulate the committee's thinking about possible improvements to teacher licensure. Mary Diez of Alverno College and Ann Harman of the National Board for Professional Teaching Standards were particularly helpful.

Three recent teacher education graduates—Joycelyn Hagaans, Tesharra Starling, and VaShaun Harper from Albany State University—described for the committee their experience as test takers and provided an important perspective on the process. Joan Baratz-Snowden of the American Federation of Teachers and Nesa Cappelle of the National Education Association discussed testing issues with the committee from the perspective of their memberships.

The committee commissioned several papers to provide a range of views on evaluating licensure systems. Linda Crocker of the University of Florida, Mary Hatwood Futrell of George Washington University, Dan Goldhaber of the Urban Institute, Richard Jaeger of the University of North Carolina-Greensboro, P. Richard Jeanneret of Jeanneret and Associates, and Diana Pullin of Boston University were generous in sharing their thoughts and research.

The committee commissioned several annotated reviews of the research literature, all of which were extremely informative and helpful. Research on the validity of currently used teacher licensure tests was conducted by Amy Antani and Jennifer Zieleskiewicz of the Illinois Institute of Technology. Peter Youngs of the University of Wisconsin reviewed the research on relationships between teacher licensure tests and teacher performance. Daniel Silverman of the University of Pennsylvania reviewed the literature on teacher compensation and teacher supply. Kara Schmitt of the Michigan State Department of Education prepared a paper comparing credentialing examinations for professions other than teaching.

Richard Wright of Dartmouth University provided data on the disparate impact of licensure tests in a number of occupations.

The committee contracted with the Oscar and Luella Buros Center for Testing and the University of Nebraska to conduct reviews of the technical quality of teacher licensure tests. James Impara from the Buros Center headed this project and provided written reports, oral testimony, and ad hoc advice. The committee is very grateful for his help.

The committee owes special thanks to Michael Kolen from the University of Iowa, who provided expert advice on numerous topics, particularly test quality and test evaluation. He also drafted and reviewed material for the committee.

Andy Baumgartner of the William Robinson Center in Augusta, Georgia, and John Bruer of the James S. McDonnell Foundation were members of the committee in the early phases of the project but were unable to continue until the end. The committee is grateful for their important insights on teacher quality, teacher development, and teacher licensure.

Several committee members chaired topical subcommittees that took responsibility for overseeing individual chapters in the final report. Barbara Plake, Abigail Hughes, Mary Kennedy, Pamela Moss, and Kenneth Wolpin carried out these extra responsibilities with wisdom and energy. Barbara Plake also chaired committee meetings in my absence. I greatly appreciate the extra effort these individuals put in.

A number of former and current members of the Board on Testing and Assessment provided sage advice and expert guidance on an ongoing basis. In particular, Lauress Wise met frequently with the committee and provided thoughtful guidance. Carl Kaestle and Robert Hauser made very useful comments on the process.

Senior staff members of the National Research Council helped the committee move the project forward. Michael Feuer, executive director of the Center for Education, enthusiastically backed the project and lent his wisdom and advice at key stages. Pasquale DeVito, director of the Board on Testing and Assessment, provided substantive advice and assistance. Eugenia Grohman's knowledge and experience with the report review and committee processes were invaluable. Kirsten Sampson Snyder provided expert assistance on the review and production of the report.

The committee's staff worked extremely hard and skillfully to help produce this report. Karen Mitchell, Kaeli Knowles, Judith Koenig, and Robert Rothman helped ensure that the meetings were informative and productive and developed numerous drafts and revisions. Dorothy Majewski, senior project assistant, handled the logistics of the report with indefatigable competence and good cheer.

This report has been reviewed in draft form by individuals chosen for their diverse perspectives and technical expertise, in accordance with procedures approved by the Report Review Committee of the National Research Council. The purpose of this independent review is to provide candid and critical comments that will assist the institution in making the published report as sound as possible and to ensure that the report meets institutional standards for objectivity, evidence, and responsiveness to the study charge. The review comments and draft manuscript remain confidential to protect the integrity of the deliberative process.

We thank the following individuals for their participation in the review of this report: Joan Baratz-Snowden, American Federation of Teachers; Pascal D. Forgione, Jr., Austin Independent School District; Claude Goldenberg, California State University, Long Beach; Daniel Goldhaber, The Urban Institute; Edward H. Haertel, Stanford University; Asa G. Hilliard III, Georgia State University; Janis Lariviere, University of Texas, Austin; Robert L. Linn, University of Colorado; Paul Sackett, University of Minnesota; and Dan B. Walker, San Jose State University.

Although the reviewers listed above provided many constructive comments and suggestions, they were not asked to endorse the conclusions or recommendations nor did they see the final draft of the report before its release. The review of this report was overseen by Richard Murnane, Harvard University, and Duncan Luce, University of California, Irvine. Appointed by the National Research Council, they were responsible for making certain that an independent examination of the report was carried out in accordance with institutional procedures and that all review comments were carefully considered. Responsibility for the final content of this report rests entirely with the authoring panel and the institution.

This book is dedicated to the memory of Richard M. Jaeger, whose intellect, dedication, and friendship were rare gifts to the committee, the board, and the educational measurement community all over the world.

David Z. Robinson, *Chair*
Committee on Assessment and Teacher Quality

Contents

BACKGROUND PAPERS PROVIDED TO THE COMMITTEE*

*These background papers are not printed in this volume but are available online. Go to *http://www.nap.edu* and search for Testing Teacher Candidates.

Executive Summary

Americans have adopted a reform agenda for their schools that calls for excellence in teaching and learning (Goals 2000: Educate America Act of 1994, P.L. 103-227; Improving America's Schools Act, 1994, P.L. 103-328; Council of Chief State School Officers, 1998). School officials across the nation are hard at work targeting instruction at high levels for all students. Gaps remain, however, between the nation's educational aspirations and student achievement (Jencks and Phillips, 1998; Rothstein, 1998; U.S. Department of Education, 1996b, 1997a, 1997b, 1997c, 1998b, 1999a). To address these gaps, policy makers have recently focused on the qualifications of teachers and the preparation of teacher candidates (National Commission on Teaching and America's Future, 1996; U.S. Department of Education, 1999b).

Increasingly, states are testing candidates who want to become teachers. Forty-two states require teacher candidates to pass one or more tests to earn a license. States use licensure tests for admission to teacher education, as a condition of graduation, and for the initial licensure of teachers. Failure rates on current tests are not insubstantial, particularly for racial/ethnic minority candidates. These tests have significant consequences for teacher candidates and potentially for America's students and schools.

Teacher licensure tests also play a critical role in the recently enacted Teacher Quality Enhancement Grants for States and Partnerships (Title II). The law seeks to improve teacher quality. One of the goals of the new law is to use teacher licensure tests to hold higher education institutions and states accountable for the quality of teacher preparation and licensing. The law requires states to issue report cards on their tests and licensure policies, to identify low-performing

1

teacher preparation programs, to report statewide passing rates on licensure tests for their teacher candidates, and to report the numbers of individuals teaching who have waivers of state licensure requirements. States are also required to report the passing rates of candidates at each teacher education institution and, based on these, to rank teacher education programs or place them in quartiles. The law requires teacher education institutions to report on the quality of their teacher preparation programs, to report their students' passing rates on state teacher licensure tests, to compare the institutions' passing rates to the state's average passing rates, and to indicate whether their programs have been designated as low performing.

The law's requirements create a mechanism that could limit federal funding to teacher preparation programs from which states have withdrawn approval or funding because the programs are low performing. The law prohibits these programs from enrolling students who receive federal financial aid under Title IV of the Higher Education Act. The institutions also are ineligible to receive professional development funds under the law. The law's provisions have met with notable resistance from some states and higher-education institutions that question whether its requirements provide a sound basis for determining the quality of teacher preparation and licensure programs.

THE COMMITTEE'S CHARGE

The importance of efforts to improve teaching quality and the difficulty of this work recently led the U.S. Department of Education to request that the National Academy of Sciences empanel the Committee on Assessment and Teacher Quality under the aegis of the Board on Testing and Assessment. In early 1999 the committee was asked to examine the appropriateness and technical quality of teacher licensure tests currently in use and to consider alternatives for developing and assessing beginning teacher competence. The committee also examined the merits of using licensure test results to hold institutions of higher education and states accountable for the quality of teacher preparation and licensure.

CONCLUSIONS AND RECOMMENDATIONS

Do Current Tests Measure Beginning Teacher Competence Appropriately and in a Technically Sound Way?

Defining Competent Beginning Teaching

Definitions of what teachers should know and be able to do have changed over time as society's values have changed, and they will continue to do so. The job of teaching students to learn and use new information, develop and apply skills, and think critically is highly complex and demanding. Teachers need to motivate and engage all students, including students from varied backgrounds and those with different learning and language needs. In addition to being responsible for student learning, teachers are expected to provide safe and nurturing classrooms, to serve as good role models, and to engage parents and the community in the business of their schools. Teachers need a wide range of knowledge, skills, abilities, and dispositions to perform these many complex tasks.

There is no single agreed-upon definition of what competencies a beginning teacher should have. Different professional organizations and many states have recently developed standards for teachers. The fact that different states have affiliations with these national and regional standards development efforts suggests some agreement between states about standards for teacher competence. Given that states have different educational standards for students, have teacher candidate pools with different characteristics, and that licensing of teachers is a state responsibility, it is not surprising that there is some variation in the knowledge and skills that states seek for beginning teachers.

Designing Tests for Initial Licensure

The primary goal of licensing beginning teachers is to ensure that all students have competent teachers. Teacher licensing is under the authority of individual states. There are 51 unique licensure systems in the United States; they share some commonalties, however. As in other professions, teacher licensing relies on more than tests to judge whether candidates have the knowledge, skills, abilities, and dispositions to practice responsibly. Teacher candidates generally must fulfill education requirements, successfully complete practice teaching, and receive the recommendations of their preparing institutions. These requirements help ensure that a broad range of competencies are considered in licensing new teachers.

Initial teacher licensure tests are designed to identify candidates with some of the knowledge and skills needed for minimally competent beginning practice. The tests currently used measure basic skills, general knowledge, content knowledge, and knowledge of teaching strategies. They are designed to separate teacher candidates who are at least minimally competent in the areas assessed from those who are not. Initial teacher licensure tests do not provide information to distinguish moderately qualified from highly qualified teacher candidates nor are they designed to test all of the competencies relevant to beginning practice.

States decide whether and what tests to use to license beginning teachers. Each of the 42 states that require tests uses a different combination of them, uses them at different points in a candidate's education, and sets its own passing scores. Several hundred different initial licensure tests are currently in use. Two test developers—Educational Testing Service (ETS) and National Evaluation Systems (NES)—develop the vast majority of these tests.

Conclusions

- Because a teacher's work is complex, even a set of well-designed tests cannot measure all of the prerequisites of competent beginning teaching. Current paper-and-pencil tests provide only some of the information needed to evaluate the competencies of teacher candidates.
- States have gradually adopted tests for teacher licensure, and test developers have made various tests available over time. Therefore, it is not surprising that states have adopted a variety of tests to license beginning teachers.
- Appropriate, technically sound tests are difficult and costly to develop. Collaborations among states participating in the Interstate New Teacher Assessment and Support Consortium and other states, professional associations, and test developers bring the intellectual and financial resources of several organizations to this difficult work.

Recommendations

- It is crucial that states use multiple forms of evidence in making decisions about teacher candidates. Licensure systems should be designed to rely on a comprehensive but parsimonious set of high-quality indicators.
- States, test developers, and professional organizations should continue exploring joint development of initial teacher licensing tests for the knowledge and skill areas they have in common. Federal and state governments and private organizations should appropriate funds to support this kind of collaboration.

Making Decisions About Candidates Based on Licensure Tests

States set passing scores on licensure tests based on judgments about the levels of knowledge and skill needed for minimally competent beginning teaching. Although many states rely on commonly used standard-setting procedures, there is little documentation about these procedures and how states actually use this information in arriving at a final decision about passing scores. In attempts to raise teacher standards, some states have recently raised their passing scores on particular tests. Some report having set passing scores that are higher than those of other states.

On all of the tests the committee reviewed, minority candidates had lower passing rates than nonminority candidates on their initial testing attempts. Though differences between the passing rates of candidate groups eventually decrease because many unsuccessful test takers retake and pass the tests, eventual passing rates for minority candidates are still lower than those for nonminority test takers.

Initial licensure tests are only one factor influencing the supply of new teachers. The quality and size of the pool of new teachers depend on many things, including recruiting efforts, other licensing requirements, labor market forces, licensing reciprocity, teacher salaries, and the conditions under which teachers work.

Conclusions

- States differ in how high they set passing scores. The committee does not know the extent to which this variation in passing scores reflects differences among states in standard-setting methods; state teaching and learning standards; the characteristics of applicant pools; or different concerns about measurement error, teacher quality, or teacher supply.
- To the extent that the tests provide accurate measurements, setting higher passing scores would be expected to increase the proportion of teacher candidates in the hiring pool who are competent in the knowledge and skills measured by the tests, although higher passing scores will tend to lower the number of candidates who pass the test. To the extent that test scores have measurement error, setting higher passing scores could eliminate competent candidates.
- Reducing the number of new licensed teachers could require districts to make difficult choices, such as hiring uncredentialed teachers, increasing class sizes, or increasing salaries to attract licensed teachers from other districts and states.
- The lower passing rates for minority teacher candidates on current licensure tests pose problems for schools and districts in seeking a qualified and diverse teaching force. Setting substantially higher passing scores on licensure tests is likely to reduce the diversity of the teacher applicant pool, further adding to the difficulty of obtaining a diverse school faculty.

Recommendations

- States should follow professionally accepted standard-setting methods and document the methods they use to set passing scores on initial licensure tests. This documentation should describe the work of standard-setting panels and the basis on which policy decisions were made by the officials setting the final passing scores. Documentation should be publicly available to users and other interested parties.
- If states raise passing scores as a way to increase the competence of new teachers, they should examine not only the impact on teacher competence but also the effects of raising passing scores on applications to teacher education programs, on the supply of new teachers, and on the diversity of the teaching force.

Evaluating Licensing Tests

Solid technical characteristics and fairness are key to the effective use of tests. The work of measurement specialists, test users, and policy makers suggests criteria for judging the appropriateness and technical quality of initial teacher licensure tests. The committee drew on these to develop criteria it believes users should aspire to in developing and evaluating initial teacher licensure tests. The committee used these evaluation criteria to evaluate a sample of five widely used tests produced by ETS. The tests the committee reviewed met most of its criteria for technical quality, although there were some areas for improvement. The committee also attempted to review a sample of NES tests. Despite concerted and repeated efforts, though, the committee was unable to obtain sufficient information on the technical characteristics of tests produced by NES and thus could draw no conclusions about their technical quality.

Conclusions

- The committee's criteria for judging test quality include the following: tests should have a statement of purpose; systematic processes should be used in deciding what to test and in assuring balanced and adequate coverage of these competencies; test materials should be tried out and analyzed before operational decisions are made; test administration and scoring should be uniform and fair; test materials and results should be protected from corruptibility; standard-setting procedures should be systematic and well documented; test results should be consistent across test forms and scorers; information about tests and scoring should be available to candidates; technical documentation should be accessible for public and professional review; validity evidence should be gathered and presented; costs and feasibility should be considered in test development and selection; and the long-term consequences of licensing tests should be monitored and examined.
- The profession's standards for educational testing say that information sufficient to evaluate the appropriateness and technical adequacy of tests should be made available to potential test users and other interested parties. The committee considers the lack of sufficient technical information made available by NES and the states to evaluate NES-developed tests to be problematic and a concern. It is also significant because NES-developed tests are administered to very large numbers of teacher candidates.
- The initial licensure tests currently in use rely almost exclusively on content-related evidence of validity. Few, if any, developers are collecting evidence about how test results relate to other relevant measures of candidates' knowledge, skills, and abilities.
- It is important to collect validity data that go beyond content-related

validity evidence for initial licensing tests. However, conducting high-quality research of this kind is complex and costly. Examples of relevant research include investigations of the relationships between test results and other measures of candidate knowledge and skills or on the extent to which tests distinguish candidates who are at least minimally competent from those who are not.

- The processes used to develop current tests, the empirical studies of test content, and common-sense analyses suggest the importance of at least some of what is measured by these initial licensure tests. Beginning teachers should know how to read, write, and do basic mathematics; they should know the content areas they teach.

- Little research has been conducted on the extent to which scores on current teacher licensure tests relate to other measures of beginning teacher competence. Much of the research that has been conducted suffers from methodological problems that interfere with making strong conclusions about the results. This makes it hard to determine what effect licensure tests might have on improving the actual competence of beginning teachers.

Recommendations

- States should strive to use the committee's or similar evaluation criteria when developing and evaluating tests for use in initial teacher licensure systems.

- When states are selecting from among existing tests for initial teacher licensure, they should obtain and carefully consider field test and any available operational data regarding reliability, validity, cost/feasibility, and fairness as part of their decision-making process. When states are developing licensing tests, they should collect and weigh this evidence in making decisions about the final form of the test and its use.

- The degree of disparate impact should be an important consideration when states are deciding which licensure test to use for various decisions about candidate competence.

- States and test developers should provide technical documentation to users, scholars, and the public about the reliability, validity, and disparate impact of their tests. Field test or any available operational data should be used to document the technical quality of tests.

- The technical information used in deciding on a test normally should be made publicly available before tests are actually used to make decisions about individuals. If technical data are not provided by the end of the first administration year, states should not use information from these tests to make licensing decisions.

- State agencies contracting for test development should specify the technical information they require. Because of the importance of these data for the technical evaluation of the tests, state agencies should request sufficient technical data and timely delivery of documentation. State agencies should ensure their clear authority to release this information to users and others for the purpose of objectively evaluating the technical quality of the tests, the resulting scores, and the interpretations based on them.

- States should arrange for independent evaluations of their current tests and teacher licensure systems and make the results of these independent examinations of their systems available for outside review.
- The committee encourages the federal government and others to conduct research on the extent to which teacher licensure tests distinguish between beginning teachers who are at least minimally competent and those who are not regarding the knowledge and skills the tests are intended to measure. This research should include evidence on a broad range of teacher competencies. Such research is likely to improve the development of teacher licensure tests. Within the limits of privacy law, states should make their raw data available to the research community to facilitate development and validity research on initial teacher licensure tests.

Should Teacher Licensure Tests Be Used to Hold States and Institutions of Higher Education Accountable for the Quality of Teacher Preparation and Licensure?

Holding Programs Accountable

A new federal law called the Teacher Quality Enhancement Grants for States and Partnerships (Title II) was enacted in 1998 to achieve four goals: to improve student achievement; to improve the quality of the current and future teaching force by improving the preparation of prospective teachers and enhancing professional development activities; to hold institutions of higher education accountable for preparing beginning teachers to have the necessary teaching skills and to be highly competent in the academic content areas in which they plan to teach; and to recruit highly qualified individuals, including individuals from other occupations.

Conclusions
- It is reasonable to hold teacher education institutions accountable for the quality of their teacher preparation programs.
- By their design and as currently used, initial teacher licensure tests fall short of the intended policy goals for their use as accountability tools and as levers for improving teacher preparation and licensing programs. The public reporting and accountability provisions of Title II may encourage erroneous conclusions about the quality of teacher preparation.

- Although the percentage of graduates who pass initial licensure tests provides an entry point for evaluating an institution's quality, simple comparisons among institutions based on their passing rates are difficult to interpret for many reasons. These include the fact that institutions have different educational missions and recruiting practices, their students have different entry-level qualifications, teacher education programs have different entry and exit testing requirements, and programs have different procedures for determining the institutional affiliations of their candidates. By themselves, passing rates on licensure tests do not provide adequate information on which to judge the quality of teacher education programs.
- Simple comparisons of passing rates across states are misleading. Many states use different tests for initial licensure or set different passing scores on the same tests. States have different policies about when a test is given or what decisions it supports.
- To fairly and accurately judge the quality of teacher education programs, federal and state officials need data on a wide variety of program characteristics from multiple sources. Other indicators of program quality might include assessment data for students in relation to course and program benchmarks, employer evaluations, and district or state evaluations of beginning teaching. Other indicators might include information on course requirements and course quality, measures of the amount and quality of field experiences, and evidence of opportunities to work with students with special learning needs and students with diverse backgrounds. Data on the qualifications of program faculty, the allocation of resources, and the adequacy of facilities might be considered. The qualifications of students at entry to teacher education programs also should be included.

Recommendations

- States should not use passing rates on initial licensure tests as the sole basis for deciding whether their teacher education programs are low performing.
- States should report multiple indicators of the quality of teacher preparation programs to federal officials in complying with Title II.
- The federal government should not use passing rates on initial teacher licensing tests as the sole basis for comparing states or teacher education programs or for withholding funds, imposing other sanctions, or rewarding teacher education programs.
- Federal officials should continue to collect the state and school data required by Title II but should not withhold funds from, otherwise sanction, or reward programs until a study is mounted of the multiple and varied data that might be used to judge the quality of teacher preparation and licensure.

How Can Innovative Measures of Beginning Teacher Competence Help Improve Teacher Quality?

Examining New Assessments

Several new and developing teacher assessment systems use a variety of testing and assessment methods, including assessments of teaching performance. These include multiple measures of candidates' knowledge, skills, abilities, and dispositions. In these systems, assessments are integrated with professional development and with ongoing support of prospective or beginning teachers.

Conclusion

- New and developing assessment systems warrant investigation for addressing the limits of current initial teacher licensure tests and for improving teacher licensure. The benefits, costs, and limitations of these systems should be investigated.

Recommendations

- Research and development of broad-based indicators of teacher competence, not limited to test-based evidence, should be undertaken; indicators should include assessments of teaching performance in the classroom, of candidates' ability to work effectively with students with diverse learning needs and cultural backgrounds and in a variety of settings, and of competencies that more directly relate to student learning.
- When initial licensure tests are used, they should be part of a coherent developmental system of preparation, assessment, and support that reflects the many features of teacher competence.

1

Introduction

Americans have adopted a reform agenda for their schools that calls for excellence in teaching and learning (Goals 2000: Educate America Act of 1994, P.L. 103-227; Improving America's Schools Act, 1994, P.L. 103-328; Council of Chief State School Officers, 1998). School officials across the nation are hard at work targeting instruction at high levels for all students. Gaps remain, however, between the nation's educational aspirations and student achievement (Jencks and Phillips, 1998; Rothstein, 1998; U.S. Department of Education, 1996b, 1997a, 1997b, 1997c, 1998b, 1999a). To address these gaps, policy makers have recently focused on the qualifications of teachers and the preparation of teacher candidates (National Commission on Teaching and America's Future, 1996; U.S. Department of Education, 1999b).

These issues took center stage in the 2000 presidential election. George W. Bush became president with a promise to put education first and leave no child behind (2001). He unveiled a series of proposals to increase student achievement and improve teacher quality. President Bush echoed his predecessor's call for improving the quality of teachers. In his 1996 State of the Union Address, President Clinton called for "dedicated, outstanding teachers, who know their subject matter, are effectively trained, and know how to teach to high standards." His Secretary of Education, Richard Riley, highlighted aspects of a revised Elementary and Secondary Education Act during his annual state of American Education speech (1999). He called on states and school districts to address teacher quality and make improvements in the recruitment, preparation, and training of teachers. The 105th Congress also highlighted teacher preparation and initial teacher licensure as critical targets for improvement. They called for the use of tests to license beginning teachers and the creation of incentives and sanctions to change teacher education. These two policy targets are among those addressed by a new federal law (P.L. 105-244).

These recent initiatives and the new administration provide an opportunity for the nation to clarify its thinking about the preparation of teacher candidates to meet current and upcoming demands for additional teachers. They raise questions about the appropriateness and soundness of current measures of teacher competence and about the roles of federal and state governments and higher education in assuring the quality of teacher preparation and teacher licensure.

PROBLEM STATEMENT

Educational Reform

In 1996, President Clinton, the nation's governors, and American business professionals met at the National Education Summit to renew their commitment to achieving high academic standards for American students and schools (Achieve, 1997). States responded by developing and strengthening their content and performance standards for student learning and by adopting standards-based tests to help drive and assess reform. Threaded throughout these reforms was the important promise to educate all students at high levels.

Innovators and educators across the nation are now implementing and refining these reforms (U.S. Department of Education, 1999b; National Research Council, 1999c; Council of Chief State School Officers, 1998; Baker and Linn, 1997; Massell et al., 1997). They have begun to link their standards for student learning to more challenging standards for teachers and to the objectives of teacher education (Cohen and Spillane, 1993; Smith and O'Day, 1991; National Association of State Directors of Teacher Education and Certification, 2000b). Darling-Hammond et al. (1999:2) explain what these reforms require of teachers:

> This new mission for education requires substantially more knowledge and radically different skills for teachers. . . . In order to create bridges between common, challenging curriculum goals and individual learners' experiences and needs, teachers must understand cognition and the many different pathways to learning. They must understand child development and pedagogy as well as the structures of subject areas and a variety of alternatives for assessing learning . . . If all children are to be effectively taught, teachers must be prepared to address the substantial diversity in the experiences children bring with them to school—the wide range of languages, cultures, exceptionalities, learning styles, talents, and intelligences that in turn [require] an equally rich and varied repertoire of teaching strategies. In addition, teaching for universal learning demands a highly developed ability to discover what children know and can do, as well as how they think and how they learn, and to match learning and performance opportunities to the needs of individual children.

Five years ago the National Commission on Teaching and America's Future (1996:5) developed an agenda for improved teaching. In *What Matters Most: Teaching for America's Future*, the commission called for teachers with the knowledge and skills needed to help all students reach high and rigorous standards. The commission set a goal for the United States. By the year 2006, the nation must "provide all students in the country with what should be their educational birthright: access to competent, caring, and qualified teachers."

To help reach this goal, the commission asked for sweeping changes in teacher education, licensure, and support, as well as reform of teacher recruitment and retention; reform of teacher preparation; mentoring and support systems for new teachers; and innovative teacher evaluation, reward, and development systems. These recommendations and those of earlier groups, including the National Council for the Accreditation of Teacher Education (NCATE, 1992), the Interstate New Teacher Assessment and Support Consortium (INTASC, 1992), and the National Board for Professional Teaching Standards (NBPTS, 1994), have accelerated efforts to reform teacher preparation and assessment.

State Initiatives

These national efforts parallel work at the state level. States have been examining and bolstering their teacher standards and licensure systems (U.S. Department of Education, 1999b; National Association of State Directors of Teacher Education and Certification, 2000b). Many states have reexamined the basic skills, general knowledge, subject matter knowledge, and knowledge about pedagogy they want beginning teachers to master (Council of Chief State School Officers, 2000). Many have also adopted or are developing challenging new teacher standards. Over half of the states have joined together under the auspices of INTASC to develop model policies for reforming teacher preparation and licensure. Many states are in the process of aligning newly developed teaching standards with their licensure requirements, including coursework requirements, requirements for disciplinary majors or minors, and student teaching criteria. Some states also are aligning their licensure tests with these challenging new standards.

Forty-two states currently use tests in licensing beginning teachers to support varied decisions about teacher candidates. States use teacher licensure tests as a standard for entry into teacher training programs or student teaching, to certify successful completion of teacher training, or to control the initial licensure of teachers (National Association of State Directors of Teacher Education and Certification, 2000b). Every state selects its own tests and establishes its own passing scores.

There are several hundred teacher licensure tests currently in use. They vary from basic skills tests in reading, writing, and mathematics to tests of subject matter knowledge, general knowledge, and knowledge of teaching strategies. Test formats vary from multiple-choice questions to open-ended questions to performance assessments. Like licensure tests in other professional fields, these tests are designed to identify candidates with the knowledge and skills that experts believe are minimally necessary.

These tests have significant consequences for teacher candidates and potentially for America's students and schools. On some of the more widely used initial licensure tests, average failure rates are approximately 15 percent (Gitomer et al., 1999). Average failure rates are higher, however, for racial/ethnic minority applicants, in some states, and in some subject areas (Gitomer et al., 1999; U.S. Department of Education, 2000a).

Despite their importance and widespread use, little is known about the impact of these tests on states' recent efforts to improve teaching and learning. Little information about the technical soundness of teacher licensure tests appears in the published literature. Little research exists on the extent to which licensure tests identify candidates with the knowledge and skills necessary to be minimally competent beginning teachers. Information is needed about the soundness and technical quality of the tests that states use to license their teachers.

Federal Initiatives

In addition to professional and state efforts, the federal government is taking a more active role in teacher quality efforts than it did in the past. In 1998 Congress amended Title II of the Higher Education Act to provide funds for teacher quality initiatives proposed by states and partnerships of higher education institutions, high-need school districts, and other agencies. Under Title II new provisions call for reform of teacher preparation, reform of licensure requirements, enhanced teacher recruitment efforts, and alternatives to traditional teacher education. The law also lays out public reporting and accountability requirements for states and teacher education programs. It creates a mechanism that limits federal funding to teacher preparation programs from which states have withdrawn approval or financial support. (See Appendix A for the text of Title II, the Teacher Quality Enhancement Grants to States and Partnerships.)

Under the reporting and evaluation provisions of Title II, every state is required to create a system for identifying and helping low-performing teacher preparation programs. The law requires states to report annually their low-performing institutions and those at risk of being designated as such. The law requires states to document the passing rates of candidates at each teacher education institution and, based on these, to rank or place the state's teacher education programs in quartiles. The law also requires states to issue report cards describing their test and other licensure requirements, reporting the statewide passing rates of their teacher candidates, and reporting the number of individuals teaching with waivers of state licensure requirements.

Title II requires teacher education programs to separately provide institutional reports on the quality of their teacher preparation efforts, including passing rates on state teacher licensure tests, comparisons of institutional results with state average passing rates, an indication of whether the institution has been designated as low performing, and information on teacher education requirements. All of this information is to be included in institutional publications, including promotional materials, school catalogs, and information sent to prospective employers. Low-performing institutions from which states have withdrawn approval or support are prohibited from enrolling students who receive financial aid under Title IV of the Higher Education Act. They are also ineligible to receive professional development funds under the law.

These requirements face opposition from states and higher education institutions (Interstate New Teacher Assessment and Support Consortium, 1999; American Association of State Colleges and Universities, 1999, 2000a; American Association of Colleges for Teacher Education, 2000; Teacher Education Accreditation Council, 2000). Critics question whether the requirements of the law provide a sound basis for determining the quality of teacher education programs (Blair, 1999). They also question whether passing rates on initial teacher licensure tests should weigh so heavily in reports of program quality. They argue that teacher licensure tests provide only a limited view of program quality and that passing rates on licensure tests are not comparable across states and institutions (American Association of State Colleges and Universities, 2000a; American Council on Education, 1999).

COMMITTEE'S CHARGE AND STUDY METHODS

Because of these important efforts and the difficulty of this work, the U.S. Department of Education requested that the National Academy of Sciences investigate the technical, educational, and legal issues surrounding the use of current tests in licensing beginning teachers and to consider alternative measures of beginning competence. The Committee on Assessment and Teacher Quality was convened in 1999 under the aegis of the Board on Testing and Assessment. In response to its charge, the committee sought to answer three questions:

- Do current initial teacher licensure tests measure beginning teacher competence appropriately and in a technically sound way?
- Should teacher licensure tests be used to hold states and institutions of higher education accountable for the quality of teacher preparation and licensure?
- How can innovative measures of beginning teacher competence help improve teacher quality?

This report presents the committee's findings, conclusions, and recommendations.

National Research Council Study Process

The members of the Committee on Assessment and Teacher Quality represent a broad range of expertise, experience, and perspectives. The committee was composed and procedures were instituted to achieve balance, independence, and protection against bias. Members represent the fields of teaching, teacher education, measurement, licensure, economics, and law.

The committee worked over the course of 20 months to define its scope, review the relevant scientific literature, study testing and licensure program practices, and commission test reviews and papers. The committee issued an interim report in 2000. It then deliberated and worked toward consensus on the conclusions and recommendations presented here. The committee's work was conducted with the oversight of the Board on Testing and Assessment and the National Academy of Sciences.

Nature of the Evidence

In conducting its work, the committee collected information and data related to policies, practice, and research on initial teacher licensure. It examined the published research literature on teacher quality, teacher testing, and professional licensure; reviewed state and federal policies on licensure testing and teacher licensure; and examined current licensure tests, their uses, and states' policies on setting passing scores on those tests. The committee also sought data on the quality of current tests, the relationships between test results and teacher competence, and the consequences of current tests and licensure systems. The committee looked at examples of innovative teacher licensure programs in the United States and at licensure in other professions. It gathered information on teacher licensure in Germany, Japan, Canada, Australia, New Zealand, France, and the United Kingdom to fuel its thinking about alternative systems. It reviewed licensure programs in nursing, physical therapy, accounting, social work, engineering, architecture, land surveying, law, and medicine.

The committee sponsored a number of activities, including a workshop on teacher licensure in selected states. It solicited testimony from state policy makers about INTASC and NBPTS efforts, and from staff of the leading test development agencies. The committee interviewed teacher candidates; commissioned papers on evaluation criteria for teacher licensure tests; consulted with and commissioned analyses from experts in measurement, licensure, economics, and law; and commissioned bibliographical reviews on test validity issues in initial teacher licensure and on teacher supply. It also sought technical documentation from test developers and commissioned an evaluation of selected tests by the Oscar and Luella Buros Center for Testing.

Discussion of the state of the evidentiary base on teacher licensure testing provides an important prelude to the chapters that follow. As suggested in the beginning of this chapter, policy and practice on teacher licensure testing in the United States are nascent and evolving. Education policy makers and practitioners are hard at work implementing broad education reforms and reform in teacher development, assessment, and support. Policy and practice are changing faster than their effects can be examined. Present programs have not been stable long enough to be examined for their intended and unintended effects. Hence, the data the committee consulted regarding current programs and policies are incomplete.

Furthermore, researchers hold differing views on the evidence that is relevant, necessary, and sufficient to judge the appropriateness and technical quality of teacher licensure tests. Some view currently collected data on the technical characteristics of licensure tests as sufficient (Jaeger, 1999; Stoker and Impara, 1995; Popham, 1992); others do not (Haertel, 1991; Haney et al., 1987; Pullin, 1999; Sireci and Green, 2000). Some consider it impossible to collect data on the relationships between initial teacher licensure tests and teacher competence; others consider it difficult but not impossible. Research is hampered by the difficulty of defining and constructing measures of teacher competence, the difficulty of defining and constructing measures of minimally competent beginning teaching, and the absence of information on teaching proficiency for many individuals who fail licensing tests.

The paucity of data and these methodological challenges made the committee's examination of teacher licensure testing difficult. There were a number of questions the committee wanted to answer but could not, either because they were beyond the scope of this study, the evidentiary base was inconclusive, or the committee's time and resources were insufficient. These included questions about:

• whether current tests really separate out competent from incompetent beginning teachers;
• whether present tests and passing scores are too easy or too hard;
• whether current licensure requirements make sense across the different levels of schooling (K-5, 6-8, 9-12) and subject areas;
• whether there is as much variation across states in the knowledge and skills needed to be minimally competent as differences in state passing scores suggest;
• whether initial teacher licensure tests appropriately or inappropriately limit supply, both in the aggregate and for minority candidates; and
• whether teacher licensure systems should be centralized to consolidate states' development resources and allow candidates to more easily move across states.

The committee poses these as questions to the field.

This report and its findings, conclusions, and recommendations represent the unanimous consensus of a 15-member committee of scholars. The report does not document all of the literature and testimony the committee reviewed, nor does it fully chronicle the committee's deliberations. The committee viewed its mission as one of analyzing and distilling the primary and secondary literature and other direct evidence to produce a summary report useful to policy makers and other audiences.

OVERVIEW OF THE REPORT

Chapter 2 describes the knowledge, skills, abilities, and dispositions that competent teachers demonstrate. In Chapter 3 current systems for licensing teacher candidates and the licensure tests that states use are described. Included are case studies of initial teacher licensing in several states. Chapter 4 presents the committee's framework for evaluating teacher licensure tests. Chapter 5 uses the framework to examine several widely used tests. Chapter 6 examines the extent to which tests can and cannot improve teacher competence and supply. Chapter 7 examines the newly enacted Title II, the Teacher Quality Enhancement Grants for States and Partnerships, and discusses the use of licensure test results for program accountability. Chapter 8 presents options for improving the assessment of teacher candidates. The report ends with the committee's recommendations for policy makers, teacher testers, and teacher educators regarding the use of existing tests to assess teacher candidates and to evaluate teacher preparation.

2

Defining Teacher Quality

Defining teacher quality is fundamental to understanding the role of licensure tests in promoting it. This chapter discusses the variety of ways in which teacher quality has been defined and describes the standards that form the basis for some of the current definitions. It suggests that the knowledge and skills used by competent teachers are many and varied.

To learn whether or how licensure tests might promote teacher quality, the committee believes it is important to distinguish teacher quality from teaching quality. States and local districts play an important role in promoting teaching quality. If schools are not well organized and supportive, it is possible that even good teachers will not be successful (Raudenbush et al., 1992). Successful teaching depends on many factors, including the level of instructional resources available, staffing levels, continuing professional development, and support from administrators and parents (Johnson, 1990). The school and community forces that shape teachers' practices and student learning are numerous and important.

This chapter examines teacher quality—the knowledge, skills, abilities, and dispositions of teachers. Defining teacher quality is no simple task, though, because the criteria for doing so vary from person to person, from one community to another, and from one era to the next. This chapter begins with a review of some of the country's most prominent historical definitions of teacher quality. It then discusses current definitions of teacher competence by describing themes that are common to the teaching standards that have been developed by states, national organizations, and organizations that accredit teacher preparation programs.

We use the standards of the Interstate New Teacher Assessment and Support Consortium (INTASC), the National Council for Accreditation of Teacher Education (NCATE), and the National Board for Professional Teaching Standards (NBPTS) to discuss current conceptions of teacher quality. INTASC is a consortium of state education agencies promoting standards-based reform through the development of licensing standards for beginning teachers. INTASC provides a vehicle for states to work together on licensing standards and assessments for beginning teachers. NCATE has been strengthening standards for teacher education programs, recently incorporating the performance standards developed by INTASC in the development of standards for accreditation of teacher education programs. NBPTS has developed standards for advanced certification, describing what accomplished teachers should know and be able to do. NBPTS has established a national voluntary system to assess and certify teachers to meet its standards. These various standards represent contemporary views of teacher quality and are relied on, in part, for the discussion below of what teachers need to know and do to promote student learning.

PAST DEFINITIONS OF TEACHER QUALITY

Teaching is, first and foremost, a cultural activity, and notions of teacher quality have changed over time as American society has shifted its values and concerns. Moreover, at any given time, different individuals and groups can hold very different ideas about teacher quality. A review of past definitions of teacher quality can provide a context for understanding contemporary definitions.

Teachers Should Personify Virtue

One popular criterion for teacher quality is high moral character. Teachers are often expected to be good role models for students and to represent the highest standards of social propriety. This view of teacher quality was especially widespread in the early 1900s. At that time, teachers were often placed on pedestals, so to speak, as were ministers. When a teacher entered a room, people stopped talking and became self-conscious and embarrassed. To illustrate the importance of moral character in teaching, Willard Waller, writing in 1932, provided this interesting contract that teachers in one community were expected to sign:

> • I promise to take a vital interest in all phases of Sunday-school work, donating of my time, service, and money without stint for the uplift and benefit of the community.
> • I promise to abstain from all dancing, immodest dressing and any other conduct unbecoming a teacher and a lady.
> • I promise not to go out with any young men except insofar as it may be necessary to stimulate Sunday-school work.

- I promise not to fall in love, to become engaged, or secretly married.
- I promise not to encourage or tolerate the least familiarity on the part of any of my boy pupils.
- I promise to remember that I owe a duty to the townspeople who are paying my wages, that I owe respect to the school board and the superintendent that hired me, and that I shall consider myself at all times the willing servant of the school board and the townspeople (p. 43).

While this contract is quite dated, the notion that virtue is important is still widely discussed, and entire books are devoted to the place of ethics and moral behavior in contemporary teaching (van Manen, 1991; Noddings, 1984; Tom, 1980).

Teachers Should Transmit Cultural and Educational Values

Another definition of teacher quality emphasizes a broader range of personality and character traits—such as curiosity, enthusiasm, and compassion. Interest in personality traits was especially widespread in the decades immediately following World War II, partly in response to popular psychoanalytical theories and partly in response to concerns that America needed to ensure that it would not be susceptible to the totalitarian influences that had captivated other countries (Adorno et al., 1950; McGee, 1955). Each personality trait had its own rationale, and each was the subject of a variety of efforts to develop measures that could be used in screening candidates for teaching. For example, one theory held that a certain kind of personality, the *authoritarian personality*, was especially susceptible to fascist influences. The authoritarian personality was defined as someone who respected social hierarchy and felt unusually strong admiration and loyalty to those in positions of authority (Adorno et al., 1950). Associated with this broader social concern was a concern about the extent to which teachers might be fostering authoritarian values in school and a belief that American society would benefit if teachers' personalities were the antithesis of the authoritarian personality. Thus, there was a great deal of interest in finding a way to measure authoritarian values and to use those measures to screen teaching candidates.

It is worth noting that researchers working during this period generally assumed that gains in student achievement were *not* good indicators of teacher quality because they represented far too narrow a range of outcomes. It was assumed that, in addition to fostering student learning, teachers served as moral role models and that they instilled a variety of social values in their students. Consequently, when researchers tried to evaluate their measures of teachers' personal qualities, they usually looked for evidence of a relationship to observed practices or to principals' ratings of teachers, rather than evidence of a relationship to student achievement (Getzels and Jackson, 1963).

Teachers Should Competently Teach the Prescribed Curricula

Another definition of teacher quality focuses on teachers' skills rather than their morality or personality traits. This approach to teacher quality was especially widespread in the post-Sputnik era when American policy makers sponsored numerous curriculum design efforts and wanted teachers to implement the programs exactly as specified.

Pursuing the idea of the teacher with technical skills, researchers in the next decades focused on observing teachers in their classrooms, at first to see how well they were implementing specific curricula and later to document specific teaching practices that seemed to be associated with gains in students' test scores (Brophy and Good, 1986). This latter body of work focused on discrete practices such as questioning and lesson pacing. This research came to be known as "process-product" research, since it sought relationships between classroom processes and the product of gains in student achievement. This movement marked the first time that student achievement became a widely accepted criterion for teacher quality. The goal of this research was to identify specific behaviors that other teachers could emulate. Researchers focused on such skills as question asking, lesson pacing, and clarity in explanations.

It is important to recall, too, that early in this country's educational history, Americans were operating separate school systems for black students and white students and did not pay much attention to the needs of other nonwhite groups in education policies and practices. Most discussions about teacher quality, at least until the 1960s, referred mainly to white teachers teaching white students. The situation changed somewhat in the 1950s and 1960s, after the Supreme Court's *Brown v. Board of Education* decision. Even then, though, discussions among mostly white scholars and politicians tended to focus more on the distribution of education resources than on questions of teacher quality.

CURRENT DEFINITIONS OF TEACHER COMPETENCE

These examples demonstrate how definitions of teacher quality have varied across time. In the 1980s and 1990s, Americans—particularly American policy makers—developed yet another definition of teacher quality. Today's definition of teacher quality differs from its predecessors in several ways. First, it acknowledges the diversity of the student population in a way not previously done. Second, it asks for a level of instruction that is more intellectually rigorous and meaningful than has traditionally been the case. These definitions of teacher quality are less concerned with teachers' character traits or technical proficiency and more concerned with teachers' ability to engage students in rigorous, meaningful activities that foster academic learning for all students. Finally, current statements on teacher quality are standards based and define the knowledge, skills, and dispositions that teachers should demonstrate.

Recent attempts to define teacher quality have sought ways to broadly represent the views of the field and to benefit teacher development and assessment. Although the field does not unanimously support the teaching standards that have resulted, a significant degree of professional consensus is implied by the wide adoption of standards for beginning teachers, for the accreditation of teacher education programs, and for accomplished teachers. Several factors—both internal and external to the fields of education and teacher preparation—have coalesced to impel the development of teacher standards.

Current Standards for Teacher Competence

Three organizations have been particularly active in establishing standards for teacher quality, and all have relied on both research and consensus-building procedures to do so. The first, NBPTS, was created in 1987 and has developed a national, voluntary system for testing and rewarding accomplished teaching. NBPTS provides certificates to teachers seeking advanced credentials. INTASC was created shortly after NBPTS. The consortium of states working with INTASC has developed "National Board-compatible" licensing standards and assessments for beginning teachers. The standards developed by NBPTS and INTASC are linked to one another and to the student standards developed by national disciplinary organizations and states.

INTASC and NBPTS have used consensus models to develop teacher standards. In developing their core standards, both have worked with teachers and other experts in child development, teacher education, and the academic disciplines. They formed standards development committees to examine the literature on teaching, learning, and best practices and to describe what beginning and accomplished teachers need to know and be able to do. They drafted teaching standards that identify the knowledge, skills, abilities, and dispositions needed to teach. The draft standards were broadly vetted with teachers, teacher educators, and relevant professional bodies. They were critiqued at professional meetings and in focus group sessions. Revisions to the core standards were made to reflect the input and describe the consensus of the field. The consensus-based development models used by INTASC and NBPTS seek to identify competencies about which there is consensus in the field.

This work resulted in NBPTS's five propositions for accomplished teachers and INTASC's model standards for beginning teachers. NCATE's standards are aligned with the INTASC principles. Because of the research that guided development of the standards and to the consensus model that the organizations used to garner support from the field for those standards, the committee chose to use them to describe current conceptions of teacher competence. The INTASC, NCATE, and NBPTS standards appear in Appendix B of this volume. Readers interested in additional information about the research utilized during the development of these standards can refer to *What Teachers Should Know and Be Able to Do* (NBPTS, 1994), *Model Standards for Beginning Teacher Licensing and Development* (INTASC, 1992), and *Standards, Procedures and Policies for the Accreditation of Professional Education Units* (NCATE, 1997).

Themes from Standards for Teachers

All three sets of standards examine teaching in light of learning. They explicitly acknowledge that teachers' actions or performances depend on many kinds of knowledge and on dispositions to use that knowledge and to work with others to support the learning and success of all students. These initiatives incorporate knowledge about teaching and learning that supports a view of teaching as complex, contingent on students' needs and instructional goals, and reciprocal—that is, continually shaped and reshaped by students' responses to learning events. The standards take into account the teaching challenges posed by a student body that is multicultural and multilingual. The standards recognize the learning styles of special-needs students and of students who possess different learning styles. By reflecting new subject matter standards for students and the demands of diverse learners, as well as the expectation that teachers should collaborate with colleagues and parents in order to succeed, the standards define teaching as a collegial, professional activity that responds to considerations of subjects, content, and students.

The three sets of standards are substantively connected and represent a continuum of development along a teacher's career path. The INTASC standards describe the knowledge, skills, abilities, and dispositions of beginning teachers. The NCATE standards are targets for the approval of teacher education programs and describe the knowledge and skills of teacher candidates. The NBPTS standards describe accomplished teaching. In the next section, central themes that emerge across the standards are described. Because the categories of teacher competence of the NBPTS standards are broader and therefore fewer in number, the committee used them here to organize discussion of the themes.

Teachers Are Committed to Their Students and Students' Learning

A central theme across the three sets of standards is that teachers should be committed to their students and their students' learning. Teachers should act on the belief that all students can learn and should develop and use curricula that encourage students to see, question, and interpret ideas. To ensure that all students do learn, teachers should understand how the developmental levels of their students affect learning and how classroom instruction should be modified to reflect students' needs. They should foster students' self-esteem, motivation, civic responsibility, and respect for others.

To accommodate and respond to the needs of all their students, teachers should also understand and modify instruction to incorporate learning opportunities for students with learning disabilities; visual and perceptual disabilities; and speech, physical, and mental challenges. To fully understand their students and how they learn, teachers should recognize the ways in which cultural backgrounds and other sources of diversity shape students' perspectives on the content and process of learning. The standards say teachers should understand how students' personal and family backgrounds shape their talents and perspectives. This is especially important because today's students come from varied cultural backgrounds. According to the National Center for Education Statistics (2000), racial/ethnic minority students made up 22 percent of the country's student population in the early 1970s. In 1998 the percentage of students from minority backgrounds enrolled in public schools had increased to 37 percent. The excerpts in Box 2-1 from the INTASC, NCATE, and NBPTS standards explain these ideas more fully. The full texts of the standards are contained in Appendix B.

BOX 2-1
Teachers Are Committed to Their
Students and Students' Learning

INTASC: The teacher understands how children learn and develop, and can provide learning opportunities that support their intellectual, social, and personal development. The teacher understands how learning occurs—how students construct knowledge, acquire skills, and develop habits of mind—and knows how to use instructional strategies that promote student learning. . . . The teacher appreciates individual variation within each area of development, shows respect for the diverse talents of all learners, and is committed to help them develop self-confidence and competence. . . . The teacher assesses individual and group performance in order to design instruction that meets learners' current needs in each domain (cognitive, social, emotional, moral, and physical) and that lead to the next level of development.

The teacher understands how students differ in their approaches to learning and creates instructional opportunities that are adapted to diverse learners. The teacher understands and can identify differences in approaches to learning and performance, including different learning styles, multiple intelligences, and performance modes and can design instruction that helps use students' strengths as the basis for growth. . . . The teacher believes that all children can learn at high levels and persists in helping all children achieve success. . . . The teacher identifies and designs instruction appropriate to students' stages of development, learning styles, strengths, and needs.

The teacher uses knowledge of effective verbal, nonverbal, and media communication techniques to foster active inquiry, collaboration, and supportive interaction in the classroom. The teacher appreciates the cultural dimensions of communication, responds appropriately, and seeks to foster culturally sensitive communication by and among all students in the class. . . . The teacher knows how to ask questions and stimulate discussion in different ways for particular purposes, for example, probing for learner understanding, helping students articulate their ideas and thinking processes, promoting risk taking and problem solving, facilitat-

continues

BOX 2-1 *Continued*

ing factual recall, encouraging convergent and divergent thinking, stimulating curiosity, helping students to question.

NCATE: Candidates reflect a thorough understanding of professional and pedagogical knowledge and skills delineated in professional, state, and institutional standards, as shown in their development of meaningful learning experiences to facilitate student learning for all students. They reflect on their practice and make necessary adjustments to enhance student learning. They know how students learn and how to make ideas accessible to them. They consider school, family, and community contexts in connecting concepts to students' prior experience and applying the ideas to real-world problems.

NBPTS: Accomplished teachers are dedicated to making knowledge accessible to all students. They act on the belief that all students can learn. They treat students equitably, recognizing the individual differences that distinguish one student from another and taking account of these differences in their practice. They adjust their practice based on observation and knowledge of their students' interests, abilities, skills, knowledge, family circumstances, and peer relationships. Accomplished teachers understand how students develop and learn. They incorporate the prevailing theories of cognition and intelligence in their practice. They are aware of the influence of context and culture on behavior. They develop students' cognitive capacity and their respect for learning. Equally important, they foster students' self-esteem, motivation, character, civic responsibility, and their respect for individual, cultural, religious and racial differences.

SOURCES: Interstate New Teacher Assessment and Support Consortium, 1992; National Council for Accreditation of Teacher Education, 2000b; National Board for Professional Teaching Standards, 1994. Used by permission of the authors. NCATE reserves all rights. The full texts of the standards are contained in Appendix B. The text included here is from the core principles of the standards. INTASC and NBPTS have content-specific standards as well.

Teachers Have Deep Subject Matter Knowledge

Another important theme of the standards is the need for deep subject matter knowledge. Teachers should know the substance and structure of the disciplines they teach. They should be able to translate difficult substantive ideas into terms that students can understand, to diagnose students' understandings and misunderstandings, and to develop explanations, examples, and representations, including learning activities themselves, that are appropriate for students' levels of understanding. INTASC, NCATE, and NBPTS standards on the need for subject matter knowledge appear in Box 2-2.

BOX 2-2
Teachers Have Deep Subject Matter Knowledge

INTASC: The teacher understands the central concepts, tools of inquiry, and structures of the discipline(s) he or she teaches and can create learning experiences that make these aspects of subject matter meaningful for students. The teacher understands major concepts, assumptions, debates, processes of inquiry, and ways of knowing that are central to the discipline(s) s/he teaches. . . . The teacher realizes that subject matter knowledge is not a fixed body of facts but is complex and ever evolving. S/he seeks to keep abreast of new ideas and understandings in the field. . . . The teacher effectively uses multiple representations and explanations of disciplinary concepts that capture key ideas and link them to students' prior understanding.

The teacher plans instruction based upon knowledge of subject matter, students, the community, and curriculum goals. The teacher understands learning theory subject matter, curriculum development, and student development and knows how to use this knowledge in planning instruction to meet curriculum goals. . . . The teacher believes that plans must always be open to adjustment and revision based on student needs and changing circumstances. . . . The teacher creates lessons and activities that operate at multiple levels to meet the developmental and individual needs of diverse learners and help each progress.

NCATE: Teacher candidates have in-depth knowledge of the subject matter that they plan to teach as described in professional, state, and institutional standards. They demonstrate their knowledge through inquiry, critical analysis, and synthesis of the subject.

Teacher candidates reflect a thorough understanding of pedagogical content knowledge delineated in professional, state, and institutional standards. They have in-depth understanding of the subject matter that they plan to teach, allowing them to provide multiple explanations and instructional strategies so that all students learn. They present the content to students in challenging, clear, and compelling ways and integrate technology appropriately.

NBPTS: Teachers know the subjects they teach and how to teach those subjects to students. Accomplished teachers have a rich understanding of the subject(s) they teach and appreciate how knowledge in their subject is created, organized, linked to other disciplines, and applied to real-world settings. While faithfully representing the collective wisdom of our culture and upholding the value of disciplinary knowledge, they also develop the critical and analytical capacities of their students. Accomplished teachers command specialized knowledge of how to convey and reveal subject matter to students. They are aware of the preconceptions and background knowledge that students typically bring to each subject and of strategies and instructional materials that can be of assistance. They understand where difficulties are likely to arise and modify their practice accordingly. Their instructional repertoire allows them to create multiple paths to the subjects they teach, and they are adept at teaching students how to pose and solve their own problems.

SOURCES: Interstate New Teacher Assessment and Support Consortium, 1992; National Council for Accreditation of Teacher Education, 2000b; National Board for Professional Teaching Standards, 1994. Used by permission of the authors. NCATE reserves all rights.

BOX 2-3
Teachers Manage and Monitor Student Learning

INTASC: The teacher understands and uses a variety of instructional strategies to encourage students' development of critical thinking, problem solving, and performance skills. The teacher understands the cognitive processes associated with various kinds of learning (e.g., critical and creative thinking, problem structuring and problem solving, invention, memorization and recall) and how these processes can be stimulated. . . . The teacher values flexibility and reciprocity in the teaching process as necessary for adapting instruction to student responses, ideas, and needs. . . . The teacher carefully evaluates how to achieve learning goals, choosing alternative teaching strategies and materials to achieve different instructional purposes and to meet student needs (e.g., developmental stages, prior knowledge, learning styles, and interests).

The teacher understands and uses formal and informal assessment strategies to evaluate and ensure the continuous intellectual, social, and physical development of the learner. The teacher understands the characteristics, uses, advantages, and limitations of different types of assessments (e.g., criterion-referenced and norm-referenced instruments, traditional standardized and performance-based tests, observation systems, and assessments of student work) for evaluating how students learn, what they know and are able to do, and what kinds of experiences will support their further growth and development. . . . The teacher is committed to using assessment to identify student strengths and promote student growth rather than to deny students access to learning opportunities. . . . The teacher appropriately uses a variety of formal and informal assessment techniques (e.g., observation, portfolios of student work, teacher-made tests, performance tasks, projects, student self-assessments, peer assessment, and standardized tests) to enhance her or his knowledge of learners, evaluate students' progress and performances, and modify teaching and learning strategies.

The teacher uses an understanding of individual and group motivation and behavior to create a learning environment that encourages positive social inter-

---

Teachers Manage and Monitor Student Learning

To ensure that students progress, teachers should know how to identify learning goals and choose from a variety of teaching and learning strategies that will engage students in the learning process. This includes selecting the necessary educational resources (computers, books, and audiovisual equipment), selecting the most appropriate instructional role (instructor, facilitator, coach, or audience), and effectively implementing instructional strategies in the classroom. Occurring simultaneously with the management of student learning is the monitoring of student learning through ongoing assessment of student progress. Hence, teachers should be aware of the different kinds of assessments that can be used in the classroom, such as criterion-referenced and norm-referenced tests, traditional standardized and performance-based tests, observation systems, and portfolios of student work. The standards in Box 2-3 describe the knowledge, skills, and dispositions teachers need to manage and monitor student learning.

action, active engagement in learning, and self-motivation. The teacher can use knowledge about human motivation and behavior drawn from the foundational sciences of psychology, anthropology, and sociology to develop strategies for organizing and supporting individual and group work. . . . The teacher understands how participation supports commitment and is committed to the expression and use of democratic values in the classroom. . . . The teacher creates a smoothly functioning learning community in which students assume responsibility for themselves and one another, participate in decision making, work collaboratively and independently, and engage in purposeful learning activities.

NCATE: Teacher candidates accurately assess and analyze student learning, make appropriate adjustments to instruction, monitor student learning, and have a positive effect on learning for all students.

NBPTS: Teachers are responsible for managing and monitoring student learning. Accomplished teachers create, enrich, maintain, and alter instructional settings to capture and sustain the interest of their students and to make the most effective use of time. They also are adept at engaging students and adults to assist their teaching and at enlisting their colleagues' knowledge and expertise to complement their own. . . . They know how to engage groups of students to ensure a disciplined learning environment and how to organize instruction to allow the schools' goals for students to be met. They are adept at setting norms for social interaction among students and between students and teachers. They understand how to motivate students to learn and how to maintain their interest even in the face of temporary failure.

SOURCES: Interstate New Teacher Assessment and Support Consortium, 1992; National Council for Accreditation of Teacher Education, 2000b; National Board for Professional Teaching Standards, 1994. Used by permission of the authors. NCATE reserves all rights.

Teachers Are Reflective About Their Teaching

Teachers make decisions that affect their students' learning throughout the day and over the course of the school year. To feel comfortable with their decisions, competent teachers evaluate these decisions and experiences and make continual adjustments in their curricular plans in response to students' progress. They revise their own repertoire of behaviors, classrooms rules, and learning activities as they learn more about how their students tend to respond to these things.

The standards call for teachers to be reflective about their practice. Teachers should use classroom observation, information about students, the professional literature, colleagues, and other resources as sources for evaluating the outcomes of their teaching. They should experiment with, reflect on, and revise their practice to improve their effectiveness in meeting students' needs and achieving instructional goals. To be reflective requires teacher candidates and accomplished teachers to be self-directed, to engage in critical thinking about

BOX 2-4
Teachers Are Reflective About Their Teaching

INTASC: The teacher is a reflective practitioner who continually evaluates the effects of his/her choices and actions on others (students, parents, and other professionals in the learning community) and who actively seeks out opportunities to grow professionally. The teacher understands methods of inquiry that provide him/her with a variety of self-assessment and problem-solving strategies for reflecting on his/her practice, its influences on students' growth and learning, and the complex interactions between them. . . . The teacher is committed to seeking out, developing, and continually refining practices that address the individual needs of students. . . . The teacher uses classroom observation, information about students, and research as sources for evaluating the outcomes of teaching and learning and as a basis for experimenting with, reflecting on, and revising practice.

NBPTS: Teachers think systematically about their practice and learn from experience. Accomplished teachers are models of educated persons, exemplifying the virtues they seek to inspire in students—curiosity, tolerance, honesty, fairness, respect for diversity, and appreciation of cultural differences—and the capacities that are prerequisites for intellectual growth: the ability to reason and take multiple perspectives to be creative and take risks and to adopt an experimental and problem-solving orientation. Accomplished teachers draw on their knowledge of human development, subject matter and instruction, and their understanding of their students to make principled judgments about sound practice. Their decisions are not only grounded in the literature but also in their experience. They engage in lifelong learning, which they seek to encourage in their students. Striving to strengthen their teaching, accomplished teachers critically examine their practice, seek to expand their repertoire, deepen their knowledge, sharpen their judgment, and adapt their teaching to new findings, ideas, and theories.

SOURCES: Interstate New Teacher Assessment and Support Consortium, 1992; National Board for Professional Teaching Standards, 1994. Used by permission of the authors.

their teaching, and to be open and responsive to feedback received from other professional colleagues. The standards in Box 2-4 address reflective teaching.

Teachers Are Members of a Broader Community

The final theme of the standards recognizes that teaching does not occur in a vacuum. Students and any individual classroom are part of a larger context both within and outside the school. The teacher needs to understand the role of the school and the staff in the broader community. Specifically, the teacher understands how factors in students' environments outside school, such as family circumstances, community environments, health, and economic conditions, may influence students' lives and learning. To this end, the teacher makes a concerted effort to establish relationships with students' parents and guardians. Within the school, the teacher also participates in collegial activities designed to make the entire school a cohesive unit and a productive learning environment. Box 2-5 provides excerpts from the INTASC, NCATE, and NBPTS standards.

These standards illustrate the wide range of knowledge, skills, abilities, and dispositions that contemporary educators believe competent teachers must possess and demonstrate in the classroom. Competent teachers are committed to their students and students' learning, possess deep subject matter knowledge, effectively manage and monitor student learning, are reflective about their teaching, and are members of the broader school community. The standards are useful in providing a framework of the complexities and multiple dimensions of teaching, yet, as

---

BOX 2-5
Teachers Are Members of a Broader Community

INTASC: The teacher fosters relationships with school colleagues, parents, and agencies in the larger community to support students' learning and well-being. The teacher understands how factors in the students' environment outside of school (e.g., family circumstances, community environments, health and economic conditions) may influence students' lives and learning. . . . The teacher is concerned about all aspects of a child's well-being (cognitive, emotional, social, and physical) and is alert to signs of difficulties. . . . The teacher establishes respectful and productive relationships with parents and guardians from diverse home and community situations and seeks to develop cooperative partnerships in support of student learning and well-being.

NCATE: Candidates' work with students, families, and communities reflects the dispositions expected of professional educators as delineated in professional, state, and institutional standards. Candidates recognize when their own dispositions may need to be adjusted and are able to develop plans to do so.

NBPTS: Teachers are members of learning communities. Accomplished teachers contribute to the effectiveness of the school by working collaboratively with other professionals on instructional policy, curriculum development and staff development. They can evaluate school progress and the allocation of school resources in light of their understanding of state and local educational objectives. They are knowledgeable about specialized school and community resources that can be engaged for their students' benefit and are skilled at employing such resources as needed. Accomplished teachers find ways to work collaboratively and creatively with parents, engaging them productively in the work of the school.

SOURCES: Interstate New Teacher Assessment and Support Consortium, 1992; National Council for Accreditation of Teacher Education, 2000b; National Board for Professional Teaching Standards, 1994. Used by permission of the authors. NCATE reserves all rights.

mentioned earlier, there is not complete consensus in the field about these standards. Concerns with the standards have included challenges to the research base that supports the NCATE standards (Ballou and Podgursky, 1999) and issues about the breadth of the statements that define the standards (Richardson, 1994; Roth, 1996).

The breadth of the standards causes problems in developing assessments, as their broad nature leaves open a variety of interpretations (Roth, 1996). This makes it difficult to translate the standards into test specifications and to develop assessments of the intended skills. The ongoing development of content-specific standards by NBPTS and INTASC begins to address this issue. Also, it is not explicitly stated what level of performance the standards relate to—the ideal, normative, or minimum? A third concern relates to a teacher's ability to demonstrate all of the behaviors denoted in the INTASC standards. As Richardson (1994:17) states: "Is it possible for a beginning teacher to attain the deep knowledge and understanding of classrooms, students, context, and subject matter implied in these principles?"

The next chapter shows how the field has attempted to develop teacher tests and assessments based on standards of teacher competence. The NBPTS assessments examine the performance of experienced teachers and are not the focus of this report. This report is about testing for initial licensure. Initial licensing tests are not intended to test for advanced levels of performance or for all of the knowledge and skills characteristic of accomplished teachers. They are intended to test the knowledge and skills of entry-level teachers. Building on the teaching competencies outlined in current teacher standards, Chapter 3 describes the procedures that states use to identify the knowledge and skills needed for minimally competent beginning practice. It examines current state tests and other initial licensure requirements.

CONCLUSION

Definitions of what teachers should know and be able to do have changed over time as society's values have changed, and they will continue to do so. The job of teaching students to learn and use new information, develop and apply skills, and think critically is highly complex and demanding. Teachers need to motivate and engage all students, including students from varied backgrounds and those with different learning and language needs. In addition to being responsible for student learning, teachers are expected to provide safe and nurturing classrooms, serve as good role models, and to engage parents and the community in the business of their school. Teachers need a wide range of knowledge, skills, abilities, and dispositions to perform these many complex tasks.

The quality of teaching in a school depends on more than just individual teacher quality. It also depends on factors such as the amount and quality of instructional resources available, teacher professional development, staffing, and support from administrators and parents.

There is no single agreed-upon definition of what competencies a beginning teacher should have. Different professional organizations and many states have recently developed standards for teachers. The fact that different states have affiliations with these national and regional standards development efforts suggests some agreement between states about standards for teacher competence. Given that states have different educational standards for students, have teacher candidate pools with different characteristics, and that licensing of teachers is a state responsibility, it is not surprising that there is some variation in the knowledge and skills that states seek for beginning teachers.

3

Testing and Licensing Beginning Teachers

Teacher licensure is under the authority of individual states. The goal of initial teacher licensure is to ensure that all students have competent teachers. Given the complexity of teaching and differences in states' current efforts to improve teaching and learning, it is not surprising that the landscape for teacher licensing is complex. States impose numerous and varied requirements on candidates for licensure. States require candidates to fulfill education and supervised teaching requirements, pass required tests, provide evidence of good character, and meet other licensure requirements. Furthermore, states use many different licensure tests in different ways.

This chapter describes initial teacher licensing—the licensing decisions made before a teacher enters the classroom on an unsupervised basis for the first time. This chapter begins with a brief discussion of licensing in other professions and of the differences between teacher licensing and licensing in other fields. The committee then describes teacher licensure systems, the tests used by states, and the decisions about candidates they support. The committee closes with examples of teacher preparation, testing, and licensure in seven states.

Here and elsewhere in the report the committee distinguishes between tests and assessments. The committee defines tests as paper-and-pencil measures of knowledge and skill; tests are evaluated and scored using standardized processes. Assessments are broader. While assessments can include standardized paper-and-pencil measures, they may also include performance-based evidence, such as portfolios, videotapes, and observation records. Assessments can be collections of different sorts of evidence, systematically gathered over time, to inform particular decisions or interpretations.

PROFESSIONAL LICENSING

Many professions use licensing systems to select individuals into their fields and to prevent those considered incompetent from practicing. As defined in 1971 by the U.S. Department of Health, Education, and Welfare, licensure is "the process by which an agency of government grants permission to persons to engage in a given profession or occupation by certifying that those licensed have attained the minimal degree of competency necessary to ensure that the public health, safety, and welfare will be reasonably well protected" (p. 7). Licensure is a state function. States regulate more than 500 professions, from real estate appraisers to electricians to architects. Licensure requirements for a given profession may vary across states, and states may vary in the professions they regulate.

Professions generally promote quality practice in three ways: through professional accreditation of preparation programs, through state licensing of applicants to the profession, and through certification of practitioners. Professions use accreditation to examine their preparation programs and to attempt to ensure that they provide high-quality instruction and practice opportunities. Licensing serves as a gateway to the profession, allowing only those who have met minimum standards of competence to practice. For some professions, certification is granted to those who demonstrate exemplary knowledge and skill. For example, in the medical profession, certification generally is professional recognition of higher standards of accomplishment and typically is associated with advanced study and practice. A national professional body, such as the American Board of Internal Medicine, the American Board of Emergency Medicine, or the National Board for Professional Teaching Standards usually grants certification.

Tests often play an important role in licensure systems and in what candidates study and learn to prepare for licensure and practice (Darling-Hammond et al., 1999). Licensing tests are designed "to provide the public with a dependable mechanism for identifying practitioners who have met particular standards" (American Educational Research Association et al., 1999:156). Typically, panels of professionals determine the knowledge and skills that are critical for safe and effective performance, with an emphasis on the knowledge and skills that should be mastered prior to entering the profession (Stoker and Impara, 1995; American Educational Research Association et al., 1999). The test specifications for licensure examinations make explicit at least part of what professions consider worth knowing and how it should be known and demonstrated.

Specifications for licensure tests may also recognize advances in professional knowledge. Licensing exams are viewed as a means for ensuring that advances in professional knowledge are incorporated into professional education programs. For example, one way that fields such as medicine, engineering, and psychology ensure that new research knowledge gets used is by including it on licensing examinations, specialty board examinations, and accreditation guidelines for professional schools, hospitals, or other training sites. Although tests are prominent in licensing systems, it is important to recognize that they are only one part of the overall quality control system that most professions have developed (National Association of State Directors of Teacher Education and Certification, 2000b).

Professional regulations generally address requirements in three areas: education, experience, and testing. The education component is intended to ensure that candidates have encountered the broad base of knowledge they will need to draw on when making decisions in professional practice. The supervised experience component allows candidates to learn the complex art of applying knowledge to specific problems of practice, to make judgments, to weigh and balance competing considerations, and to develop practical skills and put them to use.

Professions generally include education, experience, and testing components in their licensing requirements but vary in the amounts of education and experience they require and in the sequence in which the requirements must be met. In deciding on specific education, experience, and testing requirements, professions evaluate the extent to which each element is likely to lead to public protection. The required levels of education, experience, and testing are intended to reflect the knowledge and skills needed for entry-level practice and not to be so high as to be unreasonably limiting (Schmitt, 2000; American Educational Research Association et al., 1999).

To learn more about licensing in other professions, the committee commissioned a paper on licensure requirements in seven fields. The goal was to learn (1) how other professions handle licensing requirements; (2) what other professions require with regard to education, experience, and testing; and (3) whether the requirements of other professions suggest ways to improve teacher licensure. The committee focused on professions that generally require a bachelor's degree for entry into the profession because these professions were expected to offer useful analogies to education.

Table 3-1 compares licensure requirements for seven professions: architects, certified public accountants (CPAs), professional engineers, land surveyors, physical therapists, registered nurses, and social workers. For each profession the state is the licensing agent. For each profession there is also variability in the education and experience that states require for licensure. For example, there are four categories of practice for social workers: Basic, Intermediate, Advanced, and Clinical. States differ in the level of practice that they regulate. The 34 states that offer licenses to social workers with bachelor's degrees (the Basic level) have 19 different combinations of education and experience requirements (Schmitt, 2000). For CPA candidates, over half of the states require two years of practical experience for a license and a few require three years (American Institute of Certified Public Accountants and National Association of State Boards of Accountancy, 1998). For architects about a quarter of states require graduation from an accredited five-year architecture program; other states accept alternative ways for satisfying the education requirements <www.ncarb.org>. These differences are analogous to the different state education and experience requirements for teachers.

There is a difference, however, between states' licensure testing requirements for the seven professions and the licensure testing requirements for teaching. For each of the seven professions examined, the same test or series of tests are used by all states (although some states augment a national examination with additional state components). For six of these professions (all but social work), the passing standards on the test(s) are the same across states (Schmitt, 2000). The situation is very different in education where testing requirements differ by state, subject area, and grade level and the passing standards vary from state to state.

Table 3-1 also provides data on alternate paths into the seven professions. A number of the professions studied have varying degree requirements for alternate routes to licensing. Some accept experience in lieu of the education requirements. About half the states allow engineers to substitute experience for an engineering degree, although the experience requirement is substantial (e.g., over 10 years; National Council of Examiners for Engineering and Surveying, 2000). Prospective architects can also substitute experience for education. Over half the states allow architect candidates to be licensed with a bachelor's degree or a high school diploma, in combination with experience/training (although typically candidates must have a combination of eight years' experience and education <www.ncarb.org>. Several states accept various combinations of education and experience in lieu of a bachelor's degree in order for prospective accountants to sit for the licensing exam (American Institute of Certified Public Accountants and National Association of State Boards of Accountancy, 1998). This is another area in which teaching is similar to the other professions studied.

Some of the seven professions allow individuals to practice without a license, but they place limitations on what unlicensed individuals are allowed to do. Unlicensed architects can design certain structures, although only licensed architects can seal a design. Unlicensed individuals can work as accountants, although they cannot use the CPA designation. In some jurisdictions, registered nurses and physical therapists who have completed the education requirements can receive temporary licenses prior to fulfilling the examination requirements (Schmitt, 2000). Teaching is similar to other professions in this regard. Unlicensed teachers can work in private schools in some states (National Association of State Directors of Teacher Education and Certification, 2000b; U.S. Department of Education, 2000b). Also, many states allow unlicensed individuals to teach in public schools for a fixed period when there are too few licensed teachers to staff existing classes.

TEACHER LICENSURE

The teaching profession and individual states impose standards through program approval, teacher education admission and course requirements, testing, and initial licensure to promote quality practice.

TABLE 3-1   Comparison of Licensing Requirements for Teaching and
Other Professions[a]

| Profession | Requirements | | |
	Education	Experience	Examination
Teaching	All states require a bachelor's degree in teacher education or a content area; most have post-baccalaureate alternative routes to enter teaching.	Most states require student teaching; length of student teaching experience varies from 9 to 18 weeks.[b]	Over 600 exams in use; most states require one or more tests of basic skills, general knowledge, subject matter knowledge, or pedagogical knowledge.
Architects[e]	About one-quarter of the states require a five-year degree from an NCARB-accredited program; others accept alternative ways of satisfying the education requirements.	Most states require that the Intern Development Program standards be met (5,600 hours of defined experience)	One exam with nine sections: predesign; general structures, lateral forces, mechanical and electrical systems, materials and methods; construction documents and services, site planning, building planning, and building technology.
Certified public accountants[f]	Most states require a bachelor's degree. Most require 150 hours of education prior to taking the test.	Most states require experience, generally between one and three years.	Four exams: Auditing, Financial Accounting and Reporting, Business Law and Professional Responsibility, and Accounting and Reporting; must pass all parts; over half the states require an exam or professional course in ethics.
Professional engineers[g]	Most states require a bachelor's degree in engineering.	All states require experience along with engineering degree, generally four years.	Two-part exam; Fundamentals of Engineering (FE) is first step and can be taken before degree completion; Principles of Engineering (PE) is the second step and is usually taken after degree completion; about half the states also require jurisprudence, ethics, or specialty exams.

Exam Format/Cost	Experience Accepted in Place of Education Requirements	Practice Without Completing All Licensing Requirements	Continuing Education (CE) Requirements
Primarily multiple-choice and constructed-response.	B.A. is a minimum requirement for all states. Experience and education requirements for states' alternative licensure programs vary widely.	Most states allow unlicensed individuals to waive one or more licensing requirements to teach temporarily[c]	Most states require CE.[d]
Computer simulation; six multiple-choice sections; three vignette sections with graphics problems; $981; sections can be taken at different times.	Less than one-quarter accept training in lieu of education; typically need combination of 8 years' education and experience.	Unlicensed individuals can work as architects, but limitations are placed on the types of work permitted (e.g., size of structure, type of structure); unlicensed individuals cannot seal a design or use the title.	Not required in most states; a few require 12 hours per year.
Multiple-choice, essay, matching, short-answer, fill-in the-blank; 15 hours, two days; test fee varies from state to state.	A few states allow a combination of experience and education to be substituted for the bachelor's degree in order to sit for the exam.	Unlicensed individuals can work as accountants but cannot use the CPA designation or perform the attest function.	Most states require 40 hours CE per year.
Multiple-choice and problems; 16 disciplines; eight hours per part; open book for PE exam but restrictions vary across states; $50 to $75 for FE; $100+ for PE.	About half the states allow experience to be substituted for an engineering degree; most require over 10 years.	Unlicensed individuals can work as engineers, but limitations are placed on the types of work permitted; unlicensed individuals cannot seal a drawing or use the title.	Less than half of the states require CE requirements.

continues

TABLE 3-1   Continued

Profession	Requirements		
	Education	Experience	Examination
Land surveyors[g]	Most require a bachelor' degree in land surveying.	Over half the states require those with a degree from an accredited program to also have field experience.	Two tests: Fundamentals of Land Surveying (FLS) and Principles and Practice of Land Surveying (PLS); most states also require a jurisprudence exam.
Physical therapists[h]	All states require graduation from an accredited PT program; after 2002, only post-baccalaureate programs will be accredited.	A few states require clinical practice.	One exam; a few states require oral or practical exam prior to licensure.
Registered nurses[j]	Most states require either an associate's degree, a bachelor of science in nursing, or graduation from NY Regents external degree program.	No states have experience requirements.	One exam.
Social workers[k]	Four categories of practice; states vary in the level(s) of practice they regulate. Requirements vary according to level of practice. Most states require at least a bachelor's in social work for the basic level of practice, although some accept nonsocial work degrees.	Experience requirements vary according to the level of practice.	Four levels of exams: Basic, Intermediate, Advanced, and Clinical; candidates take only one exam for each level of licensure.

[a] This table summarizes information in a paper prepared for the committee by Kara Schmitt. The full electronic version of the paper can be obtained by contacting the author at karaschmitt@hotmail.com.

[b] From National Association of State Directors of Teacher Education and Certification (2000b:Table B-22).

[c] From Education Week, Quality Counts (2000:52).

[d] From National Association of State Directors of Teacher Education and Certification (2000b:E-1).

[e] From National Council of Architectural Registration Boards (1998); NCARB member board requirements. Washington, DC: National Council of Architectural Registration Boards; and <www.ncarb.org>.

[f] From American Institute of Certified Public Accountants and National Association of State Boards of Accoun-

Exam Format/Cost	Experience Accepted in Place of Education Requirements	Practice Without Completing All Licensing Requirements	Continuing Education (CE) Requirements
Multiple-choice; eight hours for FLS, $175; six hours for PLS, $265.	A few states accept experience in place of education.	Unlicensed individuals can work as surveyors, but limitations are placed on the types of work permitted; unlicensed individuals cannot seal a drawing or use the title.	About half the states require CE, generally 6 to 15 hours per year.
Computer-based multiple-choice; four hours; $285.	Experience cannot be substituted for education.	About half of the states allow individuals who have completed the educational requirements to practice (temporarily) prior to passing the test.	About half the states require CE (one to four CE units).
Computer-adaptive; multiple-choice; five hours; $120	No states accept experience in lieu of education.	About half of the states allow individuals who have completed the educational requirements to practice (temporarily) prior to passing the test; some states allow individuals to take the LPN exam while training for RN and to practice as an LPN until becoming an RN.	About half of the states require CE for license renewal.
Computer-based multiple-choice; four hours; $110 per level	Most states do not accept experience in lieu of education.	Four levels of practice that define a progression of education/experience requirements.	Most states require CE, usually 15 to 20 hours every two years.

tancy (1998). *Digest of state accountancy laws and state board regulations.* New York: American Institute of Certified Public Accountants and <www.aicpa.org>.

g From National Council of Examiners for Engineering and Surveying (2000) <www.ncees.org>.

h From American Physical Therapy Association. (1997). *State licensure reference guide.* Washington, DC: American Physical Therapy Association and <www.fsbpt.org>.

j From Yocom et al. (1999) <www.ncsbn.org>.

k From American Association of State Social Work Boards (1998) <www.aswb.org>.

Accreditation and Approval of Teacher Education Programs

As in other fields, accreditation of teacher education programs is a mechanism for examining and attesting to the quality of programs (National Council for the Accreditation of Teacher Education, 1997). However, unlike other professions, national professional accreditation is not required in teacher education. The majority of states recognize only teacher preparation programs from institutions that are regionally accredited. Fewer than 40 percent of teacher education programs are nationally accredited (U.S. Department of Education, 2001).

All states require teacher preparation programs to obtain state approval based on policies and standards set by them. These standards establish criteria that, if met, authorize the program to prepare and recommend teacher candidates for state licensure. The teacher preparation approval standards often also incorporate specific state-required courses or competencies necessary to obtain a state license. These approval standards and license requirements are unique to each state. Fourteen states have established independent professional standards boards or commissions with responsibility for establishing licensure standards, and all but three of these boards have authority to approve teacher preparation programs (National Association of State Directors of Teacher Education and Certification, 2000b).

The process for approving programs varies by state. Some states conduct a paper review of the curriculum. Others do an on-site review based on adopted standards, primarily process measures organized around students, faculty, and program resources (e.g., number of faculty, degree status, student admission criteria, diversity of students and faculty, professional development funds). Some states (such as Indiana, Connecticut, Ohio, North Dakota, and Minnesota) have approval criteria that are performance or competency based; they examine how a program endeavors to ensure that teacher candidates acquire specific knowledge and skills. Sometimes they also examine program outcomes, such as teachers' and employers' perceptions of their adequacy of the programs, graduation rates, and job placement rates.

In over 40 states, teacher preparation programs in colleges and universities may obtain both state approval and national accreditation or may substitute national accreditation by the National Council for the Accreditation of Teacher Education (NCATE) for state approval. NCATE began accrediting teacher education programs in 1954 (NCATE, 2000a). It represents 33 specialty professional associations of teachers, teacher educators, content specialists, and local and state policy makers. NCATE introduced new outcome-based accreditation standards in 2000 (see Chapter 2 and Appendix B). Currently, 12 states require accreditation using the NCATE standards and more than 40 states have partnerships that encourage professional accreditation.

A new organization called the Teacher Education Accrediting Council (TEAC) has proposed to take a different approach to accreditation. TEAC proposes to conduct academic audits against institutions' own standards using evidence collected by the institution and to use those standards to judge program quality. TEAC has applied to the U.S. Department of Education and the Council for Higher Education Accreditation for recognition as an accrediting agency but has not yet received this recognition.

State-Specified Admission Requirements for Teacher Education

Some states also address teacher quality by specifying standards for admission to teacher education programs. Thirty-five states specify entrance requirements for their teacher preparation programs (National Association of State Directors of Teacher Education and Certification, 2000b). Almost all include meeting a basic skills standard. Additional requirements may include minimum grade point averages, subject area majors, and certain coursework.

State-Specified Course Requirements in Teacher Education

States specify the coursework their teacher candidates should take and the competencies they must demonstrate. Thirty-seven states specify some required coursework in English, humanities, social sciences, natural sciences, and mathematics, although the specific course requirements may differ for elementary or multiple-subject teachers and single-subject teachers (National Association of State Directors of Teacher Education and Certification, 2000b). Some states require that a subject area major be completed prior to entering teacher preparation.

Most teacher preparation programs include a mix of courses and field experiences (National Association of State Directors of Teacher Education and Certification, 2000b). The coursework usually includes teaching strategies and methodology, social foundations, development and learning, curriculum and instruction, classroom management, and student assessment. Some states also include the teaching of reading, use of technology, cultural diversity, school organization, and school improvement course requirements.

Instead of specifying course requirements, some states have identified competencies or performance standards to be demonstrated by program completers (Alaska, Alabama, California, Minnesota, North Dakota, Texas, West Virginia, Connecticut and Ohio; National Association of State Directors of Teacher Education and Certification, 2000b). These competencies generally follow the tenets of the states' teaching standards or the Interstate New Teacher Assessment and Support Consortium (INTASC) and other nationally developed standards statements.

Although most states also specify the type and amount of supervised teaching experience candidates must complete, there is variability in state requirements. Some states require some experience in schools before the student teaching experience begins; others do not. Thirty states have field experience requirements before student teaching. For student teaching, states require between 9 and 18 weeks of supervised teaching (National Association of State Directors of Teacher Education and Certification, 2000b). Most professions, including medicine, architecture, psychology, and engineering, require more extensive supervised clinical experience (Darling-Hammond et al., 1999).

Tests

As noted earlier, in addition to these requirements, 42 states require candidates to pass one or more tests of basic skills, general knowledge, subject matter knowledge, or teaching knowledge (National Association of State Directors of Teacher Education and Certification, 2000b). Among states that use tests, the type and number of required tests run the gamut from one test of basic skills (e.g., Alabama) to four different types of tests, including basic skills, subject matter knowledge, pedagogical content knowledge and pedagogical knowledge tests (e.g., Michigan, Colorado). Within types, more than one test may be required. For example, California requires two subject matter tests for high school teachers who have not completed an approved subject matter program.

In some states, licensing tests are tied to the granting of a degree; in others they are not. In states where tests are not required for graduation, candidates can successfully complete a teacher preparation program and graduate, but if they fail a state's test(s), they cannot get a standard teaching license. In states where tests are required for degree conferral, candidates can successfully complete all of the institutional requirements for graduation but leave without a degree because they fail the licensing test; these candidates also lack a license to teach in that state's public school system.

States' Alternative Preparation Programs for Teachers

A majority of states also have supplemented college and university preparation programs for licensure with postbaccalaureate alternative routes for candidates to enter teaching from other fields (Feistritzer and Chester, 2000). These routes are called alternative because they provide options to the four-year undergraduate programs that were the only routes to licensure in many states until the 1990s. Although varying greatly, these routes generally include an entrance requirement for content expertise and experience in the field. The programs range from requiring a preservice program of teacher education (usually 9 to 15 months) to programs offering 3 to 12 weeks of instruction prior to granting a limited teaching license, such as an intern license or a temporary or emergency license, while other requirements are completed. Some states also provide individually tailored programs based on reviews of the academic and professional backgrounds of each candidate. Alternative programs are provided by states, local districts, or institutions of higher education. In most cases, teachers from these programs are required to pass the same tests as those who become teachers through traditional routes.

Other State Licensing Requirements

Additional state licensing requirements can include U.S. citizenship, minimum age, character recommendations, or oaths of allegiance (National Association of State Directors of Teacher Education and Certification, 2000b). A small number of states require criminal background checks. Each state has guidelines governing the types of prior offenses that would prohibit licensure. Generally, prospective teachers with misdemeanors can be licensed, while those with felony records cannot.

Types of State Teaching Licenses

The majority of states have a two- or three-tiered licensure process with additional requirements tied to obtaining each type of license (National Association of State Directors of Teacher Education and Certification, 2000b). Thirty-one states require an initial license (valid for two to five years) and the attainment of a standard professional license based on fulfillment of additional requirements. Another 13 states offer an optional advanced certificate. Only three states grant a lifetime license at the advanced level. Although most of the additional licensing requirements center around completing advanced degrees or continued professional development, some states (such as Ohio, North Carolina, and Connecticut) require demonstration of competent teaching practice to obtain the next level of license. Awarding licenses based on progressively increasing education, experience, and performance requirements is another way that states try to improve the quality of teaching.

By their nature, licensure requirements reduce the supply of credentialed teachers. In some subjects and jurisdictions, given current hiring practices and current levels of teacher compensation, the supply of credentialed teachers is below the numbers needed to staff existing classes (U.S. Department of Education, 2000b, 2001). This is particularly true in mathematics, science, bilingual education, and special education and in some urban and rural communities.

In responding to these conditions, almost all states issue various kinds of restricted licenses, allowing districts and schools to hire teachers on a temporary or emergency basis for a number of reasons. Some require a demonstration that the district cannot find credentialed teachers (National Association of State Directors of Teacher Education and Certification, 2000b; U.S. Department of Education, 2000a, 2001). Some states issue emergency or temporary licenses to individuals who have met some requirements, such as holding a bachelor's degree, passing a basic skills test, or holding a license from another state, yet who have not fulfilled all of the licensure requirements for that state. State rules differ as to which licensure requirements may be waived for teachers using temporary or emergency credentials.

In all but three states requiring basic skills testing, basic skills test requirements may be waived or delayed for temporary or emergency licenses (National Association of State Directors of Teacher Education and Certification, 2000b). Subject matter test requirements may be waived or delayed in all but one of the states that require them. In some cases these waiver policies may mean that districts can hire teachers who have failed licensure tests. However, most available data do not indicate which requirements temporary or emergency credentialed teachers have met and which they have not met.

Although the numbers of employed teachers who have temporary or emergency credentials vary across states, the numbers are substantial in some states and some districts or fields within states. In the *Initial Report of the Secretary on the Quality of Teacher Preparation* (U.S. Department of Education, 2000a), 39 states provided data on the numbers of individuals in 1998 who were teaching with waivers. Using their own definitions for teaching waivers, 16 of the 39 states had waiver rates greater than 2 percent. Eight of these had waiver rates higher than 5 percent, and some were just over 17 percent.

States' Provisions for Licensure Portability

Currently, 40 states, the District of Columbia, and Puerto Rico participate in the National Association of State Directors of Teacher Education and Certification Interstate Contract (National Association of State Directors of Teacher Education and Certification, 2000a). The purpose of the contract is to help new teachers obtain licenses in other states based on their completion of a state-approved teacher education program or conferral of a state license. States participating in the contract will issue a license to candidates trained or licensed elsewhere but may specify additional requirements such as tests or courses to be completed within a given time period. States do have the option of granting full reciprocity through the contract. There also are regionally specified portability agreements that may stipulate additional licensing requirements to be met over time (e.g., Missouri, Oklahoma, Iowa, Nebraska, Kansas, South Dakota, and Arkansas have a regional compact; Maryland, the District of Columbia, New Jersey, Pennsylvania, and Delaware have a reciprocity agreement; New York and the six New England states also have a portability agreement).

Beginning Teacher Support Programs

The support provided to beginning teachers varies nationwide. Although 28 states report providing beginning teachers with a support system, the process is voluntary in 10 states, and state funding is provided only in 10 to 12 states (National Association of State Directors of Teacher Education and Certification, 2000b). Mentors and support teams are usually selected at the district level based on state or local criteria, and the amount of training provided also varies greatly.

The role of beginning teacher support programs is to provide help and guidance during the first few years of teaching, generally through the first stage of licensure. Only a few support models include an assessment component that determines continuation of a teacher's license based on a set of performance standards (such as Connecticut, Indiana, Oklahoma, and Mississippi). The majority of models provide support only or include a formative evaluation of the beginning teacher, usually conducted by the support team, including the school principal.

Hiring

Public school districts generally select their teachers from available pools of licensed candidates. Most districts use additional information about the quality of applicants to make hiring decisions. Such information sometimes includes evidence of teaching performance (e.g., videotape, demonstration lesson), the ability to develop lessons that reflect diverse student needs, and responses to interview questions about teaching specific to the culture and community of the district.

CURRENTLY USED LICENSURE TESTS

The states that require teachers to pass one or more tests to earn a license vary widely in their practices (National Association of State Directors of Teacher Education and Certification, 2000b). States have chosen different examinations based on conceptions of the knowledge and skills they expect teachers to demonstrate. Within teaching areas, states also use different tests because they work with different test developers or because, at the time a state specified its testing requirements, it chose from among existing tests, and newer-generation tests were introduced later (Angus, 2001). Different examinations test different aspects of teacher knowledge. Some measure basic skills or liberal arts knowledge, others test subject matter knowledge in teaching areas, and still others test knowledge of teaching strategies. States also vary in the way they use licensure tests to evaluate teacher candidates. In some states, tests are used for admission to teacher education programs and for graduation, while in other states testing is required only for initial licensure.

As is the case with the licensing tests used in other professions, teacher licensure tests focus on the knowledge and skills identified by panels of educators as critical for entry into the profession. They cover the material considered to be *minimally* necessary for beginning teaching. Teacher licensure tests are not designed to distinguish moderately qualified teachers from highly qualified teachers. They are not constructed to predict the degree of teaching success a beginning teacher will demonstrate. The tests focus on the knowledge and skills necessary for competent beginning teaching, not on advanced levels or on the full set of knowledge and skills that licensing boards might like candidates to have. Thus, initial licensing tests are designed to discriminate at the score level that separates minimally competent from incompetent beginning practitioners. They do not possess the kinds of measurement qualities needed to make distinctions at the higher performance levels.

The following descriptions of initial teacher licensure tests and their uses rely on recent reports by the U.S. Department of Education (2000a), the National Association of State Directors of Teacher Education and Certification (2000b), and the Council of Chief State School Officers (2000). These reports describe the state of practice one to two years ago; current practices may differ.

Types of Tests Used by States

There are two primary commercial producers of teacher licensure tests—the Educational Testing Service (ETS) and National Evaluation Systems (NES). Thirty-two states use one or more components of the ETS-produced series called Praxis (U.S. Department of Education, 2000a; National Association of State Directors of Teacher Education and Certification, 2000b). When the committee began its work, eight states used tests specifically designed by NES for their prospective teachers (National Association of State Directors of Teacher Education and Certification, 1999); additional states are now developing tests with NES. Some states develop their own tests, and some use a combination of state-developed and contractor-produced tests. Table 3-2 shows the number of states that require each of five different types of licensure tests—basic skills, general knowledge, subject matter knowledge, pedagogical knowledge, and subject-specific pedagogical knowledge tests—as well as the test producers.

Table 3-3 presents the numbers of tests in use in 1998/1999 and shows that states use over 600 different tests. ETS administers 144 different tests (Educational Testing Service, 1999e). NES has developed over 400 different teacher tests for its client states (U.S. Department of Education, 2000a). Again, some states develop their own tests. The data show that there are 40 different basic skills tests in use. Over half of these are custom developed by NES. ETS offers paper-and-pencil and computer-based versions of its basic skills tests. Currently, only a few general knowledge tests are being used by states. There are over 500 different subject matter tests. Three-quarters of these are specifically developed for or by states. ETS provides 126 different subject matter tests, covering over 50 different subject areas. Presently, there are 17 pedagogical knowledge tests in use, in addition to a small number of subject-specific pedagogical knowledge tests. Appendix C lists the tests offered by each test developer. The content and format of these tests are described next.

TABLE 3-2 Numbers of States Using Different Types of Initial Licensure Tests, by Test Developer, 1998-1999[a]

| Test Developer | Test Type | | | | | |
	Basic Skills	General Knowledge	Subject Matter Knowledge	Subject-Specific Pedagogical Knowledge[b]	Pedagogical Knowledge[b]	Total Number of States[c]
ETS	28[d]	10[e]	20	20	7	32
NES	9	4	9	6		8[f]
State[g]	1		2	2		2
Total	38	14	31	28	7	42

[a]Data are from the U.S. Department of Education (2000), the National Association of State Directors of Teacher Education and Certification (2000b), and Educational Testing Service (1999d). There are data discrepancies across sources and across tables within sources. The data in this and the next table represent our understanding of the data from these sources and from information obtained from state web sites and licensing officials.

[b]State tests were classified as subject-specific pedagogical knowledge tests only if test titles indicated they were. Other tests may include items testing both content and pedagogical knowledge.

[c]Row totals show the numbers of states working with ETS, NES, and developing their own tests. The data in the cells of the rows do not sum to the totals because some states use several types of tests.

[d]Includes Pre-Professional Skills Test, Computer-Based Test, and one Core Battery test.

[e]The General Knowledge test is one component of the Core Battery test.

[f]Ten states were listed as NES, states in the 2000b National Association of State Directors of Teacher Education & Certification Guide. However, Oregon is not included here because it primarily uses ETS tests; and Oklahoma's test development program was in transition when our study began.

[g]Several states and higher-education institutions have chosen to develop some or all of their teacher licensure tests.

TABLE 3-3 Numbers of Different Initial Licensure Tests, by Test Type and Test Developer, 1998-1999[a]

Test Developer	Test Type					Total Number of States[c]
	Basic Skills	General Knowledge	Subject Matter Knowledge	Subject-Specific Pedagogical Knowledge	Pedagogical Knowledge[b]	
ETS	7[c]	1[d]	126	4[d]	6	144
NES	27	4	362	12		405
State[e]	6		69	1		76
Total	40	5	557	17	6	625

[a]Data are taken from the U.S. Department of Education, (2000a), the National Association of State Directors of Teacher Education and Certification, (2000b), and Educational Testing Service, (1999d). There are data discrepancies across sources and across tables within sources. The data in this table represent our understanding the data from these sources and from other information obtained from state websites and licensing officials.

[b]State tests were classified as subject-specific pedagogical knowledge tests only if test titles indicated they were. Other tests may include items testing both content and pedagogical knowledge.

[c]Includes Pre-Professional Skills Test, Computer-Based Test, and one Core Battery test.

[d]Includes Principles of Learning and Teaching test and one Core Battery test.

[e]Several states and higher-education institutions have chosen to develop some or all of their teacher licensure tests

Basic Skills

As can be seen in Table 3-2, more states use tests of basic literacy, communication, and mathematics skills than any other type of test. Thirty-eight states require teacher candidates to meet minimum state requirements on a basic skills test before earning initial licenses (U.S. Department of Education, 2000a; National Association of State Directors of Teacher Education and Certification, 2000b). Twenty-eight of these use Praxis I, the first part of the Praxis series (Educational Testing Service, 1999d), which measures basic knowledge in mathematics, reading, and writing. There are both paper-and-pencil and computer-based versions. Ten other states have chosen basic skills tests specifically developed for their teacher candidates. In nine of these states the basic skills test is designed by NES (U.S. Department of Education, 2000a; National Association of State Directors of Teacher Education and Certification, 2000b). Five other states require candidates to fulfill the basic skills requirement before entering teacher education but give higher education institutions leeway in selecting which tests to use.

General Knowledge

Fourteen states administer tests of general knowledge, which are generally tests of undergraduate-level liberal arts content. New York, for example, administers the Liberal Arts and Sciences Test (LAST) <www.highered.nysed.gov>. LAST covers scientific and mathematical processes, historical and social scientific awareness, artistic expression and the humanities, communication skills, and written analysis and expression. New Mexico gives the Teacher General Knowledge test, and Oklahoma requires the Oklahoma General Education Test. The Praxis II series includes Core Battery tests, which have three parts: General Knowledge, Professional Knowledge, and Communication Skills. The General Knowledge test includes social studies, mathematics, literature and fine arts, and science items. The Professional Knowledge and Communications Skills tests, which are tests of teaching skill, are described below.

Subject Matter Knowledge

Twenty-one states require teacher candidates to take one or more tests of subject matter knowledge (U.S. Department of Education, 2000a; National Association of State Directors of Teacher Education and Certification, 2000b). As with the basic skills tests, states can choose from among several options for this purpose. The Praxis II series includes some 126 subject-area examinations, including accounting, biology, driver education, French, mathematics, physical education, and psychology (Educational Testing Service, 1999d). The states that use tests designed for them by NES also cover a range of subject areas (U.S.

Department of Education, 2000a; National Association of State Directors of Teacher Education and Certification, 2000b). For example, New York offers 24 subject exams, while Michigan administers over 70. NES has developed over 360 different subject matter tests, including tests in social studies, art, Russian, music, reading, and agriculture.

ETS recently announced that it will be collaborating with the National Council for Accreditation of Teacher Education to revamp the Praxis II subject area Tests (National Association of State Directors of Teacher Education and Certification, 1999). The goal of the revisions is to more closely align the content of Praxis tests with the teaching standards written by subject matter associations and to include more items on pedagogy.

Pedagogical Knowledge

Pedagogical knowledge tests examine prospective teachers' knowledge of learning and development, educational psychology, classroom management, instructional design and delivery techniques, and evaluation and assessment. They cover such topics as organizing content knowledge for student learning, creating an environment for learning, teaching for student learning, and teacher professionalism. Twenty-eight states use tests to assess candidates' subject-specific knowledge of teaching strategies (U.S. Department of Education, 2000a; National Association of State Directors of Teacher Education and Certification, 2000b). Two states require teacher education programs to assess pedagogical knowledge. Twenty states use a component of Praxis II called the Principles of Learning and Teaching tests, which are designed for three grade levels: grades K-6, 5-9, and 7-12 (Educational Testing Service, 1999d).

The Professional Knowledge test of the ETS Core Battery tests examines candidates' knowledge of four teaching functions: planning instruction, implementing instruction, evaluating instruction, and managing the learner and the learning environment. The Communication Skills test assesses candidates' knowledge of aspects of the teacher education curriculum and their ability to listen, read, and write well.

NES has also developed pedagogical knowledge tests for several states, including Arizona, Colorado, New York, Texas, and Illinois (National Association of State Directors of Teacher Education and Certification, 2000b). In New York, teachers must pass the Assessment of Teaching Skills-Written, which measures candidates' knowledge of the learner, instructional planning and assessment, instructional delivery, and the professional environment <www.highered.nysed>. The Examination for the Certification of Educators in Texas (ExCET) combines subject matter knowledge with the professional knowledge expected of entry-level teachers <www.excet.nesinc.com>.

Florida has designed its own test for assessing prospective teachers' pedagogical knowledge <www.firn.edu/doe>. Candidates for initial certification take the Florida Professional Education Test, which covers five content areas: personal development, appropriate student behavior, planning instruction, implementing instruction, and evaluating instruction. Alternatively, candidates can take the Praxis Professional Knowledge Test.

California has a new pedagogical test for prospective reading teachers called the Reading Instruction Competence Assessment (RICA) <www.ctc.ca.gov>. RICA assesses the knowledge and skills essential for providing effective reading instruction to students. It includes four domains, which cover planning and organizing reading instruction based on ongoing assessment, developing phonological and other linguistic processes related to reading, developing reading comprehension and promoting independent reading, and supporting reading through oral and written language development. RICA is offered as a paper-and-pencil test and as a video-based performance assessment.

INTASC states are developing a new pedagogical knowledge test called the Test of Teaching Knowledge (TTK) for teacher candidates. This test is scheduled for administration in 2002 (J. Miller, INTASC, personal communication, 2000). Field test materials for the TTK include open-ended items about learning, development, and motivation; teaching scenarios and artifacts; and samples of student work that attempt to evaluate whether teacher candidates understand the fundamentals of child development, motivation and behavior, learning theory, the identification of common learning difficulties, principles of classroom management, and strategies for assessment.

The field test version of the TTK includes a case study exercise and a folio review as well as constructed-response questions based on INTASC principles. In the case study a detailed narrative about a classroom situation is described, while the folio review exercise presents a collection of documents related to one particular classroom instructional sequence. Questions following the exercises ask candidates to describe appropriate instructional strategies that address and support different learning styles or to describe effective classroom management styles of individual, small-group, or whole-class work. Other items ask candidates to write letters to parents explaining plans for organizing classroom work for their students, considering curriculum goals, and knowledge about child and adolescent development.

Subject-Specific Pedagogical Knowledge

Another kind of teacher knowledge that includes dimensions of content and pedagogy is called subject-specific pedagogical knowledge (Shulman, 1986). Subject-specific pedagogical knowledge goes beyond knowledge of subject matter to include ways of representing and formulating topics that make them understandable to students. It also includes an understanding of what makes learning a topic easy or difficult for students—for example, misconceptions about the solar system that might impede learning about astronomy.

The Praxis II series includes subject-specific pedagogical content knowledge tests in biology, foreign language, mathematics, physical science, social studies, and Spanish (Education Testing Service, 1999d). Only seven states require prospective teachers to take tests of pedagogical knowledge.

Concerns About Current Tests

A number of questions have been raised by the field about whether current tests measure what they purport to measure. For example, while requiring a basic skills test might seem like a straightforward matter, there are substantial differences in which skills various tests actually measure, in how different they are, and in how much consensus there is about the importance of tested skills. Recent controversy about the Massachusetts Educator Certification Test (MECT) provides a case in point (Haney et al., 1999). The MECT included an item that asked candidates to transcribe an excerpt of the Federalist papers dictated to them by audiotape. This test question produced widespread debate about the job relatedness of the test (Melnick and Pullin, 2000; Haney et al., 1999).

Tests of subject matter knowledge raise additional questions. For example, should a test of subject matter knowledge for teacher candidates measure the content that candidates will be expected to teach in the K-12 curriculum or should it measure a more ambitious set of understandings achieved at the college level? Should content be tested through multiple-choice items that sometimes demand recall of specific facts or should candidates demonstrate that they can generate information and apply knowledge in situations that demand reasoning and integration of ideas? Different tests currently in use resolve these questions in different ways with different results for who passes and what they know (Darling-Hammond et al., 1999; Shulman, 1987).

Several tests of pedagogical knowledge have been criticized for their inability to evaluate how teaching knowledge would be applied in complex contexts, favoring instead items requiring the recognition of facts within subject areas, knowledge of school law and bureaucratic procedures, and recognition of the "correct" teaching behavior in a situation described in a short scenario of only one or two sentences. Tests that rely on multiple-choice or short-answer responses to brief statements of professional problems may fail to represent the complexity of the decision-making process. The example in Box 3-1 from the Praxis II series illustrates this problem (Educational Testing Service, 1996:15).

It is possible from the question's wording and an understanding of the test's expectations that B is the "right" answer, but in reality the answer would likely depend on the curriculum and student context. A thoughtful teacher making real-world decisions would need to know many things not treated in the question. What was the point of the assignment? Was the drawing the central task or a peripheral aspect of a task focused more centrally on writing or science? Did the curriculum goals and the use of class time really allow the teacher to go out

BOX 3-1
Sample Praxis II Item

A third-grade student who is attempting to draw a spaceship stops drawing and asks the teacher to draw it. Of the following teacher responses, which would best provide for this student's continued learning and growth?

(A) Drawing the spaceship for him so that he can continue his picture.
(B) Having the student observe models of spaceships and giving him some pointers about drawing.
(C) Asking the best student artist to provide help.
(D) Having another student draw the spaceship for him.
(E) Assuring the student that the drawing is fine for his purpose.

SOURCE: Educational Testing Service, 1996:15.

and find spaceship models and give a mini art lesson? What are the opportunity costs of this approach? What caused the student's question? Did he really have difficulty with drawing or did he simply want the teacher's attention at that moment? Depending on the social and academic goals of the class, the teacher might want to encourage peer tutoring (answer C) rather than devoting time to this herself.

Aside from the fact that intelligent and thoughtful teacher candidates could think of circumstances under which any of the given answers might be the most appropriate, it is not clear what value getting the "right" answer here has in demonstrating important knowledge or skill for teaching. Furthermore, suggesting to teacher candidates that there is one right answer to such a question could be counterproductive rather than supportive of developing a sophisticated practice since it fails to treat the important issues of curriculum goals, context, and student needs. Others have questioned the way current tests separate questions about subject matter from questions about teaching knowledge. This is viewed as problematic by some who see the interrelations between subject matter knowledge and knowledge of learning as critical to teaching. Some tests that have tried to examine subject matter knowledge as it is applied to teaching have had difficulty doing so in a manner viewed as closely related to the act of teaching.

TEST RESULTS SUPPORT DIFFERENT DECISIONS ABOUT CANDIDATES

States vary in the way they use initial licensure tests to evaluate teacher candidates (National Association of State Directors of Teacher Education and Certification, 2000b). The differences reflect the decisions that test information supports. As noted earlier, some states use the tests for admission into teacher education, others as a prerequisite for student teaching or as a condition of graduation, and others for the initial licensure of teachers. Many teacher candidates take multiple tests. Table 3-4 shows the different decisions that states and institutions support with teacher licensure test results.

Initial Licensure Requirements in Seven States

To help illustrate the different ways that licensure tests are used to make decisions about teacher candidates, initial teacher licensure systems in seven states are described below. The cases demonstrate the different ways in which initial licensure tests are used to make decisions about teacher candidates. Two states have no testing requirements for licensure (Idaho and Wyoming); two require only basic skills testing; three require basic skills and subject matter tests for licensure (California, Maryland, and Connecticut). Table 3-5 summarizes the seven systems, showing the initial licensure requirements for teacher candidates in elementary education. More complete descriptions of teacher licensure in these states appear in Appendix D. Some states also have induction programs.

TABLE 3-4   Numbers of States Using Initial Teacher Licensure Tests to Support Varied Decisions About Candidates in 1998-1999[a]

	Basic Skills	Subject Matter Knowledge	Pedagogical Knowledge	Subject-Specific Pedagogical Knowledge
Admission to teacher education[b]	19	3	0	0
Eligibility for student teaching or degree conferral[c]	1	3	2	2
Licensure	18	25	26	5
Total	38	31	28	7

[a]Data are from the National Association of State Directors of Teacher Education and Certification (2000b), especially Tables G-1 and G-3. In some cases, contradictory information appeared across the guide's tables; data were reconciled here to the extent possible. In some cases, states reviewed and revised policies after supplying information for the guide. The National Association of State Directors of Teacher Education and Certification guide does not document the uses of general knowledge tests. Some data also came from Educational Testing Service (1999d).

[b]ACT, SAT, or state precollege tests are required for admission to teacher education programs in some states or at some institutions in states without entry testing requirements.

[c]These data appeared in comment fields in the National Association of State Directors of Teacher Education and Certification guide (2000b) and were not systematically gathered. More states may use current tests for these purposes, and states and institutions may use test results for additional purposes.

In addition to differences in the use of tests, these case studies suggest some of the multiple criteria that states use to award initial licenses as well as the variations among states in their views of the knowledge and skills required for beginning teaching. Like six other states, Idaho and Wyoming have no testing requirements. Table 3-5 shows that candidates in Connecticut and Nebraska must pass a basic skills test to enter teacher education. In California, candidates take a basic skills test for diagnostic purposes before entering teacher education and must pass the same test before obtaining an initial license. In Alaska and Maryland, teacher candidates must pass a basic skills test before earning a license. Several of the states with basic skills test requirements use Praxis I. Alaska, Nebraska, Maryland, and Connecticut all do so, but they set different passing scores. There is a seven-point difference, for example, in the reading passing scores required in Nebraska and Maryland. Similarly, there is a difference in the math passing scores required by Alaska and Maryland, although both states require teacher candidates to pass Praxis I for initial licensure. California requires teacher candidates to pass the California Basic Educational Skills Test, developed by NES.

Teacher candidates in California, Connecticut, and Maryland also must pass relevant subject matter tests to earn an initial license. As illustrated in Table 3-5, elementary teacher candidates in California must pass the Multiple Subjects Assessment for Teachers, which includes content knowledge and content area exercises and measures knowledge in seven content areas. Connecticut and Maryland both use tests from the Praxis II series to test elementary teacher candidates, with Connecticut requiring candidates to pass Elementary Education: Curriculum, Instruction and Assessment, and Elementary Education Content Area Exercises. Maryland also requires candidates to pass Elementary Education Content Area Exercises (with a different passing score than Connecticut) but uses a different test to assess content knowledge; Maryland uses the Elementary Education: Content Knowledge test.

Although Idaho and Wyoming have no testing requirements for initial teacher licensure, they have other requirements for earning a teaching license. Like the other five states, they require teacher candidates to have completed an approved teacher education program and to have met specific coursework requirements. Idaho asks teacher candidates to demonstrate computer competency before obtaining an initial license. Wyoming requires a course on the U.S. Constitution and on its state constitution. Alaska and California also require U.S. Constitution courses. Several states require teacher candidates to complete special education courses (Nebraska, Maryland, and Connecticut) or a multicultural course prior to earning an initial teacher license (Alaska). Some states also require candidates to fulfill residency requirements and to verify recent teaching experience. Most states require candidates to demonstrate good moral character and/or the absence of a criminal record.

TABLE 3-5 Initial Licensure Requirements in Seven States[a]

States	Required Tests	Passing Scores	Decisions About Students Supported by Test Scores	Other Requirements for Initial Licensure
Idaho[b]	None required[c]			• Graduation from an approved teacher education program • Meet state coursework requirements • Demonstrate computer competency • Good moral character
Wyoming[d]	None required[c]			• Graduation from an approved teacher education program • Completeon of a course on the U.S Constitution and the Wyoming constitution

Alaska[e]	Praxis I
	Paper/Pencil or Computer-Based Tests (CBT) accepted
		reading = 175;
		writing = 174;
		math = 173
		
		[CBT:
		reading = 322;
		writing = 321;
		math = 318]
			Licensure	• Graduation from an approved teacher education program
				• Fulfill recency/residency requirement
				• Completion of a course in Alaska studies and multicultural/cross-cultural education
				• Good moral character

Nebraska[f]	Praxis I
	Paper/Pencil or Computer-Based Tests (CBT) accepted
		reading = 170;
		writing = 171;
		math = 172
		
		[CBT
		reading = 316;
		writing = 318;
		math = 316]
			Entry into teacher education program	• Graduation from an approved teacher education program
				• Complete a special education course
				• Adhere to Nebraska's standards of Conduct and Ethics
				• Fulfill training requirement in human relations
				• Fulfill recency/residency requirement
				• No criminal record (no felony convictions or misdemeanor convictions involving abuse, neglect, or sexual misconduct)

Or

	Test	Score	Stage	Additional Requirements
	Content Mastery Exam for Educators (CMEE)	CMEE = 850 (composite score)		
California[g]	California Basic Educational Skills Test (CBEST)	Composite score of 123, with a minimum score of 37 in each section: reading, math, and writing	Entry into teacher education program (most traditional teacher education programs)	• Completion of an approved teacher preparation program • Completion of a course or an exam on the U.S. Constitution • Completion of a teaching of reading course • Completion of a health education course, including nutrition and cardiopulmonary resuscitation
	Reading Instruction Competence Assessment (RICA)	RICA Composite score = 311		
	Elementary Teachers: Multiple Subjects Assessment for Teachers (MSAT) (a) Content Knowledge (b) Content Areas Exercises	Content knowledge = 156 Content area exercises = 155		
Maryland[h]	Praxis I Paper/Pencil or Computer-Based Tests (CBT) accepted	reading = 177; writing = 173; math = 177 [CBT: reading = 325; writing = 319; math = 322]	Licensure	• Graduation from an approved teacher education program • Completion of a special education course • Good moral character

continues

TABLE 3-5 Continued

States	Required Tests	Passing Scores	Decisions About Students Supported by Test Scores	Other Requirements for Initial Licensure
	Praxis II for elementary teachers: Elementary Education Content Knowledge	Elementary School: Content Knowledge = 136	Licensure	
	Elementary Education Content Area Exercises	Content exercises = 150		
Connecticut[i]	Praxis I (CBT only)	reading = 324; writing = 318; math = 319	Entry into teacher education programs	• Graduation from an approved teacher education program • Completion of a special education course • Completion of a U.S. history course
	Praxis II (for elementary teachers): Elementary Education: Curriculum, Instruction and Assessment	163	Licensure	
	Elementary Education Content Area Exercises	148		

a Table includes tests and other requirements for initial licensure only. Connecticut and other states have induction and beginning teacher support programs that have additional assessment requirements.

b Higher education institutions in the state require students to pass a basic skills test before entering teacher education, although this is not a state requirement. Idaho State Department of Education, Certification Department <www.sde.state.id.us/certification/>.

c Higher education institutions in the state require students to pass a basic skills test before entering teacher education, although this is not a state requirement.

d Wyoming State Department of Education, Certification Department <www.k12.wy.us/ptsb/index>.

e Alaska State Department of Education, Certification Department <www.eed.state.ak.us/TeacherCertification>.

f Nebraska State Department of Education, Certification Department <www.nde.state.ne.us/TCERT/TCERT.html>.

g California Commission on Teacher Credentialing <www.ctc.ca.gov>.

h Maryland State Department of Education, Certification Department <www.msde.state.md.us/certification/index.htm>.

i Connecticut State Department of Education, Certification Department <www.state.ct.us/sde/dtl/cert/index.htm>.

The admission criteria for teacher education programs also can differ at institutions within a state and in some cases even exceed the state's requirement for initial licensure. For example, Maryland does not require basic skills testing for entry to teacher education, yet some institutions in the state require students to pass Praxis I (at the state's established passing score for licensure) to enter their programs. In Idaho and Wyoming, where there are no testing requirements, some higher-education institutions require a basic skills test for admission to their teacher education programs; different tests are used by different institutions.

A review of the case studies in Appendix D also reveals some variation in the curriculum of teacher education programs across states. Several states (Idaho, Maryland) have adopted the National Association of State Directors of Teacher Education and Certification standards as the basis for the curriculum in their teacher education programs, while other states (California, Nebraska) require that the curriculum of teacher education programs be aligned to standards adopted by the state. Additionally, states vary in the amount of education required to earn an initial teaching license. For example, in California most traditional teacher education programs require completion of a baccalaureate program before admission to a one-year preparatory program. In most states a teaching license can be obtained after completion of an undergraduate program.

In most of the states reviewed by the committee, initial licensure is contingent on institutional recommendations for candidates; this is especially true in states without testing requirements. Yet in some states (California and Maryland) alternative routes to initial licensure have been established that allow individuals to begin teaching (with supervision) without having completed a teacher education program. Candidates are typically granted an emergency or intern teaching certificate for the academic year. The alternative routes can include university internship programs, district internship programs, preinternship programs, and resident teacher programs. In some programs, candidates need to meet state testing requirements before beginning the alternate program and entering the classroom, while in other programs candidates can teach while fulfilling state testing requirements for the initial license.

SETTING PASSING SCORES

Passing scores on licensure tests are important because they help determine access to the profession. States set their own passing scores The passing scores currently required by different states are given in Appendix C (National Association of State Directors of Teacher Education and Certification, 2000b; U.S. Department of Education, 2000a). The standard-setting models used to estimate minimally competent performance are discussed below. Information used by policy makers to set final passing scores also is described.

Standard-Setting Methods

Most states set passing scores on teacher licensure tests by asking panels of educators to identify the level of content and teaching knowledge that they judge to be minimally necessary for beginning practice. Several methods for setting passing scores are currently used (Jaeger, 1989; Mills, 1995; Plake, 1998; Horn et al., 2000). The modified Angoff (1971) model is the most widely used method for setting standards on multiple-choice tests. It is used by ETS states. With this method, panelists estimate the proportion of minimally qualified candidates who would be able to answer each test question correctly. The standard is established by summing these proportions across questions. Though this approach is widely used in licensure testing, its methods and the meaningfulness of the standards it produces have been questioned (National Research Council, 1999b). Analysts argue that the estimation task given to panelists is too difficult and confusing, that the results vary significantly by question type, and that the method sometimes yields results that are not believable.

Other methods are used to set standards on open-ended test questions. Estimating the performance of minimally competent candidates on questions for which responses are graded along a continuum (i.e., not just right or wrong), such as on essay questions, is more complex (Educational Testing Service, 1999b). The methods used on these items are not as well researched as those used with multiple-choice items, and there is less agreement in the field about which methods are appropriate.

States using ETS exams either use item-level pass/fail procedures or a benchmark paper selection approach (Educational Testing Service, 1997). For the former, panelists look at the scoring tables for open-ended items and make estimates of the numbers of points minimally competent candidates can be expected to earn on each question. Then they are given input on the actual performance of the candidate population. Experts are given an opportunity to revise their initial estimates. The final averages across panelists are used as the recommended passing scores for open-ended questions.

The benchmark paper selection approach calls for panels of educators to examine a preselected range of candidate responses and judge which work is indicative of the minimally competent candidate; often, panelists select the two papers that best represent this work. Sometimes panelists are given data on the actual performance of candidates after their first selection of papers and are allowed to make revised selections if they wish to after seeing the data. The scores of benchmark papers are averaged across panelists to generate the recommended passing score for the open-ended questions.

In some states the results of these standard-setting studies are then provided to state officials for the final determination of passing scores (Educational Testing Service, 1999b). The panelists recommend passing scores to a policy body, such as the state board of education or the commissioner's office. That body usually makes the final decision based on the panelists' recommendations and other information, including the standards of neighboring states, historical passing rates in their own state, eventual passing rates (as distinct from first-time passing rates), possible decision errors for candidates scoring at or near the proposed passing score, the impact of different standards on the passing rates of minority groups, and a desire to raise or lower standards in response to concerns about teacher quality and supply (Horn et al., 2000). These factors are similar to those influencing standards in other fields (Jasanoff, 1998).

The extent to which states follow the standard-setting models described here is not known. It is known that research on standard-setting methods indicates that passing scores may vary as a function of several factors, such as the methods used to set the standard, the particular panelists who participate in the process, and the training and instructions the panelists receive (Kane, 1994; Horn et al., 2000). Indeed, on different occasions even the same panelists may arrive at different standards for the same test (Norcini and Shea, 1992). Various criteria, such as high agreement among different panels, have been suggested for evaluating the quality of standard-setting processes (Kane, 1994; Cizek, 1996). The professional *Standards for Educational and Psychological Testing* say that technically-sound standard-setting studies are systematic, both in the procedures used and in the way the panelists are chosen (American Educational Research Association et al., 1999). Standard-setting studies all should be well-documented, providing information on the panelists, the methods, and the results.

No data were found in the published literature to document states' particular practices. In order to better characterize and discuss states' various standard-setting procedures, the committee fielded a survey on standard-setting methods in teacher licensure as part of its study. State licensing officials were asked about the methods used in their standard-setting studies, about the composition of their standard-setting panels, and about the decision models and data used by policy makers in setting final passing scores. The questions appear below in Box 3-2.

The committee did not get enough responses to its survey to support useful descriptions of states' practices. Responses to questions about the standard-setting methods that states use and about their panels were low. Responses to questions about the methods and data used by policy bodies in setting final passing scores were particularly low. Little is known about how states arrive at final decisions about passing scores.

It is known, however, that several state policy bodies have recently raised passing scores on their licensure tests (Educational Testing Service, 1998b, 2000). Others have reported setting passing scores on newly adopted tests that exceed those set by other states using the same tests (Archer, 1998; The Ohio Wire, 2/18/98; Education World, 2000). These policies have accompanied teacher quality initiatives and make the standards for passing more stringent.

BOX 3-2
Survey of Standard-Setting Methods for Initial Teacher
Licensure Examinations

1. There are several methods used to set performance standards, or cut scores, on tests. Which method most closely describes the method used by your state to set a passing standard for your initial teacher licensure examination(s)? If your state uses different methods for different tests, please mark all methods used:

____ Modified Angoff. For each item or exercise, panelists indicate the proportion of minimally competent examinees who would be able to answer the item satisfactorily. The standard is established by summing these proportions across all items or exercises.

____ Bookmarking. This method is used for both multiple-choice and constructed-response tests. Test items are arranged in descending order of difficulty and panelists place "bookmarks" immediately after the last item that all minimally competent examinees should be expected to know.

____ Judgmental policy capturing. This method is used for tests such as performance assessments and test batteries that contain items or exercises that have a score scale of three or more points (rather than simply right/wrong). Panelists review profiles of scores and provide judgments about the performance level of each examinee. Statistical analysis is used to yield a recommended standard for each panelist.

____ Nedelsky's method. This method is used with multiple-choice tests. For each item, panelists eliminate all response options that the minimally competent examinee should be able to eliminate and records the reciprocal of the remaining number of responses. (If a panelist eliminates two out of five response options, three options would remain and the panelist would record "1/3").

____ Ebel's method. This method is used with multiple-choice tests. Test items are classified in a two-dimensional grid of item difficulty and item relevance. Each cell of the grid indicates how many items are at a given level of difficulty and relevance. Panelists indicate the proportion of items in each cell that a minimally competent examinee should answer correctly.

____ Contrasting groups. Panelists engage in discussion and agree on what constitutes minimally acceptable performance. They then identify candidates who, in their judgment, are clearly above the standard and those who are clearly below the standard. The examination is administered to both groups of examinees, score distributions are plotted for the two groups, and the performance standard is set at the point of intersection between the two score distributions.

____ Other (please describe)

Composition of the Standard-Setting Panel

2. How many panelists typically serve on your state's standard-setting panel?

____

3. What is the composition of your state's standard-setting panel? Please indicate the approximate percentage of your state's standard-setting panel represented by each type of person listed below.

continues

BOX 3-2 *Continued*

____ Teachers
____ Principals
____ District-level curriculum specialists
____ University-level content experts
____ Teacher educators
____ Professional association representatives (e.g., National Council of Teachers of English, National Council of Teachers of Mathematics, International Reading Association, etc.)
____ Business representatives
____ Parents
____ Other (please describe)

Review of the Recommended Passing Standard

4. After the standard-setting panel recommends a passing standard, what happens next?

____ Nothing. The panel's recommended standard is adopted as the final standard.
____ An automatic adjustment based on the standard error is applied to the panel's recommended standard.
____ The panel's recommended standard is reviewed by a technical advisory committee.
____ The panel's recommended standard is reviewed by the state department of education.
____ The panel's recommended standard is reviewed by a professional standards board.
____ Other (please describe)

Changes to the Recommended Standard

5. If you indicated that the technical advisory committee, state department, professional standards board, or other body has the authority to modify the standard-setting panel's recommended standard, which of the following best describes the experience in your state?

____ The standard has not been changed.
____ The standard has been adjusted upward based on the standard error.
____ The standard has been adjusted upward based on other considerations.
____ The standard has been adjusted downward based on the standard error.
____ The standard has been adjusted downward based on other considerations.

Current Standards

Current passing scores on several widely used Praxis tests appear in Table 3-6. For each test, the lowest passing score currently in use by a state is shown in the first data column. The percentiles associated with these passing scores in the national candidate population are given in the second data column. Column

TABLE 3-6 Range of Passing Scores for States Using Selected Praxis Tests, 1998-1999

Praxis Test[a]	Lowest Passing Score	National Percentile Equivalent for Lowest Score	Highest Passing Score	National Percentile Equivalent for Highest Score
PPST: Reading	169	10	178	43
PLT: K-6	152	6	169	34
Middle School English/Language Arts	145	6	164	29
Mathematics: Proofs, Models & Problems, Part 1	139	22	154	46
Biology Content Knowledge, Part 1	139	4	161	32
Biology Content Knowledge, Part 2	135	25	156	68

[a] These tests were selected because currently they are widely used; they represent a range of test types, content, item types, and levels of schooling; and they are not currently scheduled for retirement. Scores range from 100 to 200 on these tests.

three shows the most stringent passing scores set by states for each of the tests, and data column four shows the associated national percentiles.

Table 3-6 shows substantial variation among states in the passing scores set for teacher examinations. For example, state passing scores on the Principles of Learning and Teaching (PLT): K-6 test range from 152 to 169 on a scale of 100 to 200. A score of 152 on the test places candidates at about the 6th percentile on the national distribution; a score of 169 places examinees at about the 34th percentile. That is, in one state, teacher candidates can pass the PLT testing requirement for licensure by scoring slightly above the 6th percentile of candidates in the national distribution. In another, applicants for licensure must score above the bottom third of the national candidate population on the PLT to satisfy the licensing requirement.

Variations in passing scores for states using the same tests show the states' differing minimum requirements for entry-level teaching. It is not known whether differences in passing scores on current tests reflect methodological differences in the standard-setting process, differences in the judgments of state panels about the minimum requirements for beginning teachers, or policy makers' adjustments to panelists' recommendations. Also not known is the extent to which differences in states' teaching and learning standards or differing concerns about decision errors, teacher quality, or teacher supply influence variability across states.

The large variation in passing standards that occurs among states that use the same test is not a phenomenon unique to teacher tests. For example, the differences in passing standards among states are larger for the law bar exam than they are on Praxis I, and these differences occur even though virtually every state claims that its bar exam is testing for minimum or basic competency to practice law (Wightman, 1998). States differ in the specific bar exam test score level of proficiency that they believe corresponds to this standard. The same is true in teaching.

CONCLUSION

The primary goal of licensing beginning teachers is to ensure that all students have competent teachers. Teacher licensing is under the authority of individual states. There are 51 unique licensure systems in the United States, with some commonalties however. As in other professions, teacher licensing relies on more than tests to judge whether candidates have the knowledge, skills, abilities, and dispositions to practice responsibly. Teacher candidates generally must fulfill education requirements, successfully complete practice teaching, and receive the recommendations of their preparing institutions. These requirements help ensure that a broad range of competencies are considered in licensing new teachers.

Initial teacher licensure tests are designed to identify candidates with some of the knowledge and skills needed for minimally competent beginning practice. The tests currently used measure basic skills, general knowledge, content knowledge, and knowledge of teaching strategies. The tests are designed to separate teacher candidates who are minimally competent in the areas assessed from those who are not. Initial teacher licensure tests do not provide information to distinguish moderately qualified from highly qualified teacher candidates nor are they designed to test all of the competencies relevant to beginning practice.

States decide whether to use tests and what tests to use to license beginning teachers. Each of the 42 states that requires tests uses a different combination of them, uses them at different points in the candidate's education, and sets its own passing scores on them. Several hundred different initial licensure tests are in current use. Two test developers, Educational Testing Service (ETS) and National Evaluation Systems (NES), develop the vast majority of these tests.

States set passing scores on licensure tests based on judgments about the levels of knowledge and skill needed for minimally competent beginning teaching in their state. Although many states rely on commonly used standard-setting procedures, there is little documentation about these procedures and how states actually use this information in arriving at a final decision about passing scores. In attempts to raise teacher standards, some states have recently raised their passing scores on particular tests. Some report having set passing scores that are higher than those of other states.

The committee draws the following conclusions from these findings:

- Because a teacher's work is complex, even a set of well-designed tests cannot measure all of the prerequisites of competent beginning teaching. Current paper-and-pencil tests provide only some of the information needed to evaluate the competencies of teacher candidates.
- States have gradually adopted tests for teacher licensure, and test developers have made various tests available over time. Therefore, it is not surprising that states have adopted a variety of tests to license beginning teachers.
- States differ in how high they set passing scores. The committee does not know the extent to which this variation in passing scores reflects differences among states in standard-setting methods; state teaching and learning standards; the characteristics of applicant pools; or different concerns about measurement error, teacher quality, or teacher supply.
- Appropriate, technically sound tests are difficult and costly to develop. Collaborations among states participating in the Interstate New Teacher Assessment and Support Consortium and other states, professional associations, and test developers bring the intellectual and financial resources of several organizations to this difficult work.

4

Developing an Evaluation Framework for Teacher Licensure Tests

This chapter builds on the work of measurement specialists, test users, and policy makers by laying out criteria for judging the appropriateness and technical quality of initial licensing tests. The committee presents an evaluation framework that suggests criteria for examining test characteristics and testing practices.

CRITERIA FOR EVALUATING TESTS

The *Standards for Educational and Psychological Testing* (American Educational Research Association et al., 1999) provide guidelines for evaluating educational and psychological tests. Likewise, the *Principles for the Validation and Use of Personnel Selection Procedures* (Society for Industrial and Organizational Psychology, 1987) and the *Uniform Guidelines for Employee Selection Procedures* (U.S. Equal Employment Opportunity Commission et al., 1978) provide guidelines for developing educational, psychological, employment, certification, and licensure tests and for gathering validity evidence about their uses. These publications reflect widespread professional consensus on criteria for evaluating tests and testing practices.

Early in its tenure the committee commissioned papers by experts in measurement, teacher education, industrial/organizational psychology, and education law, including Linda Crocker (1999), Mary Futrell (1999), Daniel Goldhaber (1999), Richard Jaeger (1999), Richard Jeanneret (1999), and Diana Pullin (1999)[1]. Based

---

[1]These papers can be obtained by contacting the National Academy of Science's public access office at <publicac@nas.edu>.

on professional guidelines and their own work, these individuals have suggested criteria for evaluating teacher licensure tests. The committee used the three sets of published guidelines and the six commissioned papers to develop a framework for evaluating teacher licensure tests. This framework, which relies heavily on the Crocker paper, suggests criteria for test development and evaluation. The framework includes criteria for stating the purposes of testing; deciding on the competencies to test; developing the test; field testing and analyzing results of the test; administering and scoring tests; protecting tests from corruptibility; setting standards; attending to reliability and related issues; reporting scores and providing documentation; conducting validation studies; determining feasibility and costs; and studying the long-term consequences of the broader licensure program. These criteria are discussed below after a discussion of validity, which is an overriding concern in all evaluations of tests.

VALIDITY EVIDENCE

The 1999 standards say that "validity refers to the degree to which evidence and theory support the interpretations of test scores entailed by proposed uses of tests" (American Educational Research Association, et al., 1999:9) and that the primary purpose of licensure testing is "to ensure that those licensed possess knowledge and skills in sufficient degree to perform important occupational activities safely and effectively" (pg. 156). The standards explain that the type of evidence needed to establish a test's validity is a matter of professional judgment: "Professional judgment guides decisions regarding the specific forms of evidence that can best support the intended interpretation and use" of test scores (pg. 11).

The 1999 standards note that at the present time validity research on licensure tests focuses "mainly on content-related evidence, often in the form of judgments that the test adequately represents the content domain of the occupation" (pg. 157). Typically, validity evidence for employment and credentialing tests includes a clear definition of the occupation or specialty, a clear and defensible delineation of the nature and requirements of the job, and expert judgments on the fit between test content and the job's requirements. Procedurally, test sponsors conduct job analyses to define occupations and develop test specifications (blueprints) for licensure tests. These are studies of the knowledge, skills, abilities, and dispositions needed to perform job duties and tasks. Studies of content relevance are then conducted to determine whether the knowledge and skills examined by the tests are relevant to the job and are represented in the test specifications. These data are generally obtained by having subject matter experts rate items on how well they reflect the test specifications, testing objectives, and responsibilities of the job (Impara, 1995; Smith and Hambleton, 1990; Sireci, 1998; Sireci and Green, 2000). Typically, sensitivity reviews also are conducted to determine if irrelevant characteristics of test questions or test forms are likely to provide unfair advantages or disadvantages to particular groups of test takers (Sireci and Green, 2000). These sensitivity reviews also rely on expert judgment and are designed to remove potentially offensive materials from test forms.

Many researchers contend that these kinds of studies are sufficient to examine the validity of licensure and employment tests and argue that it is unnecessary and even impossible to obtain data that go beyond content-related evidence of validity (Jaeger, 1999; Stoker and Impara, 1995; Popham, 1992). For other types of tests in education and psychology, the 1999 standards and the measurement community suggest collecting additional evidence for a test's intended interpretations and uses. For college admissions tests, for example, the measurement and higher-education communities seek data on the extent to which scores on admissions tests predict students' performance in college. For these and other types of educational and psychological tests, the profession expects to have data that demonstrate the relationships between test results and the criterion of interest.

Jaeger (1999) and others hold their ground for teacher licensure tests, however. Jaeger argues that criterion-related evidence of validity is "incongruent with fundamental interpretations of results of teacher certification testing, and that the sorts of experimental or statistical controls necessary to produce trustworthy criterion-related validity evidence [are] virtually impossible to obtain" (pg. 10). Similarly, Popham (1992) says that, "although it would clearly be more desirable to appraise teacher licensure tests using both criterion-related and content-related evidence of validity, this is precluded by technical obstacles, as well as the enormous costs of getting a genuinely defensible fix on the instructional competence of a large number of teachers." The feasibility of identifying in a professionally acceptable way teachers who are and are not minimally competent is unknown.

The technical obstacles to this kind of research are not insubstantial. Several researchers have described the measurement and design difficulties associated with collecting job-related performance information for beginning teachers. Measuring beginning teacher competence credibly and adequately distinguishing between minimally competent and minimally incompetent beginning practice is problematic (Sireci and Green, 2000; Smith and Hambleton, 1990; Haney et al., 1987; Haertel, 1991). Researchers explain that competent performance is difficult to define when candidates are working in many different settings (Smith and Hambleton, 1990). They also note that using student achievement data as criterion measures for teacher competence is problematic because it is difficult (1) to measure and isolate students' prior learning from the effects of current teaching, (2) to isolate the contemporaneous school and family resources that interact with teaching and learning, (3) to match teachers' records with student data in some school systems, and (4) to follow teachers and students over time and take multiple measurements in today's time- and resource-constrained schools. The 1999 standards note an additional obstacle, saying that "criterion measures are generally not available for those who are not granted a license" (pg. 157). This is an important limitation.

However, some of these same researchers say that, although content-related evidence is essential for establishing the validity of teacher licensure tests, more is needed (e.g., Haertel, 1991; Haney et al., 1987; Poggio et al., 1986; Pullin, 1999; Sireci and Green, 2000). These researchers argue that it should be possible to demonstrate that teacher licensure tests have some power to identify minimally competent beginning teachers. They call for empirical evidence on the relationships between performance on teacher licensing tests and other relevant variables. These researchers say that, even though content-related evidence provides useful information about the adequacy of content representation, it is very restrictive in the overall validity evidence that it communicates.

This group of researchers applies the recommendations of the standards for validity research on educational and psychological tests to the licensure testing arena. The 1999 standards suggest, but do not require, gathering additional validity evidence for educational and psychological tests, such as evidence on the fit between the intended interpretations of test scores and (a) the processes in which examinees engage as they respond to assessment exercises; (b) the patterns of relationships among assessment exercises and assessment components; and (c) correlations with measures of the same and different constructs, including examining differences in performance across known groups. According to the standards, "content-related evidence . . . [of validity] may be supplemented with other forms of evidence external to the test" (pg. 157). These data can be collected through research on the performance strategies candidates use in responding to test questions or on the extent to which interrelationships between test questions support the conceptual frameworks that guide test development. Smith and Hambleton (1990) point out that investigations of the underlying structure of the subtests that comprise licensing examinations might be useful. Validity evidence could also be based on examinations of the relationships between licensure test scores and scores on other tests measuring the same (or different) knowledge and skills. Validity research also might examine the scores of test takers expected to differ in their knowledge of tested content—for example, teacher education students and students in other fields. A final type of validity research might include studies of the relationships between licensure test scores and teaching competence. For example, this research might look at licensure test results and the teaching performance of licensed beginning teachers and candidates holding emergency teaching licenses after failing licensing tests.

In his discussion of new forms of teacher assessment, Haertel (1991) suggests that the newer kinds of teacher assessments currently being introduced may lead to new kinds of criterion data, such as more systematic classroom observation data or ratings of portfolio entries. These types of data might be used to examine patterns of relationships among different criterion measures. Using these types of data, researchers could generate and test hypotheses about expected patterns of relationships among different criterion measures (Smith and Hambleton, 1990). According to Haertel, "if multiple, diverse forms of evidence converge in identifying the same candidates as high or low in particular areas of teaching expertise, the case for the validity of all of them is strengthened" (pg. 24).

Some researchers have already collected this kind of evidence for teacher licensure tests. Among the relevant measures they and others have identified for teacher licensure tests are candidates' self-perceptions of their knowledge in the domains measured by licensing examinations, grade point averages in teacher education programs, performance evaluations in student teaching, and performance differences between groups known to be more and less knowledgeable about teaching (Poggio et al., 1986; Smith and Hambleton, 1990; Sireci, personal communication, University of Massachusetts, January 15, 2001). A study by Poggio and colleagues (1986) is cited by several researchers (Sireci and Green, 2000; Stoker and Impara, 1995) as an example of an investigation that gathered useful data on the relationship between licensure test results and other measures of candidate knowledge. Poggio and colleagues obtained evidence of validity by comparing the performance of education and noneducation majors at the University of Kansas on one of the precursor tests to Praxis—the National Teachers Examination Test of Professional Knowledge.

The committee contends that current licensing and employment conditions provide new opportunities to collect criterion-related evidence for teacher licensure tests. As noted in the previous chapter, teacher candidates who fail licensure tests can and do teach in private schools in some states. Candidates who fail licensure tests teach with emergency licenses in the public school systems of many states. In fact, in some states and districts, large numbers of individuals teach with emergency licenses. These labor conditions allow researchers to contrast the job performance of those who have passed licensure tests with those who have not.

Furthermore, as noted earlier, some states have recently raised their passing scores. The job performance of those hired under the new higher standards can be compared to the performance of teachers hired under the lower passing standards. In addition, different states have established different passing standards for the same tests. These different licensing requirements afford a natural opportunity to look for differences in the competency levels of beginning teachers. Identifying methods for collecting reliable and valid measures of teachers' competency and interpreting such data for these candidate groups are likely to be difficult. Nonetheless, these conditions provide opportunities to collect criterion data for teacher licensure tests that might be informative and that are unavailable in many other professions.

Clearly, there is disagreement in the field about the type of validity evidence that should be collected for teacher licensure tests. The committee contends that it is important to collect data that go beyond content-related evidence of validity for initial licensure tests. Examples of relevant research include investigations of the relationships between test results and other measures of candidate knowledge and skill or on the extent to which tests distinguish minimally competent candidates from those who are not (coupled with a professionally acceptable method of identifying teachers who are and those who are not competent). The committee recognizes the complexity and likely costs of high-quality research of this type but believes that it is important to expand the knowledge base about teacher licensure testing.

EVALUATION FRAMEWORK

This broader conception of validity is reflected in the committee's framework for evaluating teacher licensure tests. The framework does not necessarily call for validity studies that examine the relationships between performance on the tests and future performance in the classroom. However, the committee does consider whether empirical evidence has been collected on the relationships between performance on licensure exams and other concurrent measures of knowledge and skills similar to those covered on the exams.

Issues of fairness also are prominent in the committee's evaluation framework. The committee subscribes to the principle that each examinee should be tested in an equitable manner. Examinees should have adequate notice, equal access to sponsor-provided information about tests, high-quality standardized testing conditions, and assurance of accurate results. Further, issues of cultural diversity have a serious impact on all aspects of teaching, and differences in test results for minority and majority candidates have a notable impact on the composition of the teaching force. Cultural diversity and fairness issues are highlighted in every component of the evaluation framework that follows. The committee acknowledges that the evaluation criteria set forth here describe the ideal to which tests should aspire and that current tests are unlikely to fully achieve all of the evaluation criteria. The criteria are described below.

Purpose of Assessment

Proper development and use of an assessment require that its purposes are clearly stated and prioritized from the beginning. Assessment development activities can then follow. Of particular importance is a statement of the intended testing population. Regarding purpose, then, the criteria are:

- the statement of purpose and rationale for the assessment should be clear;
- multiple uses should be prioritized to guide assessment development and validation;
- purposes should be communicated to all stakeholders;
- issues associated with cultural diversity should be incorporated into statements of purpose; and

- the intended testing population (e.g., candidates who have recently completed coursework) should be clearly stated.

Competencies to be Assessed

To assure fairness and gather content-related evidence of validity, a systematic process should be used in deciding which competencies to assess and then delineate. This process might include a thorough analysis of those aspects of the work of teachers that are necessary for safe, appropriate, and effective practice. The description of what is to be assessed should be clear, complete, and sufficiently specific to be used by assessment developers. The criteria are:

- a systematic process should be used to decide on the competencies to be assessed;
- the competencies to be assessed should encompass a range of settings and activities in which teachers will be expected to work;
- the qualifications and backgrounds of the experts used to decide on the competencies should be appropriate and representative of the grade levels, subject areas, teaching settings, genders, and racial/ethnic characteristics of the licensing field;
- issues associated with cultural diversity and disabilities should be incorporated into developing competencies to be assessed; and
- the resulting statement of competencies to be assessed should be clear.

Developing the Assessment

This clear description of what is to be assessed should then be used to develop assessments that provide balanced and adequate coverage of the competencies. The assessment should be pilot tested as part of the development process. The committee's criteria include the following:

- the development process should ensure balance and adequate coverage of relevant competencies;
- the development process should ensure that the level of processing required (cognitive relevance) of the candidates is appropriate;
- the assessment tasks, scoring keys, rubrics, and scoring anchor exemplars should be reviewed for content accuracy, clarity, relevance, and technical quality;
- the assessment tasks, scoring keys, rubrics, and scoring anchor exemplars should be reviewed for sensitivity and freedom from biases that might advantage or disadvantage candidates from particular geographic regions, cultures, or educational ideologies or those with disabilities;
- the developers and reviewers should be representative, diverse, and trained in their task;

• the exercises, instructions, and rubrics should be piloted as part of development; and

• the test forms should be piloted for timing and feasibility of the assessment process for candidates.

Field Testing and Exercise Analysis

After preliminary versions of the assessments have been constructed, they should be field tested on representative samples of candidates. Assessment analysis is conducted after field testing and after the assessment is administered operationally. To the extent feasible, the analysis should include an assessment of the adequacy of functioning of the assessment exercises and an examination of responses for differential item functioning for major population groups. In particular, the criteria for this phase include the following:

• the assessments should be field tested on an adequate sample that is representative of the intended candidates;

• where feasible, assessment responses should be examined for differential functioning by major population groups to help ensure that the exercises do not advantage or disadvantage candidates from particular geographic regions, races, gender, cultures, or educational ideologies or with those disabilities;

• assessment analysis (e.g., item difficulty and discrimination) methods should be consistent with the intended use and interpretation of scores; and

• clearly specified criteria and procedures should be used to identify, revise, and remove flawed assessment exercises.

Administration and Scoring

Appropriate administration conditions, scoring processes, quality control procedures, confidentiality requirements, and procedures for handling assessment materials should be used. Clear policies on retaking the examination and on the appeals process should be communicated to candidates. In particular, the committee's criteria include the following:

• proctors and scorers should be appropriately qualified;

• uniform assessment conditions should be provided for candidates to test under standard conditions;

• appropriate accommodations should be made for candidates with disabilities;

• scorers of performance assessments and other kinds of open-ended test responses should be appropriately recruited and trained, including being trained to score responses from a culturally diverse group of candidates;

- appropriate scoring models for individual exercises and the total assessment should be clearly described and appropriately implemented;
  - quality control procedures for the scoring process should be maintained;
  - confidentiality and security of candidate performances should be protected;
  - appropriate procedures should be used for archival, disposal, and return of products or performances;
  - a clear policy on retaking the assessment should be stated for candidates who do not pass, including information on whether or not parts that were passed need to be retaken;
  - a clearly stated appeals process should exist; and
  - candidates should be provided with a pass/fail decision prior to the deadline for registration for the next administration of the test.

Protection from Corruptibility

Procedures should be used to ensure that candidates' products are authentic, that assessment materials are secure, and that inappropriate coaching strategies do not improve scores. In particular, the committee's criteria include the following:

- instructions and procedures should be in place to ensure the authenticity of candidates' responses;
- administrative procedures should protect the security of test items and scoring rubrics from copying or plagiarism;
- coaching strategies that are inappropriate or inconsistent with the knowledge and skills tested do not improve performance;
- sanctions for possible candidate improprieties related to the assessment should be specified; and
- if the assessment is designed to be secure, there should be a sufficient number of exercises and forms available to maintain the assessment over time and to accommodate any retake policy, and effective design should be in place for limiting exercise exposure over time, particularly for memorable exercises.

Standard Setting

Standard-setting processes lead to decision rules about who passes an assessment. These processes should be systematic and should involve a representative group of qualified individuals. Consistent with the purposes of licensure, standards should be based on the knowledge and skills judged necessary for minimally acceptable beginning practice. The committee's criteria specify that:

- a systematic reasoned approach should be used to set standards and should be available for public review;

- the standard-setting process should be clearly documented;
- professionally qualified panelists should participate in the standard-setting process;
- the composition of the standard-setting panels should reflect the diversity of the candidate population;
- a check should be made on the reproducibility of the standards set on other test forms with other expert panels;
- the standards should depend on the knowledge and skills previously determined to be necessary for minimally competent beginning teaching;
- a systematic procedure should be in place for evaluating the standards and should be available for public review; and
- external evidence of the validity of the standard should be gathered to document its appropriateness, if feasible.

Consistency, Reliability, Generalizability, and Comparability

The consistency of results across different forms of an assessment, different raters, and other relevant components should be studied and documented. Where appropriate, procedures for equating scores on different forms of an assessment should be used. In particular, the committee's criteria include the following:

- procedures should be in place to ensure that decisions are reliable, that is, that they are consistent across different forms, different raters, and different times of assessment and for different examinee groups. These procedures should include statistical equating of forms, procedures for training raters, and procedures for arriving at consensus among raters;
- the consistency of decisions should be estimated and reported, taking into account various sources of error, including different assessment exercises, different raters, and different times of assessment;
- misclassification rates should be estimated and reported for the entire population and by population groups defined by gender, racial/ethnic status, and other relevant characteristics; and
- defensible designs and procedures should exist for equating alternate assessment forms.

Score Reporting and Documentation

Candidates should be provided a study guide, including sample assessments and guidelines regarding scoring procedures prior to administration of an assessment. Technical documentation should be available for public and professional review. Appropriate score reporting procedures should be used. In particular, the committee's criteria include the following:

- guidelines for scoring, score interpretation, and sample assessments should be provided to candidates preparing for the examination;
- procedures used to combine scores on multiple parts of the assessment to determine overall scores should be reported to candidates;
- technical documentation should exist on test development, scoring, interpretation and evidence of reliability and validity, scaling, norming, test administration, score interpretation, and the means by which passing scores are determined; technical documentation provides relevant information on the assessment and should be available for public and professional review;
- a systematic procedure should exist for candidates to request score verification or rescoring;
- score reporting systems should be pretested with representative candidates to assure they are understandable;
- a policy should exist for reporting scores for candidates who have been provided with testing accommodations;
- group performance should be reported for major population groups defined by gender, racial/ethnic status, and other relevant characteristics; and
- a policy should exist for making data available for research and policy studies.

Validation Studies

At the time an assessment is first released, the development process should be clearly described, and content-related evidence of validity should be presented along with any other empirical evidence of validity that exists, plans for collecting additional logical and empirical validity evidence should be provided and updated or modified as needed, results from these additional validation studies should be reported as soon as the data are available, in particular, the committee's criteria include the following:

- a comprehensive plan for gathering logical and empirical evidence for validation should specify the types of evidence that will be gathered (e.g., content-related evidence, data on the test's relationships to other relevant measures of candidate knowledge and skill, and data on the extent to which the test distinguishes between minimally competent and incompetent candidates), priorities for the additional evidence needed, designs for data collection, the process for disseminating results, and a time line;
- the validation plan should include a focus on the fairness of the assessment for candidates and on disparate impacts for major candidate population groups; the plan should specify examination of the initial and eventual passing rates;
- major stakeholders should have input into the validation plan, and assessment experts should review the plan against current professional standards;
- the plan should require periodic review of accumulated validity evidence by external reviewers and appropriate follow-up;

- evidence should be provided regarding implementation of the validity plan including results of studies undertaken to collect validity evidence and gather fairness data;
  - the validity evidence should be reported as studies are conducted; and
  - assessment experts should review the results of the validity studies against current professional standards.

Costs and Feasibility

Costs and feasibility should be important considerations in the development of any assessment. An analysis of costs and feasibility should consider all components of the testing program, including test development, administration, applicant assessment time, scoring, and reporting. The analysis should be documented. In particular, the committee's criteria specify that:

- the assessments should be accomplished in a cost-effective manner that considers logistics, space, and the personnel requirements of test administration;
  - applicant testing time, processing time, and fees should be considered;
  - scoring and reporting should be done in cost-effective ways and in a reasonable amount of time; and
  - a legal review of the test should be conducted and the exposure to legal challenge considered.

Long-term Consequences of a Licensure Program

Assessments should be used in the context of a total licensure program. In addition, assessments may be used for purposes other than licensure. A systematic effort should be made to study the consequences of the use of assessments in this broader context. In particular:

- a systematic effort should be made to learn the ways in which individual candidates may benefit and/or be harmed from participation in the licensure process;
  - the impact of the licensure process on underrepresented groups and on diversity in the teaching profession should be examined;
  - major stakeholder groups should be surveyed as to their perspective on the licensure program;
  - the impact of the process on teacher supply and retention should be evaluated;
  - evidence of the effects of licensure programs on the achievement of students taught by licensed teachers should be examined;
  - evidence should be sought of shifts in the academic talent of those entering the field of teaching;

- the impact of the licensure program on the content of teacher education curricula should be studied; and
- to the extent feasible, evidence should be collected to demonstrate whether individuals who passed the test possess more of the tested knowledge and skills than do those who failed.

CONCLUSION

Solid technical characteristics and fairness are key to the effective use of tests. The work of measurement specialists, test users, and policy makers suggests criteria for judging the appropriateness and technical quality of initial teacher licensure tests. The committee drew on these to develop criteria it believes users should aspire to in developing and evaluating initial teacher licensure tests.

As the committee's evaluation criteria make clear, assessment development, evaluation, and use are complex and beset with practical issues. Furthermore, as noted earlier, there is some disagreement among measurement experts about the type of validity evidence that is necessary for teacher licensure tests. Throughout its evaluation framework, the committee has stressed the necessity of adequate documentation as well as the importance of informing candidates about procedures.

- The committee's criteria for judging test quality include the following: tests should have a statement of purpose; systematic processes should be used in deciding what to test and in assuring balanced and adequate coverage of these competencies; test material should be tried out and analyzed before operational decisions are made; test administration and scoring should be uniform and fair; test materials and results should be protected from corruptibility; standard-setting procedures should be systematic and well documented; test results should be consistent across test forms and scorers; information about tests and scoring should be available to candidates; technical documentation should be accessible for public and professional review; validity evidence should be gathered and presented; costs and feasibility should be considered in test development and selection; and the long-term consequences of licensing tests should be monitored and examined.

5

Evaluating Current Tests

This chapter examines current teacher licensure tests. The committee uses its evaluation framework to evaluate several widely used initial licensure tests and presents the results of the evaluation here, along with the sampling criteria used to select the tests it reviewed.

As noted in Chapter 3, most of the commonly used teacher licensure tests come from the Educational Testing Service (ETS) or National Evaluation Systems (NES). In addition, some state education agencies or higher-education institutions develop tests for their states. Since the majority of tests used are from ETS's Praxis series or NES, the committee focused its review on tests developed by these two publishers. A measurement expert was commissioned under the auspices of the Oscar and Luella Buros Center for Testing to provide technical reviews of selected teacher licensure tests. A subset of available tests was selected for review.

SELECTING TEACHER LICENSURE TESTS FOR REVIEW

Selecting Praxis Series Tests

In negotiations with ETS, a number of factors were considered in selecting Praxis tests for review. Assessments in both the Praxis I and Praxis II series were considered for technical review. Altogether, the following factors were considered in selecting Praxis tests to review. The committee wanted the review to:

- include one Praxis I test;
- include both content and pedagogical knowledge Praxis II tests;
- include tests that have both multiple-choice and open-ended formats;
- cover the full range of teacher grade levels (e.g., K-6, 5-9, 7-12);
- include, if possible, language arts/English, mathematics, science, and social studies content tests;
- include tests that are in wide use; and
- consider shelf life, that is, not include tests that are near "retirement."

The final set of tests was chosen by the committee through discussions with ETS and the Buros Center for Testing. From the Praxis I set of assessments, the Pre-Professional Skills Test: Reading (paper-and-pencil administration) was selected for review. From Praxis II the committee selected four tests for review: the Principles of Learning and Teaching (K-6); Middle School English/Language Arts; Mathematics: Proofs, Models, and Problems, Part 1; and Biology: Content Knowledge Test, Parts 1 and 2.

Selecting NES Tests

To obtain material on NES-developed tests, the committee contacted NES and the relevant state education agencies in the states listed as using NES tests in the *2000 NASDTEC Manual*.[1] Efforts to obtain sufficient technical information for the committee to evaluate the tests similar to what the committee received from ETS were unsuccessful for NES tests. As a result, NES-developed tests are not included in the committee's review and the committee can make no statements about their soundness or technical quality.

The committee's inability to comment on NES-developed tests is significant. First, NES-developed tests are administered to very large numbers of teacher candidates (R. Allen, NES, personal communication, July 26, 1999). Second, the disclosure guidelines in the joint *Standards for Educational and Psychological Testing* specify that "test documents (e.g., test materials, technical manuals, users guides, and supplemental materials) should be made available to prospective test users and other qualified persons at the time a test is published or released for use" (American Educational Research Association et al., 1999:68). Consistent with the 1999 standards, and as it did with ETS, the committee requested information sufficient to evaluate the appropriateness and technical adequacy of NES-developed tests. In response to the committee's request, an NES

---

[1] New York, Massachusetts, Arizona, Michigan, California, Illinois, Texas, and Colorado were listed as NES states in the *2000 NASDTEC Manual*. Oregon uses ETS and NES tests. Oklahoma's test development program was in transition when the committee's study began.

representative informed it that the requested materials were "under the control and supervision" of its client states and that the committee should seek information directly from the state agencies (R. Allen, NES, correspondence, September 4, 1999).

Following the tenets of the 1999 standards, the committee then requested the following data from several state agencies (D. Z. Robinson, committee chair, correspondence, August 8, 2000):

> . . . technical information on state licensing tests, including the processes involved in the tests' development (including job analysis and the means by which job analyses are translated into tests), technical information related to scoring, interpretation and evidence of validity and reliability, scaling and norming, guidelines of test administration and interpretation, and the means by which passing scores are determined . . . sufficient documentation to support judgments about the technical quality of the test, the resulting scores, and the interpretations based on the test scores.

In communications with the states, at least two state agencies reported their understanding that the requested technical information could not be disclosed to the committee because of restrictions included in their contracts with NES. Colorado's Office of Professional Services, for example, pointed the committee to the following contract language (E. J. Campbell, Colorado Office of Professional Service, correspondence, September 19, 2000):

> Neither the Assessment, nor any records, documents, or other materials related to its development and administration may be made available to the general public, except that nonproprietary information, such as test objectives and summary assessment results may be publicly disseminated by the State. Except as provided above and as contemplated by Paragraph 15, or as required by a court of competent jurisdiction or other governmental agency or authority, neither the State nor the Contractor, or its respective subcontractor(s), employees, or agents may reveal to any persons(s) any part of the Assessment, any part of the information collected during the Project, or any results of the Project, or any Assessment, without the prior written permission of the other party.

Despite multiple contacts with many of the relevant state agencies over several months, the committee received very little of the requested technical information. Several state agencies provided registration booklets and test preparation guides and one state provided a summary of passing rates. California officials provided technical documentation for one of its 40 tests, but the committee concluded that the documentation did not include sufficient information for a meaningful technical evaluation.

In addition to contract restrictions on disclosure, state education agencies gave various reasons for not providing to the committee some or all of the requested material, including the following: the technical information was not readily accessible; the technical information appears in a form that would not be useful to the committee; the technical documentation was not yet complete; and planned revisions of state assessments would limit the usefulness of current test review. Several state agencies simply declined to provide some or all of the requested information to the committee.

The committee's lack of success in obtaining sufficient technical material on NES tests currently in use precludes a meaningful technical evaluation by the committee of the quality of these tests or an assessment of their possible adverse impact. The committee urges efforts to ensure that users and other interested parties can obtain sufficient technical information on teacher licensure tests in accordance with the joint 1999 *Standards*.

EVALUATING THE PRAXIS SERIES TESTS

In this section the overall strengths and weaknesses of the selected Praxis tests are discussed in relation to the committee's evaluation framework. The analysis is based on technical reviews prepared by the Buros Center for Testing of the five Praxis tests. The reviews were provided to the committee and shared with ETS in July 2000. The full text of each is available in the electronic version of the committee's report on the World Wide Web at *www.nap.edu*. The reviews are briefly summarized below.

Although separate documentation was provided by ETS for the tests reviewed, additional documentation was provided on general test development procedures by ETS. The *ETS Standards for Quality and Fairness* (1999a) serve as the guide for all test development by ETS. Updated in 1999, they were developed to supplement the *Standards for Educational and Psychological Testing* (American Educational Research Association et al., 1999). In many cases these generic test development procedures formed the basis of information regarding the specific Praxis tests, and additional specific information was provided to support test development of the individual tests. As a result these generic procedures should be considered as the foundation on which the respective individual assessments were developed.

For Praxis, test development begins with an analysis of the knowledge and skills beginning teachers need to demonstrate (Educational Testing Service, 1999e). These analyses draw on standards from national disciplinary organizations, such as the National Council of Teachers of Mathematics (1989) and the National Research Council (1996), state standards for students and teachers, and the research literature. The knowledge and skill listings which result are then used to survey teachers about their views on the importance and criticality of potential content. Using the information received from these surveys, test specifications describing the content of the tests are developed. Test questions that meet the specifications are written by ETS developers and then reviewed for accuracy and clarity. ETS staff also review items for potential bias, with attention to possible inappropriate terminology, stereotyping, underlying assumptions, ethnocentrism, tone, and inflammatory materials. Occasionally, external reviews also are conducted, but this is not systematic. Test forms are then constructed to reflect the test's specifications.

Once tests are constructed, passing standards are set (Educational Testing Service, 1999b). States that conduct standard-setting studies determine the scores required for passing. As noted in Chapter 3, passing scores are based on educators' views of minimally competent teaching performance and policy makers' goals for improvements in teaching and teacher supply.

Detailed manuals are prepared for the Praxis tests and are provided to test administrators and supervisors. There are separate manuals for standard administrations and those tailored to the needs of candidates with learning or physical disabilities. Manuals also detail security procedures for the tests and test administration.

Overall Assessment of Praxis Tests

With a few exceptions, the Praxis I and Praxis II tests reviewed meet the criteria for technical quality articulated in the committee's framework. This is particularly true regarding score reliability, sensitivity reviews, standard setting, validation research (although only content-related evidence of validity was provided), costs and feasibility, and test documentation.

However, several areas were of concern to the committee. For three of the tests, concerns remain about the content specifications. For two of these tests the job analysis information was dated; for another the development may not be sensitive to the grade-level focus of the test; for the last test there is ambiguity about the possible inclusion of noncontent-relevant material. Only one of the tests reviewed has information on differential item functioning. In four of the five tests reviewed, information on equating strategies is either lacking, inadequate, or problematic. These issues are detailed below. Although these areas of concern are important and need attention by the test developer, all five of these tests do meet the majority of review criteria set forth in this report.

Praxis I: Pre-Professional Skills Test (PPST) in Reading

The PPST in Reading meets all of the review criteria. The test shows strong evidence of being technically sound. The procedures for test development, equating, reliability, and standard setting are consistent with current measurement practices (see Box 5-1). However, since the job analysis on which the content of the test is based is over 10 years old, a study should be conducted to examine whether the components included from the previous job analysis are still current and appropriate and whether additional skills should be addressed.

BOX 5-1
Technical Review Synopsis
Pre-Professional Skills Test (PPST):
Reading (Paper-and-Pencil Administration)

Description: Forty multiple-choice items; one-hour administration. In some states the test is administered prior to admission to a teacher preparation program; in other states it may be administered at any time prior to obtaining an initial license.

Purpose of the Assessment: To measure ability to understand and evaluate written messages.

Competencies to Be Assessed: Two broad categories are covered: Literal Communication (55%) and Critical and Inferential Comprehension (45%).

Developing the Assessment: Based on a 1988 job analysis and reviews by an external advisory committee.

Field Testing and Exercise Analysis: Average item difficulties range from 0.72 to 0.80; average item-to-total correlations are in the 0.50 range. Differential item functioning analyses were conducted by considering various pairings of examinee groups. Only a few problematic items were noted. Following ETS's standard practice, sensitivity reviews are conducted by specially trained staff members.

Administration and Scoring: Administration is standardized; all examinees have one hour to complete the 40-item test. Training is provided for administrators for standard and accommodated administrations. ETS has a clear policy for score challenges; however, decisions regarding pass/fail status are the state's responsibility. Policies regarding retakes, due process, and so forth reside at the state level.

Protection from Corruptibility: Special procedures are in place to ensure the security of test materials.

Standard Setting: Modified Angoff was used with panels of size 25 to 40. Panelists are familiar with the job requirements and are representative of the state's educators in terms of gender, ethnicity, and geographic region.

Consistency, Reliability, Generalizability, and Comparability: Common-item, nonequivalent group equating is used to maintain comparability of scores and pass/fail decisions across years and forms. Internal consistency estimates range from 0.84 to 0.87; limited information is provided on conditional standard errors of measurement at possible passing scores. States set different passing scores on the reading tests, so classification rates are peculiar to states and, in some cases, licensing years within states.

Score Reporting and Documentation: Results are reported to examinees in about four weeks (along with a booklet that provides score interpretation information); examinees can have their results sent to up to three recipients. Guides, costing $18 each, contain released tests with answers and explanations and test-taking strategies. Other information (including *Tests at a Glance,* which contains information on the content and structure of the test, types of questions on the test, and sample questions with explanations of answers) is available at no cost. General information about the Praxis program can be accessed through ETS's website. However, there is no single, comprehensive, integrated technical manual for tests in the Praxis series.

Validation Studies: Content-related evidence of validity was reported, based on a 1992 study. Limited evidence is provided on disparate impact by gender and racial/ethnic groups. In 1998 to 1999, across all states, passing rates were 86% for white examinees, 65% for Hispanic examinees, and 50% for African American examinees. Test-taker pools were not large enough to report passing rates for Asian examinees.

Cost and Feasibility: There are no special logistical, space, or personnel requirements for the paper-and-pencil administration. For 2000 to 2001, there was a $35 nonrefundable registration fee and a $25 fee for the test.

Study of Long-Term Consequences of Licensure Program: No information was reported on the long-term consequences of the PPST reading test as a component of a total licensure program.

Overall Evaluation: Overall, the PPST in Reading shows strong evidence of being technically sound. The procedures for test development, equating, validation, reliability, and standard setting are consistent with current measurement practices. The job analysis is over 10 years old, and validity evidence was based on a limited content study.

SOURCE: Impara, 2000d.

Principles of Learning and Teaching (K-6) Test

The Principles of Learning and Teaching (PLT) (K-6) test is well constructed and has moderate to good technical qualities. The procedures for test development and standard setting are consistent with current measurement practices (see Box 5-2). Two areas of concern were raised for the test—statistical functioning and fairness. Some of the indicators of statistical functioning of the test items are problematic. In particular, correlations of individual items with overall test performance (biserial correlations) are low for a test of this kind. In addition, no studies of differential item functioning are reported for scores. With regard to the fairness criterion, no material is provided on methods used to equate alternate forms of the test—an issue that is especially important because, across years, candidates appear to be performing better. Because of the lack of equating information, it is unclear whether this results from a better-prepared candidate population or from easier test forms across years. Also, because the test is a mix of multiple-choice and open-ended questions, the equating strategies are not straightforward. The job analysis for the test is over 10 years old.

Middle School English/Language Arts Test

The Middle School English/Language Arts test is well constructed and has reasonably good technical properties. The procedures for test development and standard setting are consistent with current measurement practices (see Box 5-3). Three areas of the Middle School English/Language Arts test are identified as

BOX 5-2
Technical Review Synopsis
Principles of Learning and Teaching (PLT) (K-6) Test

Description: Forty-five multiple-choice items; six constructed response tasks; two-hour administration. The test is designed for beginning teachers and is intended to be taken after a candidate has almost completed his or her teacher preparation program.

Purpose of the Assessment: To assess a beginning teacher's knowledge of a variety of job-related criteria, including organizing content knowledge for student learning, creating an environment for learning, teaching for student learning, and teacher professionalism.

Competencies to Be Assessed: Organizing Content Knowledge for Student Learning (28%), Creating a Learning Environment (28%), Teaching for Student Learning (28%), Teacher Professionalism (16%).

Developing the Assessment: Based on a 1990 job analysis and reviews by an external advisory committee.

Field Testing and Exercise Analysis: Average item difficulties are typically 0.70; average item-to-total correlations are in the mid-30s. No differential item functioning analyses were reported. Following ETS's standard practice, sensitivity reviews are conducted by specially trained staff members.

Administration and Scoring: Administration is standardized; all examinees have two hours to complete the test. Training is provided for administrators for standard and accommodated administrations. ETS has a clear policy for score challenges; however, decisions regarding pass/fail status are the state's responsibility. Policies regarding retakes, due process, and so forth reside at the state level.

Protection from Corruptibility: Special procedures are in place to ensure the security of test materials.

Standard Setting: Modified Angoff for the multiple-choice items was used with panels of size 25 to 40. Panelists are familiar with the job requirements and are representative of the state's educators in terms of gender, ethnicity, and geographic region. Either a benchmark or an item-level pass/fail method was used with the constructed-response questions.

Consistency, Reliability, Generalizability, and Comparability: No information is provided on what method was used to maintain comparability of scores across years and forms. Interrater reliability estimates on constructed-response items are all greater than 0.90; overall reliability estimates range from 0.72 to 0.76. Limited information is reported on conditional standard errors of measurement at possible passing scores. States set different passing scores on the test, so classification error rates are peculiar to state and year.

Score Reporting and Documentation: Results are reported to examinees in about six weeks (along with a booklet that provides score interpretation information); examinees can have their results sent to up to three recipients. No interpretive guide specific to this test is available. Some information (including *Tests at a Glance*, which contains information on the content and structure of the test, types of questions on the test, and sample questions with explanations of answers) is available at no cost. General information about the Praxis program can be accessed through ETS's website. However, there is no single, comprehensive, integrated technical manual for tests in the Praxis series.

Validation Studies: Content-related evidence of validity is reported. Limited evidence is provided on disparate impact by gender and racial/ethnic groups. In 1998 to 1999, across all states, passing rates were 86% for white examinees, 65% for Hispanic examinees, 82% for Asian examinees, and 48% for African American examinees.

Cost and Feasibility: There are no special logistical, space, or personnel requirements for the paper-and-pencil administration. For 2000 to 2001, there was a $35 nonrefundable registration fee and an $80 fee for the test.

Study of Long-Term Consequences of Licensure Program: No information was reported on the long-term consequences of the test as a component of a total licensure program.

Overall Evaluation: Overall, the test is well constructed and has moderate to good psychometric properties. The procedures for test development, validation, and standard setting are all consistent with current measurement practices. No information was provided on equating alternate forms of the test, and validity evidence is limited to content-related evidence.

SOURCE: Impara, 2000e.

BOX 5-3
Technical Review Synopsis
Middle School English/Language Arts Test

Description: Ninety multiple-choice items; two constructed-response tasks; two-hour administration. The test is designed for beginning teachers and is intended to be taken after a candidate has almost completed his or her teacher preparation program.

Purpose of the Assessment: To measure whether an examinee has the knowledge and competencies necessary for a beginning teacher of English/language arts at the middle school level.

Competencies to Be Assessed: Reading and Literature Study (41%), Language and Linguistics (18%), Composition and Rhetoric (41%).

Developing the Assessment: Based on a 1996 job analysis, the purpose of which was to determine the extent that a job analysis undertaken earlier for secondary teachers would apply to middle school teachers and reviews by an external advisory committee.

Field Testing and Exercise Analysis: Average item difficulties were typically 0.73; average item-to-total correlation was 0.37. No differential item functioning analyses are reported. As is ETS's standard practice, sensitivity reviews are conducted by specially trained staff members.

Administration and Scoring: Administration is standardized; all examinees have two hours to complete the test. Training is provided for administrators for

continues

BOX 5-3 *continued*

standard and accommodated administrations. ETS has a clear policy for score challenges; however, decisions regarding pass/fail status are the state's responsibility. Policies regarding retakes, due process, and so forth reside at the state level.

Protection from Corruptibility: Special procedures are in place to ensure the security of test materials.

Standard Setting: Modified Angoff was used for the multiple-choice items using panels of size 25 to 40. Panelists are familiar with the job requirements and are representative of the state's educators in terms of gender, ethnicity, and geographic region. Either a benchmark or an item-level pass/fail method was used with the constructed-response questions.

Consistency, Reliability, Generalizability, and Comparability: No information was provided on the method used to maintain comparability of scores across years and forms. Interrater reliability on constructed-response items was 0.89; overall reliability was estimated at 0.86. Limited information was reported on conditional standard errors of measurement at possible passing scores. States set different passing scores, so classification error rates are specific to states and years.

Score Reporting and Documentation: Results are reported to examinees in about six weeks (along with a booklet that provides score interpretation information); examinees can have their results sent to up to three recipients. No specific interpretive guide is available for this test. Some information (including *Tests at a Glance*, which contains information on the content and structure of the test, types of questions on the test, sample questions with explanations of answers) is available at no cost. General information about the Praxis program can be accessed are representative of the state's educators in terms of gender, ethnicity, and geographic region. Either a benchmark or an item-level pass/fail method" was used with the constructed-response questions.

Consistency, Reliability, Generalizability, and Comparability: No information is provided on what method was used to maintain comparability of scores across years and forms. Interrater reliability estimates on constructed-response items are all greater than 0.90; overall reliability estimates range from 0.72 to 0.76. Limited information is reported on conditional standard errors of measurement at possible passing scores. States set different passing scores on the test, so classification error rates are peculiar to state and year.

Score Reporting and Documentation: Results are reported to examinees in about six weeks (along with a booklet that provides score interpretation information); examinees can have their results sent to up to three recipients. No interpretive guide specific to this test is available. Some information (including *Tests at a Glance*, which contains information on the content and structure of the test, types of questions on the test, and sample questions with explanations of answers) is available at no cost. General information about the Praxis program can be accessed through ETS's website. However, there is no single, comprehensive, integrated technical manual for tests in the Praxis series.

Validation Studies: Content-related evidence of validity is reported. Limited evidence is provided on disparate impact by gender and racial/ethnic groups. In 1998 to 1999, across all states, passing rates were 86% for white examinees, 65%

for Hispanic examinees, 82% for Asian examinees, and 48% for African American examinees.

Cost and Feasibility: There are no special logistical, space, or personnel requirements for the paper-and-pencil administration. For 2000 to 2001, there was a $35 nonrefundable registration fee and an $80 fee for the test.

Study of Long-Term Consequences of Licensure Program: No information was reported on the long-term consequences of the test as a component of a total licensure program.

Overall Evaluation: Overall, the test is well constructed and has moderate to good psychometric properties. The procedures for test development, validation, and standard setting are all consistent with current measurement practices. No information was provided on equating alternate forms of the test, and validity evidence is limited to content-related evidence.

SOURCE: Impara, 2000c.

showing possible weaknesses in relation to the evaluation framework. First, since the test is derived directly from the High School English/Language Arts test, it is not clear whether the item review process is sufficient and relevant to the middle school level. Second, as with the PLT (K-6) test, no information is provided on differential item functioning for scores across identified groups of examinees. Finally, as with the PLT (K-6) test, information is lacking on the equating strategies used. This test combines multiple-choice and open-ended item formats, which complicates the equating process.

Mathematics: Proofs, Models, and Problems, Part 1 Test

The Mathematics: Proofs, Models, and Problems, Part 1 test is well constructed and has reasonably good technical properties. The test development and standard-setting procedures are consistent with current measurement practices (see Box 5-4). Specifications for the test are unclear, and it appears that the test may include material not directly related to the content specifications. If this is the case, the possibility of score contamination is a concern because performance by some candidates might be distorted by noncontent-specific information included in the test questions. Furthermore, the test contains open-ended questions, and interrater score agreement is lower than desired for some of these questions. Similar concerns are noted for the PLT (K-6) and Middle School English/Language Arts tests. No information is reported on differential item functioning for this test. Fairness is also a concern because the equating method is questionable if forms have dissimilar content. In addition, sample sizes are too low to have confidence in the accuracy of the equating results.

BOX 5-4
Technical Review Synopsis
Mathematics: Proof, Models, and Problems, Part 1 Test

Description: Four constructed-response tasks (one mathematical proof, one developing a mathematical model, two problem solving); one-hour administration. The test is designed for beginning teachers and is intended to be taken after a candidate has almost completed his or her teacher preparation program.

Purpose of the Assessment: To measure the mathematics knowledge and competencies necessary for a beginning teacher of secondary mathematics.

Competencies to Be Assessed: To solve the four problems, examinees must understand and be able to work with mathematical concepts, reason mathematically, integrate knowledge of different areas of mathematics, and develop mathematical models of real-life situations.

Developing the Assessment: Based on a 1989 job analysis and through reviews by an external advisory committee.

Field Testing and Exercise Analysis: Average scores for the two problem-solving items (out of a possible 10) are 7.8 and 3.7; mathematical proof average score is 5.4; average for the mathematical model question is 5.0. Intertask correlations range from a low of 0.12 to a high of 0.32. No differential item functioning analyses are reported. ETS's standard practice is to conduct sensitivity reviews by specially trained staff members.

Administration and Scoring: Administration is standardized; all examinees have two hours to complete the test. Training is provided for administrators for standard and accommodated administrations. ETS has a clear policy for score challenges; however, decisions regarding pass/fail status are the state's responsibility. Policies regarding retakes, due process, and so forth reside at the state level.

Protection from Corruptibility: Special procedures are in place to ensure the security of test materials. Competencies from other content areas may be required to solve the problems. This could confound score interpretations.

Standard Setting: ETS uses either a benchmark or an item-level pass/fail method with constructed-response questions. Neither method is well documented in the literature, and there is no specific report for the applications of these methods for this test.

Consistency, Reliability, Generalizability, and Comparability: Total raw scores on the test are equated through raw scores on a multiple-choice test using a chained equipercentile procedure. The equating is based on very small samples. Interrater reliability on constructed-response items is in the mid-0.90s. Classification error rates are peculiar to state and year.

Score Reporting and Documentation: Results are reported to examinees in about six weeks (along with a booklet that provides score interpretation information); examinees can have their results sent to up to three recipients. Guides, costing $31 each, contain released tests with answers, explanations, and test-taking strategies. Other information (including *Tests at a Glance*, which contains information on the content and structure of the test, types of questions on the test, sample questions with explanations of answers) is available at no cost. General information about the Praxis program can be accessed through ETS's website.

There is no single, comprehensive, integrated technical manual for tests in the Praxis series.

Validation Studies: Content-related evidence of validity is reported. Differential passing rates are reported only for white and African American examinees (due to small sample sizes). In 1998 to 1999, across all states, the average passing rate for white examinees was 82% and for African American examinees 53%.

Cost and Feasibility: There are no special logistical, space, or personnel requirements for the paper-and-pencil administration. For 2000 to 2001, there is a $35 nonrefundable registration fee and a $70 fee for the test.

Study of Long-Term Consequences of Licensure Program: No information is reported on the long-term consequences of Mathematics: Proofs, Models, and Problems, Part 1 as a component of a total licensure program.

Overall Evaluation: Overall, the test is well constructed and has reasonably good psychometric properties. The procedures for test development, validation, and standard setting are consistent with current measurement practices. The equating strategy is problematic, especially given the small sample sizes. The cost of the study guide may be prohibitive for some candidates.

SOURCE: Impara, 2000b.

Biology: Content Knowledge Tests, Parts 1 and 2

The Biology: Content Knowledge Tests, Parts 1 and 2 seem to be well constructed and have moderate to good psychometric properties. The test development and standard-setting procedures are consistent with current practice (see Box 5-5). There was a lack of information on differential item functioning reported for the biology tests. No information was provided regarding the equating of alternate forms of the test (this was the base form). Only limited statistical data are available.

EXAMINING DISPARATE IMPACT

Test fairness issues are important to test quality. In this section of the report, the committee examines data for racial/ethnic minority and majority teacher candidates on several teacher licensing tests; compares these data to data from other large-scale tests; and discusses issues of test bias, the consequences of disparate impact, and the policy implications of the data.

Historically and currently, African American and Hispanic candidates usually have substantially lower passing rates on teacher licensure tests than white candidates (Garcia, 1985; George, 1985; Goertz and Pitcher, 1985; Graham, 1987; Rebell, 1986; Smith, 1987; Gitomer et al., 1999; Mehrens, 1999; Brunsman et al., 1999; Brunsman et al., 2000; Carlson et al., 2000). The size of the gap in passing

BOX 5-5
Technical Review Synopsis
Biology: Content Knowledge Tests, Parts 1 and 2

Description: Each test consists of 75 multiple-choice items; each test is designed to be administered in one hour. These tests are designed for beginning teachers and are intended to be taken after a candidate has almost completed a teacher preparation program.

Purpose of the Assessment: To measure the knowledge and competencies necessary for a beginning teacher in biology in a secondary school.

Competencies to Be Assessed: Part 1: Basic Principles of Science (17%); Molecular and Cellular Biology (16%); Classical Genetics and Evolution (15%); Diversity of Life, Plants, and Animals (26%); Ecology (13%); and Science, Technology, and Society (13%). Part 2: Molecular and Cellular Biology (21%); Classical Genetics and Evolution (24%); Diversity of Life, Plants, and Animals (37%); and Ecology (18%).

Developing the Assessment: Based on a 1990 job analysis and reviews by an external advisory committee.

Field Testing and Exercise Analysis: Part 1: Average item difficulties range from 0.64 to 0.70; average item-to-total correlations are in the mid-0.40s. Part 2: Average item difficulties range from 0.53 to 0.57; average item-to-total correlations are in the upper 0.30s. Differential item functioning analyses were not conducted due to small samples. ETS's standard practice is to conduct sensitivity reviews by specially trained staff members.

Administration and Scoring: Administration is standardized; all examinees have one hour to complete each of the 75-item tests. Training is provided for administrators for standard and accommodated administrations. ETS has a clear policy for score challenges; however, decisions regarding pass/fail status are a state responsibility. Policies regarding retakes, due process, and so forth reside at the state level.

Protection from Corruptibility: Special procedures are in place to ensure the security of test materials.

Standard Setting: Modified Angoff was used with panels of size 25 to 40. Panelists are familiar with the job requirements and are representative of the state's educators in terms of gender, ethnicity, and geographic region.

Consistency, Reliability, Generalizability, and Comparability: Equating is used to maintain comparability of scores and pass/fail decisions across years and forms, although the specific method is not specified. Internal consistency estimates are in the mid-0.80s for both tests; limited information was provided on conditional standard errors of measurement at possible passing scores. Classification error rates are specific to state and year.

Score Reporting and Documentation: Results are reported to examinees in about six weeks (along with a booklet that provides score interpretation information); examinees can have their results sent to up to three recipients. Guides, costing $16 each, contain released tests with answers, explanations, and test-taking strategies. Other information (including *Tests at a Glance,* which contains information on the content and structure of the test, types of questions on the test, and sample questions with explanations of answers) is available at no cost. General information about the Praxis program can be accessed through ETS's website. There is no single, comprehensive, integrated technical manual for tests in the Praxis series.

Validation Studies: Content-related evidence of validity is reported, based on a 1992 study. Limited evidence is provided on disparate impact by gender and racial/ethnic groups. In 1998 to 1999, across all states, average passing rates were 91% for white examinees, 34% for African American examinees; and 71% for Asian examinees for Part 1; test-taker pools for Hispanic candidates were not large enough to report passing rates. For Part 2, average passing rates by examinee groups were as follows: white, 70%; African American, 24%; Hispanic, 35%; Asian, 74%.

Cost and Feasibility: There are no special logistical, space, or personnel requirements for the paper-and-pencil administration. For 2000 to 2001, there was a $35 nonrefundable registration fee and fees of $45 each for Parts 1 and 2.

Study of Long-Term Consequences of Licensure Program: No information was reported on the long-term consequences of the tests as components of a total licensure program.

Overall Evaluation: Overall, these tests seem to be well constructed with moderate to good psychometric properties. The procedures for test development, validation, and standard setting are all consistent with current measurement practices. The job analysis is dated, and no information is provided on the procedures used to equate scores on different forms of these tests.

SOURCE: Impara, 2000a.

rates varies across tests and states. Before discussing these differences, issues to be considered in comparing racial/ethnic minority and majority group data on teacher licensure tests are noted. These issues bear on the use of licensure tests to make decisions about teacher candidates. The committee considers fairness issues in using licensure tests to judge program quality in Chapter 7.

METHODOLOGICAL NOTE ABOUT COMPARISONS

First-Time and Eventual Passing Rates

Within all racial/ethnic groups, first-time test takers of teacher licensure tests generally have higher passing rates than do repeaters. Moreover, as a byproduct of the differences in passing rates among groups, a larger percentage of minority applicants are likely to be repeaters than are nonminority candidates. Hence, comparisons of average scores and passing rates among groups that are based on a single administration of a test (or on the last test taken during a given year) do not give a complete picture of group differences. Comparisons based on a single test administration are likely to inflate differences in passing rates among groups.

Because of the importance of this distinction, some analysts prefer to emphasize eventual passing rates in examining test fairness issues in licensure decision making; the eventual passing rate is the percentage of a group that passes after several attempts. This approach focuses on the passing rate that corresponds to the percentage of candidates meeting the testing requirements for licensure—at some point in time, if not on the first attempt. Conversely, other analysts focus on initial passing rates, the rates of first-time test takers. The first-time testing group includes four sets of individuals: (1) initial testers who pass, (2) initial testers who fail and never retry the licensing test, (3) test takers who initially fail but eventually pass the licensing test, and (4) test takers who repeat but never pass the licensing test. Initial passing rates are important. Candidates' initial unsuccessful attempts cause delays and additional costs, even for those who eventually pass. The committee contends that both initial and eventual testing results are important.

Data Combined Across States

Comparisons of passing rates for racial/ethnic groups that are based on data aggregated across states can present interpretation problems. A number of factors, such as differences among states in their passing scores and the characteristics of their minority and majority teacher candidates make such data difficult to interpret. Consequently, the committee suggests that readers use extra caution in interpreting the results of any comparisons that aggregate data across states.

Test Scales

Different tests have different scoring scales. Consequently, scores must be converted to a common metric in order to determine whether a gap in average scores between two groups is larger on one test than another. This is usually accomplished by reporting the difference in scores between groups in terms of standard deviation units. The standard deviation difference is computed by dividing the difference between the mean scores for two groups by the standard deviation of the scores. (For readers who are not familiar with this metric, a one standard deviation difference in average scores between groups would roughly correspond to about 75 percent of the high-scoring group having scores that are higher than 75 percent of those in the low-scoring group. Thus, although a one standard deviation difference is quite large, there is still some overlap in the scores of the groups.)

DIFFERENCES BETWEEN MINORITY AND MAJORITY EXAMINEES ON LARGE-SCALE TESTS

As a frame of reference for the discussion that follows, it is useful to note that the differences in average scores among racial/ethnic groups on the teacher licensure tests the committee examined are generally similar to the differences found among these groups on other tests. In one review of test data, Hedges and Nowell (1998) found that the average scores of African American and white test takers on a large number of secondary-level tests differed by 0.82 to 1.18 standard deviation units. Similar differences have been found on the National Assessment of Educational Progress tests (U.S. Department of Education, 1998b). On the 1999 Scholastic Assessment Test (SAT), the difference in average scores between African Americans and white test takers was one standard deviation on the mathematics section and 0.89 standard deviation units on the verbal section (College Entrance Examination Board, 1999).

DIFFERENCES BETWEEN MINORITY AND MAJORITY TEACHER CANDIDATES ON THE SAT

Differences in SAT scores among prospective teachers provide another point of comparison for differences among racial/ethnic groups on teacher licensure tests. ETS recently reported SAT data for over 150,000 teacher candidates who took the Praxis I and Praxis II tests between 1994 and 1997. ETS matched their data to the records of those who took the SAT between 1977 and 1997. The last SAT record was used for individuals who took the SAT more than once (some individuals retake the SAT with the goal of improving their scores). Table 5-1 shows the average SAT scores of Praxis examinees. The mean and standard

TABLE 5-1　Average SAT Scores for Praxis Test Takers by Population Group, 1994-1997

	Praxis I Examinees[a]			Praxis II Examinees[b]		
Ethnicity	N	SAT Math	SAT Verbal	N	SAT Math	SAT Verbal
African American	3,603	413	428	11,510	424	440
Asian American	1,277	517	490	3,810	534	508
Hispanic	602	459	476	5,352	465	473
White	27,506	501	514	135,035	505	518

[a]Average SAT math and verbal scores for Praxis I examinees were 491 and 503, respectively.
[b]Average SAT math and verbal scores for Praxis II examinees were 498 and 510, respectively.
SOURCE: Gitomer, et al. (1999).

deviations of the SAT scores are 500 and 100, respectively, for the general SAT-taking population.

Table 5-1 shows that African American and Hispanic Praxis I examinees have lower average SAT scores than Asian American and white teacher candidates. The same pattern of results is seen for Praxis II takers. The next table presents standard deviation differences for these tests and groups. Table 5-2 shows the differences in mean SAT scores between white and racial/ethnic minority teacher candidates. The difference between white and African American Praxis I examinees is slightly less than one standard deviation on both the math and the verbal sections of the SAT. The difference between white and Hispanic students is about half this size. For Praxis II examinees the pattern is similar. These standard deviation differences are likely to be conservative estimates because the standard deviation of SAT scores for the total SAT-taking population was used in the computations; this standard deviation is likely to be larger than the standard deviation of SAT scores for Praxis I and II test takers. (SAT standard deviation data were not reported for Praxis test takers.)

The mean differences in SAT performance between African American and white Praxis examinees are slightly smaller than those reported for the broader SAT-taking population. This may reflect restriction in range for the groups; that is, the individuals whose records were used in this analysis were college entrants and thus a relatively capable subset of the total SAT-taking population. It may reflect the fact that the SAT records used in this analysis were eventual records obtained by searching SAT records for a 20-year period for Praxis test takers' last SAT records. As just noted, it also may reflect a difference in the standard deviation of SAT scores for the total SAT-taking population compared to the group that took the Praxis tests. Whether these restrictions play out differently for minority and majority test takers is unknown.

TABLE 5-2   Differences Between Average SAT Scores of Minority and White Praxis I and II Test Takers in Standard Deviation Units, 1994-1997

Differences Between Whites and:	Praxis I Examinees		Praxis II Examinees	
	SAT Math	SAT Verbal	SAT Math	SAT Verbal
African Americans	0.88	0.86	0.81	0.78
Asian Americans	−0.16	0.24	−0.29	0.10
Hispanics	0.42	0.38	0.40	0.45

DIFFERENCES BETWEEN MINORITY AND MAJORITY CANDIDATES ON TEACHER LICENSING TESTS

Average Scores

Though licensure testing programs generally report passing rates rather than average scores for their candidates, the committee was able to obtain group means from ETS for the Praxis tests it reviewed earlier in this chapter (Educational Testing Service, prepared March 22, 2001). Tables 5-3 and 5-4 report data for the Pre-Professional Skills Test in Reading and the Principles of Learning and Teaching (K-6) test. There were too few test takers in some population groups to report average score data for the Middle School/English Language Arts test, the Mathematics: Proof, Models, and Problems: Part 1 test, and Parts 1 and 2 of the Biology Content Knowledge test. These Praxis I and PLT data are from the 1998/1999 administrations of the tests and include the most recent testing records for candidates testing more than once during that period. For both tests, average scores for the groups are presented in Table 5-3, and the differences between group averages (in standard deviation units) are given in Table 5-4. Some of the limitations of these data are described below.

Table 5-3 shows that the average scores of minority candidates on the PPST in Reading and the PLT (K-6) for 1998/1999 were lower than those of white candidates. Table 5-4 shows that the difference between the average scores of African American and white test takers on the 1998/1999 PPST in reading was 1.2 standard deviations. The difference between Hispanic and white average scores for 1998/1999 was 0.7 standard deviations. The difference in the average scores of African American and white candidates on the PLT (K-6) test for

TABLE 5-3   Average Praxis Scores for 1998-1999 Test Takers by Racial/Ethnic Group

Ethnicity	PPST: Reading		PLT (K-6)	
	N	Mean^a	N	Mean^b
African American	5,296	172	1,617	159
Asian American	1,114	175	359	169
Hispanic	848	175	206	165
White	38,868	179	15,743	173

^{a}The most recent scores were included for examinees repeating PPST: Reading in 1998/1999; mean, 178; standard deviation, 6.

^{b}The most recent scores were included for examinees repeating PLT (K-6) in 1998/1999; mean, 172; standard deviation, 12.

SOURCE: Data provided to the committee by Educational Testing Service on March 22, 2001.

TABLE 5-4 Differences Between the Average Praxis Scores of Minority and White Test Takers in Standard Deviation Units, 1998-1999

Differences Between Whites and:	PPST Reading	PLT: K-6
African Americans	1.2	1.2
Asian Americans	0.7	0.3
Hispanics	0.7	0.7

1998/1999 was 1.2 standard deviations; the average difference between Hispanic and white examinees was 0.7.

Several methodological characteristics of the data may affect the group differences. The first is that the Praxis records used in this analysis combine testing data for first-time examinees with data for those retesting during the application year. The data do not take into account the performance of those in the cohort who retest successfully after the application year. Moreover, the data include the later results for individuals who tested unsuccessfully before the 1998/1999 application year. Application-year reports like these tend to exaggerate group differences because minority examinees tend to be overrepresented in the repeat test-taking population. The average scores for minority test takers are depressed by the inclusion of greater numbers of repeaters who, by definition, are lower scoring.

Second, some earlier mentioned characteristics of the SAT dataset for Praxis examinees affect comparisons between these data and the data in Table 5-2. The SAT analyses included 20 years of data, allowing more retesting opportunities and higher scores for some candidates. Further, standard deviation differences for SAT scores in Table 5-2 were calculated by using the SAT population standard deviation, not the standard deviation of SAT scores for Praxis test takers.

Data reports that combine testing records for first-time examinees with those of repeaters are called concurrent reports. The vast majority of state agencies report data for their licensure tests as concurrent reports.

Licensure testing programs generally report passing rates instead of average scores for their candidates because passing rates show about how many candidates have access to the profession. ETS states generally report passing rate data for the Praxis tests. NES states typically do as well. Passing rate data are described next.

Passing Rates

Table 5-5 shows passing rates for the two tests discussed above. It gives the average passing rates on PPST: Reading and PLT (K-6) by racial/ethnic group for 1998/1999 test takers. The candidate data are a subset of those used for Table

TABLE 5-5 Praxis Passing Rates for Test Takers by Racial/Ethnic Group, 1998-1999

Ethnicity	PPST: Reading[a]		PLT (K-6)[c]	
	N	% Passing[b]	N	% Passing
African American	3,874	50	1,219	48
Asian American	670	59	280	82
Hispanic	375	65	163	65
White	21,944	86	12,569	86

[a]Data for 29 states and U.S. Department of Defense Dependents Schools were included.

[b]Average passing rates were calculated by averaging across the passing rates resulting from the application of state passing scores to data for students reporting data to their respective states. States were equally weighted in computing the averages. Note that the number of candidates taking each test exceeds the number reporting data back to a state. For the Praxis II test, 90 to 100% of examinees reported scores to their states. For the PPST reading test, the percentages reporting by racial/ethnic group ranged from 50 to 80%. There was no discernable relationship between the groups' reporting rates and passing rates.

[c]Data for 12 states were included.

SOURCE: Data provided to the committee by Educational Testing Service on August 17, 2000.

5-3 because some candidates take Praxis but do not report their scores back to their states. PPST data are reported in Table 5-3 for candidates reporting scores back to the 29 states using it in 1998/1999; PLT data are shown for candidates reporting scores to 12 states. For the PLT test, between 90 and 100 percent of examinees reported scores to their states in 1998/1999. For PPST: Reading the percentages reporting by racial/ethnic group ranged from 50 to 80 percent. There was no discernable relationship between the groups' reporting rates and the passing rates on PPST: Reading. Average passing rates were calculated by applying state passing scores to data for students reporting scores to their respective states. This provided instate passing rates; instate passing rates were then averaged across states. States were equally weighted in computing the averages. The differences between group passing rates on the two tests are shown in Table 5-6.

TABLE 5-6 Differences Between Praxis Passing Rates for Minority and White Test Takers, 1998-1999

Differences Between Whites and:	PPST Reading	PLT (K-6)
African Americans	36[a]	38
Asian Americans	27	4
Hispanics	21	21

[a]Difference in percentages.

The data in Table 5-5 show substantial disparities between the passing rates of white and minority test takers on both tests. As Table 5-6 shows, the gap between African American and white test takers in 1998/1999 was 36 percentage points on the PPST reading test and 38 on the PLT (K-6) test. For Hispanics the differences were 21 percent on both tests. For Asian Americans the differences were 27 and 4 percent, respectively.

Like the data in Tables 5-3 and 5-4, these data have limitations. They are subject to two types of misinterpretation due to data aggregation. As already noted, they confound the scores for initial and repeat test takers. Group differences may be amplified by the fact that repeat test takers are more likely to be minority group members than majority candidates. The data also may misrepresent similarities and differences in passing rates across groups within states. These average passing rates combine data on passing rates across states using the same tests (based on states' own passing scores, which vary). Some states have different demographic profiles. For example, Texas has a higher percentage of Hispanic candidates than many other states. One group may be more or less likely than another to test in states with relatively low passing scores. The combination of different passing scores and different demographic profiles across states makes direct comparisons of the passing rates across groups problematic.

Nonetheless, the pattern in these results is similar to the patterns observed between minority and majority examinees on the National Board for Professional Teaching Standards (NBPTS) assessments. Certification rates of slightly over 40 percent for white teachers have been reported (Bond, 1998). The reported certification rate for African American teachers was 11 percent, some 30 percent lower than the passing rate for white teachers. The NBPTS assessments are performance based and differ in format from the Praxis tests. The NBPTS assessments and the differences between them and conventional tests are described in Chapter 8.

The pattern in the Praxis results is also seen on licensure tests in certain other professions. For example, a national longitudinal study of graduates of American Bar Association-approved law schools found initial passing rates on the bar exam to be 61 percent for African Americans, 81 percent for Asians, 75 percent for Hispanics, and 92 percent for whites (Wightman, 1998). The corresponding eventual passing rates (after as many as six attempts) were 78, 92, 89, and 97 percent, respectively. Thus, the 31 percentage point difference between passing rates for African Americans and whites on initial testing shrank to a 19-point gap after as many as six attempts. The differences between Hispanics and whites dropped from 17 percentage points to 8. These data also must be interpreted with care, however. Like the Praxis results, data were aggregated across states that have very different passing scores and compositions of minority candidates. To illustrate, although states have different essay sections, almost all of them use the same multiple-choice test. On that test, minority students in one large western state had substantially lower scores than their white classmates. Nevertheless, they still had higher scores than the mostly white candidates in another state. These states also had quite different passing standards and different percentages of minority candidates.

Analogous data are found for medical licensure tests (but because the same passing score is used nationwide, these data are less subject to concerns about misinterpretations of aggregated data). On the first part of the medical tests, a difference of 45 percentage points has been reported for initial passing rates of white and African American medical students, but the difference in their eventual passing rates dropped to 11 points. Similarly, the 25 percentage point difference in initial passing rates between these groups on the second part of the exam dropped to a 9-point difference in eventual passing rates (Case et al., 1996).

The initial and eventual passing rates for lawyers and physicians may be affected by their common use of intensive test preparation courses for these exams. Test preparation courses are less widely available for teacher licensure tests. There may be other differences between these doctoral-level licensing tests and teacher licensure tests that play out differently for minority and majority examinees.

The committee was able to obtain information on initial and eventual passing rates for teacher licensure tests from only two states—California and Connecticut. These two datasets avoid some of the interpretation problems posed by aggregating data across states. They also allow examination of group differences for candidates' first attempts and for test takers' later attempts. Eventual passing rates are important because they are determinative; they relate fairly directly to the licensure decision. Again, the initial rates are important too, since candidates who initially fail but eventually pass may experience delays and additional costs in securing a license.

Table 5-7 shows the number and percentage of candidates who passed the California Basic Education Skills Test (CBEST) on their first attempt in 1995/1996 and the percentage of the 1995/1996 cohort that passed the CBEST by the end of the 1998/1999 testing year. Table 5-9 provides analogous data for California's Multiple Subjects Assessment for Teachers (MSAT) examination. First-time passing rates on the 1996/1997 test are given, along with passing rates for that cohort by 1998/1999. Tables 5-8 and 5-10 give group differences for these tests.

Table 5-7 shows that initial passing rates for 1995/1996 minority candidates on the CBEST exam were lower than for white examinees. The difference between African American and white initial passing rates was 38 percentage points. The gap between rates for Mexican Americans and whites was 28 percentage points, and the difference between Latinos/other Hispanics and whites was 22 percentage points. The passing rates for all groups increased after initially unsuccessful candidates took the test one or more additional times; and as the eventual rates show, the differences between passing rates for minority and majority groups decreased. The gap between African American and white candidates' CBEST passing rates fell from 38 percentage points to 21. The gap

TABLE 5-7   Passing Rates for the CBEST by Population Group, 1995-1996 Cohort

Ethnicity	First-Time Passing Rates		Eventual Passing Rates	
	N^a	% Passing	N	% Passing
African American	2,599	41	2,772	73
Asian American	1,755	66	1,866	87
Mexican American	3,907	51	4,344	88
Latino or other Hispanic	2,014	47	2,296	81
White	25,928	79	26,703	94

aThe size of the 1995-1996 cohort differs for the first-time and eventual reports because first-time rates consider candidates who took all three CBEST sections on their first attempt; eventual rates consider candidates who took each CBEST section at least once by 1998/1999.

SOURCE: Data from Carlson et al., (2000).

between Mexican Americans and whites dropped from 28 to 6 points, and the gap between Latino/other Hispanic examinees and white candidates dropped from 22 to 13 percentage points.

From these data, eventual passing rates tell a different story than do initial rates. The committee contends that both sets of data need to be included in policy makers' judgments about the disparate impact of tests for licensing minority and majority group teacher candidates.

For the MSAT, initial and eventual passing rates for all groups were lower than CBEST passing rates. In addition, passing rates for minority candidates were lower than majority passing rates on the MSAT. The difference between African American and white candidates on the first MSAT was 49 percentage points. By the end of the 1998/1999 testing year, the difference dropped to 42 percent. A 35 percentage point difference between Mexican American and white candidates on the first attempt dropped to 26 percentage points by the end of the third year. The difference for Latino/other Hispanic and white candidates dropped from 33 to 22 percentage points.

Tables 5-11, 5-12, 5-13, and 5-14 provide similar data for Connecticut teacher candidates. The structure of the Connecticut data set differs from that of the California data in that, passing rates are shown for all Connecticut candidates who tested between 1994 and 2000. For the California analyses, the records of first-time candidates in a given year were matched to any subsequent testing attempts made in the next several years. The Connecticut analyses begin with initial testers in 1994, and the data set follows these individuals over the next six years. The data set also includes initial testers from 1995; the records of these candidates are matched to any retest attempts occurring in the next five years.

TABLE 5-8   Differences Between CBEST Passing Rates for Minority and White California Candidates, 1995-1996 Cohort

Differences Between Whites and:	First-Time Passing Rates	Eventual Passing Rates
African Americans	38[a]	21
Mexican Americans	28	6
Latinos or other Hispanics	22	13
Asian Americans	13	7

[a]Difference in percentages.

TABLE 5-9   Passing Rates for the MSAT by Population Group, 1996-1997 Cohort

Ethnicity	First-Time Passing Rates		Eventual Passing Rates	
	N^a	% Passing	N	% Passing
African American	424	24	424	46
Asian American	543	62	543	81
Mexican American	989	38	989	62
Latino or other Hispanic	428	40	428	66
White	7,986	73	7,986	88

[a]The size of the 1995-1996 cohort differs for the first-time and eventual reports because first-time rates consider candidates who took all three CBEST sections on their first attempt; eventual rates consider candidates who took each CBEST section at least once by 1998/1999.

SOURCE: Data from Brunsman et al. (1999).

TABLE 5-10 Differences Between MSAT Passing Rates for Minority and White California Candidates, 1996-1997 Cohort

Differences Between Whites and:	First-Time Passing Rates	Eventual Passing Rates
African Americans	49[a]	42
Mexican Americans	35	26
Latinos or other Hispanics	33	22
Asian Americans	11	7

[a]Difference in percentages.

TABLE 5-11 Passing Rates for Praxis I: Computer-Based Test by
Population Group, 1994-2000 Connecticut Candidates

	First-Time Passing Rates		Eventual Passing Rates	
Ethnicity	*N*	% Passing	*N*	% Passing
African American	354	48	452	55
Asian American	96	54	227	66
Hispanic	343	46	442	59
White	8,852	71	10,035	81

SOURCE: Data provided to the committee by the State of Connecticut Department of Education on
February 9, 2001. See text for a description of this dataset.

TABLE 5-12 Differences Between Praxis I: Computer-Based Test
Passing Rates for Minority and White Connecticut Candidates, 1994-2000

Differences Between Whites and:	First-Time Passing Rates	Eventual Passing Rates
African Americans	23[a]	26
Asian Americans	17	15
Hispanics	25	22

[a]Difference in percentages.

TABLE 5-13 Passing Rates on the Praxis II: Elementary Education
Tests by Population Group, for 1994-2000 Connecticut Candidates

	First-Time Passing Rates		Eventual Passing Rates	
Ethnicity	*N*	% Passing	*N*	% Passing
African American	64	33	122	64
Asian American	38	66	48	83
Hispanic	66	54	95	78
White	2,965	68	3,877	89

SOURCE: Data provided to the committee by the State of Connecticut Department of Education on
February 9, 2001. See the text for a description of this dataset.

TABLE 5-14   Differences Between Praxis II: Elementary Education Tests Passing Rates for Minority and White Connecticut Candidates, 1994-2000

Differences Between Whites and:	First-Time Passing Rates	Eventual Passing Rates
African Americans	35	25
Asian Americans	2	6
Hispanics	14	11

[a]Difference in percentages.

Likewise, records for first-time candidates from 1996 are included along with any retest records generated in the next four years. Similarly, first-time takers from 1997, 1998, and 1999 are included with retesting records from the next three, two, and one years, respectively. For each candidate initially testing between 1994 and 2000, the latest testing record is considered the eventual testing record. Because of this structure, candidates testing unsuccessfully for the first time in 2000 and passing in 2001 or later do not have their later successful attempts included in the analysis. Therefore, the reported eventual passing rates in Tables 5-11 through 5-14 are conservative estimates.

The Connecticut results show some of the same patterns as the California data. Minority passing rates were lower than majority passing rates on the initial and eventual administrations for both tests. The differences decreased for Hispanic and Asian American candidates on Praxis I and for African American and Hispanic test takers on the Praxis II Elementary Education tests. The differences between African American and white candidates on the Praxis I tests increased slightly from the initial testing to the eventual testing.

Although data for only a small number of tests are reported in Tables 5-7 through 5-14, in each case they showed that minority teacher candidates had lower average scores and lower passing rates than nonminority candidates. These differences exist on the initial attempts at licensure testing. The gaps decrease but do not disappear when candidates have multiple testing opportunities. The committee does not know how well these results generalize to those of other states. The committee contends that data on initial and eventual passing rates for minority and majority candidates should be sought from other states so that a broader picture of disparate impact on teacher licensure tests can be developed.

THE MEANING OF DISPARITIES

The differences in average scores and passing rates among groups raise at least two important questions. First, do the scores reflect real differences in competence or are the tests' questions biased against one or more groups? Second, are the inferences drawn from the test results on specific tests (i.e., that some candidates have mastered some of the basic knowledge, skills, and abilities that are generally necessary to practice competently) sufficiently well grounded to justify the social outcomes of differential access to the teaching profession for members of different groups?

Bias

The finding that passing rates for one group are lower than those of another is not sufficient to conclude that the tests are biased. Bias arises when factors other than knowledge of a test's content result in systematically higher or lower scores for particular groups of test takers. There are a number of factors that contribute to possible test bias: item bias, appropriateness of test content, and opportunity to learn issues.

Some researchers have found evidence of cultural bias on teacher tests that are no longer is use, especially tests of general knowledge (Medley and Quirk, 1974; Poggio et al., 1985, 1986). These findings have led to speculation that tests which rely more heavily on general life experiences and cultural knowledge than on a specific curriculum that can be studied may unfairly disadvantage candidates whose life experiences are substantially different from those of majority candidates. This would especially be the case if the content and referents represented on certain basic skills or general knowledge tests, for example, were more commonly present in the life experiences of majority candidates (Bond, 1998). At least some developers of teacher licensure tests, though, put considerable work into eliminating bias during test construction. Items are examined for potentially biasing language or situations, and questionable items often are repaired or removed (Educational Testing Service, 1999a). Additionally, items that show unusually large differences among groups are reexamined for bias. Items that show such differences may be removed from scoring. There is disagreement among committee members about the effectiveness of the statistical and other procedures used by test developers to reduce the cultural bias that might be present in test items. Some committee members contend that these procedures are effective in identifying potentially biased items, whereas others are more skeptical about these methods' ability to detect biased questions. Some members worry that the procedures are not systematically applied.

Other researchers have reservations about the content of pedagogical knowledge tests. They argue that expectations about appropriate or effective teaching behaviors may differ in different kinds of communities and teaching settings and that tests of teacher knowledge that rely on particular ideologies of teaching (e.g., constructivist versus direct instruction approaches) may be differentially valid for different teaching contexts. Items or expected responses that overgeneralize notions about effective teaching behaviors to contexts in which they are less valid may unfairly disadvantage minority candidates who are more likely to live and work in these settings (Irvine, 1990; Ladson-Billings, 1994; Delpit, 1996).

Perhaps most important, the fact that members of minority groups have had less access to high-quality education for most of this country's history (National Research Council, 2001), and that disparate impact occurs across a wide range of tests could suggest that differential outcomes reflect differential educational opportunities more than test bias. In addition to uneven educational opportunities, some contend that these differences may relate to differences between groups in test preparation and test anxiety (Steele, 1992). At the same time, concerns have been raised that the disparities in candidate outcomes on some teacher licensing tests exceed those on other tests of general cognitive ability (Haney et al., 1987; Goertz and Pitcher, 1985). One explanation for these larger historical differences is that there have been geographic differences in the concentrations of test takers of different groups taking particular tests and that these are correlated with differences in educational opportunities available to minorities in different parts of the country (Haney et al., 1987). This hypothesis also may explain why differences among groups are much smaller on some teacher tests than on others and why the pattern for Hispanics does not necessarily follow that for African Americans.

Another explanation is that minority candidates for teaching are drawn disproportionately from the lower end of the achievement distribution among minority college students. Darling-Hammond et al. (1999) suggest this could arise if the monetary rewards of teaching are especially low for minority group members relative to other occupations to which they now have access.

Consequences

When there are major differences in test scores among groups, it is important to evaluate the extent to which the tests are related to the foundational knowledge needed for teaching or to a candidate's capacity to perform competently as a teacher. If minority candidates pass the test at a lower rate than their white peers, the public should expect that there is substantial evidence that the test (and the standard represented by the passing scores that are in effect) is appropriate. For example, the test should be a sound measure of the foundational skills needed for teaching, such as basic literacy skills or subject matter knowledge, that teachers need to provide instruction effectively or should accurately assess skills that make a difference in teacher competence in the classroom. This concern for test validity should be particularly salient when large numbers of individuals who are members of historically underrepresented minority groups have difficulty passing the tests.

Lower passing rates for minority candidates on teacher licensure tests mean that a smaller subset of the already small numbers of minority teacher candidates will move into the hiring pool as licensees and that schools and districts will have smaller pools of candidates from which to hire. This outcome poses problems for schools and districts in seeking a qualified and diverse teaching force. Currently, 13 percent of the teaching force is minority, while minority children make up 36 percent of the student population (U.S. Department of Education, 2001). There are many reasons to be concerned about the small numbers of minority teachers (Darling-Hammond and Sclan, 1996). The importance of minority teachers as role models for minority and majority students is one source of concern. Second, minority teachers can bring a special level of understanding to the experiences of their minority students and a perspective on school policies and practices that is important to include. Finally, minority teachers are more likely to teach in central cities and schools with large minority populations (Choy et al., 1993; National Education Association, 1992). Because minority teachers represent a relatively larger percentage of teacher applicants in these locations, a smaller pool of minority candidates could contribute to teacher shortages in these schools and districts.

There are different perspectives on whether these problems should be the focus of policy attention and, if so, what should be done about them. From a legal perspective, evidence of disparate outcomes does not, by itself, warrant changes in test content, passing scores, or procedures. While Title VII of the Civil Rights Act of 1964 says that employment procedures that have a significant differential impact based on race, sex, or national origin must be justified by test users as being valid and consistent with business or educational necessity, court decisions have been inconsistent about whether the Civil Rights Act applies to teacher licensing tests. In two of three cases in which teacher testing programs were challenged on Title VII grounds, the courts upheld use of the tests (in South Carolina and California), ruling that evidence of the relevance of test content was meaningful and sound. Both courts ruled that the tests were consistent with business necessity and that valid alternatives with less disparate impacts were not available. [2]

In the third case, Alabama discontinued use of its teacher licensing test based on findings of both disparate impact and the failure of the test developer to meet technical standards for test development. The court pointed to concerns about content-related evidence of validity and to arbitrary standards for passing scores as reasons for overturning use of the test. These cases and other licensure and employment testing cases demonstrate that different passing rates do not, by themselves, signify unlawful practices. The lawfulness of licensure tests with disparate impact comes into question when validity cannot be demonstrated.

---

[2]In its interim report (National Research Council, 2000), the committee reported the ruling in a case involving the California Basic Educational Skills Test (*Association of Mexican American Educators v. California*, 183, F.3d 12055, 1070-1071, 9th Cir., 1999). The court subsequently set aside its own decision and issued a new ruling on October 30, 2000 (*Association of Mexican American Educators v. California*, 231 F.3d 572, 9th Cir., en banc). The committee did not consider this ruling.

POLICY OPTIONS

The disadvantages that many minority candidates face as a result of their teacher licensure test scores is not a small matter. These disparate outcomes also affect society in a variety of ways. The committee contends that the effects of group differences on licensure tests are so substantial that it will be difficult to offset their impact without confronting them directly. To the extent that differences in test performance are a function of uneven educational opportunities for different groups, reducing disparities in the educational opportunities available to minority candidates throughout their educational careers is an important policy goal. This will take concerted effort over a sustained period of time. In the shorter run, colleges and universities that prepare teaching candidates who need greater developmental supports may need greater resources to invest in and ensure minority students' educational progress and success.

The committee also believes it is critically important that, where there is evidence of substantial disparate impact, work must be done to evaluate the validity of tests and to strengthen the relationships between tests and the knowledge, skills, abilities, and dispositions needed for teaching. In these instances the quality of the validity evidence is very important.

CONCLUSION

The committee used its evaluation framework to evaluate a sample of five widely used tests produced by the Educational Testing Service. The tests the committee reviewed met most of its criteria for technical quality, although there were some areas for improvement. The committee also attempted to review a sample of National Evaluation Systems tests. Despite concerted and repeated efforts, though, the committee was unable to obtain sufficient information on the technical characteristics of tests produced by NES and thus could draw no conclusions about their technical quality.

On all of the tests that the committee reviewed, minority candidates had lower passing rates than nonminority candidates on their initial testing attempts. Though differences between the passing rates of candidate groups eventually decrease because many unsuccessful test takers retake and pass the tests, eventual passing rates for minority candidates are still lower than those for nonminority test takers.

The committee concludes its evaluation of current tests by reiterating the following:

- The profession's standards for educational testing say that information sufficient to evaluate the appropriateness and technical adequacy of tests should be made available to potential test users and other interested parties. The committee considers the lack of sufficient technical information made available by NES and the states to evaluate NES-developed tests to be problematic and a concern. It is also significant because NES-developed tests are administered to very large numbers of teacher candidates.

- The initial licensure tests currently in use rely almost exclusively on content-related evidence of validity. Few, if any, developers are collecting evidence about how test results relate to other relevant measures of candidates' knowledge, skills, and abilities.

- It is important to collect validity data that go beyond content-related validity evidence for initial licensing tests. However, conducting high-quality research of this kind is complex and costly. Examples of relevant research include investigations of the relationships between test results and other measures of candidate knowledge and skills or on the extent to which tests distinguish candidates who are at least minimally competent from those who are not.

- The processes used to develop current tests, the empirical studies of test content, and common-sense analyses suggest the importance of at least some of what is measured by these initial licensure tests. Beginning teachers should know how to read, write, and do basic mathematics; they should know the content areas they teach.

- The lower passing rates for minority teacher candidates on current licensure tests pose problems for schools and districts in seeking a qualified and diverse teaching force. Setting substantially higher passing scores on licensure tests is likely to reduce the diversity of the teacher applicant pool, further adding to the difficulty of obtaining a diverse school faculty.

6

Using Licensure Tests to Improve Teacher Quality and Supply

Licensure tests are only one factor that influences the overall quality of teachers and teaching. Changes in the quality and effectiveness of teachers depend on many things. Salaries and working conditions affect who enters teaching, as do schooling conditions. The quality of teacher education and of professional development influences teachers' knowledge and skills. Furthermore, as noted earlier, teaching rests on more than teachers; school organizational factors such as use of time, quality of curriculum materials, and student/ teacher ratios affect the quality of teaching.

The belief that testing can improve the quality of the teaching force is based on an assumption that the tests used are good measures of the competencies needed for effective teaching and that their salutary effects on training and selection are not outweighed by negative consequences for supply (including, for example, eliminating competent teachers from the pool and dissuading some from considering teaching). As discussed below, some tests measure qualities that are reasonably related to aspects of teacher effectiveness. However, there are questions about the extent to which different tests capture the way this knowledge is actually used in teaching. There is a paucity of evidence concerning the ability of teacher licensure tests to distinguish minimally competent candidates from those who are not.

This chapter presents a theoretical model suggesting that the quality of prospective beginning teachers depends on a number of factors, including the accuracy of licensure tests in distinguishing between those who would be competent and those who would not; the actual and perceived opportunity costs to applicants of licensure testing, the level of teachers' salaries and working conditions, and the attractiveness of labor market alternatives. These effects are discussed by building a logical argument based on an economic model of occupational choice. A discussion of the evidentiary base for the relationship between licensure tests and teacher competence follows the description of the model. The measurement and research design challenges that mark this field of research are discussed, and some empirical findings are reviewed.

LICENSING TESTS AND THE QUANTITY AND QUALITY OF TEACHERS

This section is based on an economic model of supply and demand for teachers.[1] The theory is used to both understand the potential consequences of licensure testing for the quality and quantity of beginning teachers and provide guidance as to the kind of information and empirical analysis needed to conduct a quantitative assessment of those consequences. The analysis assumes that beginning teachers have met whatever other licensing requirements exist (e.g., completion of an accredited teacher education program) prior to attempting to meet the testing requirement. The counterfactual, in which passing a test is not a requirement for licensure, assumes that in the absence of a licensure test the hiring practices of school districts would lead to a teacher work force with a higher proportion of "unqualified" teachers.[2]

As already noted, teacher licensure testing is intended to distinguish between those who are competent to enter the classroom in terms of the skills measured by the test and those who are not. Ideally, tests would do this, as in other professions, by limiting the supply of teachers only to those who are competent.

The supply side of the model assumes that individuals choose between teaching and other occupations according to which provides the larger expected (net) benefit, wages, and nonmonetary forms of compensation after education and other training costs are paid.[3] As a baseline case, consider the situation where there is no test; in that case the model assumes that individuals who are potentially competent teachers are indistinguishable from those who are potentially incompetent. The net benefit to teaching in any given labor market is thus taken to be the same for all individuals independent of their potential competency.[4] However, individuals are assumed to differ in the net benefits they receive in

---

[1]A full presentation and discussion of the model are provided in Appendix E.

[2]Ballou (1996) provides some evidence that school districts do not do a particularly good job of screening candidates under current accountability systems. However, it is not known whether the same would be true under a different accountability system (e.g., one based on student performance). It is beyond the scope of this report to consider alternatives to the current licensure system.

[3]The net benefits may also include psychic rewards.

[4]To simplify the analysis, the possibility that psychic benefits to teaching might differ according to potential competency is ignored.

alternative occupations. Increasing the compensation of teachers would thus lead to an increase in the supply of both competent and incompetent individuals.[5] To the extent that those who would be competent as teachers can obtain higher wages in alternative occupations than those who are not competent, the incentive for those who are competent to enter teaching will be less than for those who are not competent at any given level of teacher wages.[6] The proportion of those choosing teaching who would be competent would depend on the difference in the distributions of net benefits in alternative occupations between potentially competent and potentially incompetent teachers.

By its nature, licensure testing increases the costs of entering an occupation. Licensure tests require payment of testing fees, allocation of time and effort to prepare for the tests, and, given a nontrivial failure rate, create uncertainty about obtaining employment in teaching. Moreover, the cost of failure is increased by specialized coursework required for licensure in teaching. To the extent that these education courses have a lower market payoff outside teaching than would alternative courses an individual might have completed had the teaching occupation not been chosen, an opportunity cost is incurred. Individuals who fail licensure tests, and thus do not get teaching jobs, will receive lower wages in alternative jobs compared to the wages they would have received had they taken courses in pursuit of alternative occupations. The total cost of the licensure test thus includes this difference in wages.

The direct cost of a licensure test, as well as the opportunity cost that arises in the case of failure, makes the teaching occupation less attractive relative to alternative occupations than it would be in the absence of a test.[7] In general, if all else is equal, the greater the cost that licensure tests impose on teacher candidates, the smaller will be the supply of both potentially competent and potentially incompetent teachers.

Due to errors in measurement, tests are not perfectly accurate and reliable. In theory a "perfect" test is one with a passing score set such that every candidate who scores at or above that level is truly competent in the skills measured and that every candidate who scores below that level is not. An "imperfect" test, however, does not have such a passing score. Instead, for any given passing

---

[5]There is considerable empirical evidence that the supply of teachers is increasing in the wage that is offered. (see e.g., Manski 1987; Ballou and Podgursky, 1997; and Stinebrikner, forthcoming).

[6]Generally, this difference would lead to a greater proportion of incompetent than competent persons choosing teaching. However, the fact that competence in teaching may be positively related to wages in alternative occupations does not imply that increasing teachers' wages will attract relatively more competent than incompetent people, although the supply of both would increase. For technical reasons the model assumes that the proportion of competent to incompetent people who choose teaching is invariant to increases in teacher wages.

[7]This conclusion ignores the argument that the prestige of the profession may be augmented by its becoming more selective, which may increase its attractiveness. It is assumed that to the extent this positive effect exists, it does not dominate the negative effect of the direct costs of the test.

score on an imperfect test, some who are not competent will still score above the passing level and therefore will be misclassified as competent; this type of error is called the type 1 error of the test. Some candidates who are truly competent will score below the passing level and will be mistakenly classified as incompetent, which is known as the type 2 error. A perfect test classifies everyone correctly and has no type 1 or type 2 errors.

The inability of a test to determine competency with perfect accuracy magnifies the actual cost of the test. The greater the probability that a candidate will fail the test (regardless of competence), the greater will be the perceived cost of the test.[8] For example, in the model, if the direct cost of the test is $500 (including the monetary and test preparation costs) and the probability of passing is 0.5, the perceived cost of the test will be equivalent to that of a perfect test in which the direct cost is $1,000.[9] In the case of truly incompetent individuals the perceived cost of the higher failure rate (which lowers type 1 errors) will reduce the supply of incompetent teacher candidates in the total pool. For truly competent individuals the higher the probability that they will mistakenly be classified as not competent (the higher the type 2 error), the more they will be discouraged from entering the teaching profession.

A perfect test would discourage only incompetent individuals from entering the teaching occupation. In that case the supply of beginning teachers would all be competent, although the number of competent individuals who choose to enter teaching will be reduced if the direct costs of the test are substantial.[10] An imperfect test discourages both incompetent and competent individuals from choosing teaching. If the failure rate is higher for those who are incompetent (than it is for the competent) and the cost of the test is not greater for the competent (than for the incompetent), the test will tend to increase the proportion of competent individuals in the total supply.

In addition to the effect of test costs on the potential supply, licensing tests affect the actual supply of teachers after they have completed their educational preparation. Depending on the accuracy of the test (the extent to which it correctly distinguishes between competent and incompetent individuals), the share of competent individuals excluded or incompetent individuals admitted will vary.

---

[8]In the case of those who are incompetent, this probability is one minus the type 1 error; for those who are competent, it is the type 2 error.

[9]The opportunity cost is multiplied by the odds of failure (the probability of failure divided by the probability of passing), which are less than one if the failure rate is below 0.5 and greater than one if it is above 0.5 (see Appendix E).

[10]In the formal model it is assumed that people know whether they are competent as well as what the true failure probability is (i.e., the type 1 and type 2 errors of the test). These assumptions, although clearly too strong, may be considerably weakened without affecting the main conclusions of the model.

To the extent that some competent individuals are misclassified by an imperfect test (type 2 error), the supply of competent teachers will be reduced.

Reducing the supply of teachers may be a desirable outcome of licensure testing as long as the proportion of competent teachers in the total supply increases sufficiently. The passing score of a test will directly affect the overall supply of teachers as well as the proportion who are competent. Setting a low passing score will tend to have a small effect on supply both because many candidates pass the test and because the perceived cost of the test differs little from the actual cost due the high chance of passing. Relative to no licensure test, a low passing score will tend not to alter the proportion of competent teachers by very much. Raising the passing score will tend to reduce the supply of both competent and incompetent teachers, as a higher proportion of both are labeled by the test as incompetent and as the perceived cost rises. Since passing scores are continually raised, it becomes more and more likely that the supply of competent teachers will decrease more than the supply of incompetent teachers because fewer incompetent people presumably score at higher levels.[11]

Some states require tests at many points in the process of teacher preparation and some require more than one subject matter test. Some require additional assessments of teaching knowledge and skill in the first year or two of teaching. If just 10 percent of test takers fail each test in a series of, say, five it would be possible to eliminate 50 percent or more of the potential teaching force from the pool of license-eligible individuals. At any of these junctures, if most of the remaining teachers are competent, raising the passing score will eliminate mostly teachers who are competent.

The number of new teachers employed and the resulting number that are competent depend not only on the supply of teachers but also on the demand for new teachers. The model of demand assumes that communities care about the achievement of their children, which is positively related to the number of competent teachers that are employed, but that they face alternative uses for their scarce resources. Assuming that communities face a competitive labor market for teachers and that their total expenditures are constrained by their tax revenues, it is shown, as is standard, that the demand for teachers falls with the level of compensation. In addition, it is shown that the demand for teachers at any given level of compensation depends on the proportion of competent teachers in the supply. Indeed, the theory implies that an increase in the proportion of com-

---

[11]Consider a test that is perfect at one unique (optimal) passing score. If the passing score is set below that point, there will be a nonzero type 1 error. Raising it from that point up to the optimal passing score will eliminate only incompetent people, and the type 1 error will fall. Raising the passing score beyond the optimal point will eliminate only competent people, creating a nonzero type 2 error.

petent teachers in the supply will never lead to a fall in the demand for teachers (at the same wage) sufficient to reduce the number of competent teachers that would be employed.

To understand the implications of the supply and demand models for teacher employment, consider again a perfect test. If the cost of the test is small, the supply of teachers is reduced exactly to the number of competent people who would choose teaching absent the test. The increase in the proportion of beginning teachers who are competent to unity may either increase or decrease the overall demand for teachers. However, the change in demand, regardless of whether it increases or falls, will never be such that the number of competent teachers employed falls below what it was without the test. If instead test takers bear a substantial cost, inducing some competent people to choose an alternative occupation relative to the case without a test, although the proportion of competent people must still increase to unity given that the test is perfect, the number of competent teachers employed may actually fall relative to the case in which there is no test.

Restrictions on supply also increase wages and other forms of compensation. However, if a test is highly accurate, so that almost all teachers who pass it are competent, and if it is of low cost, so that the attractiveness of teaching is not unduly adversely affected, the resulting increase in wages will reflect the true scarcity of competent teachers. Furthermore, as described above, the combined effect of the test on supply and demand will be to increase the number of competent beginning teachers and thus to increase student learning. On the other hand, if the test is highly imperfect, so that the proportion of competent teachers in the total (smaller) supply is not altered much by the test, or the test is viewed by teacher candidates as especially onerous and costly (e.g., because the failure rate is high even for competent teachers), the resulting increased wages will reflect mainly an artificially created scarcity. An artificial scarcity can also be created even with a highly accurate test if the passing score is raised to a point where most of those being eliminated from the supply are competent. In either case, there could be fewer competent teachers relative to having no test and student learning may be diminished.

The theoretical model is ambiguous as to whether licensure tests are efficacious in improving teacher competency. To determine the quantitative effects of licensure tests on the overall supply of new teachers and on their competency requires a great deal of information. It is necessary to know not only about the accuracy of the test (i.e., its type 1 and type 2 errors) but also about the direct and opportunity costs to the test takers, the alternative market opportunities of potential teachers, the constraints on the tax revenues of school districts, and the effects on student learning of alternative uses of school funds.

As is clear, establishing what constitutes optimal licensure testing in a given state is a complex issue. This complexity is multiplied when taking a national perspective that considers the effect that one state's licensure testing requirement can have on teacher supply and competency and thus on student learning in other states. Reciprocity across states in the licensing of teachers is quite limited, because different states require different tests or have established different passing scores for the same test. This lack of reciprocity has several consequences. First, it reduces the attractiveness of teaching as an occupation because it increases the cost of changing jobs across states. Second, it creates barriers to mobility that impede the responsiveness of teachers to changes in the demand for teachers across states.[12] Finally, individual states, by taking independent uncoordinated actions, can affect the labor market for teachers in other states without knowledge or consideration of those effects. On the other hand, states have intentionally different objectives in their testing policies and requirements for licensure, which may be one reason that voluntary reciprocity agreements are limited. The extent to which coordination in state policies should be fostered is an important issue for examination.

This analysis has assumed that only licensed teachers are employed in public schools. As discussed in Chapter 3, though, almost all states permit waivers of their licensure rules to allow school districts to hire teachers on an emergency basis under certain circumstances. To the extent that those waivers are used, the restriction that licensure tests impose on the supply of teachers will be loosened and the effects discussed above will be mitigated (i.e., the potential gains from accurate licensure testing will be reduced as might be the potential losses from inaccurate and costly testing).

RESEARCH ON TEACHER LICENSING TESTS AND TEACHER COMPETENCE

Questions about test validity are key to the analysis described above. The extent to which teacher licensure tests identify candidates with the knowledge and skills minimally needed for competent practice is a key concern. The content of teacher tests generally is determined through logical and empirical processes (Educational Testing Service, 1999a, 1999e). Educators are asked to identify the knowledge, skills, abilities, and dispositions that are minimally needed for teaching. Tests are constructed to align with these specifications. Standards are set for performance on tests in order to differentiate those candidates who have sufficient levels of competence to practice from those who do not. Scores on the tests are used by policy makers to help decide which candidates are licensed.

---

[12]While K-12 enrollments are anticipated to increase by more than 10 percent in many states in the West and South by the year 2007, in most parts of the Northeast and Midwest enrollments are expected to decline (U.S. Department of Education, 1996a). This may be a particularly acute concern as student enrollments have been growing in some parts of the country and shrinking in others, while the distribution of trained teachers is uneven across states.

Whether these practices result in tests that actually identify individuals who will become minimally competent beginning teachers is an important question. Research on the relationship between scores on teacher licensure tests and measures of teacher performance should provide some answers. To examine this question, the committee commissioned a review of the literature on the relationships between teacher licensure tests and teacher competence (Youngs, 2000). Electronic databases in education, psychology, and economics were searched; metanalyses and literature reviews were examined to identify other potentially relevant articles, books, and chapters; and researchers were contacted to learn about current or other recent research.

Initially, the search was limited to evidence about teacher licensure tests currently in use. This search strategy uncovered no relevant research. Some currently used tests are newly introduced and have not been in place long enough to support research. Next, the literature was examined for research on retired teacher licensure tests. This yielded a small body of studies, including work by Ferguson (1991), Ferguson and Brown (2000), Strauss and Sawyer (1986), Summers and Wolfe (1975), Sheehan and Marcus (1978), and Ayers and Qualls (1979). Finally, the search criteria were expanded to include research on the relationship between teacher performance and tests of the content domains currently measured by teacher licensure tests. This approach yielded additional information and expanded the committee's analysis to include research that might inform questions about the relationship between performance on teacher licensure tests and teacher competence (Ehrenberg and Brewer, 1995; Ferguson and Ladd, 1996; Bassham, 1962; Rothman, 1969; Begle, 1972; Rowan et al., 1997; Clary, 1972). Thirteen studies were found.

The search could have been expanded to include studies of the relationship between teacher performance and teachers' knowledge and skills in the areas that licensure tests examine, regardless of how the knowledge and skills are measured. This approach would have allowed the broadest possible range of indicators of teacher characteristics, including the number of courses that candidates took, whether candidates majored or minored in the subject taught, and the highest degree level obtained. The committee elected to not undertake this search; readers are referred to reviews in *Teacher Quality and Student Achievement: A Review of State Policy Evidence* (Darling-Hammond, 2000), *A License to Teach* (Darling-Hammond et al., 1999), and elsewhere.

There were substantial interpretive problems with the body of evidence uncovered. This type of research is very difficult to mount because of measurement and research design issues. Although it is difficult to examine the relationship between scores on teacher licensure tests and teaching quality, it is certainly possible and important to do so. Analyses of the relationships between scores on teacher licensure tests and effectiveness in the classroom would provide a better understanding of what the tests do and do not measure.

To understand the difficulties involved in determining the extent to which teacher characteristics affect student achievement, it is useful to describe a paradigm in which the existing analyses fall. One can think of student achievement as measured at any grade level as the outcome of the school and family resources provided to children over their lifetimes, not just within the grade level at which the measurement is taken. Because the qualities of the educational institutions and the availability of family-supplied resources that are complementary to achievement (e.g., books, computers, tutors) are generally not unrelated to each other, researchers have recognized the importance of obtaining measures of "inputs" into the production of student achievement from all of these sources even when their interest is in estimating the impact of only a single input, such as teacher subject matter knowledge. However, data are limited; researchers do not have measures of all of these inputs and measures of the ones they do have are often imperfect.

For instance, many studies compare district-wide or school-wide average teacher test scores with comparable averages in students' test scores. Often the data on which these studies are based have only crude measures of family inputs. Moreover, researchers tend not to include in their analyses inputs, both of schools and families, prior to the grade level at which achievement is measured. It is, therefore, likely that districts or schools whose students score better than would be predicted given the observed school and family inputs are also districts or schools whose students have available to them important inputs that were not measured. To the extent that districts that serve higher scoring students, beyond that of their measured inputs, also employ higher scoring teachers (whatever the reason), the relationship between teacher test scores and student achievement will be confounded. That is, some of the effect of the omitted inputs that cause student achievement to be higher will be attributed to higher teacher test scores.

Other studies examine the issue using matched student-teacher data at the individual student level, rather than relying on district- or school-wide averages. The advantage of these data is that, with observations of many students within a district or school, district- or school-level inputs that are not measured can nevertheless be accounted for by making use of within-school (or within-district) variation. Thus, the problem that teachers are not randomly employed in districts (or in schools within districts) with respect to unmeasured inputs that influence student achievement is circumvented with such data. However, it may still be true that teacher assignments within districts, or even schools, are related to student achievement that is due to unmeasured inputs or student abilities, and such nonrandom assignment would again confound the effect of teacher test scores. Although the availability of such data generally reduces the extent to which there are omitted factors that affect student achievement, it is not possible to say that the bias due to nonrandom teacher assignment is lessened by the use of matched student-teacher data without further assertions about the teacher assignment process.

Having matched student-teacher data does not preclude the necessity to account for the cumulative nature of student learning. Test score measurements at a single point in time (grade level) would be related not only to the characteristics of the current teacher and current family-provided inputs but also to the characteristics of past teachers and past family inputs (even prior to school attendance and arguably back to a child's conception). There is no source of data that meets that requirement. One way researchers have attempted to circumvent this data limitation is by exploiting the availability of achievement measures at more than one point in time. Such studies look at the relationship of changes in achievement between two grade levels to school and family inputs applied between the measurements, the so-called value-added approach found in the education production function literature (Hanushek, 1986). The seemingly plausible argument that because the teacher's task is to add knowledge to what students already know, one can ignore teacher and other inputs prior to the initial measurement, however, is in fact only valid under additional assumptions about how rapidly the effects of prior inputs diminish over time. Moreover, while measuring initial achievement "controls" for all of the inputs that went into the determination of initial achievement (in a specific way), it is still possible that there are omitted school and family inputs that affect (the change in) achievement, that are known to the school, and that are related to teacher assignment.

Measurement problems also complicate this research. Much is said in this report about the difficulty of measuring teachers' effectiveness in the classroom; it has been noted that there is no commonly accepted valid and fair measure of effective teaching. Research is further hampered by the difficulty of accurately distinguishing minimally competent from minimally incompetent classroom practice. In Chapter 2 it is said that most current teaching standards do not specify whether the knowledge and skills they describe are to be demonstrated by minimally competent or more proficient beginning teachers. It is difficult to measure minimally competent performance in the absence of a clear definition. Most of the studies described below use student achievement as a proxy for teacher performance. Even comprehensive, highly reliable measures of student learning are incomplete indicators of teaching effectiveness. Available student achievement measures are considered narrow by some researchers and lacking in detail (Porter et al., 2000). One study uses principals' ratings of teacher performance.

A final design obstacle in this field of research follows from discussion of measurement problems. The absence of job performance information for unlicensed examinees is a notable limitation. The criterion of greatest interest to research on the relationship between licensure test results and job performance is a measure of minimally competent beginning teaching. Because candidates who fail licensure tests generally are ineligible for licensure and employment as classroom teachers, job performance information is unavailable for them. However, the fact that unlicensed individuals are now hired in relatively large numbers by private schools and by public schools on an emergency basis makes possible the collection of job performance information for candidates scoring below passing levels. As noted earlier, well over half of the states permit individuals to begin teaching without meeting licensure test requirements, some for as long as the district says it cannot find qualified applicants (U.S. Department of Education, 2000a; Blair, 1999; Education Week, 2001). Job performance information is obtainable for these individuals. In addition, as states raise the passing scores on their tests, it will be possible to compare the performance of teachers who failed to those who did not fail under the new higher passing score.

These important measurement and research design problems limit the inferences that can be drawn from the existing research. The degree of bias in estimates of teacher effects associated with the use of these different sources of data, district averages, school averages, cross-sectional matched student-teacher data, and longitudinal matched student-teacher data that is likely to arise from nonrandom teacher assignment is unknown. The degree of error associated with incomplete and imperfect measurement also is unknown. All of the studies that the committee uncovered have one or more design and measurement limitations. Table 6.1 describes the studies and documents their measurement and design characteristics.

Table 6.1 describes for each study the measure of teacher performance used by the researchers. Eleven of the studies used student achievement tests as measures of teacher competence; all reported student test results on a continuous scale. One study used principals' evaluations of teachers' job performance. The table also describes the teacher licensure or other tests of teachers used by the researchers. Five studies examined teacher licensure tests, and seven looked at teachers' performance on tests measuring some of the same knowledge and skills examined by licensure tests (e.g., ACT test). As with the student test data, all but one set of teacher results were reported on a continuous scale. The table additionally notes whether researchers included other teacher data, like degree type or racial/ethnic status, as measures of other characteristics potentially related to teacher performance. The table shows whether baseline data were available to describe students' academic achievement prior to the teachers' work with them. Likewise, it shows whether other student, school, or family data, such as teacher/pupil ratios, poverty levels, or language status, were available for study. The table also shows whether teachers, schools, or districts were the unit of analysis in the research and gives sample sizes for the studies. It notes the amount of time that elapsed between teacher testing and measurement of their performance in the classroom. Finally, the table documents the statistical procedures used by the researchers and records their interpretations of the data.

The remainder of this chapter provides a description of the findings from this body of evidence as the original authors presented them. Some readers will find problematic some of the inferences these researchers drew from the data, as does the committee. However, the committee would like to provide the reader with a sense of the research and the research findings it uncovered. What follows is a review of findings from research on tests of the knowledge and skills exam-

TABLE 6.1　Research on Tests of Teachers and Teaching Outcomes

	Outcome Variables			Other Variables			
Study	Student Achievement Measure	Teacher Evaluation by Principal	Teacher Test	Other Teacher Variables	Baseline Student Achieve-ment Measure	Other Student Variables	School Variables
Basic Skills or General Knowledge							
Ehrenberg and Brewer (1995)	Verbal and nonverbal test, reading and math test (test names not provided)		Verbal aptitude test (test name not provided)	√		√	√
Ferguson (1991); Ferguson and Brown (2000)	Texas Educational Assessment of Minimum Skills (reading, math)		Texas Examination of Current Administrators and Teachers (reading, writing, professional knowledge)	√		√	√
Ferguson and Ladd (1996); Ferguson and Brown (2000)	Basic Competency Test, Stanford Achievement Test (reading, math)		American College Test (English, reading, math, science)	√	For school analysis		√
	Basic Competency Test, Stanford Achievement Test (reading, math)		American College Test (English, reading, math, science)		Used data for third and fourth graders as baseline for district analysis		

Study Characteristics						Findings
Family Vari-ables	Unit of Analysis	Sample Charac-teristics	Sample Size	Time Between Teacher Test and Outcome Measure	Statistical Procedure Used	Estimated Relation-ship Between Teacher Test Data and Student Test Data or Principal's Evaluation
√	School	Schools that had grades 3 and 6 or 9 and 12	969 elementary schools, 256 secondary schools		Synthetic gain scores (mean test scores of upper grades in a school minus mean test scores of lower grades in same school)	Positive and statistically significant for both elementary and secondary schools (higher verbal scores of teachers were associated with higher gains in scores for white, but not black, high school students)
√	District	All Texas school districts: Houston, Dallas, and very small districts	Ranged from 857 districts for grades 11 to 890 districts for grade 1	Within academic year and then 2 and 4 years later	Multiple regression	Positive and statistically significant
√	School	Schools with both third and fourth grades in same school	Grade 4 cohort students, data available for only ¼ of teachers across schools; (690 schools); only 35 schools (of 690) with full data for teachers	ACT (from entrance to college, so time since ACT varies among teachers)		Positive and statistically significant for teachers' scores on reading at school level; positive but not significant for math
	District		127 school districts			Positive and stastically significant results for students' math test scores

continues

TABLE 6.1   Continued

	Outcome Variables			Other Variables			
Study	Student Achievement Measure	Teacher Evaluation by Principal	Teacher Test	Other Teacher Variables	Baseline Student Achievement Measure	Other Student Variables	School Variables
Subject Matter Knowledge							
Bassham (1962)	California Achievement Test (reading, math)		Test of Basic Mathematical Understanding	√	√		√
Rothman (1969)	Test on Understanding Science, Project Physics Achievement Test, Science Welch Process Inventory		Test of Selected Topics in Physics, Test on Understanding Science	√	√		
Begle (1972)	Mathematics Inventory (I-IV)		Algebra Inventory (Forms A and B) and Abstract Algebra Inventory (Form C)		√		
Pedagogical Knowledge							
Clary (1972)	Science Research Associates Achievement Series in Reading		Inventory of Teacher Knowledge of Reading	√			

	Study Characteristics					Findings
Family Variables	Unit of Analysis	Sample Characteristics	Sample Size	Time Between Teacher Test and Outcome Measure	Statistical Procedure Used	Estimated Relation-ship Between Teacher Test Data and Student Test Data or Principal's Evaluation
	Teacher	Grade 6 teachers in an urban school district (14,000 students; 28 teachers)	28 grade 6 teachers in an urban school district (14,000 students)	Within academic year	Multiple regression	Positive and statistically significant for above average, but not below average, students
	Teacher	All students of participating teachers (number of students not provided)	51 high school physics teachers randomly selected from a list of 17,000	Within academic year	Canonical correlation	Positive and statistically significant relationship between teachers' test scores and students' scores
	Teacher	Teachers from across the country who participated in National Science Foundation summer institutes and grade 9 students	308 math teachers	Within a calendar year	Multiple regression	Significant positive but modest relationship between teachers' test scores and students' understanding of algebra, but not for student achievement
	Teacher	Most (23 of 25) grade 4 teachers in one district	23 grade 4 teachers		Multiple regression	Positive and statistically significant

continues

TABLE 6.1   Continued

	Outcome Variables			Other Variables			
Study	Student Achievement Measure	Teacher Evaluation by Principal	Teacher Test	Other Teacher Variables	Baseline Student Achievement Measure	Other Student Variables	School Variables
Summers and Wolfe (1975)	Iowa Test of Basic Skills		National Teacher Examination: Common Examination (general and professional knowledge)	√	√	√	√
Sheehan and Marcus (1978)	Metropolitan Reading Test (vocabulary, math), Iowa Test of Basic Skills (vocabulary, math)		Weighted Common Examinations Total (NTE; general and professional knowledge)	√	√		√ (controlled for background factors by entering pre-test measures first)
Ayers and Qualls (1979)		Evaluation by Supervisor form	Weighted Common Examinations Total (NTE; general and professional knowledge) Education in the Elementary School	√			
Strauss and Sawyer (1986)	Norm-Referenced Achievement (reading, math)		National Teacher Examination (plus five other non-teacher-related variables)		√	√	√

ined by current teacher licensure tests: (a) basic skills and general knowledge, (b) subject matter knowledge, (c) pedagogical knowledge, and (d) pedagogical content knowledge.

Study Characteristics						Findings
Family Vari-ables	Unit of Analysis	Sample Charac-teristics	Sample Size	Time Between Teacher Test and Outcome Measure	Statistical Procedure Used	Estimated Relation-ship Between Teacher Test Data and Student Test Data or Principal's Evaluation
√	School		Urban elementary schools (103 schools)	Used a school average of grade 6 teachers' scores; time since test varies based on experience of teacher	Multiple regression	Negative and statistically significant but small
√ (controlled for back-ground factors by entering pretest measures first)	Teacher	Students not randomly selected; class average of students	119 teachers, 1,836 students	Range of teacher experience (1-40 years); time varied since taking NTE	Stepwise regression	Positive and significant association with students' math and reading; relationships disappeared when teachers' race was considered
	Teacher	Elemen-tary and secon-dary teachers	84 elementary and 49 secondary teachers	Generally one year	Correla-tional (compared means and standard deviations)	Mixed, small correlations
√	District	High school juniors	145 districts in North Carolina (105 districts with capital stock info)		Production function	Significant but modest relationship between teacher test scores and student achievement

Tests of Basic Skills and General Knowledge

Three sets of researchers examined the relationships between teachers' performance on basic skills or general knowledge tests and student achievement: Ehrenberg and Brewer (1995), Ferguson (1991), and Ferguson and Ladd (1996).

Ferguson and Brown (2000) reexamined data from the two earlier Ferguson studies. One study examined teacher licensure test results (Ferguson, 1991), and the others examined other tests of basic skills. Ferguson (1991) studied teachers' performance on the Texas licensing test, the Texas Examination of Current Administrators and Teachers (TECAT), which measures reading and writing skill, including verbal ability and research skills, as well as a limited body of professional knowledge. Ferguson found that the following four district average teacher and school variables were related to student performance on the Texas Educational Assessment of Minimum Skills examinations in reading and mathematics: TECAT scores, teachers' experience, number of students per teacher, and percentage of teachers with master's degrees. TECAT scores were found to account for 20 to 25 percent of all variation across districts in student average scores.

Ferguson and Ladd (1996) conducted similar district-level analyses in Alabama but used ACT scores (not scores on a licensing examination) as measures of teacher ability. School average scores for teachers on the ACT test were related to student achievement but less so than for the earlier TECAT study. Ehrenberg and Brewer (1995) also found positive relationships between teachers' performance on basic skills tests and student achievement, though results varied for elementary and high school students and by students' racial/ethnic status.

Subject Matter Knowledge

Research has also examined the relationships between teachers' subject matter knowledge and their competence. Four sets of researchers looked at the relationship between tests of teachers' subject matter knowledge and student achievement: Bassham (1962), Rothman (1969), Begle (1972), and Rowan et al. (1997). Bassham studied the relationship between teachers' performance on a Test of Basic Mathematical Understandings and students' mathematics gains on pre- and posttests over the course of a year. This researcher found a significant relationship between teachers' and students' scores only for students of above-average achievement. Rothman (1969) reported a significant positive relationship between teachers' and student' performance on some measures of science and physics knowledge. Begle found different relationships from year to year and class to class between teacher scores on the algebra inventory test and student achievement. Rowan et al. reported a positive and significant relationship between students' performance on the 1998 National Educational Longitudinal Study (NELS) math achievement test and their teachers' responses to a one-item measure of mathematics knowledge on the NELS teacher questionnaire.

Pedagogical Knowledge

Five studies examined the relationship between teacher pedagogical knowledge, as measured by paper-and-pencil tests, and their performance in the classroom: Clary (1972), Summers and Wolfe (1975), Sheehan and Marcus (1978), Ayers and Qualls (1979), and Strauss and Sawyer (1986). Four studies used student achievement test data as measures of teacher competence, and one used supervisor evaluations. Clary examined teachers' understanding of how to teach reading, as evaluated by an Inventory of Teacher Knowledge of Reading, in relation to students' reading achievement on pre- and posttests from the Science Research Associates Reading Achievement Series. The author reported statistically significant relationships between pedagogical knowledge and student performance, concluding that "there is a direct relationship between the person who exhibits proficient knowledge about teaching reading and that person's success in producing students who make an appreciable amount of progress in reading achievement" (p. 15).

Four sets of researchers—Summers and Wolfe (1975), Sheehan and Marcus (1978), Ayers and Qualls, (1979), and Strauss and Sawyer (1986)—examined pedagogical knowledge as tested by the National Teacher Examinations (NTE), precursors to the current Praxis tests. Strauss and Sawyer looked at the relationships between students' test scores and teachers' performance on the NTE. The authors included data on six inputs in their examination of these relationships; they looked at the number of teachers in each of 145 school districts, the number of students per district, the number of high school students interested in postsecondary education in each district, the racial/ethnic composition of the schools, the value of the districts' capital stock, and teachers' test scores. A modest positive and statistically significant relationship was found between district average NTE scores and student test scores.

Two other studies looked at the relationship between NTE scores and student achievement test data. One found a small negative and statistically significant relationship between school average teacher and student scores (Summers and Wolfe, 1975). The other reported a positive significant relationship between teachers' and students' scores, but when teacher race was used as a control variable, teacher scores showed no effect on student achievement (Sheehan and Marcus, 1978). Ayers and Qualls (1979) reported small positive and small negative correlations between teachers' NTE scores and principals' ratings of teacher competence.

Pedagogical Content Knowledge

As noted earlier, the idea of pedagogical content knowledge is relatively new to education discourse. Prior to the mid-1980s, discussions of teacher knowledge tended to distinguish subject matter knowledge from knowledge of teaching or of students. No studies were found that examined licensure tests of pedagogical content knowledge. Other researchers have examined questions similar to those addressed by the studies discussed above including Andrews et al. (1980) and Hanushek (1986).

DIRECTIONS FOR RESEARCH

Teaching is a public enterprise. The public has an important interest in the quality of its teaching force and in current initiatives to improve teaching and learning. The committee encourages the federal government and others to conduct research that has the potential to improve the quality of licensure tests and, possibly, the capabilities of the beginning teacher work force.

In Chapters 4 and 5 the committee discussed the kinds of data that might provide supportive empirical evidence for the validity of teacher licensure tests. These include data on the relationships between test results and other measures of candidate knowledge and skill and data on the extent to which licensure tests distinguish minimally competent candidates from those who are not. The committee also described several licensing and employment conditions that permit observations of job performance for candidates who fail licensing tests. The committee explained that job performance data are now available for unlicensed candidates who are teaching with emergency licenses. Data are also available for candidates who passed licensure tests under different passing standards. These are fairly recent conditions for entering the teaching profession, and they provide an important opportunity to collect job-related evidence for candidates scoring above and below passing scores on the tests. This chapter describes and illustrates the difficulty of mounting this research. However, the measurement and research design problems that mark this research are not unique to teacher licensure tests. They characterize research on many other social science questions as well.

Given the complexity of these issues, it would be valuable to undertake an interagency study to define needed research. Representatives from the U.S. Department of Education, National Science Foundation, U.S. Department of Health and Human Services, National Institute of Child Health and Development, U.S. Department of Labor, and the Census Bureau should be appointed to define research aimed at examining and improving the quality of teacher licensure tests, teacher licensing, and, potentially, the capabilities of the new teacher work force. Representatives should include educators, child development specialists, labor economists, statisticians, demographers, anthropologists, and others.

These individuals should be charged with defining a multidisciplinary, multiple-methods research program. Representatives should specify the primary and secondary research questions, sampling designs, measurement tools, data collection methods, and data triangulation and analysis techniques to be used. They should specify a broad-based omnibus research program that begins collecting data on students and their families at a very early age; collects information on students' physical and intellectual development, family characteristics, and school achievement; and follows students over time. The research should track students in and out of classrooms and schools, collecting relevant data on teacher and school characteristics. It should collect information about teachers' backgrounds, education, and licensure; it should catalog school resources.

The research should examine licensure testing, beginning teacher performance, and student learning. Representatives should look at existing data sources, such as the National Center for Education Statistics Early Childhood Longitudinal Survey (www.nces.ed.gov/ecls) and the Bureau of Labor Statistics National Longitudinal Surveys of Youth-Child Data (www.states.bls.gov.nlsy79ch.htm), to evaluate their utility and build on any useful data collection systems.

CONCLUSION

Initial licensure tests are only one factor influencing the supply of new teachers. The quality and size of the pool of new teachers depend on many things, including recruiting efforts, other licensing requirements, labor market forces, licensing reciprocity, teacher salaries, and the conditions under which teachers work.

The committee's analysis of teacher quality and supply issues leads to the following conclusions:

- To the extent that the tests provide accurate measurements, setting higher passing scores would be expected to increase the proportion of teacher candidates in the hiring pool who are competent in the knowledge and skills measured by the tests, although higher passing scores will tend to lower the number of candidates who pass the tests. To the extent that test scores have measurement error, setting higher passing scores could eliminate competent candidates.
- Reducing the number of newly licensed teachers could require districts to make difficult choices, such as hiring uncredentialed teachers, increasing class sizes, or increasing salaries to attract licensed teachers from other districts and states.
- Setting substantially higher passing scores on licensure tests is likely to reduce the diversity of the teacher applicant pool, further adding to the difficulty of obtaining a diverse school faculty.
- Little research has been conducted on the extent to which scores on current teacher licensure tests relate to other measures of beginning teacher competence. Much of the research that has been conducted suffers from methodological problems that interfere with making strong conclusions about the results. This makes it hard to determine what effect licensure tests might have on improving the actual competence of beginning teachers.

7

Using Licensure Tests for Accountability

Earlier chapters examine the use of teacher licensure tests in identifying candidates with some of the knowledge and skills needed for minimally competent beginning practice. This chapter looks at policy makers' other ambitions for teacher licensure tests, such as using them to help teacher education institutions focus on the knowledge and skills considered critical for beginning teaching and to hold higher-education institutions and states accountable for the quality of teacher preparation and licensure programs. In the current policy context, licensure tests are being used to identify competent teacher candidates, communicate what beginning teachers need to know and be able to do, and evaluate the quality of teacher preparation and licensure programs. These are broad and ambitious goals.

FOCUSING TEACHER EDUCATION ON
IDENTIFIED COMPETENCIES

Teacher licensure tests have the potential to influence teacher preparation institutions in several ways. Some assert—and the committee agrees—that initial licensure tests can have positive effects on teacher education if the tests support states' teaching and learning standards and if performance on them relates to teachers' performance in the classroom (Melnick and Pullin, 2000). Initial licensure tests signal to teacher education programs the content and pedagogical knowledge considered prerequisite to minimally competent beginning teaching. They can draw attention to the advances in research and professional knowledge recognized by the test. The committee has tried to examine these issues.

As noted in Chapter 6, as yet there is little information on the relationship between results on initial licensure tests and other indicators of candidates' competence. However, there is some evidence on the relationship between the content of licensure tests and states' teaching standards. The test adoption process followed by states using Educational Testing Service (ETS) tests and the test construction procedures used by National Evaluation Systems (NES) suggest that licensure tests have some correspondence to states' standards. The test adoption process undertaken by states administering ETS tests calls for comparisons of states' needs and tested content. States administering ETS tests are asked to make a judgment that the tests they select correspond to their teaching and learning goals. In states that contract with NES for test development, tests are developed according to the states' specifications. Alignment between initial licensure tests and state teaching and learning standards is an important prerequisite to coherent developmental systems for teacher preparation, assessment, and support.

It is also possible that licensure tests can have negative effects on teacher education. Several logical arguments can be made. If licensure tests oversimplify teaching knowledge or emphasize types of knowledge or practice that are not universally associated with effective teaching or do so in a manner that discourages teachers from learning to be diagnostic in relation to different students' needs, they might have negative effects. However, as to negative effects, there is a paucity of data. Some data are available on possible testing effects in Massachusetts. Flippo and Riccards (2000) report changes by some Massachusetts colleges and universities in response to the recent disappointing performance of Massachusetts candidates on the state's new licensure exam (Haney et al., 1999) and to recent federal attention to initial teacher licensure testing. These institutions report aligning course content to test specifications, adding workshops on test preparation, and imposing testing requirements for admission to teacher education programs. These changes would not necessarily be cause for concern except that in Massachusetts there may be a perceived misalignment between the content of the licensing test and the knowledge and skills identified as important for teaching (Haney et al., 1999; Melnick and Pullin, 2000). As noted earlier, the first administration of Massachusetts' new test gave notable weight in scoring to candidates' responses to a test item asking for transcription of one of the Federalist papers from audiotape, a task not highly related to the central tasks of teaching. It is possible that poorly designed tests could serve to water down teacher education curricula in institutions where officials are more desirous of having graduates pass the test than of preparing well-qualified teachers (Flippo and Riccards, 2000).

The committee does not have enough evidence to judge whether, on balance, current tests and the regulations that surround them are likely to improve teacher preparation or divert teacher education from untested content in problematic ways. It will also be important to monitor the impact of new licensure tests and licensure requirements on teacher education curricula and to examine the conditions under which tests are used. Given currently available data on the impact of initial licensure tests on teacher education programs, it is unclear whether and under what conditions licensure tests can and do improve teacher education.

HOLDING STATES AND HIGHER EDUCATION INSTITUTIONS ACCOUNTABLE

In 1998 Congress amended Title II of the Higher Education Act (HEA) to promote teacher quality in two ways (P.L. 105-244). Teacher quality enhancement grants were authorized for states and for partnerships including at least an institution of higher education and a high-need school district. Additionally, public reporting and accountability requirements were established for states receiving funds authorized by the law and for institutions of higher education with teacher preparation programs enrolling students receiving aid under the HEA.

The law has several purposes (see Box 7-1). The overriding purpose is to improve student achievement. To this end, the federal government seeks improvement in the preparation of prospective teachers and the quality of professional development for current teachers. The law also holds institutions of higher education with teacher preparation programs accountable for preparing teachers who have the necessary teaching skills and content knowledge. Additionally, it encourages efforts to recruit qualified individuals into teaching, including those now in other occupations.

The teacher quality enhancement grants for states and partnerships may be used to address the purposes of Title II in several ways. States are permitted to use the funds for implementing reforms to hold institutions of higher education with

---

BOX 7-1
Title II Purposes

• Improve student achievement.
• Improve the quality of the current and future teaching force by improving the preparation of prospective teachers and enhancing professional development activities.
• Hold institutions of higher education accountable for preparing teachers who have the necessary teaching skills and are highly competent in the academic content areas in which the teachers plan to teach, such as mathematics, science, English, foreign languages, history, economics, art, civics, government, and geography, including training in the effective uses of technology in the classroom.
• Recruit highly qualified individuals, including individuals from other occupations, into the teaching force.

SOURCE: Higher Education Reauthorization Act, 1998.

teacher preparation programs accountable for preparing new teachers who will be competent to teach in their planned areas. Funds can be used to reform teacher certification or licensure requirements. Grants can be used to establish, expand, or improve alternatives to traditional routes to certification or licensure in teacher preparation programs. Additionally, funds can be used to develop and implement new ways to recruit highly qualified teachers, provide financial rewards to those who are highly effective, and remove those who are not competent.

Partnerships can use their grants for an array of activities. A partnership can address problems in integrating the efforts of schools of arts and sciences and schools of education in preparing new teachers who are highly knowledgeable in relevant content areas. A partnership can work to provide clinical experiences in preservice teacher programs. A partnership can also create and implement improved professional development programs and can work to improve the recruitment of highly qualified individuals into teaching.

The federal government is investing $75 million in these new initiatives in the first year and $98,000,000 in each of the second and third fiscal years.

Accountability and Evaluation Provisions

Title II created a new accountability system of reports on the quality of teacher preparation. This system requires institutions of higher education to report annually to states, states to report annually to the U.S. Department of Education, and the Secretary of Education to report annually to the Congress and the public on the quality of teacher preparation. Institutions are to report by April 7 of each year the passing rates of their teacher education graduates on state-required assessments; the average passing rates of all graduates in the state; and selected program characteristics, such as the numbers of enrolled students, faculty/student ratios, and whether a teacher preparation program has been identified as low performing by the state. All of this information is to be included in institutional publications such as promotional materials, school catalogs, and information sent to prospective employers. Institutions can be fined $25,000 for failing to report in a timely and accurate manner.

States are to aggregate institutional reports and report to the U.S. Department of Education by October 7 of each year. Each state report is to rank teacher preparation programs by quartiles on the passing rates of their graduates on licensure tests. Information on state requirements for teacher certification or licensure is to be presented, and states must identify any institutions identified as low performing or at risk of being so identified based on criteria they select. See Box 7-2.

Finally, the Secretary of Education is to prepare an annual report to Congress and the public on the quality of teacher preparation starting in April 2002. This report is to include information on state requirements for certification or licensure as well as information on efforts to improve the quality of teacher preparation and the teacher force.

BOX 7-2
State Reporting Provisions

The law specifies that state report cards should include:

- a description of the teacher certification and licensure assessments, and any other certification and licensure requirements, used by the state;
- the standards and criteria that prospective teachers must meet in order to attain initial teacher certification or licensure and to be certified or licensed to teach particular subjects or particular grades within the state;
- a description of the extent to which the assessments and requirements are aligned with the state's standards and assessments for students;
- the percentage of teaching candidates who passed each of the assessments used by the state for teacher certification and licensure, and the passing score on each assessment that determines whether a candidate has passed that assessment;
- the percentage of teaching candidates who passed each of the assessments used by the state for teacher certification and licensure, disaggregated and reported in quartiles, by the teacher preparation program in the state from which the teaching candidate received the candidate's most recent degree, which shall be made available widely and publicly;
- information on the extent to which teachers in the state are given waivers of state certification or licensure requirements, including the proportion of such teachers distributed across high- and low-poverty school districts and across subject areas;
- a description of the state's alternative routes to teacher certification, if any, and the percentage of teachers certified through alternative certification routes who pass state teacher certification or licensure requirements;
- a description of proposed criteria for assessing the performance of teacher preparation programs within institutions of higher education in the state, including indicators of teaching candidates' knowledge and skills; and
- information on the extent to which teachers or prospective teachers in the state are required to take examinations or other assessments of their subject matter knowledge in the area or areas in which the teacher provides instruction, the standards established for passing any such assessments, and the extent to which teachers or prospective teachers are required to receive a passing score on such assessments in order to teach in specific subject areas or grade levels.

SOURCE: Higher Education Reauthorization Act, 1998.

To receive funds under the HEA, states are to develop procedures to identify and assist, through the provision of technical assistance, low-performing programs of teacher preparation in institutions of higher education. As Box 7-2 shows, states are to include in their annual reports a list of any such institutions identified, and any institution so identified must report this designation in its

Title II and other public reports. States are responsible for selecting the criteria they use to identify low-performing institutions. Title II says that states may use the passing rates of graduates in determining low performance but are not required to do so. The law also says that, if an institution looses state approval or state funding for its teacher preparation program because of low performance, it will lose its eligibility for certain federal funds. Such institutions will be ineligible for funding by the U.S. Department of Education for professional development. Further, teacher preparation programs will not be permitted to accept or enroll any student receiving aid under Title IV of the HEA.

The stakes for noncompliance with the law or for poor performance are high. Institutions can be fined $25,000 for failing to report in a timely and accurate manner. Non-reporting states can loose funding authorized under the Higher Education Act. If states withdraw program approval or terminate funding, teacher education programs can lose grant funds and are ineligible to enroll teacher candidates who receive federal aid. At stake are federal fines and federal aid to teacher education programs and students. Declining student enrollments and decreasing support from the professional community and public also are possible consequences for low-performing schools.

The new law has met with notable resistance from states and the higher education community (Interstate New Teacher Assessment and Support Consortium, 1999; American Association of State Colleges and Universities, 1999, 2000a; American Association of Colleges for Teacher Education, 2000; Teacher Education Accreditation Council, 2000). Critics argue that teacher licensure tests provide only a limited view of program quality; that passing rates on licensure tests are not comparable across states and across institutions; and that the data are difficult to collect, verify, and report.

The U.S. Department of Education (2000b) has developed a reference guide to help states and institutions of higher education learn about and comply with the law. The *Reference and Reporting Guide for Preparing State and Institutional Reports on the Quality of Teacher Preparation* includes definitions, forms, and time tables. It suggests data-reporting procedures and includes questionnaires that states and institutions must use to report. It provides guidance on data interpretation. The Guide also includes a list of possible supplementary indicators of program quality for states and institutions.

Concerns About the Accountability and Evaluation Provisions

The National Center for Education Statistics of the U.S. Department of Education has worked closely with representatives from the states and higher education to develop standard definitions and uniform reporting methods for the data required by the law. Procedures to track candidates' testing histories, check institutional affiliation data, and verify data have been instituted and are described in the *Guide*. However, there remain a number of important data collection and reporting problems for states and institutions (Interstate New Teacher Assessment and Support Consortium, 1999; American Association of State Colleges and Universities, 1999, 2000a; American Association of Colleges for Teacher Education, 2000; Teacher Education Accreditation Council, 2000). Some of the problems are fairly fundamental and raise legitimate questions about the interpretability of the data that will be reported. These are described next. The *Reference and Reporting Guide* includes some similar cautionary statements about data interpretation.

For institutions and states, collecting and reporting required data are made difficult by:

- the need to report degree and licensure requirements, waiver categories, and types of licenses in standardized ways;
- the need to verify the institutional affiliations reported by test takers;
- the need to track over time the testing records of individuals who retest;
- the need to determine the pertinent institutional affiliations of students who have attended multiple institutions;
- the large numbers of tests for which states have data;
- insufficient numbers of examinees per test and population group to obtain reliable aggregated results;
- the need to aggregate data across categories of tests; and
- the absence of previous state and institutional data collections on these federally required data.

These difficulties may make it hard to interpret the reported data and hard to draw meaningful conclusions about candidates' mastery of tested content.

The law requires states to report passing rate data for all tests that are used in more than one state and that have sufficient numbers of test takers. Institutions are required to report passing rate data for all tests for which they have adequate numbers of candidates. It is likely that policy makers and others will use these data to make inferences about the relative quality and rigor of preparation and licensure systems; however, comparability across states and institutions is questionable.

Differences among state testing systems are likely to make comparisons of passing rates misleading; these differences include:

- considerable variability among states in the tests required for licensure;
- even when tests are the same, states set different passing scores;
- states administer tests at different points in teacher education (e.g., before admission, before graduation, after degree conferral); and
- states attach different stakes to passing (e.g., no passing requirements, passage required for student teaching, passage required for licensure).

This diversity across states makes passing rate comparisons among them misleading. For states using different examinations, comparing passing rates is highly problematic because differences in the content, format, and margins of error of the tests limit reasonable inferences about relative performance (National Research Council, 1999a). Comparing results for states using the same tests with different passing scores also is problematic because the numbers passing in each state are partly determined by the passing scores in effect. Furthermore, differences in the way tests are used by states make it virtually impossible to meaningfully compare passing rates from different licensure tests (National Research Council, 1999). Passing rates are partially determined by the decisions about teacher candidates that the scores support. States that require Praxis I for entry into teacher preparation will have 100 percent passing rates on Praxis I, while states that require it at licensure are likely to have lower rates. Passing rates are comparable only for states using the same tests with the same passing scores to support the same decisions.

For the tests reviewed in Chapter 5, only three allow comparisons across states. For these tests multiple states use them with the same passing scores to support the same candidate decisions. When states' current passing scores and uses are considered for the Mathematics: Proofs, Models, and Problems, Part 1 test, only two states can compare their own passing rates to those of one other state. The same is true for the Biology: Content Knowledge, Part 1 test. No comparisons are possible for the Principles of Learning and Teaching test, the Middle School English/Language Arts test, or the Biology: Content Knowledge, Part 2 test. On the Pre-professional Skills Test (PPST) in Reading, four states can each compare their own passing rates to those of one other state; a total of 12 states can compare their own passing rates to those of two other states; and five states can compare their own passing rates to those of four others. However, the PPST tests provide little information about the quality of teacher preparation. They examine basic skills considered prerequisite to, not the result of, teacher education. Because these tests were selected by the committee for this report from among ETS's more commonly administered tests, fewer comparisons will be possible, in general, on the other Praxis tests. Comparisons of passing rates for NES states or others using state-specific tests are not meaningful.

In addition to passing rates for individual tests, the *Reference and Reporting Guide* says passing rates are to be aggregated and reported across tests within various test categories, i.e. basic skills tests, subject matter tests, pedagogy tests, special populations tests (special education, English as a second language), other content tests, and performance tests. Passing rates are also to be aggregated and reported across all required tests. The committee is highly doubtful that these aggregated and summary scores can support meaningful conclusions about program quality. Combining data from different tests, with different passing scores, given at different times, to support different candidate decisions will create summary scores with unknown meaning.

Institutional comparisons within states pose similar problems. Though passing rates provide a useful point of entry for investigating possible sources of strong and weak performance, they can be taken at face value only in some cases. Passing rates may not be comparable across teacher preparation programs within a state because of institutional factors such as:

- different missions and recruiting practices,
- differences in the entry-level characteristics of students,
- different entry and exit testing requirements in teacher education,
- variability in the procedures used to determine appropriate affiliations for students who attend multiple institutions or who do not identify institutional affiliations,
- differences in the numbers of students who retest, and
- differential score instability associated with small test-taking pools.

Because some teacher candidates take subject matter coursework at different institutions, passing rates on the subject matter tests may not indicate very much about the quality of a teacher preparation program. Even within institutions, faculty in the arts and sciences departments who teach subject matter courses to teacher candidates may be differentially willing to attend to the content of licensing tests.

Differences in the entry-level characteristics of teacher candidates at different institutions also pose an important problem for comparability. Higher passing rates at one institution may simply indicate that admitted students had better prior educational opportunities than those admitted to another institution. For example, a teacher education institution that draws students from underrepresented groups, some of whom score relatively poorly on college entrance tests of basic skills, will likely need to provide instruction in basic skills. Even with this instruction, it might be more difficult for such teacher candidates to pass the basic skills and other teacher licensure tests. According to Title II criteria, however, such an institution could appear to be a poor or even a failing institution even though students may have had more learning opportunities and accomplished more while in the program than, say, students in a program with higher admissions requirements. Passing rates may say very little about the quality of education at an institution in the absence of information about candidates' mastery levels when entering the program.

Differences in the percentage of students who retest at different institutions pose additional problems for comparability. As discussed in Chapter 5, the test-taking population of every school includes initial testers who pass, initial testers who fail and never retry the licensing test, test takers who initially fail and eventually pass the licensing test, and test takers who repeat but never pass the licensing test. Institutions are asked to report passing rates just after program completion and, starting in 2004, three years after completion. The proportion of candidates in each of the first-time and repeating groups in a reporting year is likely to be related to the institution's overall passing rate. Differences in their proportions across institutions will make passing rate data difficult to compare.

The data collection and interpretation problems posed by Title II are not insubstantial. On their own, initial licensure tests fall short as indicators of program quality. In complying with Title II, test score information should be supplemented with other information about the characteristics and quality of programs. The U.S. Department of Education (2000b) suggests that data on other measures be reported, including demographic data on teacher education students and program completers, job placement rates in fields of eligibility, numbers of completers with National Board for Professional Teaching Standards certification, and information on the goals of teacher education programs. Other supplementary indicators might include data on the entry-level academic characteristics of teacher education students and program completers, job retention rates for graduates, numbers of placements in high-need schools and fields, and employer evaluations.

CONCLUSION

The Teacher Quality Enhancement Grants for States and Partnerships was enacted to achieve four goals: to improve student achievement; to improve the quality of the current and future teaching forces by improving the preparation of prospective teachers and enhancing professional development activities; to hold institutions of higher education accountable for preparing teachers who have the necessary skills and are highly competent in the academic content areas in which they plan to teach; and to recruit highly qualified individuals, including individuals from other occupations, into the teaching force.

Given its analysis of the objectives and requirements of the law, the committee concludes that:

- It is reasonable to hold teacher education institutions accountable for the quality of teacher preparation programs.
- By their design and as currently used, initial teacher licensure tests fall short of the intended policy goals for their use as accountability tools and as levers for improving teacher preparation and licensing programs. The public reporting and accountability provisions of Title II may encourage erroneous conclusions about the quality of teacher preparation.
- Although the percentage of graduates who pass initial licensure tests provides an entry point for evaluating an institution's quality, simple comparisons among institutions based on their passing rates are difficult to interpret for many reasons. These include the fact that institutions have different educational missions and recruiting practices, their students have different entry-level qualifications, teacher education programs have dif-

ferent entry and exit testing requirements, and programs have different procedures for determining the institutional affiliations of their candidates. By themselves, passing rates on licensure tests do not provide adequate information on which to judge the quality of teacher education programs.

- Simple comparisons of passing rates across states are misleading. Many states use different tests for initial licensure or set different passing scores on the same tests. States have different policies about when a test is given or what decisions it supports.

- To fairly and accurately judge the quality of teacher education programs, federal and state officials need data on a wide variety of program characteristics from multiple sources. Other indicators of program quality might include assessment data for students in relation to course and program benchmarks, employer evaluations, and district or state evaluations of beginning teaching. Other indicators might include information on course requirements and course quality, measures of the amount and quality of field experiences, and evidence of opportunities to work with students with special learning needs and students with diverse backgrounds. Data on the qualifications of program faculty, the allocation of resources, and the adequacy of facilities might be considered. The qualifications of students at entry to teacher education programs also should be included.

8

Improving Teacher Licensure Testing

As described in Chapter 1, many states have adopted or are developing challenging new teacher standards. These standards define teacher performance in terms of the competencies teachers should demonstrate; they focus on the teacher's ability to engage students in rigorous, meaningful activities that foster academic learning. As part of their reforms in teacher education and licensure, states are attempting to align newly developed teaching standards with their licensure requirements. Traditionally, teacher licensure has required candidates to complete an approved teacher preparation program and to pass the state's required tests. As noted in Chapter 3, however, the tests currently in wide use for beginning teacher licensure measure only a subset of the knowledge and skills important for practice.

Many in the profession have recently called for systematic collection of evidence about the actual teaching performance of prospective and new teachers (Darling-Hammond et al., 1999; Klein and Stecher, 1991; Tell, 2001). They have asked for evaluations that examine what teachers actually do in the classroom and in planning for instruction. They have called for assessments that require prospective and new teachers to perform in situations that are both more lifelike and more complex than those posed by paper-and-pencil tests. They argue that performance assessments are used in other fields to license practitioners. In licensing lawyers, for example, the Multistate Performance Examination includes performance assessments that pose tasks beginning lawyers would be expected to accomplish, including writing persuasive memos, briefs, witness examination plans, and closing arguments <www.ncbex.org>. In medicine, computer-based simulations are used for the third stage of licensure testing <www.usmle.org>, and an assessment that uses standardized patients[1] is being piloted for use during the second stage of licensure testing (Swanson et al., 1995).

States are now beginning to explore performance-based assessment of prospective and beginning teachers' competence. For example, as noted in Chapter 3, 10 states are participating in the Interstate New Teacher Assessment and Support Consortium's (INTASC) Performance Assessment Development Project to develop prototypical classroom performance assessments that can be used to evaluate new teachers' performance against INTASC's professional standards <www.ccsso.org>. In California, prospective teachers can take the Reading Instruction Competence Assessment as a video-based performance assessment <www.ctc.ca.gov/profserv/examinfo/ricaexam.html>. In Connecticut, beginning teachers prepare discipline-specific teaching portfolios for second-stage licensure. In this chapter the committee describes assessments that are used and assessment research that is under way nationally and in several states.

It is important to clarify certain terms used in this chapter. Readers are reminded of the distinction made earlier between testing and assessment. The committee defines tests as paper-and-pencil measures of knowledge and skill; performance on them is evaluated and scored using a standardized process. Assessment is considered to be a broader term and a broader enterprise than testing. While assessment encompasses standardized paper-and-pencil measures, it also refers to other kinds of performance-based evidence. Moreover, it may describe a collection of different kinds of evidence, systematically gathered over time, to inform particular decisions or interpretations.

Selecting Assessment Cases

The committee's initial search for performance-based assessment identified only one state that used performance assessments operationally to make initial licensure decisions. The committee then expanded its search to include performance assessments used by teacher education programs to warrant teacher education students' competence and performance assessments used in second-stage licensure and certification. The committee selected four cases to illustrate different relevant assessments of teacher performance. They and the systems in which they have been developed and implemented are described here.

The committee chose to study the assessments of the National Board for Professional Teaching Standards (NBPTS) because its subject-specific portfolio and assessment center exercises are among the most established and prominent

---

[1]Standardized patients are nonphysicians taught to portray patients in a standardized, consistent fashion. Examinees interact with standardized patients as though interviewing and examining real patients. Standardized patients are trained to complete checklists and rating forms to summarize their observations of the examinee's skill in the targeted areas.

of performance-based teacher assessments. These assessments are used to certify the accomplishment of experienced teachers. They provide an existence proof that performance-based assessment can be implemented on a large scale for assessing teacher competence. The NBPTS assessments have instigated and provide a basis for the work of INTASC and several states.

The committee also examined Connecticut's subject-specific portfolio assessments. Connecticut's assessments are of interest because they emulate the NBPTS assessments and were developed in collaboration with INTASC. These assessments are taken by beginning teachers during their second and/or third years of teaching as part of second-stage licensure. Additionally, the committee studied Ohio's work with the Educational Testing Service (ETS) on the PATHWISE Classroom Induction Program-Praxis III and the Praxis III performance-based assessment. These systems are of interest because they use direct observations of classroom practice and are intended for use by more than one state. Like the Praxis I and II tests, these ETS products theoretically are viable options for many states. These programs are geared toward new teachers, with Praxis III intended for use in second-stage licensure.

Finally, the committee studied Alverno College's integrated ongoing learning and assessment program for teacher candidates. Alverno's program is of interest because it provides an example of a system in which a party other than a state or district could warrant teacher competence. In fact, licensing tests are used in Alverno College's home state (Wisconsin), but the committee wanted to push its thinking about models in which teacher education institutions warrant candidates' capabilities.

The committee's intention in studying these cases was to pose multiple viable models for consideration in judging teacher competence.[2] The committee wanted to address how these different assessment systems work to support evidence-based decisions about teacher competence and, ultimately, a well-qualified and diverse work force. Given the limited scope of what is assessed by conventional licensure tests, the committee also wanted to encourage further research into the development and evaluation of performance-based assessment systems in teaching.

Not all of these assessment systems are in full operation. For instance, performance-based assessment systems for teachers in Connecticut and Ohio—states that lead the nation in the use of such systems—are still under development, and much of the planned validity evidence is not yet available. Even the NBPTS, which has many assessments fully operationalized, is still developing standards

---

[2]In choosing among alternatives to conventional licensing procedures and in keeping within its charge, the committee remained within the framework of licensing systems. The committee therefore did not conduct an analysis of wholly market-based solutions in which licensure is not a prerequisite for employment and decision making is decentralized to the school or district level.

and assessments in other subject areas and is considering modifications to streamline existing assessments (D. Gitomer, ETS, personal communication, 2000). Thus, although the committee believes these practices may hold promise, currently available evidence does not allow evaluation of them in the same way conventional tests are evaluated in Chapter 5.

To guide its data-gathering efforts and to facilitate cross-case comparisons, the committee developed a list of program features to be described (see Box 8-1). Information about each of these features is included if available and relevant. Each case description is based on documents available from the agency or institution that is the focus of the case and on interviews with key personnel. Wherever possible, supporting documentation, such as in-house research reports or implementation guides, was obtained.[3]

NEW AND DEVELOPING SYSTEMS

This section presents a synopsis of each case, focusing in particular on relevant performance-based assessments and professional development activities, if any. Complete case descriptions, including references to the full range of data collection and professional development activities undertaken by the state or institution, along with relevant citations, are provided in Appendix F.

NBPTS Certification

The NBPTS provides an example of a large-scale, high-stakes, performance-based assessment of teaching that draws on portfolio and assessment center exercises. The board has developed a series of performance-based assessments for voluntary certification of accomplished teachers. Certification is available in 30 fields according to the subject taught and the developmental level of the students.

The philosophy behind NBPTS's conception of accomplished teaching is reflected in its five core "propositions":

- teachers are committed to students and their learning;
- teachers know the subjects they teach and how to teach those subjects to students;

---

[3]Each case is presented from the perspective of the particular institution or agency primarily responsible for the performance assessment. While in some cases there is regular monitoring of the other parts of the system (e.g., the state accredits teacher education institutions), in other cases the focal agency or organization may only lay out expectations and/or make assumptions about other components of the system with which it is not directly involved (e.g., the National Board suggests and publicizes local support initiatives but does not take responsibility for implementing or monitoring them). Given limited resources, the committee did not obtain independent information about the other components of the system.

BOX 8-1
Features of Case Studies

Statement of Teaching Qualities
- What are the teaching qualities that orient the system?

Support for Prospective and Beginning Teachers
- What is the nature of development and support available for teachers before, during, and after the assessment?
- What is the nature and extent of preparation that is available for the mentors and assessors of teachers?

Performance-Based Assessments
- What are the strategies for collecting information on the qualities to be assessed?
- What is the timing, sequencing, and context for the assessments or other data collection activities?
- Who conducts the evaluation? How are evaluators trained?
- What methods are used to determine the level of performance or qualities considered sufficient for licensure?

Coherence of the System
- How are multiple pieces of evidence about a beginning teacher, including assessment and nonassessment information, combined and used in making the overall licensure decision?
- What role is played by the various institutions within the system—the state, teacher preparation institutions, local schools and districts, and external organizations within the system?
- To what extent do the various conceptions of quality, development and support opportunities, assessments, and program evaluation activities form a coherent whole?

Validity Research Program
- What is done to evaluate the validity of the assessments or other information about the candidate?
- To what extent are standard-setting methods evaluated?
- What is the nature of external reviews or audits of assessment and support activities? To what extent are external perspectives solicited?
- What is known about the impact of the assessment and support system on diversity in the teaching force?
- What kinds of program evaluations are conducted?
- What efforts are undertaken to examine the quality of the teaching force that results from the system?
- In what ways are the assessment, program evaluation, and outcome information used to improve the system?
- What is the nature and availability of documentation for public and professional review?

- teachers are responsible for managing and monitoring student learning;
- teachers think systematically about their practice and learn from experience; and
- teachers are members of learning communities.

For each certification area, content standards are based on these propositions. The content standards are developed by committees comprised of experienced teachers in particular certification areas and others with expertise in relevant areas, such as child development, teacher education, and particular academic disciplines. The content standards guide all aspects of assessment development.

Each assessment consists of a portfolio completed by candidates at their school sites and a set of exercises to be completed at an assessment center. The school-based portfolio consists of two parts: (1) three entries that are classroom based and include two videos that document the candidate's teaching practice through student work and (2) one entry that combines the candidate's work with students' families, the community, and collaboration with other professionals. The six assessment center exercises require candidates to demonstrate their knowledge of subject matter content.

Each assessment task is scored in accordance with a rubric prepared during the development phase and later illustrated with multiple benchmarks (sample responses) at each performance level. The rubrics encompass four levels of performance on a particular task with the second-highest level designated as meeting the standard. Most exercises are scored independently by two trained assessors. Exercise scores are weighted and summed to form a total. To make certification decisions, the total score is compared to a predetermined passing score that is uniform across certificates. The uniform performance standard was set by NBPTS following a series of empirical studies using different methods of standard setting.

States and local education agencies have their own policies regarding how NBPTS-certified teachers are recognized and rewarded. Although NBPTS's direct involvement in professional development and support activities is limited, it does encourage and support locally initiated activities.

NBPTS maintains an ongoing program of psychometric research into the technical quality of its assessments. Evidence routinely gathered for each assessment includes documentation of the development process, estimates of reliability and measurement error, expert judgments about the fit between the assessments and the content standards, examination of disparate impact, and evidence of the validity of the scoring process. Additional special studies address such issues as examining potential sources of disparate impact to rule out concerns about bias (Bond, 1998b), considering whether alternative means of assessment (e.g., direct observations and interviews, samples of student work) can reproduce classifications of candidates as certified or not, and comparing the professional activities of teachers who have and those who have not received NBPTS certification

(Bond et al., 2000). Additional information on these studies can be found at the NBPTS's website <www.nbpts.org> and in professional journals.

Connecticut's Beginning Teacher Induction Program

Connecticut, working in collaboration with INTASC, exemplifies a state that has implemented a licensing system that relies on performance-based assessments. Connecticut's Beginning Educator Support and Training Program is a comprehensive three-year induction program that involves both mentoring and support for beginning teachers and a portfolio assessment. The philosophy behind Connecticut's program is that effective teaching involves mastery of both content and pedagogy. This philosophy is reflected in Connecticut's Common Core of Teaching, which in intended to present a comprehensive view of the accomplished teacher. The Common Core of Teaching specifies what teachers should know, how they should apply their knowledge, and how they should demonstrate professional responsibility (see Appendix F). The Common Core of Teaching guides state policies related to preservice training, induction, evaluation, and the professional growth of all teachers. The state also has subject-specific standards.

The preservice training requirements for prospective teachers are specified in terms of a set of competencies as distinct from a list of required courses. The competencies encompass the body of knowledge and skills the state believes individuals should develop as they progress through the teacher education program. Prospective teachers must pass Praxis I to enter a teacher preparation program and Praxis II to be recommended for licensure.

During their first three years of teaching, beginning teachers receive support from school- or district-based mentors and through state-sponsored professional development activities. During their second year, teachers must compile and submit a discipline-specific teaching portfolio. In the portfolio, teachers document their methods of lesson planning, teaching, assessment of student learning, and self-reflection in a 7- to 10-day unit of instruction. The portfolio includes information from multiple sources, such as lesson logs, videotapes of teaching, teacher commentaries, examples of student work, and formal and informal assessments. The state offers seminars that instruct teachers in ways to meet professional standards through the portfolio process.

Scorers are trained to evaluate the portfolios using criteria based on content-focused teaching standards. Portfolio scorers receive up to 70 hours of training and must meet a proficiency standard before being eligible to score. If the portfolio does not meet the acceptable standards, the teacher is provided with another opportunity to submit a portfolio during the third year of teaching. If a teacher fails to meet the standard by then, he or she is ineligible to apply for a Connecticut provisional certificate and cannot teach in Connecticut public schools. To regain certification, such an individual must successfully complete a formal program of study approved by the state.

Connecticut has an extensive ongoing program of research that includes job analyses, the collection of content- and construct-related evidence of validity, reliability and generalizability research, an examination of program consequences, and sensitivity reviews and bias analyses for each content area. Studies have included (1) examinations of the relationships between teachers' performance on the portfolio assessment and other quantitative information about teachers, such as their undergraduate grade point averages, SAT scores, and Praxis I and II scores; (2) on-site case studies of beginning teacher performance; (3) expert review of portfolios; and (4) the relationship between portfolio performance and student achievement in reading, language arts, and mathematics. Surveys of mentors, portfolio assessors, school administrators, principals, beginning teachers, and higher-education faculty are conducted annually to examine program effectiveness and impact. Additional details about the studies conducted by Connecticut appear in Appendix F.

Ohio's Teacher Induction Program

Ohio exemplifies a state that plans to incorporate a commercially available program into its licensing system, which is being redesigned. By 2002 the state will require beginning teachers to successfully complete an entry-year program of support, including mentoring, provided by the employing district, and to pass a performance-based assessment administered by the Ohio Department of Education in order to obtain a professional teaching license. Ohio's entry-year induction program is based on the ETS-developed PATHWISE Induction Program-Praxis III Version for mentor training and mentor assistance. Ohio is calling this program the Ohio FIRST Year Program (Formative Induction Results in Stronger Teaching). The state plans to use ETS's Praxis III Classroom Performance Assessment beginning in 2002. Both Praxis III and the PATHWISE Induction Program draw on the same four teaching domains: organizing content knowledge for student learning, teaching for student learning, creating an environment for student learning, and teacher professionalism. Nineteen criteria have been developed for these domains and serve as the basis for evaluating teachers' performance (see Appendix F). Many of Ohio's state institutions have incorporated these domains into their preservice education programs, and the PATHWISE Observation System will be integrated into the preservice program.

The PATHWISE Induction Program-Praxis III Version consists of 10 structured tasks designed to encourage collaboration between beginning teachers and their mentors. One task, for example, requires beginning teachers to gather information from colleagues, journals, and texts about particular aspects of teaching and, with a mentor's guidance, to use the information to develop an instructional plan, implement it, and reflect on the experience. Another asks for individual growth plans that specify beginning teachers' plans for learning more about particular teaching practices, school or district initiatives, or other teaching challenges.

Mentors are expected to be experienced teachers who, ideally, teach the same subject or grade level in the same building as the entry-year teacher. Mentors receive training in the PATHWISE Induction Program-Praxis III Version, and their service as mentor teachers can be part of their individual professional development plans that count toward licensure renewal.

The Praxis III assessment, which is designed to be used across content areas, employs three data collection methods: direct observation of classroom practice, written materials prepared by the beginning teacher describing the students and the instructional objectives, and interviews structured around classroom observations. As part of the assessment, the beginning teacher provides written documentation about the general classroom context and the students in the class. During the observation, assessors view the teacher's practices and decisions in the classroom. Semistructured interviews with the beginning teacher before and after the observation provide assessors with an opportunity to hear the teacher reflect on his or her decisions and teaching practices and to evaluate the teacher's skill in relating instructional decisions to contextual factors. Observers are trained in observation, interpretation, and scoring of the performance assessment data.

Praxis III has been piloted for seven years in Ohio but has not yet been used for making high-stakes licensure decision. In January 2000 the State Board of Education set passing scores on Praxis III. Since Praxis III has not yet been used operationally, the available research consists of content-related evidence of validity collected as part of the test development process. The content and knowledge base covered by the PATHWISE Induction Program-Praxis III was identified by ETS through an extensive series of studies that included job analyses, a review of the literature, and a compilation of teacher licensing requirements in all 50 states. Reports on the development work for Praxis III and PATHWISE are available through ETS (Dwyer, 1994; Wesley et al., 1993; Rosenfeld et al., 1992a; 1992b, 1992c).

School districts in Ohio are expected to develop and implement their own plans for entry-year programs in accordance with state guidelines and with financial support provided from the state. Several districts in Ohio have had comprehensive induction programs in place for a number of years. For example, the Cincinnati School District has had a peer review and induction program in place since 1985, although it is undergoing change to adapt to the new state requirements. Cincinnati's program is mentioned here because it provides an example of a district developing its own induction and evaluation system and because it shares some common features with the system Ohio plans to implement statewide.

Cincinnati's system has components aimed at teacher preparation, teacher induction, and teacher evaluation and compensation. The district collaborates with the University of Cincinnati in offering a fifth-year graduate internship program that places teacher candidates in one of seven professional practice schools in Cincinnati. The interns are mentored and evaluated by career and lead teachers. The district's teacher induction program provides support and ongoing feedback to beginning teachers. The program uses experienced teachers as both mentors and evaluators of new teachers. The example of Cincinnati suggests that in addition to the role played by national, state, and local institutions, districts can play an active role in teacher assessment and licensing.

Performance-Based Teacher Education at Alverno College

In this case study the committee provides a description of teacher education and assessment as practiced at Alverno College, which undertook development of a performance-based baccalaureate degree over 20 years ago (Diez, et al., 1998). This change resulted in an overhaul of the college's curriculum and approach to teaching. The new approach is characterized by publicly articulated learning outcomes, realistic classroom activities and field experiences, and ongoing performance assessments of learning progress. Alverno's program is of interest because it provides an example of a system in which a party other than a state or district could warrant teacher competence. Thus, the focus here is on Alveno as a working program that can expand the debate about other models for warranting teacher competence.

All students enrolled at Alverno College are expected to demonstrate proficiency in the following eight ability areas: communication, analysis, problem solving, values within decision making, social interaction, global perspectives, effective citizenship, and aesthetic responsiveness (see descriptions in Appendix F). These abilities cut across discipline areas and are subdivided into six developmental levels. The six levels for each ability area represent a developmental sequence that begins with awareness of one's own performance process for a given ability and that specifies increasingly complex knowledge, skills, and dispositions.

The teacher education program at Alverno College builds on the foundation provided by the eight general education abilities. The program's performance-based standards require teacher candidates to demonstrate competency in five areas:

• *Conceptualization:* Integrating content knowledge with educational frameworks and a broadly based understanding of the liberal arts in order to plan and implement instruction.

• *Diagnosis:* Relating observed behavior to relevant frameworks in order to determine and implement learning prescriptions.

• *Coordination:* Managing resources effectively to support learning goals.

• *Communication:* Using verbal, nonverbal, and media modes of communication to establish the classroom environment and to structure and reinforce learning.

• *Integrative interaction:* Acting with professional values as a situational decision maker, adapting to the changing needs of the environment in order to develop students as learners.

These teaching abilities refine and extend the general education abilities into the professional teaching context; they define professional levels of proficiency that are required for graduation from any of the teacher education programs. While the professional teaching abilities are introduced in the first year, they receive heavy emphasis during the junior and senior years.

The program places emphasis on using knowledge effectively in a context and describes its approach as "assessment as learning." Each course is structured around the assessments and learning outcomes that must be demonstrated to claim mastery of the course material. Assessment criteria are made public, and the paths connecting particular concrete activities to general abstract abilities can easily be traced. Evaluations of students are ongoing and handled by means of course-based assessments that require Alverno students to demonstrate what they have learned through activities such as essays, letters, position papers, case study analyses, observations, and simulations. Faculty members evaluate Alverno students' performances and provide diagnostic feedback; students are also expected to evaluate themselves and reflect on their performance on any given exercise.

Coursework is intentionally sequenced to reflect developmental growth and to provide for cross-course application of concepts. For example, a mathematics methods course assessment might ask teacher candidates to (1) create a mathematics lesson for first graders that incorporates concepts from developmental psychology, (2) teach the lesson, and (3) describe the responses of the learners and the adaptations made.

Alverno's education program is characterized by extensive opportunities for field experiences. For its education majors, classroom-based field experiences progress from working one on one with students to working with small groups and entire classes. Alverno teacher candidates design lesson plans, teach the lessons, and reflect on the effectiveness of their instruction. Teacher candidates keep logs that require them to reflect on their practices and to make links between theoretical knowledge and practical application, observe processes and environments of learning, translate their content knowledge into short presentations, and begin to translate their philosophy of education into decisions about the instructional process.

Before student teaching, teacher candidates compile a portfolio consisting of samples of written work, lesson plans, videotapes of their interactions with children, and instructional materials. They develop a resume and write an analysis of a videotaped lesson. Portfolios are reviewed by teams of teachers and principals who pose questions on teaching practices to candidates. Readiness for student teaching is judged on the basis of the portfolio as well as performance during the questioning session.

Students at Alverno College are required to meet the licensing requirements of the state of Wisconsin, which currently include a basic skills test and endorsement from the institution conferring the teaching degrees. Beginning in 2004, Wisconsin will require all teacher candidates to compile portfolios that demonstrate their performance in relation to the state's teaching standards. Candidates who pass the portfolio review will be granted provisional licenses to teach for three to five years while pursuing professional development goals related to the standards.

Alverno routinely conducts internal and external reviews of its assessment instruments and practices in light of its curriculum goals and students' performance. In addition, research has examined the extent to which Alverno graduates consider themselves prepared for teaching; research has also looked at their job satisfaction and retention in the field and employers' perceptions of their qualifications (Zeichner, 2000). Research on Alverno's program is documented and widely distributed and is published in professional journals.

ANALYSIS OF ALTERNATIVES

To conclude this chapter, the committee focuses on what can be learned from a comparison of the design principles underlying the assessments reviewed here. In each of the cases involving prospective or beginning teachers, there is consistent attention to the following features that the committee considers important components of a sound licensure systems:

• There is a coherent statement about the qualities of teaching valued by the institution or agency.

• There is a means for providing evidence of a teacher's actual performance with his or her students in a classroom (either through videotapes and artifacts or direct observations).

• There is a coherent system of assessments that, taken together, cover a broad range of teaching qualities, including evidence about basic skills, content and/or pedagogical knowledge, and teaching performance. The assessments are staged at relevant points in time across a prospective teacher's preparation and beginning teaching experiences.

• There is sustained attention to the professional development and support of prospective or beginning teachers integrated with the qualities and practices covered by the assessments. Support systems draw on the capabilities of experienced teachers, thereby supporting professional development for experienced teachers as well as beginning teachers.

- For the programs that have begun or are beginning operational use, there is an ongoing program of research into the validity of these assessments and opportunity for outside professionals to review the practices.

Looking across these case studies of assessment practice, the committee also found instructive differences. While all of the selected systems involve performance-based assessments of teaching, the programs use different measurement methodologies (e.g., school-based portfolios, observation systems, assessment centers) and emphasize different aspects of teaching performance. The agency or institution responsible for implementing performance-based assessments also differs for the various cases, including two states, a professional organization, and a teacher preparation program. The particular decisions supported by the assessments differ, as do the means for combining results with other information to make decisions about teacher competence. Furthermore, the systems in which the performance assessments operate are more or less tightly coupled; in one case the performance-based assessment is a fully integral ongoing part of the learning sequence, whereas in another case the connections between assessment and support are less direct.

Looking more specifically at the performance assessment methodologies, additional differences can be noted. These include differences in the way in which the statements of teacher competence guiding the assessments are developed and characterized (e.g., professional consensus, job analysis survey); in the scope of teaching to which the assessments apply (e.g., content-specific assessments, assessments intended for teaching across content areas); and in the way responses are scored and evidence is combined to inform overall decisions. There are also differences in the way standards are set (e.g., based on actual performances or profiles of scores, embedded in scoring rubrics) and in the nature of support provided to candidates, mentors, and assessors. The balance of contextualized versus standardized forms of evidence about teaching competence also varies across these programs.

The two cases that have been in operation the longest call for special note. The NBPTS focuses on voluntary assessment of experienced teachers. For our purposes, it serves as an existence proof that centrally administered, large-scale, high-stakes assessments of teaching performance can meet professional standards of technical quality for standardized assessments. As such it provides an important model for states, districts, teacher preparation programs, or other organizations developing performance-based assessments. As noted, Connecticut already has drawn on the work of the NBPTS in developing its portfolio assessment (with some unique design features of its own).

The NBPTS's assessment also serves at least two additional purposes relevant to the committee's charge. First, it can be used to support reciprocity across states in granting licenses based on evidence of performance, albeit at the advanced practice level. It suggests possibilities for reciprocity in initial licensing.

Second, and perhaps most important, it offers opportunities for assessment and recognition of accomplished teachers, thus providing incentives for professional development and advancement across the span of a career.

The teacher education and student assessment program at Alverno College provides an existence proof of a different sort; it demonstrates that evidence-based decisions about readiness to teach can be based on assessment practices contextualized at the local level as part of a program integrating learning and assessment in a developmental sequence. Whether this sort of contextualized assessment system culminating in high-stakes decisions can be successfully implemented in a broader range of teacher education institutions is a question that deserves further study.

Research is needed to understand the impact of these different assessment choices on decisions about teaching quality. While the committee believes all design choices should be situated in an assessment with a strong program of validity research, it is not believed that these differences necessarily can or should be resolved into a single set of recommendations. The diversity is productive: it provides an important source of alternatives for triangulation and critical review and revision. As Messick (1989:88) reminds us: "The very recognition of alternative perspectives about the social values to be served, about the criteria to be enhanced, or about the standards to be achieved should be salutary in its own right. This is so because to the extent that alternative perspectives are perceived as legitimate, it is less likely that any one of these perspectives will dominate our assumptions, our methodologies, or our thinking about the validation of test use."

Some issues of concern to the committee have not been sufficiently addressed by these assessment programs. These concerns, the committee notes, are equally relevant to its review of conventional testing programs. First, very little is known about how any of these different assessments of teacher quality relate to one another or to other indicators. To be fair, the professional testing standards do not explicitly require such evidence before an assessment is put into operational use. To their credit, the NBPTS and the state of Connecticut have undertaken such studies on a small scale with specific assessments. Alverno's practices also provide routine opportunity for informal triangulation through the multitude of appraisals of any given student. Cross-fertilization among these programs and between these programs and more conventional assessment practices would be fruitful. Examining the relationships among different assessments of teacher competence would contribute relevant validity evidence by documenting commonalities and differences that can and should be explained as part of a program's overall plan for validity research.

Second, with the possible exception of Alverno, very little is known about the quality of the overall decision about competence or accomplishment. Licensure decisions rest on the combination of information across disparate sources of evidence. In most of the examples the different assessments within a given system are sequential and conjunctive; they present distinct hurdles that a teacher must pass in order to continue. Each decision has the potential to reduce the pool of prospective teachers. This represents an implicit and underexamined theory about professional development that needs further investigation.

Third, one advantage originally associated with performance-based assessment was its potential as an "antidote for differential performance between majority and minority candidates" (Bond, 1998a:28). However, the experiences of the NBPTS suggest otherwise. Differences between African Americans and whites on the NBPTS assessments mirror those seen for multiple-choice exams. Studies have examined these differences in relation to gender, years of teaching, location of teaching assignment, putative quality of the baccalaureate degree-granting institution, support during preparation for the assessment, assessment exercise type, writing load of the assessment task, assessor training, and assessor ethnicity. None of these factors have been found to fully explain the performance differences observed between African American and white teachers on these assessments (Bond, 1998a, Bond 2000; A. Harman, NBPTS, personal communication, 2001). Bond concludes that the differences "may well be traceable to more systematic factors in U.S. society at large" (1998a:254).

Fourth, none of these assessment programs examine the teaching performances of the same individuals across different contexts of teaching. The different schools and communities in which a teacher is licensed to teach offer unique challenges and opportunities, yet a teacher's performance is typically evaluated only in a single context. The committee contends that licensure systems should incorporate information about a teacher's ability to work effectively with students in a variety of settings. For instance, student teaching requirements and the assessment data they yield could be structured to assure multiple contexts that include diverse learners. Also, support and professional development may be needed when teachers (whether beginning or experienced) move into new schools and communities.

In closing, the committee believes that articulating the validity issues that these cases suggest is an important challenge for the field. In Chapter 4 the committee presents an evaluation framework for standardized forms of testing. Some of its criteria apply directly to the assessments described here. The criteria for the purposes of assessment, the competencies to be assessed, and others are meaningful and important to judgments about performance-based assessments of teacher competence. However, for other evaluation criteria, their meaning and utility are less immediately clear for these assessment forms. The developmental nature of the systems in which these assessments reside, the varied ways in which candidates demonstrate their knowledge and skills within assessment forms, the balance between the information value of these assessments and the professional development benefits that accrue to examinees and other participants, and other differences raise issues about the validity evidence needed to support them.

The committee asserts that the evaluation criteria and evidence for these assessments should be rigorous, just as rigorous as those for conventional teacher licensure tests. The committee suspects, however, that the forms of evidence that will be telling and the criteria that should guide judgments about the soundness and technical quality of the assessments described here may differ somewhat from those outlined in Chapter 4. The committee challenges test developers, practitioners, and researchers to consider its evaluation framework as well as other more conventional evaluation frameworks and to decide which criteria best apply to judgments about newer forms of assessments, which criteria have important and helpful corollaries, and where new criteria may be needed that address the particular validity issues raised by performance-based assessments. For example, consistency and generalizability are important criteria in traditional evaluation frameworks; although they might be instantiated differently, they are potentially important concepts in evaluating alternative assessments as well. The utility of other evaluation criteria that speak to the unique validity issues raised by these assessments also should be considered. Furthermore, careful study of the validity criteria used by these performance-based assessment programs might suggest additional criteria that are relevant to more conventional forms of assessment. It is beyond the committee's charge to suggest appropriate validity practices for new forms of assessment. It urges the field to do so.

CONCLUSION

Several new and developing teacher assessment systems use a variety of testing and assessment methods, including assessments of teaching performance. They include multiple measures of candidates' knowledge, skills, abilities, and dispositions. In these systems, assessments are integrated with professional development and with the ongoing support of prospective or beginning teachers.

Given its analysis of systems that employ performance-based assessments, the committee concludes:

- New and developing assessment systems warrant investigation for addressing the limits of current initial teacher licensure tests and for improving teacher licensure. The benefits, costs, and limitations of these systems should be investigated.

9

Conclusions and Recommendations

In this report the committee describes recent efforts by teacher educators, state officials, and federal policy makers to improve teacher preparation and strengthen initial teacher licensure. The committee notes that states are increasingly testing candidates for their ability to become teachers and the federal government is looking to licensure tests for leverage in changing teacher education and improving teacher quality. In the preceding chapters, the committee reviews programs that use written tests to determine whether entry-level teachers have the skills and knowledge minimally necessary for beginning teaching. The report describes a new federal law called the Teacher Quality Enhancement Grants for States and Partnerships that uses teacher licensure tests to hold teacher education programs and states accountable for the quality of their preparation and licensure systems.

In this report the committee examines three questions:

• Do current tests measure beginning teacher competence appropriately and in a technically sound way?
• Should teacher licensure tests be used to hold states and institutions of higher education accountable for the quality of teacher preparation and licensure?
• How can innovative measures of beginning teacher competence help improve teacher quality?

In this last chapter, the committee reiterates the conclusions of its analysis and presents a series of recommendations for policy makers, teacher testers, and licensure officials. The first set of recommendations speaks to the use of the current tests. The second set is about evaluating teacher education, and the final recommendations encourage new and innovative assessments.

DO CURRENT TESTS MEASURE BEGINNING TEACHER COMPETENCE APPROPRIATELY AND IN A TECHNICALLY SOUND WAY?

The committee examined four types of data in response to this question; it looked at practice and research data on the knowledge, skills, abilities, and dispositions that competent teachers demonstrate; information about current licensing systems and licensing tests; evaluation data for several widely used teacher licensure tests; and an investigation of the extent to which tests can and cannot improve teacher competence and supply.

Defining Competent Beginning Teaching

Definitions of what teachers should know and be able to do have changed over time as society's values have changed, and they will continue to do so. The job of teaching students to learn and use new information, develop and apply skills, and think critically is highly complex and demanding. Teachers need to motivate and engage all students, including students from varied backgrounds and students with different learning and language needs. In addition to being responsible for student learning, teachers are expected to provide safe and nurturing classrooms, to serve as good role models, and to engage parents and the community in the business of their schools. Teachers need a wide range of knowledge, skills, abilities, and dispositions to perform these many complex tasks.

The quality of teaching in a school depends on more than just teacher quality. Quality teaching depends on a number of factors, including the amount and quality of instructional resources available, teacher professional development, staffing, and support from administrators and parents.

There is no single agreed-upon definition of what competencies a beginning teacher should have. Different professional organizations and many states have recently developed standards for teachers. The fact that different states have affiliations with these national and regional standards development efforts suggests some agreement between states about standards for teacher competence. Given that states have different educational standards for students, have teacher candidate pools with different characteristics, and that licensing of teachers is a state responsibility, it is not surprising that there is some variation in the knowledge and skills that states seek for their beginning teachers.

Designing Tests for Initial Licensure

The primary goal of licensing beginning teachers is to ensure that all students have competent teachers. Teacher licensing is under the authority of individual states. There are 51 unique licensure systems in the United States; they share some commonalties, however. As in other professions, teacher licensing relies on more than tests to judge whether candidates have the knowledge, skills, abilities, and dispositions to practice responsibly. Teacher candidates generally must fulfill education requirements, successfully complete practice teaching, and receive the recommendations of their preparing institutions. These requirements help ensure that a broad range of competencies are considered in licensing new teachers.

Initial teacher licensure tests are designed to identify candidates with some of the knowledge and skills needed for minimally competent beginning practice. The tests currently used measure basic skills, general knowledge, content knowledge, and knowledge of teaching strategies. They are designed to separate teacher candidates who are minimally competent in the areas assessed from those who are not. Initial teacher licensure tests do not provide information to distinguish moderately qualified from highly qualified teacher candidates nor are they designed to test all of the competencies relevant to beginning practice.

States decide whether and what tests to use to license beginning teachers. Each of the 42 states that requires tests uses a different combination of them, uses them at different points in a candidate's education, and sets its own passing scores. States use initial licensure tests for admission to teacher education, as a prerequisite for student teaching, as a condition of graduation, and/or as a licensure requirement. Several hundred different initial licensure tests are currently in use. Two test developers—Educational Testing Service (ETS) and National Evaluation Systems (NES)—develop the vast majority of these tests.

Conclusions

- Because a teacher's work is complex, even a set of well-designed tests cannot measure all of the prerequisites of competent beginning teaching. Current paper-and-pencil tests provide only some of the information needed to evaluate the competencies of teacher candidates.
- States have gradually adopted tests for teacher licensure, and test developers have made various tests available over time. Therefore, it is not surprising that states have adopted a variety of tests to license beginning teachers.
- Appropriate, technically sound tests are difficult and costly to develop. Collaborations among states participating in the Interstate New Teacher Assessment and Support Consortium and other states, professional asso-

ciations, and test developers bring the intellectual and financial resources of several organizations to this difficult work.

Recommendations

- It is crucial that states use multiple forms of evidence in making decisions about teacher candidates. Licensure systems should be designed to rely on a comprehensive but parsimonious set of high-quality indicators.
- States, test developers, and professional organizations should continue exploring joint development of initial teacher licensing tests for the knowledge and skill areas they have in common. Federal and state government and private organizations should appropriate funds to support this kind of collaboration.

Making Decisions About Candidates Based on Licensure Tests

States set passing scores on licensure tests based on judgments about the levels of knowledge and skill needed for minimally competent beginning teaching. Although many states rely on commonly used standard-setting procedures, there is little documentation about these procedures and how states actually use this information in arriving at a final decision about passing scores. In attempts to raise teacher standards, some states have recently raised their passing scores for particular tests. Some report having set passing scores that are higher than those of other states.

On all of the tests the committee reviewed, minority candidates had lower passing rates than nonminority candidates did on their initial testing attempts. Though differences between the passing rates of candidate groups eventually decrease because many unsuccessful test takers retake and pass the tests, eventual passing rates for minority candidates are still lower than those for nonminority test takers.

Initial licensure tests are only one factor influencing the supply of new teachers. The quality and size of the pool of new teachers depend on many things, including recruiting efforts, other licensing requirements, labor market forces, licensing reciprocity, teacher salaries, and the conditions under which teachers work.

Conclusions

- States differ in how high they set passing scores. The committee does not know the extent to which this variation in passing scores reflects differences among states in standard-setting methods; state teaching and learning standards; the characteristics of applicant pools; or different concerns about measurement error, teacher quality, or teacher supply.

- To the extent that the tests provide accurate measurements, setting higher passing scores would be expected to increase the proportion of teacher candidates in the hiring pool who are competent in the knowledge and skills measured by the tests, although higher passing scores will tend to lower the number of candidates who pass the test. To the extent that test scores have measurement error, setting higher passing scores could eliminate competent candidates.
- Reducing the number of new licensed teachers could require districts to make difficult choices, such as hiring uncredentialed teachers, increasing class sizes, or increasing salaries to attract licensed teachers from other districts and states.
- The lower passing rates for minority teacher candidates on current licensure tests pose problems for schools and districts in seeking a qualified and diverse teaching force. Setting substantially higher passing scores on licensure tests is likely to reduce the diversity of the teacher applicant pool, further adding to the difficulty of obtaining a diverse school faculty.

Recommendations

- States should follow professionally accepted standard-setting methods and document the methods they use to set passing scores on initial licensure tests. This documentation should describe the work of standard-setting panels and the basis on which policy decisions were made by the officials setting the final passing scores. Documentation should be publicly available to users and other interested parties.
- If states raise passing scores as a way to increase the competence of new teachers, they should examine not only the impact on teacher competence but also the effects of raising passing scores on applications to teacher education, on the supply of new teachers, and on the diversity of the teaching force.

Evaluating Licensing Tests

Solid technical characteristics and fairness are key to the effective use of tests. The work of measurement specialists, test users, and policy makers suggests criteria for judging the appropriateness and technical quality of initial teacher licensure tests. The committee drew on these to develop criteria that it believes users should aspire to in developing and evaluating initial teacher licensure tests. The committee used these evaluation criteria to evaluate a sample of five widely used tests produced by ETS. The tests the committee reviewed met most of its criteria for technical quality, although there were some areas for improvement. The committee also attempted to review a sample of NES tests. Despite concerted and repeated efforts, though, the committee was unable to obtain sufficient information on the technical characteristics of tests produced by NES and thus could draw no conclusions about their technical quality.

Conclusions

- The committee's criteria for judging test quality include the following: tests should have a statement of purpose; systematic processes should be used in deciding what to test and in assuring balanced and adequate coverage of these competencies; test materials should be tried out and analyzed before operational decisions are made; test administration and scoring should be uniform and fair; test materials and results should be protected from corruptibility; standard-setting procedures should be systematic and well documented; test results should be consistent across test forms and scorers; information about tests and scoring should be available to candidates; technical documentation should be accessible for public and professional review; validity evidence should be gathered and presented; costs and feasibility should be considered in test development and selection; and the long-term consequences of licensing tests should be monitored and examined.
- The profession's standards for educational testing say that information sufficient to evaluate the appropriateness and technical adequacy of tests should be made available to potential test users and other interested parties. The committee considers the lack of sufficient technical information made available by NES and the states to evaluate NES-developed tests to be problematic and a concern. It is also significant because NES-developed tests are administered to very large numbers of teacher candidates.
- The initial licensure tests currently in use rely almost exclusively on content-related evidence of validity. Few, if any, developers are collecting evidence about how test results relate to other relevant measures of candidates' knowledge, skills, and abilities.
- It is important to collect validity data that go beyond content-related validity evidence for initial licensing tests. However, conducting high-quality research of this kind is complex and costly. Examples of relevant research include investigations of the relationships between test results and other measures of candidate knowledge and skills or on the extent to which tests distinguish candidates who are at least minimally competent from those who are not.
- The processes used to develop current tests, the empirical studies of test content, and common-sense analyses suggest the importance of at least some of what is measured by these initial licensure tests. Beginning teachers should know how to read, write, and do basic mathematics; they should know the content areas they teach.

- Little research has been conducted on the extent to which scores on current teacher licensure tests relate to other measures of beginning teacher competence. Much of the research that has been conducted suffers from methodological problems that interfere with making strong conclusions about the results. This makes it hard to determine what effect licensure tests might have on improving the actual competence of beginning teachers.

Recommendations

- States should strive to use the committee's or similar evaluation criteria when developing and evaluating tests for use in initial teacher licensure systems.
- When states are selecting from among existing tests for initial teacher licensure, they should obtain and carefully consider field test and any available operational data regarding reliability, validity, cost/feasibility, and fairness as part of their decision-making process. When states are developing licensing tests, they should collect and weigh this evidence in making decisions about the final form of the test and its use.
- The degree of disparate impact should be an important consideration when states are deciding which licensure test to use for various decisions about candidate competence.
- States and test developers should provide technical documentation to users, scholars, and the public about the reliability, validity, and disparate impact of their tests. Field test or any available operational data should be used to document the technical quality of tests.
- The technical information used in deciding on a test normally should be made publicly available before tests are actually used to make decisions about individuals. If technical data are not provided by the end of the first administration year, states should not use information from these tests to make licensing decisions.
- State agencies contracting for test development should specify the technical information they require. Because of the importance of these data for the technical evaluation of tests, state agencies should request sufficient technical data and timely delivery of documentation. State agencies should ensure their clear authority to release this information to users and others for the purpose of objectively evaluating the technical quality of the tests, the resulting scores, and the interpretations based on them.
- States should arrange for independent evaluations of their current tests and teacher licensure systems and make the results of these independent examinations of their systems available for outside review.
- The committee encourages the federal government and others to conduct research on the extent to which teacher licensure tests distinguish be-

tween beginning teachers who are at least minimally competent and those who are not regarding the knowledge and skills the tests are intended to measure. This research should include evidence on a broad range of teacher competencies. Such research is likely to improve the development of teacher licensure tests. Within the limits of privacy law, states should make their raw data available to the research community to facilitate development and validity research on initial teacher licensure tests.

SHOULD TEACHER LICENSURE TESTS BE USED TO HOLD STATES AND INSTITUTIONS OF HIGHER EDUCATION ACCOUNTABLE FOR THE QUALITY OF TEACHER PREPARATION AND LICENSURE?

Making Decisions About Programs Based on Licensure Tests

Title II of the Higher Education Act was enacted to achieve four goals: to improve student achievement; to improve the quality of the current and future teaching force by improving the preparation of prospective teachers and enhancing professional development activities; to hold institutions of higher education accountable for preparing beginning teachers to have the necessary teaching skills and to be highly competent in the academic content areas in which they plan to teach; and to recruit highly qualified individuals, including individuals from other occupations.

Conclusions

- It is reasonable to hold teacher education institutions accountable for the quality of their teacher preparation programs.
- By their design and as currently used, initial teacher licensure tests fall short of the intended policy goals for their use as accountability tools and as levers for improving teacher preparation and licensing programs. The public reporting and accountability provisions of Title II may encourage erroneous conclusions about the quality of teacher preparation.
- Although the percentage of graduates who pass initial licensure tests provides an entry point for evaluating an institution's quality, simple comparisons among institutions based on their passing rates are difficult to interpret for many reasons. These include the fact that institutions have different educational missions and recruiting practices, their students have different entry-level qualifications, teacher education programs have different entry and exit testing requirements, and programs have different procedures for determining the institutional affiliations of their candidates. By themselves, passing rates on licensure tests do not provide

adequate information on which to judge the quality of teacher education programs.

- Simple comparisons of passing rates across states are misleading. Many states use different tests for initial licensure or set different passing scores on the same tests. States have different policies about when a test is given or what decisions it supports.
- To fairly and accurately judge the quality of teacher education programs, federal and state officials need data on a wide variety of program characteristics from multiple sources. Other indicators of program quality might include assessment data for students in relation to course and program benchmarks, employer evaluations, and district or state evaluations of beginning teaching. Other indicators might include information on course requirements and course quality, measures of the amount and quality of field experiences, evidence of opportunities to work with students with special learning needs and students with diverse backgrounds. Data on the qualifications of program faculty, the allocation of resources, and the adequacy of facilities might be considered. The qualifications of students at entry to teacher education programs also should be included.

Recommendations

- States should not use passing rates on initial licensure tests as the sole basis for deciding whether their teacher education programs are low performing.
- States should report multiple indicators of the quality of teacher preparation programs to federal officials in complying with Title II.
- The federal government should not use passing rates on initial teacher licensing tests as the sole basis for comparing states and teacher education programs or for withholding funds, imposing other sanctions, or rewarding teacher education programs.
- Federal officials should continue to collect the state and school data required by Title II but should not withhold funds from, otherwise sanction, or reward programs until a study is mounted of the multiple and varied data that might be used to judge the quality of teacher preparation and licensure.

HOW CAN INNOVATIVE MEASURES OF BEGINNING TEACHER COMPETENCE HELP IMPROVE TEACHER QUALITY?

Several new and developing teacher assessment systems use a variety of testing and assessment methods, including assessments of teaching performance. These include multiple measures of candidates' knowledge, skills, abilities, and dispositions. In these systems, assessments are integrated with professional development and with ongoing support of prospective or beginning teachers.

Conclusion

- New and developing assessment systems warrant investigation for addressing the limits of current initial teacher licensure tests and for improving teacher licensure. The benefits, costs, and limitations of these systems should be investigated.

Recommendations

- Research and development of broad-based indicators of teacher competence, not limited to test-based evidence, should be undertaken; indicators should include assessments of teaching performance in the classroom, of candidates' ability to work effectively with students with diverse learning needs and cultural backgrounds and in a variety of settings, and of competencies that more directly relate to student learning.
- When initial licensure tests are used, they should be part of a coherent developmental system of preparation, assessment, and support that reflects the many features of teacher competence.

References

Achieve. (1997). *A review of the 1996 National Education Summit.* ERIC Document Reproduction Service No. ED40770: Author.

Adorno, T.W., Frenkel-Brunswik, E., Levinson, D., and Sanford, R.N. (1950). *The authoritarian personality.* New York: Harper and Brothers.

Alverno College Faculty. (1973/2000). Ability-based learning program. [Brochure]. Milwaukee, WI: Alverno College Institute.

Alverno College Institute. (1996). *Ability-based learning program teacher education.* Milwaukee, WI: Author.

American Association of Colleges for Teacher Education. (2000). Counterpoint article: *USA Today* January 31, We need time to do the job right. Available: <www.aacte.org/governmental_relations/time_do_job_right.htm> [May 7, 2001].

American Association of State Colleges and Universities. (1999). *Concerns regarding NCES draft manual.* Available: <www.aascu.org/news/bulletins/090999.htm> [May 7, 2001].

American Association of State Colleges and Universities. (2000a). *Legislative bulletins.* Available: <www.aascu.org/news/bulletins> [May 7, 2001].

American Association of State Colleges and Universities. (2000b). *An opportunity to teach: Meeting Title II teacher education reporting requirement.* Washington, DC: Author.

American Association of State Social Work Boards. (1998). *Social work laws and board regulations: A comparison guide.* Culpepper, VA: Author.

American Council on Education. (1999). Letter to Secretary Riley concerning state teacher licensure examinations. *Eye on Washington.* Available: <www.acenet.edu/washington/teacher_education/1999/08august/teacher_licensure_ltr.html> [May 7, 2001].

American Educational Research Association, American Psychological Association, and National Council on Measurement in Education. (1999). *Standards for educational and psychological testing.* Washington, DC: American Educational Research Association.

American Institute of Certified Public Accountants and National Association of State Boards of Accountancy. (1998). *Digest of state accountancy laws and state board regulations.* New York: American Institute of Certified Public Accountants.

173

American Physical Therapy Association. (1997). *State licensure reference guide.* Washington, DC: Author.

Andrews, J.W., Blackmon, C.R., and Mackey, J.A. (1980). Preservice performance and the National Teachers Exams. *Phi Delta Kappan, January,* 358-359.

Angoff, W.H. (1971). Scales, norms and equivalent scores. In R. L. Thorndike (Ed.), *Educational measurement,* 2nd ed. (pp. 508-600). Washington, DC: American Council on Education.

Angus, D.L. (2001). *Professionalism and the public good: A brief history of teacher certification.* Washington, DC: Thomas B. Fordham Foundation.

Archer, J. (1998). States raising bar for teachers despite pending shortage. *Education Week,* volume 17, March 25. Available: <www.edweek.com/ew/ewstory.cfm?slug=28praxis.h17& keywords= states%20raising%20bar> [May 7, 2001].

Ayers, J.B., and Qualls, G.S. (1979). Concurrent and predictive validity of the national teacher examinations. *Journal of Educational Research, 732,* 86-92.

Baker, E.L., and Linn, R.L. (1997). *Emerging educational standards of performance in the United States.* CSE Technical Report 437. Los Angeles, CA: University of California, National Center for Research on Evaluation, Standards, and Student Testing.

Ballou, D. (1996). Do public schools hire the best applicant? *Quarterly Journal of Economics, III(2),* 97-134.

Ballou, D., and Podgursky, M. (1997). *Teacher pay and teacher quality.* Kalamazoo, MI: W.E. Upjohn Institute.

Ballou, D., and Podgursky, M. (1999). Reforming teacher training and recruitment: A critical appraisal of the recommendations of the National Commission on Teaching and America's Future. *Government Union Review, 174.*

Bassham, H. (1962). Teacher understanding and pupil efficiency in mathematics—A study of relationship. *Arithmetic Teacher, 9,* 383-387.

Begle, E.G. (1972). Teacher knowledge and student achievement in algebra. *School_Mathematics Study Group, Report Number 9.*

Blair, J. (1999). Teacher ed. (Education) riled over federal plan. *Education Week 18* (43), 1, 32-33. Available: < www.edweek.com/ew/vol-18/43hea.h18 > [May 7, 2001].

Bond, L. (1998a). Culturally responsive pedagogy and the assessment of accomplished teaching. *Journal of Negro Education, 673,* 242-254.

Bond, L. (1998b). Disparate impact and teacher certification. *Journal of Personnel Evaluation in Education, 12*(2), 211-220.

Bond, L. (2000). *The measurement of teaching ability.* Paper prepared for the Teacher Quality Project Panel Meeting, Department of Education and American Institutes for Research, Washington, DC.

Bond, L., Jaeger, R.M., and Hatti, J.A. (2000). *Accomplished teaching: A validation of National Board Certification.* Washington, DC: National Board for Professional Teaching Standards.

Brophy, J., and Good, T.L. (1986). Teacher behavior and student achievement. In M.C. Wittrock (Ed.), *Handbook of research on teaching,* pp. 328-375. New York: MacMillan.

Brunsman, B.A., Oster, J., Tanaka, D., Carlson, R.E., and Salley, R. (1999). *Annual report on the Multiple Subjects Assessment for Teachers (MSAT).* Sacramento, CA: California Commission on Teacher Credentialing.

Brunsman, B.A., Carlson, R.E., and Tierney, D. (2000). *Annual report on the Praxis and SSAT examinations in English, Mathematics, and Social Science.* Sacramento, CA: California Commission on Teacher Credentialing.

Bush, G.W. (2001). No child left behind. Available: www.ed.gov/inits/nclb/ [May 7, 2001].

Carlson, R.E., Wright, D., McLean, M. and Sandy, M.V. (2000). *Report on the California Basic Educational Skills Test (CBEST).* Sacramento, CA: California Commission on Teacher Credentialing.

Case, S.M., Swanson, D.B., Ripkey, D.R., Bowles, L.T., and Melnick, D.E. (1996). Performance of the class of 1994 in the new era of USMLE. *Academic Medicine, 71,*10 (October Supplement), 91-93.

Choy, S.P., Bobbitt, S.A., Henke, R.R., Medrich, E.A., Horn, L., and Lieberman, J. (1993). *America's teachers: Profile of a profession*. NCES Report No. 93-025. Washington, DC: U.S. Department of Education, National Center for Education Statistics.

Cizek, G. (1996). Standard-setting guidelines. *Educational Measurement: Issues and Practice, 15*(1), 13-21, 12.

Clary, L.M. (1972). *Teacher characteristics that predict successful reading instruction*. Augusta College: ERIC Document Reproduction Service No. 174961.

Clinton, W.J. Presidential address before a joint session of the Congress on the state of the union 27 January 1996 . *Federal Register 32, 4,* 29 January 1996, 83-118.

Clinton, W.J. Presidential address before a joint session of the Congress on the state of the union 4 February 1997. *Federal Register 33, 6,* 10 February 1997, 129-162.

Cohen, D.K., and Spillane, J.P. (1993). Policy and practice: The relations between governance and instruction. In S.H. Fuhrman (Ed.), *Designing coherent education policy: Improving the system*. San Francisco, CA: Jossey-Bass.

Coleman, J.S., and others. (1966). *Equality of educational opportunity*. Washington, DC: U.S. Government Printing Office.

Connecticut State Board of Education. (2000). *Connecticut's commitment to excellence in teaching: The beginning educator support and training program*. Hartford, CT: Author.

Connecticut State Department of Education. (1999). *Connecticut's common core of teaching*. Hartford, CT: Author.

Council of Chief State School Officers. (1998). *Key state education policies on K-12 education: standards, graduation, assessment, teacher licensure, time and attendance: A 50-state report*. Washington, DC: Author.

Council of Chief State School Officers. (2000). *Key state education policies on K-12 education 2000*. Washington, DC: Author.

Crocker, L. (1999). *Evaluating teacher licensure assessment programs: Do the old criteria apply to emergent assessments?* Paper commissioned by the Committee on Assessment and Teacher Quality, Center for Education, National Research Council.

Darling-Hammond, L., and Sclan, E. (1996). Who teaches and why. In J. Sikula, T. Buttery, and E. Guyton (Eds.), *The handbook of research on teacher education*. New York: MacMillian.

Darling-Hammond, L. (2000). *Teacher quality and student achievement: A review of state policy evidence*. Seattle, WA: University of Washington, Center for the Study of Teaching and Policy.

Darling-Hammond, L., Wise, A.E., and Klein, S.P. (1999). *A license to teach*. San Francisco, CA: Jossey-Bass.

Darling-Hammond, L., Dilworth, M., and Bullmaster, M. (in press). *Educators of color*.

Delpit, L. (1996). Skills and other dilemmas of a progressive black educator. *American Educator, 20*(3), 9-11.

Diez, M.E. (1999). Critical components in the preparation of teachers. In R.A. Roth (Ed.), *The role of the university in the preparation of teachers*, pp.226-240. London: Falmer Press.

Diez, M.E., Hass. J.M., Henn-Reinke, K., Stoffels, J.A., and Truchan, L.C. (1998). Guiding coherence: Performance-based teacher education at Alverno College. In M.E. Diez (Ed.), *Changing the practice of teacher education*, pp. 41-50. Washington, DC: American Association of College for Teacher Education.

Diez, M.E., Richards, W., and Lake, K. (1994). Performance assessment in teacher education at Alverno College. In T. Warren (Ed.), *Promising practices: Teacher education in liberal arts colleges*. New York: University Press of America.

Dwyer, C.A. (1994). *Development of the knowledge base for the Praxis III: Classroom performance assessments assessment criteria*. Princeton, NJ: Educational Testing Service.

Education Week. (2000). *Quality counts 2000: Who should teach? The states decide, 19* (18), 8-9. Available: <www.edweek.com/sreports/qc00/templates/article.cfm?slug=execsum.htm& keywords=who%20should%20teach> [May 7, 2001].

Education Week. (2001, January 31). *No child left behind*, vol. 20, number 19, page Web only. Available: <www.edweek.com/ew/ewstory.cfm?slug=19bushchart_web.h20&keywords=no%20child%20left> [May 7, 2001].

Education World. (1998, September 14). *The focus on teacher standards: States raise the bar on teacher standards*. Available: <www.education-world.com/a_admin/admin080.shtml> [May 23, 2001].

Educational Testing Service. (1995a). *Pathwise*. [folder]. Princeton, NJ: Author.

Educational Testing Service. (1995b). *Pathwise classroom observation system orientation guide*. Princeton, NJ: Author.

Educational Testing Service. (1995c). *Teacher performance assessments: Assessment criteria*. Princeton, NJ: Author.

Educational Testing Service. (1996). *The Praxis series: Test at a glance*. Princeton NJ: Author. Available: <www.teachingandlearning.org/profdvlp/pathwise> [August 8, 2001].

Educational Testing Service. (1997, September). *Validation and standard-setting procedures used for tests in the Praxis series*. Princeton, NJ: Author.

Educational Testing Service. (1998a). *Guidelines for proper use of the Praxis series and related assessments*. [Booklet]. Princeton, NJ: Author.

Educational Testing Service. (1998b). *Understanding your Praxis scores 1997-98*. [Booklet]. Princeton, NJ: Author.

Educational Testing Service. (1999a). *ETS standards for quality and fairness*. [Brochure]. Princeton, NJ: Testing and Learning Division.

Educational Testing Service. (1999b). *Setting passing scores: The need for justifiable procedures*. [Brochure]. Princeton, NJ: Teaching and Learning Division.

Educational Testing Service. (1999c). *Significant decisions in testing litigation*. [Brochure]. Princeton, NJ: Teaching and Learning Division.

Educational Testing Service. (1999d). *Understanding your Praxis scores 1998-99*. [Booklet]. Princeton, NJ: Author.

Educational Testing Service. (1999e). *Validity for licensing tests*. [Brochure]. Princeton, NJ: Teaching and Learning Division.

Educational Testing Service. (2000). *Understanding your Praxis scores 1999-2000*. [Booklet]. Princeton, NJ: Author.

Ehrenberg, R.G., and Brewer, D.J. (1995). Did teachers' verbal ability and race matter in the 1960s? Coleman revisited. *Economics of Education Review, 141*, 1-21.

Engelhard, G., Myford, C.M., and Cline, F. (2000). *Investigating assessor effects in National Board for Professional Teaching Standards assessments for early childhood/generalist and middle childhood/generalist certification* (ETS RR-00-13). Princeton, NJ.

Feistritzer, C.E., and Chester, D.T. (2000). *Alternative teacher certification*. Washington, DC: National Center for Education Information.

Ferguson, R.F. (1991). Paying for public education: New evidence on how and why money matters. *Harvard Journal on Legislation, 282*, 465-498.

Ferguson, R.F., and Brown, J. (2000). Certification tests scores, teacher quality, and student achievement. In D.W. Grissmer and J.M. Ross (Eds.), *Analytic issues in the assessment of student achievement*, pp.133-156. Washington, DC: U.S. Department of Education, National Center for Education Statistics.

Ferguson, R.F., and Ladd, H.F. (1996). How and why money matters: An analysis of Alabama schools. In H.F. Ladd (Ed.), *Holding schools accountable: Performance-based reform in education*, pp. 265-298. Washington, DC: Brookings Institute.

Flippo, R.F., and Riccards, M.P. (2000, September). Initial teacher certification testing in Massachusetts: A case of the tail wagging the dog. *Phi Delta Kappan, 82*(1), 34-37.

Futrell, M.H. (1999). *Criteria for teacher licensure*. Paper commissioned by the Committee on Assessment and Teacher Quality, Center for Education, National Research Council.

Garcia, P. (1985, August). *A study on teacher competency testing and test validity with implications for minorities and the results and implication of the use of the Pre-Professional Skills Test as a screening device for entrance into teacher education programs in Texas* (NIE Grant No. NIE-G-85-0004). Washington, DC: National Institute of Education.

George, P. (1985). Teacher testing and the historically black college. *Journal of Teacher Education,* *36*(6), 54-57.

Getzels, J.W., and Jackson, P.W. (1963). The teacher's personality and characteristics. In N.L. Gage (Ed.), *Handbook of research on teaching.* Chicago: Rand McNally.

Gitomer, D.H., Latham, A.S., and Ziomek, R. (1999). *The academic quality of prospective teachers: The impact of admissions and licensure testing.* Princeton, NJ: Educational Testing Service. Available: <www.praxis.org/rschnews/research/researchrpt.html> [May 28, 2001].

Goertz, M.E., and Pitcher, B. (1985). *The impact of NTE use by states on teacher selection.* Research Report No. RR-85-1. Princeton, NJ: Educational Testing Service.

Goldhaber, D.D. (1999). *Criteria of effective teacher licensure system.* Paper commissioned by the Committee on Assessment and Teacher Quality, Center for Education, National Research Council.

Graham, P.A. (1987, April). Black teachers: A drastically scarce resource. *Phi Delta Kappan,* 598-605.

Greene, R. (1998, February 16). States raising test standards for would-be teachers. *The Ohio Wire.* Available: <www.ohio.com:80/bj/news/ohio/docs/010941.html> [February 18, 1998].

Guyton, E., and Farokhi, E. (1987). Relationships among academic performance, basic skills, subject matter knowledge and teaching skills of teacher education graduates. *Journal of Teacher Education, 385,* 37-42.

Haertel, E.H. (1991). New forms of teacher assessment. In G. Grant (Ed.), *Review of research in education, 17,* 3-29. Washington, DC: American Educational Research Association.

Haney, W.M., Madaus, G., and Kreitzer, A. (1987). Charms talismanic: Testing teachers for the improvement of education. In E.Z. Rothkopf (Ed.), *Review of research in education, 14,* 169-238. Washington, DC: American Educational Research Association.

Haney, W., Fowler, C., Wheelock, A., Bebell, D., and Malec, N. (1999). Less truth than error? An independent study of the Massachusetts teacher tests. *Educational Policy Analysis Archives,* *7*(4). [Online serial]. Available: http://epaa.asu.edu/epaa/v7n4/ [May 28, 2001].

Hanushek, E.A. (1986). The economics of schooling. *Journal of Economic Literature, 26*(3), 1141-1177.

Hedges, L.V., and Nowell, A. (1998). Black-white test score convergence since 1965. In C. Jencks and A. Phillips (Eds.), *The Black white test score gap,* pp.149-181. Washington, DC: Brookings Institution.

Higher Education Reauthorization Act. (1998). Pub. L. No. 105-244, 20 U.S.C. § 1021-1030.

Horn, C., Ramos, M, Blumer, I., and Madaus, G. (2000). *Cut scores: Results may vary.* National Board on Educational Resting and Public Policy, Monograph 1, Vol. 11. Boston, MA: Boston College.

Howell, P., and Gitomer, D.H. (2000). *What is the perceived impact of National Board scoring on assessors?* Paper presented at AERA April 2000 New Orleans.

Impara, J. (Ed.). (1995). *Licensure testing: Purposes, procedures and practices.* Lincoln, NE: Buros Institute of Mental Measurements.

Impara, J.C. (2000a). An evaluation of the bology: Content knowledge, part 1 and 2 tests. Technical Report. Paper commissioned by the Committee of Assessment and Teacher Quality, Center for Education, National Research Council.

Impara, J.C. (2000b). An evaluation of high school mathematics proofs, models, and problems, part 1 test. Technical Report. Paper commissioned by the Committee of Assessment and Teacher Quality, Center for Education, National Research Council.

Impara, J.C. (2000c). An evaluation of the middle school: English/Language arts test. Technical Report. Paper commissioned by the Committee of Assessment and Teacher Quality, Center for Education, National Research Council.

Impara, J.C. (2000d). An evaluation of the pre-professional skils test (PPST) reading test. Technical Report. Paper commissioned by the Committee of Assessment and Teacher Quality, Center for Education, National Research Council.

Impara, J.C. (2000e). An evaluation of the principles of learning and teaching (PLT) test: K-6. Technical Report. Paper commissioned by the Committee of Assessment and Teacher Quality, Center for Education, National Research Council.

Improving America's Schools Act. (1965). Title 1—Amendments to the elementary and secondary education act. Pub. L. No. 103-382, 103d Congress, 2d Session § 1-101.

Interstate New Teacher Assessment and Support Consortium (INTASC). (1992). *Model standards for beginning teacher licensing and development: A resource for state dialogue.* Washington, DC: Council of Chief State School Officers.

Interstate New Teacher Assessment and Support Consortium. (1999, Fall). INTASC tackles challenges of new Title II reporting requirements. *INTASC in Focus, 21,* 1-6.

Irvine, J.J. (1990). *Black students and school failure: Policies, practices and prescriptions.* New York: Greenwood.

Jaeger, R.M. (1989). Certification of Student Competence. *Educational Measurement,* 3rd ed., 485-514. New York: American Council on Education, Macmillian.

Jaeger, R.M. (1998). Evaluating the psychometric qualities of the National Board for Professional Teaching Standards' Assessments: A methodological accounting. *Journal of Personnel Evaluation in Education, 22,* 189-210.

Jaeger, R.M. (1999). Some psychometric criteria for judging the quality of teacher certification tests. Paper commissioned by the Committee on Assessment and Teacher Quality, Center for Education, National Research Council.

Jasanoff, S. (1998). Science and judgment in environmental standard setting. *Applied Measurement in Education, 111,* 107-120.

Jeanneret, P.R. (1999). Report to the Committee on Assessment and Teacher Quality. Paper commissioned by the Committee on Assessment and Teacher Quality, Center for Education, National Research Council.

Jencks, C., and Phillips, M. (Eds.) (1998). *The black-white test score gap.* Washington, DC: Brookings Institution.

Jerald, C., and Boser, U. (2001). Setting policies for new teachers. Education Week on the web. Available: <edweek.com/sreports/qc00/templates/article.cfm?slug=policies.htm&keywords= jerald> [May 7, 2001].

Johnson, S.M. (1990). *Teachers at work: Achieving success in our schools.* Boston: Basic Books.

Kane, M. (1994). Validating the performance standards associated with passing scores. *Review of Educational Research, 64,* 425-461.

Klein, S.P., and Stecher, B. (1991). Developing a prototype licensing examination for secondary school teachers. *Journal of Personnel Evaluation in Education, 5,* 169-190.

Ladson-Billings, G. (1994). Who will teach our children? Preparing teachers to successfully teach African-American students. In E. Hollins, J. King, and W. Hayman (Eds.), *Teaching diverse populations: Formulating a knowledge base,* pp. 129-158. Albany, NY: State University of New York.

Loacker, G., and Mentkowski, M. (1993). Creating a culture where assessment improves learning. In T. W. Banta (Ed.), *Making a difference: Outcomes of a decade of assessment in higher education,* pp. 5-24. San Francisco, CA: Jossey-Bass.

Lynch, S., Murdock, J., and Gitomer, D. (2000). *How do candidates prepare for National Board certification?* Paper presented at AERA April 2000 New Orleans

Manski, C.F. (1987). Academic ability, earnings, and the decision to become a teacher: Evidence from the National Longitudinal Study of the high school class of 1972. In D. Wise (Ed.), *Public sector payrolls,* pp. 291-312. Chicago: Chicago University Press.

Massell, D., Kirst, M.W., and Hoppe, M. (1997). *Persistence and change: Standards-based reform in nine states.* CPRE Research Report No. RR-037. Philadelphia: University of Pennsylvania, Consortium for Policy Research in Education.

McGee, H.M. (1955). Measurement of authoritarianism and its relation to teachers' classroom behavior. *Genetic Psychology Monographs, 52,* 89-146

Medley, D.M., and Quirk, T.J. (1974). The application of a factorial design to the study of cultural bias in general culture items on the National Teacher Examination. *Journal of Educational Measurement, 114,* 235-245.

Mehrens, W.A. (1999, May). The CBEST Saga: Implications for licensure and employment testing. *Bar Examiner, 68*(2), 23-32.

Melnick, S.L., and Pullin, D. (2000). Can you take dictation? Prescribing teacher quality through testing. *Journal of Teacher Education, 514,* 262-275.

Mentkowski, M. (1991). *Designing a national assessment system: Assessing abilities that connect education and work.* Milwaukee, WI: Alverno College Productions.

Mentkowski, M., and Doherty, A. (1984). Abilities that last a lifetime: Outcomes of the Alverno experience. *American Association for Higher Education Bulletin, 366,* 5-14.

Mentkowski, M. and Associates. (2000). *Learning that lasts: Integrating learning, development, and performance in college and beyond.* San Francisco, CA: Jossey-Bass.

Messick. S. (1989). Validity. In R.L. Linn (Ed.), *Educational measurement,* 3rd ed., pp. 13-103. Washington, DC: The American Council on Education and the National Council on Measurement in Education.

Mills, C.N. (1995). Establishing passing standards. *Licensure testing: Purposes, procedures, and practices.* Lincoln, NE: Buros Institute of Mental Measurements.

Moss, P.A. and Schultz, A. (1999). Risking frankness in educational assessment. *Phi Delta Kappan, 80*(9), 680-687.

National Association of State Directors of Teacher Education and Certification. (1999). *The NASDTEC manual 1998-1999: Manual on the preparation and certification of educational personnel 4th ed.* T. Andrews, and L. Andrews (Eds.). Dubuque, IA: Kendall/Hunt.

National Association of State Directors of Teacher Education and Certification. (2000a). *The NASDTEC Interstate Contract.* Available: <www.nasdtec.org/contract.html> [May 28, 2001].

National Association of State Directors of Teacher Education and Certification. (2000b). *The NASDTEC Manual on the preparation and certification of educational personnel 5th ed.* T. Andrews, and L. Andrews (Eds.). Dubuque, IA: Kendall/Hunt.

National Board for Professional Teaching Standards. (1994). *What teachers should know and be able to do.* Detroit, MI: Author.

National Board for Professional Teaching Standards (1996). *Early Adolescence/English Language Arts Standards for National Board Certification.* Southfield, MI: Author.

National Board for Professional Teaching Standards. (2001). *Next generation certificate overviews.* Arlington, VA: Author.

National Center for Education Statistics. (2000). *The condition of education 2000.* Washington, DC: National Center for Education Statistics.

National Commission on Teaching and America's Future. (1996). *What matters most: Teaching for America's future.* New York: Teachers College, Columbia University.

National Council for Accreditation of Teacher Education. (1992). Achieving NCATE accreditation: The price and the prize. *Quality Teaching 1*(3).

National Council for the Accreditation of Teacher Education. (1997). *Standards, procedures and policies for the accreditation of professional education units.* Washington, DC: Author.

National Council for Accreditation of Teacher Education. (1999). *ETS joint venture with NCATE aligns standards and assessments in teacher preparation accreditation and licensing.* Available: <www.ncate.org/newsbrfs/etsoct99.htm> [May 7, 2001].

National Council for Accreditation of Teacher Education. (2000a). *NCATE history and governance.* Available: <www.ncate.org/ncate/histgov.htm> [May 7, 2001].

National Council for Accreditation of Teacher Education. (2000b). *NCATE 2000 unit standards.* Available: <www.ncate.org/standard/m_stds.htm> [May 7, 2001].

National Council of Architectural Registration Boards. (1998). *NCARB member board requirements.* Washington, DC: Author.

National Council of Examiners for Engineering and Surveying. (2000). *1999 survey information.* Clemson, SC: Author.

National Council of Teachers of Mathematics. (1989). *Curriculum and evaluation standards for school mathematics.* Reston, VA: Author.

National Education Association. (1992). *Status of American public school teacher 1990-91.* Washington, DC: Author.

National Research Council. (1996). *National science education standards.* Washington, DC: National Academy Press.

National Research Council. (1999a). *Grading the nation's report card: Evaluating NAEP and transforming the assessment of educational progress.* J.W. Pellegrino, L.R. Jones, and K.J. Mitchell (Eds.), Committee on the Evaluation of National and State Assessments of Educational Progress. Washington, DC: National Academy Press.

National Research Council. (1999b). *Testing, teaching and learning: A guide for states and school districts.* R.F. Elmore, and R. Rothman (Eds.)., Committee on Title I Testing and Assessment. Washington, DC: National Academy Press.

National Research Council. (1999c). *Uncommon measures: Equivalence and linkage among educational tests.* M.J. Feuer, P.W. Holland, B.F. Green, M.W. Bertenthal, and F.C. Hemphill (Eds.), Committee on Equivalency and Linkage of Educational Tests. Washington, DC: National Academy Press.

National Research Council. (2000). *Tests and teaching quality: Interim report.* Committee on Assessment and Teacher Quality. Washington, DC: National Academy Press.

National Research Council. (2001). *America becoming: Racial trends and their consequences, Volume 1.* N.J. Smelser, W.J. Wilson, and F. Mitchell (Eds.), Commission on Behavioral and Social Sciences and Education. Washington, DC: National Academy Press.

Noddings, N. (1984). *Caring: A feminine approach to ethics and moral education.* Berkeley: University of California Press.

Norcini, J.J., and Shea, J.A. (1992). The reproducibility of standards over groups and occasions. *Applied Measurement in Education, 51,* 63-72.

Plake, B.S. (1998). Setting performance standards for professional licensure and certification. *Applied Measurement in Education, 11*(1), 65-80.

Poggio, J.P., Glasnapp, D.R., Miller, M.D., Tollefson, N., and Burry, J.A. (1985). *Report on the validation studies of the National Teacher Examinations core battery tests for certification of entry-level teachers in the state of Kansas.* Lawrence: Center for Educational Testing and Evaluation, University of Kansas.

Poggio, J.P., Glasnapp, D.R., Miller, M.D., Tollefson, N.,and Burry, J.A. (1986). Strategies for validating teacher certification tests. *Educational Measurement: Issues and Practice, 52,* 18-25.

Popham, W.J. (1992). Appropriate expectations for content judgments regarding teacher licensure tests. *Applied Measurement in Education, 5,* 285-301.

Porter, A.C., Youngs, P., and Odden, A. (2000). Advances in teacher assessments and their uses. In V. Richardson (Ed.). *Handbook on Research on Teaching, 4th ed.* Washington, DC: American Educational Research Association.

Pullin, D. (1999). *Criteria for evaluating teacher tests: A legal perspective.* Paper commissioned by the Committee on Assessment and Teacher Quality, Center for Education, National Research Council.

Raudenbush, S.W., Rowan, B., and Cheong, Y.F. (1992). Contextual effects on the self-perceived efficacy of high school teachers. *Sociology of Education, 65*, April, 150-167.

Rebell, M.A. (1986). Disparate impact of teacher competency on minorities: Don't blame the test takers-or the tests. *Yale Law & Policy Review, 42*, 375-403.

Richardson, J. (1994). Standards and assessments: What is their educative potential? In M.E. Diez, P. David Pearson, and V. Richardson, *Setting standards and educating teachers, a national conversation: A report from the Wingspread Conference*, pp.15-36. Washington, DC: American Association of Colleges of Teacher Education.

Riley, R.W. (1999). New Challenges, A New Resolve: Moving American Education Into the 21st Century. Sixth Annual State of American Education Speech, Long Beach, Calif., Feb. 16.

Rosenfeld, M., Freeberg, N, and Bukatko, P. (1992a). *The professional functions of secondary school teachers.* Princeton, NJ: Educational Testing Service.

Rosenfeld, M., Reynolds, A., and Bukatko, P. (1992b). *The professional functions of elementary school teachers.* Princeton, NJ: Educational Testing Service.

Rosenfeld, M., Wilder, G., and Bukatko, P. (1992c). *The professional functions of middle school teachers.* Princeton, NJ: Educational Testing Service.

Roth, R.A. (1996). Standards for certification, licensure and accreditation. In J. Sikula (Ed.), *Handbook of research on teacher education*, 2nd ed., pp. 242-278. New York: Simon & Schuster.

Rothman, A. (1969). Teacher characteristics and student learning. *Journal of Research in Science Teaching, 64*, 340-48.

Rothstein, R. (1998). *The way we were? The myths and realities of America's student achievement.* New York: Century Foundation.

Rowan, B., Chiang, F., and Miller, R.J. (1997). Using research on employees' performance to study the effects of teachers on students' achievement. *Sociology of Education, 704*, 256-284.

Schmitt, K. (2000). *An overview of credentialing.* Paper commissioned by the Committee on Assessment and Teacher Quality, Center for Education, National Research Council. Unpublished paper; to obtain a copy contact the author at karaschmitt@hotmail.com.

Sheehan, D.S., and Marcus, M. (1978). Teacher performance on the National Teacher Examinations and student mathematics and vocabulary achievement. *The Journal of Educational Research, 71*, 134-136.

Shulman, L.S. (1986). Those who understand: Knowledge growth in teaching. *Educational Researcher, 152*, 4-14.

Shulman, L.S. (1987). Knowledge and teaching: Foundation of the new reform. *Harvard Educational Review, 57*(1), 1-22.

Sireci, S.G. (1998). Gathering and analyzing content validity data. *Educational Assessment, 54*, 299-321.

Sireci, S.G., and Green, P.C. III. (2000). Legal and psychometric criteria for evaluating teacher certification tests. *Educational Measurement: Issues and Practice, 191*, 22-31, 34.

Smith, G.P. (1987). The impact of competency tests on teacher education: Ethical and legal issues in selecting and certifying teachers. In M. Haberman and J.M. Backus (Eds.), *Advances in teacher education, vol. 3*, pp. 218-249. Westport, CT: Ablex Publishing.

Smith I.L., and Hambleton, R. (1990). Content validity studies of licensing examinations. *Educational Measurement: Issues and Practice, 94*, 7-10.

Smith, M., and O'Day, J. (1991). Systemic school reform. In S. Fuhrman and B. Malen (Eds.), *The politics of curriculum and testing.* New York: Taylor and Francis.

Society for Industrial and Organizational Psychology. (1987). *Principles for the validation and use of personnel selection procedures*, 3rd ed. College Park, MD: Author.

Steele, C.M. (1992). Race and the schooling of Black Americans. *The Atlantic, 2694*, 68-78.

Stinebrinker, T R. (in press). Compensation policies and teacher decisions. *International Economic Review*.

Stoker, H.W., and Impara, J.C. (1995). Basic psychometric issues in licensure testing. In *Licensure testing: Purposes, procedures, and practices*, J.C. Impara (Ed.), Buros Institute for Mental Measurements. Lincoln: University of Nebraska-Lincoln.

Strauss, R.P., and Sawyer, E.A. (1986). Some new evidence on teacher and student competencies. *Economics of Education Review, 51*, 41-48.

Summers, A.A., and Wolfe, B.L. (1975). Do schools make a difference? *American Economic Review, 67*, 639-652.

Swanson, D.B., Norman, G.R., and Linn, R.L. (1995). Performance-Based Assessment: Lessons from the Health Professions. *Educational Researcher, 24*(5), 5-11.

Teacher Education Accreditation Council. (2000). *Prospectus for a new system of teacher education accreditation*. Available: <www.teac.org> [May 7, 2001].

Tell, C. (2001). Appreciating good teaching: A conversation with Lee Shulman. *Educational leadership, 58*(5). Available: <www.ascd.org/readingroom/edlead/0102/tell.html> [May 9, 2001].

The College Entrance Examination Board. (1999). *1999 college-bound seniors: National report*. New York: Author.

Tom, A. (1980). Teaching as a moral craft. *Curriculum Inquiry, 10*, 317-323.

U.S. Department of Education. (1997a). NAEP 1996 mathematics report card for the nation and the states: Findings from the National Assessment of Educational Progress. C. Reese, K. Miller, J. Mazzeo, J. Dossey, Eds. Washington, DC: Author.

U.S. Department of Education. (1997b). *NAEP 1996 science: Report card for the nation and the states*. C.O'Sullivan, C. Reese, J. Mazzeo, Eds. Washington, DC: Author.

U.S. Department of Education. (1998). *Promising practices: New ways to improve teacher quality*. Available: <www.ed.gov/pubs/PromPractice/index.html> [May 7, 2001].

U.S. Department of Education. (1999). *NAEP 1998 reading report card for the nations and states*. P. Donahue, K. Voelkl, J. Campbell, J. Mazzeo, Eds. Washington, DC: Author.

U. S. Department of Education. (2000). *The initial report of the Secretary on the quality of teacher preparation—Release 2*. Washington, DC: Author.

U.S. Department of Education. (2001). *Removing the barriers to improving teaching*. Washington, DC: Author.

U.S. Department of Education, National Center for Education Statistics. (1996a). *Projections of education statistics to 2007*. LACES Report No. 97-382. Washington, DC: U.S. Government Printing Office.

U.S. Department of Education, National Center for Education Statistics. (1996b). *Pursuing excellence: A study of U.S. eighth-grade mathematics and science teaching, learning, curriculum, and achievement in international context: Initial findings from the Third International Mathematics and Science Study*. LACES Report No. 97-198. Washington, DC: U.S. Government Printing Office.

U.S. Department of Education, National Center for Education Statistics. (1997). *Pursuing excellence: A study of U.S. fourth-grade mathematics and science teaching, learning, curriculum, and achievement international context: Initial findings from the Third International Mathematics and Science Study*. LACES Report No. 97-255. Washington, DC: U.S. Government Printing Office.

U.S. Department of Education, National Center for Education Statistics. (1998). *Pursuing excellence: A study of U.S. twelfth-grade mathematics and science teaching, learning, curriculum, and achievement in international context: Initial findings from the Third International Mathematics and Science Study*. LACES Report No. 98-049. Washington, DC: U.S. Government Printing Office.

U.S. Department of Education, National Center for Education Statistics. (1999). L. Lewis, B. Parsad, N. Carey, N. Bartfai, E. Farris, and B. Smerdon, *Teacher quality: A report on the preparation and qualification of public school teachers*. Washington, DC: Author.

U.S. Department of Education, National Center for Education Statistics. (2000). *Reference and reporting guide for preparing state and institutional reports on the quality of teacher preparation: Title II, Higher Education Act, NCES 2000-089.* Washington, DC: Author.

U. S. Department of Health, Education and Welfare. (1971). *Report on licensure and related health personnel credentialing.* PHEW Publication 72-11. Washington, DC: Author.

U.S. Equal Employment Opportunity Commission, Civil Service Commission, U.S. Department of Labor, and U.S. Department of Justice. (1978). Uniform guidelines on employee selection procedures. *Federal Register, 43*, August 25, 38290-38315.

Van Manen, M. (1991). *The tact of teaching: The meaning of pedagogical thoughtfulness.* London, ON: The Althouse Press.

Waller, W. (1961). *The sociology of teaching.* New York: Russell and Russell.

Wesley, S., Rosenfeld, M., and Sims-Gunzenhauser, A. (1993). *Assessing the classroom performance of beginning teachers: Teachers' judgments of evaluation criteria.* Princeton, NJ: Educational Testing Service.

Wightman, L.F. (1998). *LSAC national longitudinal bar passage study.* Newtown, PA: Law School Admission Council.

Wylie, C., Thompson, M., Sigel, I., and Gitomer, D.H. (2000). *The relationship of teaching, student learning, and NBPTS certification status.* Paper presented at AERA April 2000 New Orleans.

Yocom, C., Schmidt, A., and White, E. (1999). *Profiles of member boards—1998.* Chicago: National Council of State Boards of Nursing.

Youngs, P. (2000). *Annotated bibliography on the relationship between teachers' knowledge/ability at time of licensure and teacher quality.* Commissioned by the Committee on Assessment and Teacher Quality, Center for Education, National Research Council.

Zeichner, K. (2000). Alverno College. In L. Darling-Hammond (Ed.), *Studies in excellence in teacher education: Preparation in the undergraduate years.* Washington, DC: American Association of Colleges of Teacher Education.

APPENDIXES

Appendix A

Public Law 105-244
105th Congress

An Act

To extend the authorization of programs under the Higher Education Act of 1965, and for other purposes. <<NOTE: Oct. 7, 1998 - [H.R. 6]>>

Be it enacted by the Senate and House of Representatives of the United States of America in Congress assembled, <<NOTE: Higher Education Amendments of 1998. Grants. Inter-governmental relations. Loans.>>

Section on Title II—Teacher Quality

TITLE II—TEACHER QUALITY

SEC. 201. TEACHER QUALITY ENHANCEMENT GRANTS.

The Act is amended by inserting after title I (20 U.S.C. 1001 et seq.) the following:

TITLE II—TEACHER QUALITY ENHANCEMENT GRANTS FOR STATES AND PARTNERSHIPS

SEC. 201. PURPOSES; DEFINITIONS. <<NOTE: 20 USC 1021.>>

(a) Purposes.—The purposes of this title are to—
    (1) improve student achievement;
    (2) improve the quality of the current and future teaching force by

improving the preparation of prospective teachers and enhancing professional development activities;

(3)   hold institutions of higher education accountable for preparing teachers who have the necessary teaching skills and are highly competent in the academic content areas in which the teachers plan to teach, such as mathematics, science, English, foreign languages, history, economics, art, civics, Government, and geography, including training in the effective uses of technology in the classroom; and

(4)   recruit highly qualified individuals, including individuals from other occupations, into the teaching force.

(b)   Definitions.—In this title:
(1)   Arts and sciences.—The term 'arts and sciences' means—
(A)   when referring to an organizational unit of an institution of higher education, any academic unit that offers 1 or more academic majors in disciplines or content areas corresponding to the academic subject matter areas in which teachers provide instruction; and
(B)   when referring to a specific academic subject matter area, the disciplines or content areas in which academic majors are offered by the arts and science organizational unit.
(2)   High-need local educational agency.—The term 'high-need local educational agency' means a local educational agency that serves an elementary school or secondary school located in an area in which there is—
(A)   a high percentage of individuals from families with incomes below the poverty line;
(B)   a high percentage of secondary school teachers not teaching in the content area in which the teachers were trained to teach; or
(C)   a high teacher turnover rate.
(3)   Poverty line.—The term 'poverty line' means the poverty line (as defined by the Office of Management and Budget, and revised annually in accordance with section 673(2) of the Community Services Block Grant Act (42 U.S.C. 9902(2)) applicable to a family of the size involved.

SEC. 202. STATE GRANTS. <<NOTE: 20 USC 1022.>>

(a)   In General.—From amounts made available under section 210(1) for a fiscal year, the Secretary is authorized to award grants under this section, on a competitive basis, to eligible States to enable the eligible States to carry out the activities described in subsection (d).

(b)   Eligible State.—
(1)   Definition.—In this title, the term 'eligible State' means—
(A)   the Governor of a State; or

(B) in the case of a State for which the constitution or law of such State designates another individual, entity, or agency in the State to be responsible for teacher certification and preparation activity, such individual, entity, or agency.

(2) Consultation.—The Governor and the individual, entity, or agency designated under paragraph (1) shall consult with the Governor, State board of education, State educational agency, or State agency for higher education, as appropriate, with respect to the activities assisted under this section.

(3) Construction.—Nothing in this subsection shall be construed to negate or supersede the legal authority under State law of any State agency, State entity, or State public official over programs that are under the jurisdiction of the agency, entity, or official.

(c) Application.—To be eligible to receive a grant under this section, an eligible State shall, at the time of the initial grant application, submit an application to the Secretary that—

(1) meets the requirement of this section;

(2) includes a description of how the eligible State intends to use funds provided under this section; and

(3) contains such other information and assurances as the Secretary may require.

(d) Uses of Funds.—An eligible State that receives a grant under this section shall use the grant funds to reform teacher preparation requirements, and to ensure that current and future teachers possess the necessary teaching skills and academic content knowledge in the subject areas in which the teachers are assigned to teach, by carrying out 1 or more of the following activities:

(1) Reforms.—Implementing reforms that hold institutions of higher education with teacher preparation programs accountable for preparing teachers who are highly competent in the academic content areas in which the teachers plan to teach, and possess strong teaching skills, which may include the use of rigorous subject matter competency tests and the requirement that a teacher have an academic major in the subject area, or related discipline, in which the teacher plans to teach.

(2) Certification or licensure requirements.—Reforming teacher certification or licensure requirements to ensure that teachers have the necessary teaching skills and academic content knowledge in the subject areas in which teachers are assigned to teach.

(3) Alternatives to traditional preparation for teaching.—Providing prospective teachers with alternatives to traditional preparation for teaching through programs at colleges of arts and sciences or at nonprofit educational organizations.

(4)   Alternative routes to state certification.—Carrying out programs that—

(A)   include support during the initial teaching experience; and

(B)   establish, expand, or improve alternative routes to State certification of teachers for highly qualified individuals, including mid-career professionals from other occupations, paraprofessionals, former military personnel and recent college graduates with records of academic distinction.

(5)   Recruitment; pay; removal.—Developing and implementing effective mechanisms to ensure that local educational agencies and schools are able to effectively recruit highly qualified teachers, to financially reward those teachers and principals whose students have made significant progress toward high academic performance, such as through performance-based compensation systems and access to ongoing professional development opportunities for teachers and administrators, and to expeditiously remove incompetent or unqualified teachers consistent with procedures to ensure due process for the teachers.

(6)   Social promotion.—Development and implementation of efforts to address the problem of social promotion and to prepare teachers to effectively address the issues raised by ending the practice of social promotion.

(7)   Recruitment.—Activities described in section 204(d).

SEC. 203. PARTNERSHIP GRANTS. <<NOTE: 20 USC 1023.>>

(a)   Grants.—From amounts made available under section 210(2) for a fiscal year, the Secretary is authorized to award grants under this section, on a competitive basis, to eligible partnerships to enable the eligible partnerships to carry out the activities described in subsections (d) and (e).

(b)   Definitions.—

(1)   Eligible partnerships.—In this title, the term 'eligible partnerships' means an entity that—

(A)   shall include—

(i)   a partner institution;

(ii)   a school of arts and sciences; and

(iii)   a high-need local educational agency; and

(B)   may include a Governor, State educational agency, the State board of education, the State agency for higher education, an institution of higher education not described in subparagraph (A), a public charter school, a public or private elementary school or secondary school, a public or private nonprofit educational organization, a business, a teacher organization, or a prekindergarten program.

(2)   Partner institution.—In this section, the term 'partner institution'

means a private independent or State-supported public institution of higher education, the teacher training program of which demonstrates that—

    (A) graduates from the teacher training program exhibit strong performance on State-determined qualifying assessments for new teachers through—

        (i) demonstrating that 80 percent or more of the graduates of the program who intend to enter the field of teaching have passed all of the applicable State qualification assessments for new teachers, which shall include an assessment of each prospective teacher's subject matter knowledge in the content area or areas in which the teacher intends to teach; or

        (ii) being ranked among the highest-performing teacher preparation programs in the State as determined by the State—

            (I) using criteria consistent with the requirements for the State report card under section 207(b); and

            (II) using the State report card on teacher preparation required under section 207(b), after the first publication of such report card and for every year thereafter; or

    (B) the teacher training program requires all the students of the program to participate in intensive clinical experience, to meet high academic standards, and—

        (i) in the case of secondary school candidates, to successfully complete an academic major in the subject area in which the candidate intends to teach or to demonstrate competence through a high level of performance in relevant content areas; and

        (ii) in the case of elementary school candidates, to successfully complete an academic major in the arts and sciences or to demonstrate competence through a high level of performance in core academic subject areas.

    (c) Application.—Each eligible partnership desiring a grant under this section shall submit an application to the Secretary at such time, in such manner, and accompanied by such information as the Secretary may require. Each such application shall—

    (1) contain a needs assessment of all the partners with respect to teaching and learning and a description of how the partnership will coordinate with other teacher training or professional development programs, and how the activities of the partnership will be consistent with State, local, and other education reform activities that promote student achievement;

    (2) contain a resource assessment that describes the resources available to the partnership, the intended use of the grant funds, including a description of how the grant funds will be fairly distributed in accordance with subsection (f), and the commitment of the resources of the partnership

to the activities assisted under this title, including financial support, faculty participation, time commitments, and continuation of the activities when the grant ends; and

    (3)   contain a description of—

        (A) how the partnership will meet the purposes of this title;

        (B) how the partnership will carry out the activities required under subsection (d) and any permissible activities under subsection (e); and

        (C) the partnership's evaluation plan pursuant to section 206(b).

(d)   Required Uses of Funds.—An eligible partnership that receives a grant under this section shall use the grant funds to carry out the following activities:

    (1) Reforms.—Implementing reforms within teacher preparation programs to hold the programs accountable for preparing teachers who are highly competent in the academic content areas in which the teachers plan to teach, and for promoting strong teaching skills, including working with a school of arts and sciences and integrating reliable research-based teaching methods into the curriculum, which curriculum shall include programs designed to successfully integrate technology into teaching and learning.

    (2) Clinical experience and interaction.—Providing sustained and high quality preservice clinical experience including the mentoring of prospective teachers by veteran teachers, and substantially increasing interaction between faculty at institutions of higher education and new and experienced teachers, principals, and other administrators at elementary schools or secondary schools, and providing support, including preparation time, for such interaction.

    (3) Professional development.—Creating opportunities for enhanced and ongoing professional development that improves the academic content knowledge of teachers in the subject areas in which the teachers are certified to teach or in which the teachers are working toward certification to teach, and that promotes strong teaching skills.

(e)   Allowable Uses of Funds.—An eligible partnership that receives a grant under this section may use such funds to carry out the following activities:

    (1) Teacher preparation and parent involvement.—Preparing teachers to work with diverse student populations, including individuals with disabilities and limited English proficient individuals, and involving parents in the teacher preparation program reform process.

    (2) Dissemination and coordination.—Broadly disseminating information on effective practices used by the partnership, and coordinating with the activities of the Governor, State board of education, State higher education agency, and State educational agency, as appropriate.

    (3) Managerial and leadership skills.—Developing and implement-

ing proven mechanisms to provide principals and superintendents with effective managerial and leadership skills that result in increased student achievement.

(4) Teacher recruitment.—Activities described in section 204(d).

(f) Special Rule.—No individual member of an eligible partnership shall retain more than 50 percent of the funds made available to the partnership under this section.

(g) Construction.—Nothing in this section shall be construed to prohibit an eligible partnership from using grant funds to coordinate with the activities of more than one Governor, State board of education, State educational agency, local educational agency, or State agency for higher education.

SEC. 204. TEACHER RECRUITMENT GRANTS. <<NOTE: 20 USC 1024.>>

(a) Program Authorized.—From amounts made available under section 210(3) for a fiscal year, the Secretary is authorized to award grants, on a competitive basis, to eligible applicants to enable the eligible applicants to carry out activities described in subsection (d).

(b) Eligible Applicant Defined.—In this title, the term 'eligible applicant' means—

    (1) an eligible State described in section 202(b); or

    (2) an eligible partnership described in section 203(b).

(c) Application.—Any eligible applicant desiring to receive a grant under this section shall submit an application to the Secretary at such time, in such form, and containing such information as the Secretary may require, including—

    (1) a description of the assessment that the eligible applicant, and the other entities with whom the eligible applicant will carry out the grant activities, have undertaken to determine the most critical needs of the participating high-need local educational agencies;

    (2) a description of the activities the eligible applicant will carry out with the grant; and

    (3) a description of the eligible applicant's plan for continuing the activities carried out with the grant, once Federal funding ceases.

(d) Uses of Funds.—Each eligible applicant receiving a grant under this section shall use the grant funds—

    (1)(A) to award scholarships to help students pay the costs of tuition, room, board, and other expenses of completing a teacher preparation program;

(B) to provide support services, if needed to enable scholarship recipients to complete postsecondary education programs; and

(C) for followup services provided to former scholarship recipients during the recipient's first 3 years of teaching; or

(2)   to develop and implement effective mechanisms to ensure that high-need local educational agencies and schools are able to effectively recruit highly qualified teachers.

(e) Service Requirements.—The Secretary shall establish such requirements as the Secretary finds necessary to ensure that recipients of scholarships under this section who complete teacher education programs subsequently teach in a high-need local educational agency, for a period of time equivalent to the period for which the recipients receive scholarship assistance, or repay the amount of the scholarship. The Secretary shall use any such repayments to carry out additional activities under this section.

SEC. 205. ADMINISTRATIVE PROVISIONS. <<NOTE: 20 USC 1025.>>

(a) Duration; One-Time Awards; Payments.—

(1) Duration.—

(A) Eligible states and eligible applicants.—Grants awarded to eligible States and eligible applicants under this title shall be awarded for a period not to exceed 3 years.

(B) Eligible partnerships.—Grants awarded to eligible partnerships under this title shall be awarded for a period of 5 years.

(2) One-time award.—An eligible State and an eligible partnership may receive a grant under each of sections 202, 203, and 204 only once.

(3) Payments.—The Secretary shall make annual payments of grant funds awarded under this part.

(b) Peer Review.—

(1) Panel.—The Secretary shall provide the applications submitted under this title to a peer review panel for evaluation. With respect to each application, the peer review panel shall initially recommend the application for funding or for disapproval.

(2) Priority.—In recommending applications to the Secretary for funding under this title, the panel shall—

(A) with respect to grants under section 202, give priority to eligible States serving States that—

(i)   have initiatives to reform State teacher certification requirements that are designed to ensure that current and future teachers possess the necessary teaching skills and academic content knowledge in the subject areas in which the   teachers are certified or licensed to teach;

(ii)   include innovative reforms to hold institutions of higher education with teacher preparation programs accountable for preparing teachers who are highly competent in the academic content area in which the teachers plan to teach and have strong teaching skills; or

(iii)   involve the development of innovative efforts aimed at reducing the shortage of highly qualified teachers in high poverty urban and rural areas;

(B)   with respect to grants under section 203—

(i)   give priority to applications from eligible partnerships that involve businesses; and

(ii)   take into consideration—

(I)   providing an equitable geographic distribution of the grants throughout the United States; and

(II)   the potential of the proposed activities for creating improvement and positive change.

(3)   Secretarial selection.—The Secretary shall determine, based on the peer review process, which application shall receive funding and the amounts of the grants. In determining grant amounts, the Secretary shall take into account the total amount of funds available for all grants under this title and the types of activities proposed to be carried out.

(c)   Matching Requirements.—

(1)   State grants.—Each eligible State receiving a grant under section 202 or 204 shall provide, from non-Federal sources, an amount equal to 50 percent of the amount of the grant (in cash or in kind) to carry out the activities supported by the grant.

(2)   Partnership grants.—Each eligible partnership receiving a grant under section 203 or 204 shall provide, from non-Federal sources (in cash or in kind), an amount equal to 25 percent of the grant for the first year of the grant, 35 percent of the grant for the second year of the grant, and 50 percent of the grant for each succeeding year of the grant.

(d)   Limitation on Administrative Expenses.—An eligible State or eligible partnership that receives a grant under this title may not use more than 2 percent of the grant funds for purposes of administering the grant.

(e)   Teacher Qualifications Provided to Parents Upon Request.—Any local educational agency or school that benefits from the activities assisted under this title shall make available, upon request and in an understandable and uniform format, to any parent of a student attending any school served by the local educational agency, information regarding the qualification of the student's classroom teacher with regard to the subject matter in which the teacher provides instruction. The local educational agency shall inform parents that the parents are entitled to receive the information upon request.

SEC. 206. ACCOUNTABILITY AND EVALUATION. <<*NOTE: 20 USC 1026.*>>

(a) State Grant Accountability Report.—An eligible State that receives a grant under section 202 shall submit an annual accountability report to the Secretary, the Committee on Labor and Human Resources of the Senate, and the Committee on Education and the Workforce of the House of Representatives. Such report shall include a description of the degree to which the eligible State, in using funds provided under such section, has made substantial progress in meeting the following goals:

(1) Student achievement.—Increasing student achievement for all students as defined by the eligible State.

(2) Raising standards.—Raising the State academic standards required to enter the teaching profession, including, where appropriate, through the use of incentives to incorporate the requirement of an academic major in the subject, or related discipline, in which the teacher plans to teach.

(3) Initial certification or licensure.—Increasing success in the pass rate for initial State teacher certification or licensure, or increasing the numbers of highly qualified individuals being certified or licensed as teachers through alternative programs.

(4) Core academic subjects.—

(A) Secondary school classes.—Increasing the percentage of secondary school classes taught in core academic subject areas by teachers—

(i) with academic majors in those areas or in a related field;

(ii) who can demonstrate a high level of competence through rigorous academic subject area tests; or

(iii) who can demonstrate competence through a high level of performance in relevant content areas.

(B) Elementary school classes.—Increasing the percentage of elementary school classes taught by teachers—

(i) with academic majors in the arts and sciences; or

(ii) who can demonstrate competence through a high level of performance in core academic subjects.

(5) Decreasing teacher shortages.—Decreasing shortages of qualified teachers in poor urban and rural areas.

(6) Increasing opportunities for professional development.—Increasing opportunities for enhanced and ongoing professional development that improves the academic content knowledge of teachers in the subject areas in

which the teachers are certified or licensed to teach or in which the teachers are working toward certification or licensure to teach, and that promotes strong teaching skills.

(7) Technology integration.—Increasing the number of teachers prepared to integrate technology in the classroom.

(b) Eligible Partnership Evaluation.—Each eligible partnership receiving a grant under section 203 shall establish and include in the application submitted under section 203(c), an evaluation plan that includes strong performance objectives. The plan shall include objectives and measures for—

(1) increased student achievement for all students as measured by the partnership;

(2) increased teacher retention in the first 3 years of a teacher's career;

(3) increased success in the pass rate for initial State certification or licensure of teachers; and

(4) increased percentage of secondary school classes taught in core academic subject areas by teachers—

(A) with academic majors in the areas or in a related field; and

(B) who can demonstrate a high level of competence through rigorous academic subject area tests or who can demonstrate competence through a high level of performance in relevant content areas;

(5) increasing the percentage of elementary school classes taught by teachers with academic majors in the arts and sciences or who demonstrate competence through a high level of performance in core academic subject areas; and

(6) increasing the number of teachers trained in technology.

(c) Revocation of Grant.—

(1) Report.—Each eligible State or eligible partnership receiving a grant under this title shall report annually on the progress of the eligible State or eligible partnership toward meeting the purposes of this title and the goals, objectives, and measures described in subsections (a) and (b).

(2) Revocation.—

(A) Eligible states and eligible applicants.—If the Secretary determines that an eligible State or eligible applicant is not making substantial progress in meeting the purposes, goals, objectives, and measures, as appropriate, by the end of the second year of a grant under this title, then the grant payment shall not be made for the third year of the grant.

(B) Eligible partnerships.—If the Secretary determines that an eligible partnership is not making substantial progress in meeting the purposes, goals, objectives, and measures, as appropriate, by the end of the third year of a grant under this title, then the grant payments shall not be made for any succeeding year of the grant.

(d) Evaluation and Dissemination.—The Secretary shall evaluate the activities funded under this title and report the Secretary's findings regarding the activities to the Committee on Labor and Human Resources of the Senate and the Committee on Education and the Workforce of the House of Representatives. The Secretary shall broadly disseminate successful practices developed by eligible States and eligible partnerships under this title, and shall broadly disseminate information regarding such practices that were found to be ineffective.

SEC. 207. <<NOTE: 20 USC 1027.>> ACCOUNTABILITY FOR PROGRAMS THAT PREPARE TEACHERS.

(a) <<NOTE: Deadline.>> Development of Definitions and Reporting Methods.—Within 9 months of the date of enactment of the Higher Education Amendments of 1998, the Commissioner of the National Center for Education Statistics, in consultation with States and institutions of higher education, shall develop key definitions for terms, and uniform reporting methods (including the key definitions for the consistent reporting of pass rates), related to the performance of elementary school and secondary school teacher preparation programs.

(b) State Report Card on the Quality of Teacher Preparation.—Each State that receives funds under this Act shall provide to the Secretary, within 2 years of the date of enactment of the Higher Education Amendments of 1998, and annually thereafter, in a uniform and comprehensible manner that conforms with the definitions and methods established in subsection (a), a State report card on the quality of teacher preparation in the State, which shall include at least the following:

(1) A description of the teacher certification and licensure assessments, and any other certification and licensure requirements, used by the State.

(2) The standards and criteria that prospective teachers must meet in order to attain initial teacher certification or licensure and to be certified or licensed to teach particular subjects or in particular grades within the State.

(3) A description of the extent to which the assessments and requirements described in paragraph (1) are aligned with the State's standards and assessments for students.

(4) The percentage of teaching candidates who passed each of the assessments used by the State for teacher certification and licensure, and the passing score on each assessment that determines whether a candidate has passed that assessment.

(5) The percentage of teaching candidates who passed each of the

assessments used by the State for teacher certification and licensure, disaggregated and ranked, by the teacher preparation program in that State from which the teacher candidate received the candidate's most recent degree, which shall be made available widely and publicly.

(6) Information on the extent to which teachers in the State are given waivers of State certification or licensure requirements, including the proportion of such teachers distributed across high- and low-poverty school districts and across subject areas.

(7) A description of each State's alternative routes to teacher certification, if any, and the percentage of teachers certified through alternative certification routes who pass State teacher certification or licensure assessments.

(8) For each State, a description of proposed criteria for assessing the performance of teacher preparation programs within institutions of higher education in the State, including indicators of teacher candidate knowledge and skills.

(9) Information on the extent to which teachers or prospective teachers in each State are required to take examinations or other assessments of their subject matter knowledge in the area or areas in which the teachers provide instruction, the standards established for passing any such assessments, and the extent to which teachers or prospective teachers are required to receive a passing score on such assessments in order to teach in specific subject areas or grade levels.

(c) Initial Report.—

(1) <<NOTE: Deadline.>> In general.—Each State that receives funds under this Act, not later than 6 months of the date of enactment of the Higher Education Amendments of 1998 and in a uniform and comprehensible manner, shall submit to the Secretary the information described in paragraphs (1), (5), and

(6) of subsection (b). <<NOTE: Records.>> Such information shall be compiled by the Secretary and submitted to the Committee on Labor and Human Resources of the Senate and the Committee on Education and the Workforce of the House of Representatives not later than 9 months after the date of enactment of the Higher Education Amendments of 1998.

(2) Construction.—Nothing in this subsection shall be construed to require a State to gather information that is not in the possession of the State or the teacher preparation programs in the State, or readily available to the State or teacher preparation programs.

(d) Report of the Secretary on the Quality of Teacher Preparation.—

(1) <<NOTE: Publication. Public information.>> Report card.—The Secretary shall provide to Congress, and publish and make widely available,

a report card on teacher qualifications and preparation in the United States, including all the information reported in paragraphs (1) through (9) of subsection (b)   Such report shall identify States for which eligible States   and eligible partnerships received a grant under this title. Such report shall be so provided, published and made available not later than 2 years 6 months after the date of enactment of the Higher Education Amendments of 1998 and annually thereafter.

    (2)   Report to Congress.—The Secretary shall report to Congress—

        (A)   a comparison of States' efforts to improve teaching quality; and

        (B)   regarding the national mean and median scores on any standardized test that is used in more than 1 State for teacher certification or licensure.

    (3)   <<NOTE: Records. Publication.>> Special rule.—In the case of teacher preparation programs with fewer than 10 graduates taking any single initial teacher certification or licensure assessment during an academic year, the Secretary shall collect and publish information with respect to an average pass rate on State certification or licensure assessments taken over a 3-year period.

    (e)   <<NOTE: Records. Publication.>> Coordination.—The Secretary, to the extent practicable, shall coordinate the information collected and published under this title among States for individuals who took State teacher certification or licensure assessments in a State other than the State in which the individual received the individual's most recent degree.

    (f)   Institutional Report Cards on the Quality of Teacher Preparation.—

    (1)   <<NOTE: Deadline. Reports. Public information.>> Report card.—Each institution of higher education that conducts a teacher preparation program that enrolls students receiving Federal assistance under this Act, not later than 18 months after the date of enactment of the Higher Education Amendments of 1998 and annually thereafter, shall report to the State and the general public, in a uniform and comprehensible manner that conforms with the definitions and methods established under subsection (a), the following information:

        (A)   Pass rate.—

            (i)   For the most recent year for which the information is available, the pass rate of the institution's graduates on the teacher certification or licensure assessments of the State in which the institution is located, but only for those students who took those assessments within 3 years of completing the program.

            (ii)   A comparison of the program's pass rate with the average pass rate for programs in the State.

(iii)   In the case of teacher preparation programs with fewer than 10 graduates taking any single initial teacher certification or licensure assessment during an academic year, the institution shall collect and publish information with respect to an average pass rate on State certification or licensure assessments taken over a 3-year period.

(B)   Program information.—The number of students in the program, the average number of hours of supervised practice teaching required for those in the program, and the faculty-student ratio in supervised practice teaching.

(C)   Statement.—In States that approve or accredit teacher education programs, a statement of whether the institution's program is so approved or accredited.

(D)   Designation as low-performing.—Whether the program has been designated as low-performing by the State under section 208(a).

(2)   Requirement.—The information described in paragraph (1) shall be reported through publications such as school catalogs and promotional materials sent to potential applicants, secondary school guidance counselors, and prospective employers of the institution's program graduates.

(3)   Fines.—In addition to the actions authorized in section 487(c), the Secretary may impose a fine not to exceed $25,000 on an institution of higher education for failure to provide the information described in this subsection in a timely or accurate manner.

SEC. 208. STATE FUNCTIONS. <<NOTE: 20 USC 1028.>>

(a)   <<NOTE: Deadline. Procedures.>> State Assessment.—In order to receive funds under this Act, a State, not later than 2 years after the date of enactment of the Higher Education Amendments of 1998, shall have in place a procedure to identify, and assist, through the provision of technical assistance, low-performing programs of teacher preparation within institutions of higher education. <<NOTE: Records.>> Such State shall provide the Secretary an annual list of such low-performing institutions that includes an identification of those institutions at risk of being placed on such list. Such levels of performance shall be determined solely by the State and may include criteria based upon information collected pursuant to this title. Such assessment shall be described in the report under section 207(b).

(b)   Termination of Eligibility.—Any institution of higher education that offers a program of teacher preparation in which the State has withdrawn the State's approval or terminated the State's financial support due to the low performance of the institution's teacher preparation program based upon the State assessment described in subsection (a)—

(1)   shall be ineligible for any funding for professional development activities awarded by the Department of Education; and

(2)   shall not be permitted to accept or enroll any student that receives aid under title IV of this Act in the institution's teacher preparation program.

(c)   Negotiated Rulemaking.—If the Secretary develops any regulations implementing subsection (b)(2), the Secretary shall submit such proposed regulations to a negotiated rulemaking process, which shall include representatives of States, institutions of higher education, and educational and student organizations.

SEC. 209. GENERAL PROVISIONS. <<NOTE: 20 USC 1029.>>

(a)   Methods.—In complying with sections 207 and 208, the Secretary shall ensure that States and institutions of higher education use fair and equitable methods in reporting and that the reporting methods protect the privacy of individuals.

(b)   Special Rule.—For each State in which there are no State certification or licensure assessments, or for States that do not set minimum performance levels on those assessments—

(1)   the Secretary shall, to the extent practicable, collect data comparable to the data required under this title from States, local educational agencies, institutions of higher education, or other entities that administer such assessments to teachers or prospective teachers; and

(2)   notwithstanding any other provision of this title, the Secretary shall use such data to carry out requirements of this title related to assessments or pass rates.

(c)   Limitations.—

(1)   Federal control prohibited.—Nothing in this title shall be construed to permit, allow, encourage, or authorize any Federal control over any aspect of any private, religious, or home school, whether or not a home school is treated as a private school or home school under State law. This section shall not be construed to prohibit private, religious, or home schools from participation in programs or services under this title.

(2)   No change in state control encouraged or required.— Nothing in this title shall be construed to encourage or require any change in a State's treatment of any private, religious, or home school, whether or not a home school is treated as a private school or home school under State law.

(3)   National system of teacher certification prohibited.— Nothing in this title shall be construed to permit, allow, encourage, or authorize the Secretary to establish or support any national system of teacher certification.

SEC. 210. AUTHORIZATION OF APPROPRIATIONS. <<NOTE: 20 USC 1030.>>

"There are authorized to be appropriated to carry out this title $300,000,000 for fiscal year 1999 and such sums as may be necessary for each of the 4 succeeding fiscal years, of which—

(1) 45 percent shall be available for each fiscal year to award grants under section 202;

(2) 45 percent shall be available for each fiscal year to award grants under section 203; and

(3) 10 percent shall be available for each fiscal year to award grants under section 204."

Appendix B

Teaching Standards of the Interstate New Teacher Assessment and Support Consortium (INTASC), National Council for the Accreditation of Teacher Education (NCATE), and National Board for Professional Teaching Standards (NBPTS)

INTERSTATE NEW TEACHER ASSESSMENT AND SUPPORT CONSORTIUM[1]

The Interstate New Teacher Assessment and Support Consortium (INTASC) is a consortium of state education agencies, higher education institutions, and national educational organizations dedicated to the reform of the education, licensing, and on-going professional development of teachers. Created in 1987, INTASC's primary constituency is state education agencies responsible for teacher licensing and professional development. Its work is guided by one basic premise: An effective teacher must be able to integrate content knowledge with pedagogical understanding to assure that all students learn and perform at high levels.

Model Standards for Beginning Teachers

The INTASC model core standards for licensing teachers represent those principles which should be present in all teaching regardless of the subject or grade level taught and serve as a framework for the systemic reform of teacher preparation and professional development. The core standards are currently being translated into standards for discipline-specific teaching.

Standards for teaching mathematics were released in Spring 1995, and a draft of standards in English/language arts will soon be released. INTASC recently began developing standards for teaching science. In the next five years

---

[1]Excerpts from the Council of Chief State School Officers, 1998. Used by permission of author.

INTASC will continue crafting model standards for teaching in history/social studies, the arts, elementary education, and special education.

INTASC Core Standards

Principle #1: The Teacher Understands the Central Concepts, Tools of Inquiry, and Structures of the Discipline(s) He or She Teaches and Can Create Learning Experiences That Make These Aspects of Subject Matter Meaningful for Students.

Knowledge   The teacher understands major concepts, assumptions, debates, processes of inquiry, and ways of knowing that are central to the discipline(s) s/he teaches.

The teacher understands how students' conceptual frameworks and their misconceptions for an area of knowledge can influence their learning.

The teacher can relate his/her disciplinary knowledge to other subject areas.

Dispositions   The teacher realizes that subject matter knowledge is not a fixed body of facts but is complex and ever evolving. S/he seeks to keep abreast of new ideas and understandings in the field.

The teacher appreciates multiple perspectives and conveys to learners how knowledge is developed from the vantagepoint of the knower.

The teacher has enthusiasm for the discipline(s) s/he teaches and sees connections to everyday life.

The teacher is committed to continuous learning and engages in professional discourse about subject matter knowledge and children's learning of the discipline.

Performances   The teacher effectively uses multiple representations and explanations of disciplinary concepts that capture key ideas and link them to students' prior understandings.

The teacher can represent and use differing viewpoints, theories, "ways of knowing" and methods of inquiry in his/her teaching of subject matter concepts.

The teacher can evaluate teaching resources and curriculum materials for their comprehensiveness, accuracy, and usefulness for representing particular ideas and concepts.

The teacher engages students in generating knowledge and testing hypotheses according to the methods of inquiry and standards of evidence used in the discipline.

The teacher develops and uses curricula that encourage students to see, question, and interpret ideas from diverse perspectives.

The teacher can create interdisciplinary learning experiences that allow students to integrate knowledge, skills, and methods of inquiry from several subject areas.

Principle #2: The Teacher Understands How Children Learn and Develop, and Can Provide Learning Opportunities That Support Their Intellectual, Social and Personal Development.

Knowledge The teacher understands how learning occurs—how students construct knowledge, acquire skills, and develop habits of mind—and knows how to use instructional strategies that promote student learning.

The teacher understands that students' physical, social, emotional, moral, and cognitive development influence learning and knows how to address these factors when making instructional decisions.

The teacher is aware of expected developmental progressions and ranges of individual variation within each domain (physical, social, emotional, moral, and cognitive), can identify levels of readiness in learning, and understands how development in any one domain may affect performance in others.

Dispositions The teacher appreciates individual variation within each area of development, shows respect for the diverse talents of all learners, and is committed to help them develop self-confidence and competence.

The teacher is disposed to use students' strengths as a basis for growth and their errors as an opportunity for learning.

Performances The teacher assesses individual and group performance in order to design instruction that meets learners' current needs in each domain (cognitive, social, emotional, moral, and physical) and that leads to the next level of development.

The teacher stimulates student reflection on prior knowledge and links new ideas to already familiar ideas, making connections to students' experiences, providing opportunities for active engagement, manipulation, and testing of ideas and materials, and encouraging students to assume responsibility for shaping their learning tasks.

The teacher accesses students' thinking and experiences as a basis for instructional activities by, for example, encouraging discussion, listening and responding to group interaction, and eliciting samples of student thinking orally and in writing.

Principle #3: The Teacher Understands How Students Differ in Their Approaches to Learning and Creates Instructional Opportunities That Are Adapted to Diverse Learners.

Knowledge The teacher understands and can identify differences in approaches to learning and performance, including different learning styles, multiple intelligences, and performance modes, and can design instruction that helps use students' strengths as the basis for growth.

The teacher knows about areas of exceptionality in learning—including learning disabilities, visual and perceptual difficulties, and special physical or mental challenges.

The teacher knows about the process of second language acquisition and about strategies to support the learning of students whose first language is not English.

The teacher understands how students, learning is influenced by individual experiences, talents, and prior learning, as well as language, culture, family, and community values.

The teacher has a well-grounded framework for understanding cultural and community diversity and knows how to learn about and incorporate students' experiences, cultures, and community resources into instruction.

Dispositions The teacher believes that all children can learn at high levels and persists in helping all children achieve success.

The teacher appreciates and values human diversity, shows respect for students' varied talents and perspectives, and is committed to the pursuit of "individually configured excellence."

The teacher respects students as individuals with differing personal and family backgrounds and various skills, talents, and interests.

The teacher is sensitive to community and cultural norms.

The teacher makes students feel valued for their potential as people and helps them learn to value each other.

Performances The teacher identifies and designs instruction appropriate to students' stages of development, learning styles, strengths, and needs.

The teacher uses teaching approaches that are sensitive to the multiple experiences of learners and that address different learning and performance modes.

The teacher makes appropriate provisions (in terms of time and circumstances for work, tasks assigned, communication, and response modes) for individual students who have particular learning differences or needs.

The teacher can identify when and how to access appropriate services or resources to meet exceptional learning needs.

The teacher seeks to understand students' families, cultures, and communities and uses this information as a basis for connecting instruction to students' experiences (e.g. drawing explicit connections between subject matter and community matters, making assignments that can be related to students' experiences and cultures).

The teacher brings multiple perspectives to the discussion of subject matter, including attention to students' personal, family, and community experiences and cultural norms.

The teacher creates a learning community in which individual differences are respected.

Principle #4: The Teacher Understands and Uses a Variety of Instructional Strategies to Encourage Students' Development of Critical Thinking, Problem Solving, and Performance Skills.

__Knowledge__   The teacher understands the cognitive processes associated with various kinds of learning (e.g. critical and creative thinking, problem structuring and problem solving, invention, memorization and recall) and how these processes can be stimulated.

The teacher understands principles and techniques, along with advantages and limitations, associated with various instructional strategies (e.g. cooperative learning, direct instruction, discovery learning, whole group discussion, independent study, interdisciplinary instruction).

The teacher knows how to enhance learning through the use of a wide variety of materials as well as human and technological resources (e.g. computers, audio-visual technologies, videotapes and discs, local experts, primary documents and artifacts, texts, reference books, literature, and other print resources).

__Dispositions__   The teacher values the development of students' critical thinking, independent problem solving, and performance capabilities.

The teacher values flexibility and reciprocity in the teaching process as necessary for adapting instruction to student responses, ideas, and needs.

__Performances__   The teacher carefully evaluates how to achieve learning goals, choosing alternative teaching strategies and materials to achieve different instructional purposes and to meet student needs (e.g. developmental stages, prior knowledge, learning styles, and interests).

The teacher uses multiple teaching and learning strategies to engage students in active learning opportunities that promote the development of critical thinking, problem solving, and performance capabilities and that help students assume responsibility for identifying and using learning resources.

The teacher constantly monitors and adjusts strategies in response to learner feedback.

The teacher varies his or her role in the instructional process (e.g. instructor, facilitator, coach, audience) in relation to the content and purposes of instruction and the needs of students.

The teacher develops a variety of clear, accurate presentations and representations of concepts, using alternative explanations to assist students' understanding and presenting diverse perspectives to encourage critical thinking.

Principle #5: The Teacher Uses an Understanding of Individual and Group Motivation and Behavior to Create a Learning Environment That Encourages Positive Social Interaction, Active Engagement in Learning, and Self-Motivation.

Knowledge The teacher can use knowledge about human motivation and behavior drawn from the foundational sciences of psychology, anthropology, and sociology to develop strategies for organizing and supporting individual and group work.

The teacher understands how social groups function and influence people and how people influence groups.

The teacher knows how to help people work productively and cooperatively with each other in complex social settings.

The teacher understands the principles of effective classroom management and can use a range of strategies to promote positive relationships, cooperation, and purposeful learning in the classroom.

The teacher recognizes factors and situations that are likely to promote or diminish intrinsic motivation and knows how to help students become self-motivated.

Dispositions The teacher takes responsibility for establishing a positive climate in the classroom and participates in maintaining such a climate in the school as a whole.

The teacher understands how participation supports commitment and is committed to the expression and use of democratic values in the classroom.

The teacher values the role of students in promoting each other's learning and recognizes the importance of peer relationships in establishing a climate of learning.

The teacher recognizes the value of intrinsic motivation to students' lifelong growth and learning.

The teacher is committed to the continuous development of individual students' abilities and considers how different motivational strategies are likely to encourage this development for each student.

Performances The teacher creates a smoothly functioning learning community in which students assume responsibility for themselves and one another, participate in decisionmaking, work collaboratively and independently, and engage in purposeful learning activities.

The teacher engages students in individual and cooperative learning activities that help them develop the motivation to achieve, by, for example, relating lessons to students' personal interests, allowing students to have choices in their learning, and leading students to ask questions and pursue problems that are meaningful to them.

The teacher organizes, allocates, and manages the resources of time, space, activities, and attention to provide active and equitable engagement of students in productive tasks.

The teacher maximizes the amount of class time spent in learning by creating expectations and processes for communication and behavior along with a physical setting conducive to classroom goals.

The teacher helps the group to develop shared values and expectations for student interactions, academic discussions, and individual and group responsibility that create a positive classroom climate of openness, mutual respect, support, and inquiry.

The teacher analyzes the classroom environment and makes decisions and adjustments to enhance social relationships, student motivation and engagement, and productive work.

The teacher organizes, prepares students for, and monitors independent and group work that allows for full and varied participation of all individuals.

Principle #6: The Teacher Uses Knowledge of Effective Verbal, Nonverbal, and Media Communication Techniques to Foster Active Inquiry, Collaboration, and Supportive Interaction in the Classroom.

Knowledge   The teacher understands communication theory, language development, and the role of language in learning.

The teacher understands how cultural and gender differences can affect communication in the classroom.

The teacher recognizes the importance of nonverbal as well as verbal communication.

The teacher knows about and can use effective verbal, nonverbal, and media communication techniques.

Dispositions   The teacher recognizes the power of language for fostering self-expression, identity development, and learning.

The teacher values many ways in which people seek to communicate and encourages many modes of communication in the classroom.

The teacher is a thoughtful and responsive listener.

The teacher appreciates the cultural dimensions of communication, responds appropriately, and seeks to foster culturally sensitive communication by and among all students in the class.

Performances   The teacher models effective communication strategies in conveying ideas and information and in asking questions (e.g. monitoring the effects of messages, restating ideas and drawing connections, using visual, aural, and kinesthetic cues, being sensitive to nonverbal cues given and received).

The teacher supports and expands learner expression in speaking, writing, and other media.

The teacher knows how to ask questions and stimulate discussion in different ways for particular purposes, for example, probing for learner understanding, helping students articulate their ideas and thinking processes, promoting risk-taking and problem solving, facilitating factual recall, encouraging convergent and divergent thinking, stimulating curiosity, helping students to question.

The teacher communicates in ways that demonstrate a sensitivity to cultural and gender differences (e.g. appropriate use of eye contact, interpretation of body language and verbal statements, acknowledgment of and responsiveness to different modes of communication and participation).

The teacher knows how to use a variety of media communication tools, including audio-visual aids and computers, to enrich learning opportunities.

Principle #7: The Teacher Plans Instruction Based Upon Knowledge of Subject Matter, Students, the Community, and Curriculum Goals.

Knowledge The teacher understands learning theory, subject matter, curriculum development, and student development and knows how to use this knowledge in planning instruction to meet curriculum goals.

The teacher knows how to take contextual considerations (instructional materials, individual student interests, needs, aptitudes, and community resources) into account in planning instruction that creates an effective bridge between curriculum goals and students' experiences.

The teacher knows when and how to adjust plans based on student responses and other contingencies.

Dispositions The teacher values both long-term and short-term planning.

The teacher believes that plans must always be open to adjustment and revision based on student needs and changing circumstances.

The teacher values planning as a collegial activity.

Performances As an individual and a member of a team, the teacher selects and creates learning experiences that are appropriate for curriculum goals, relevant to learners, and based upon principles of effective instruction (e.g. that activate students' prior knowledge, anticipate preconceptions, encourage exploration and problem solving, and build new skills on those previously acquired).

The teacher plans for learning opportunities that recognize and address variation in learning styles and performance modes.

The teacher creates lessons and activities that operate at multiple levels to meet the developmental and individual needs of diverse learners and help each progress.

The teacher creates short-range and long-term plans that are linked to student needs and performance and adapts the plans to ensure and capitalize on student progress and motivation.

The teacher responds to unanticipated sources of input, evaluates plans in relation to short- and long-range goals, and systematically adjusts plans to meet student needs and enhance learning.

Principle #8: The Teacher Understands and Uses Formal and Informal Assessment Strategies to Evaluate and Ensure the Continuous Intellectual, Social, and Physical Development of the Learner.

__Knowledge__ The teacher understands the characteristics, uses, advantages, and limitations of different types of assessments (e.g. criterion-referenced and norm-referenced instruments, traditional standardized and performance-based tests, observation systems, and assessments of student work) for evaluating how students learn, what they know and are able to do, and what kinds of experiences will support their further growth and development.

The teacher knows how to select, construct, and use assessment strategies and instruments appropriate to the learning outcomes being evaluated and to other diagnostic purposes.

The teacher understands measurement theory and assessment-related issues, such as validity, reliability, bias, and scoring concerns.

__Dispositions__ The teacher values ongoing assessment as essential to the instructional process and recognizes that many different assessment strategies, accurately and systematically used, are necessary for monitoring and promoting student learning.

The teacher is committed to using assessment to identify student strengths and promote student growth rather than to deny students access to learning opportunities.

__Performances__ The teacher appropriately uses a variety of formal and informal assessment techniques (e.g. observation, portfolios of student work, teacher-made tests, performance tasks, projects, student self-assessments, peer assessment, and standardized tests) to enhance her or his knowledge of learners, evaluate students' progress and performances, and modify teaching and learning strategies.

The teacher solicits and uses information about students' experiences, learning behavior, needs, and progress from parents, other colleagues, and the students themselves.

The teacher uses assessment strategies to involve learners in self-assessment activities, to help them become aware of their strengths and needs, and to encourage them to set personal goals for learning.

The teacher evaluates the effect of class activities on both individuals and the class as a whole, collecting information through observation of classroom interactions, questioning, and analysis of student work.

The teacher monitors his or her own teaching strategies and behavior in relation to student success, modifying plans and instructional approaches accordingly.

The teacher maintains useful records of student work and performance and can communicate student progress knowledgeably and responsibly, based on appropriate indicators, to students, parents, and other colleagues.

Principle #9: The Teacher Is a Reflective Practitioner Who Continually Evaluates the Effects of His/Her Choices and Actions on Others (Students, Parents, and Other Professionals in the Learning Community) and Who Actively Seeks Out Opportunities to Grow Professionally.

Knowledge The teacher understands methods of inquiry that provide him/ her with a variety of self-assessment and problem-solving strategies for reflecting on his/her practice, its influences on students' growth and learning, and the complex interactions between them.

The teacher is aware of major areas of research on teaching and of resources available for professional learning (e.g. professional literature, colleagues, professional associations, professional development activities).

Dispositions The teacher values critical thinking and self-directed learning as habits of mind.

The teacher is committed to reflection, assessment, and learning as an ongoing process.

The teacher is willing to give and receive help.

The teacher is committed to seeking out, developing, and continually refining practices that address the individual needs of students.

The teacher recognizes his/her professional responsibility for engaging in and supporting appropriate professional practices for self and colleagues.

Performances The teacher uses classroom observation, information about students, and research as sources for evaluating the outcomes of teaching and learning and as a basis for experimenting with, reflecting on, and revising practice.

The teacher seeks out professional literature, colleagues, and other resources to support his/her own development as a learner and a teacher.

The teacher draws upon professional colleagues within the school and other professional arenas as supports for reflection, problem solving, and new ideas, actively sharing experiences and seeking and giving feedback.

Principle #10: The Teacher Fosters Relationships with School Colleagues, Parents, and Agencies in the Larger Community to Support Students Learning and Well-Being.

Knowledge The teacher understands schools as organizations within the larger community context and understands the operations of the relevant aspects of the system(s) within which s/he works.

The teacher understands how factors in the students' environment outside of school (e.g. family circumstances, community environments, health and economic conditions) may influence students' [lives] and learning.

The teacher understands and implements laws related to students' rights and teacher responsibilities (e.g. for equal education, appropriate education for handicapped students, confidentiality, privacy, appropriate treatment of students, reporting situations related to possible child abuse).

Dispositions The teacher values and appreciates the importance of all aspects of a child's experience.

The teacher is concerned about all aspects of a child's well being (cognitive, emotional, social, and physical) and is alert to signs of difficulties.

The teacher is willing to consult with other adults regarding the education and well being of his/her students.

The teacher respects the privacy of students and confidentiality of information.

The teacher is willing to work with other professionals to improve the overall learning environment for students.

Performances The teacher participates in collegial activities designed to make the entire school a productive learning environment.

The teacher makes links with the learners' other environments on behalf of students, by consulting with parents, counselors, teachers of other classes and activities within the schools, and professionals in other community agencies.

The teacher can identify and use community resources to foster student learning.

The teacher establishes respectful and productive relationships with parents and guardians from diverse home and community situations and seeks to develop cooperative partnerships in support of student learning and wellbeing.

The teacher talks with and listens to the student, is sensitive and responsive to clues of distress, investigates situations, and seeks outside help as needed and appropriate to remedy problems.

The teacher acts as an advocate for students.

NATIONAL COUNCIL FOR ACCREDITATION OF TEACHER EDUCATION[2]

Teaching children—to recognize letters, to read for the first time, to understand how a tree grows—is one of the most important jobs in America. The nation's future depends, in large part, on how well it is done.

---

[2]Excerpts from the National Council for the Accreditation of Teacher Evaluation, 2000b. Used by permission of the author. NCATE reserves all rights.

NCATE is the profession's mechanism to help establish high-quality teacher preparation. Through the process of professional accreditation of schools, colleges and departments of education, NCATE works to make a difference in the quality of teaching and teacher preparation today, tomorrow, and for the next century.

NCATE is a coalition of 33 specialty professional associations of teachers, teacher educators, content specialists, and local and state policy makers. All are committed to quality teaching, and together the coalition represents over 3 million individuals. See Table B-1.

NATIONAL BOARD FOR PROFESSIONAL TEACHING STANDARDS (NBPTS)[3]

The mission of the National Board for Professional Teaching Standards (NBPTS) is to establish high and rigorous standards for what accomplished teachers should know and be able to do; to develop and operate a national, voluntary system to assess and certify teachers who meet these standards; and to advance related education reforms for the purpose of improving student learning in American schools. Governed by a 63-member board of directors, the majority of whom are classroom teachers, the National Board is dedicated to bringing teaching the respect and recognition this important work deserves.

National Board Certification, developed by teachers, with teachers, and for teachers, is a symbol of professional teaching excellence. Offered on a voluntary basis, it complements, not replaces, state licensing. While state licensing systems set entry-level standards for beginning teachers, National Board Certification has established advanced standards for experienced teachers.

The Five Propositions of Accomplished Teaching

The National Board for Professional Teaching Standards seeks to identify and recognize teachers who effectively enhance student learning and demonstrate the high level of knowledge, skills, abilities, and commitments reflected in the following five core propositions.

Proposition #1. Teachers are Committed to Students and Their Learning.

Accomplished teachers are dedicated to making knowledge accessible to all students. They act on the belief that all students can learn. They treat students equitably, recognizing the individual differences that distinguish one student

---

[3]National Board for Professional Teaching Standards, 1994. Used by permission of author.

TABLE B-1: CANDIDATE PERFORMANCE

Standard 1. Candidate Knowledge, Skills, and Dispositions—Candidates[a] preparing to work in schools as teachers or other professional school personnel know and demonstrate the content, pedagogical, professional knowledge, skills, and dispositions necessary to help all students[b] learn. Assessments indicate that candidates meet professional, state, and institutional[c] standards.

Rubrics

Elements of Standards	Unacceptable	Acceptable	Target
Content Knowledge for Teacher Candidates (Initial and Continuing Preparation of Teachers)	Teacher candidates have inadequate knowledge of subject matter that they plan to teach as shown by their inability to give examples of important principles or concepts delineated in professional, state, and institutional standards.	Teacher candidates know the subject matter that they plan to teach as shown by their ability to explain important principles and concepts delineated in professional, state, and institutional standards.	Teacher candidates have in-depth knowledge of the subject matter that they plan to teach as described in professional, state, and institutional standards. They demonstrate their knowledge through inquiry, critical analysis, and synthesis of the subject.
Pedagogical Content Knowledge for Teacher Candidates (Initial and Continuing Preparation of Teachers)	Teacher candidates do not understand the relationship of content and pedagogy delineated in professional, state, and institutional standards in a way that helps them develop learning experiences that integrate technology and build on students' cultural backgrounds and knowledge of content so that students learn.	Teacher candidates have a broad knowledge of institutional strategies that draws upon content and pedagogical knowledge and skills delineated in professional, state, and institutional standards to help all students learn. They facilitate student learning of the subject matter through presentation of the content in clear and meaningful ways and the integration of technology.	Teacher candidates reflect a thorough understanding of pedagogical content knowledge delineated in professional, state, and institutional standards. They have indepth understanding of the subject matter that they plan to teach, allowing them to provide multiple explanations and instructional strategies so that all students learn. They present the content to students in challenging, clear, and compelling ways and integrate technology appropriately.
Professional and Pedagogical Knowledge and Skills for Teacher Candidates (Initial and Continuing Preparation of Teachers)	Candidates have not mastered professional and pedagogical knowledge and skills delineated in professional, state, and institutional standards as shown in their lack of	Candidates use their professional and pedagogical knowledge and skills delineated in professional, state, and institutional standards to facilitate learning. They consider	Candidates reflect a thorough understanding of professional and pedagogical knowledge and skills delineated in professional, state, and institutional standards, as

	knowledge of school, family, and community contexts or in their inability to develop learning experiences that draw on students' prior experience.	the school, family, and community contexts in which they work and the prior experience of students to develop meaningful learning experiences.	shown in their development of meaningful learning experiences to facilitate student learning for all students. They reflect on their practice and make necessary adjustments to enhance student learning. They know how students learn and how to make ideas accessible to them. They consider school, family, and community contexts in connecting concepts to students' prior experience and applying the ideas to real-world problems.
Disposition for ALL Candidates	Candidates are not familiar with professional dispositions delineated in professional, state, and institutional standards. They do not model these dispositions in their work with students, families, and communities.	Candidates are familiar with the dispositions expected of professionals and their work with students, families, and communities reflects the dispositions delineated in professional, state, and institutional standards.	Candidates' work with students, families, and communities reflects the dispositions expected of professional educators as delineated in professional, state, and institutional standards. Candidates recognize when their own dispositions may need to be adjusted and are able to develop plans to do so.
Student Learning for Teacher Candidates (Initial and Continuing Preparation of Teachers)	Teacher candidates do not accurately assess student learning or develop learning experiences based on students' developmental levels or prior experience.	Teacher candidates focus on students' learning as shown in their assessment of student learning, use of assessments in instruction, and development of meaningful learning experiences for students based on their developmental levels and prior experience.	Teacher candidates accurately assess and analyze student learning, make appropriate adjustments to instruction, monitor student learning, and have a positive effect on learning for all students.

[a]Candidates include persons preparing to teach, teachers who are continuing their professional development, and persons preparing for other professional roles in schools such as principals, school psychologists, and school library media specialists.

[b]All students include students with exceptionalities and of different ethnic, racial, gender, religious, socioeconomic, and regional/geographic origins.

[c]Institutional standards are reflected in the unit's conceptual framework and include candidate proficiencies.

from another and taking account of these differences in their practice. They adjust their practice based on observation and knowledge of their students' interests, abilities, skills, knowledge, family circumstances, and peer relationships.

Accomplished teachers understand how students develop and learn. They incorporate the prevailing theories of cognition and intelligence in their practice. They are aware of the influence of context and culture on behavior. They develop students' cognitive capacity and their respect for learning. Equally important, they foster students' self-esteem, motivation, character, [and] civic responsibility and their respect for individual, cultural, religious, and racial differences.

Proposition #2. Teachers Know the Subjects They Teach and How to Teach Those Subjects to Students.

Accomplished teachers have a rich understanding of the subject(s) they teach and appreciate how knowledge in their subject is created, organized, linked to other disciplines, and applied to real-world settings. While faithfully representing the collective wisdom of our culture and upholding the value of disciplinary knowledge, they also develop the critical and analytical capacities of their students.

Accomplished teachers command specialized knowledge of how to convey and reveal subject matter to students. They are aware of the preconceptions and background knowledge that students typically bring to each subject and of strategies and instructional materials that can be of assistance. They understand where difficulties are likely to arise and modify their practice accordingly. Their instructional repertoire allows them to create multiple paths to the subjects they teach, and they are adept at teaching students how to pose and solve their own problems.

Proposition #3. Teachers Are Responsible for Managing and Monitoring Student Learning.

Accomplished teachers create, enrich, maintain, and alter instructional settings to capture and sustain the interest of their students and to make the most effective use of time. They also are adept at engaging students and adults to assist their teaching and at enlisting their colleagues' knowledge and expertise to complement their own.

Accomplished teachers command a range of generic instructional techniques, know when each is appropriate, and can implement them as needed. They are as aware of ineffectual or damaging practice as they are devoted to elegant practice.

They know how to engage groups of students to ensure a disciplined learning environment and how to organize instruction to allow the schools' goals for students to be met. They are adept at setting norms for social interaction among students and between students and teachers. They understand how to motivate students to learn and how to maintain their interest even in the face of temporary failure.

Accomplished teachers can assess the progress of individual students as well as that of the class as a whole. They employ multiple methods for measuring student growth and understanding and can clearly explain student performance to parents.

Proposition #4. Teachers Think Systematically about Their Practice and Learn from Experience.

Accomplished teachers are models of educated persons, exemplifying the virtues they seek to inspire in students—curiosity, tolerance, honesty, fairness, respect for diversity, and appreciation of cultural differences—and the capacities that are prerequisites for intellectual growth: the ability to reason and take multiple perspectives, to be creative and take risks, and to adopt an experimental and problem-solving orientation.

Accomplished teachers draw on their knowledge of human development, subject matter and instruction, and their understanding of their students to make principled judgments about sound practice. Their decisions are not only grounded in the literature, but also in their experience. They engage in lifelong learning, which they seek to encourage in their students.

Striving to strengthen their teaching, accomplished teachers critically examine their practice, seek to expand their repertoire, deepen their knowledge, sharpen their judgment, and adapt their teaching to new findings, ideas, and theories.

Proposition #5. Teachers Are Members of Learning Communities.

Accomplished teachers contribute to the effectiveness of the school by working collaboratively with other professionals on instructional policy, curriculum development, and staff development. They can evaluate school progress and the allocation of school resources in light of their understanding of state and local educational objectives. They are knowledgeable about specialized school and community resources that can be engaged for their students' benefit and are skilled at employing such resources as needed.

Accomplished teachers find ways to work collaboratively and creatively with parents, engaging them productively in the work of the school.

Appendix C

Educational Testing Service (ETS) and National Evaluation Systems (NES) Teacher Licensure Tests

SOURCE: U.S. Department of Education – Release 2. 2000. *The Initial Report of the Secretary on the Quality of Teacher Preparation*. Washington, DC: Office of Postsecondary Education, U.S. Department of Education.

Appendix A: Complete List of Praxis Tests, Scores, and State Cut Scores: 1998-99

This appendix contains a listing of the Praxis assessments used by states in the teacher certification and licensure process. The Praxis Series, or Professional Assessments for Beginning Teachers, was developed and is administered by the Educational Testing Service (ETS).

There are 3 components of the Praxis Series: Praxis I—Academic Skills Assessments; Praxis II—Subject Assessments/Specialty Area, Professional Knowledge, and Core Battery tests, the Principles of Learning and Teaching (PPLT), and the Multiple Subjects Assessment for Teachers (MSAT); and Praxis III—Classroom Performance Assessment. The Academic Skills Assessments include the Pre-Professional Skills Tests (PPST) and the Computer-Based Testing (CBT) program, both of which measure basic proficiency in reading, writing, and mathematics. States set their own cut score or minimum passing score for their test takers.

BASIC SKILLS

	Praxis I: Academic Assessments						Praxis II: Core Battery		
	PPST: Mathematics	PPST: Reading	PPST: Writing	CBT: Mathematics	CBT: Reading	CBT: Writing	Communication Skills	General Knowledge	Professional Knowledge
Test Number	730	710	720	731	711	721	500	510	520
Score Range	150-190	150-190	150-190	300-335	300-335	300-335	600-695	600-695	600-695
State									
AR	169	170	171	314	316	316			642
CT				319	324	318			657
DE	174	175	173	319	322	319			
DC	*	172	171	*	319	316			
FL	175	172	171	317	321	318			646
GA	173	172	172	318	319	318			642
HI	176	175	171	321	322	316			644
IN							653	647	644
KS	174	173	172						645
KY	173	173	172	318	320	318	646	643	648
LA							645	644	648
ME	172	173	168	317	320	312	656	649	
MD							648	645	
MN	169	173	172	314	320	318			
MS	169	170	172	314	316	318			
MT	170	170	170	315	316	314			630

* = Test required—passing score not set   ** = Effective January 1999   + = Multiple scores required   a-ac = See notes at end of this appendix

APPENDIX A: LIST OF PRAXIS TESTS

MORE ON APPENDIX A ...

Appendix A: Complete List of Praxis Tests, Scores, and State Cut Scores: 1998–99, cont'd.

BASIC SKILLS, cont'd.

	Praxis I: Academic Assessments						Praxis II: Core Battery		
	PPST: Mathematics	PPST: Reading	PPST: Writing	CBT: Mathematics	CBT: Reading	CBT: Writing	Communic- ation Skills	General Knowledge	Professional Knowledge
NC	173	176	173	318	323	319			661
NE	171	170	172	316	316	318			
NH	172	174	172	317	321	318			642
NJ								649	643
NM							644	645	630
NV	170	172	172	315	319	318			649
NY							650	649	642
OH								642	
OR	175	174	171	320	321	317			653
PA							646	644	
RI							657 (g)	649 (g)	
SC	*	*	*	*	*	*			
TN	169	169	172	314	315	318			
TX	*	*	*	*	*	*			
VA	178	178	176	323	326	324			
WV	172	172	171	317	319	316			
WI	173	175	174	318	322	320	655		
DoDEA	175	177	174	320	325	320			
USVI	170	175	174	315	322	320			

APPENDIX A: LIST OF PRAXIS TESTS

Appendix A: Complete List of Praxis Tests, Scores, and State Cut Scores: 1998-99, cont'd.

PROFESSIONAL KNOWLEDGE OF TEACHING

	PLT: Grades K-6	PLT: Grades 5-9	PLT: Grades 7-12
Test Number	522	523	524
Score Range	100-200	100-200	100-200
State			
AR			
CT		163	
FL			
GA		166	
HI	163	157	157
IN			
KS			
KY			
LA			
ME			
MD			
MS	152	152	152

PROFESSIONAL KNOWLEDGE OF TEACHING, cont'd.

	PLT: Grades K-6	PLT: Grades 5-9	PLT: Grades 7-12
MO		160	160
NC	160	160	160
NJ			
NM			
NV	169		161
NY			
OH			
OR			159
PA	162		
RI			
SC			
TN	155	*	159
WV	165	154	156
DoDEA			

MORE ON APPENDIX A ...

APPENDIX A: LIST OF PRAXIS TESTS

Appendix A: Complete List of Praxis Tests, Scores, and State Cut Scores: 1998-99, cont'd.

SUBJECT AREA KNOWLEDGE

	Accounting (PA Version)	Agriculture	Agriculture (CA Version)	Agriculture (PA Version)	Art Education	Art Making	Arts Content Knowledge	Art Content, Traditions, Criticism & Aesthetics	Athletic Trainer (WV Version)	Biology
Test Number	791	700	900	780	130	131	133	132	097	230
Score Range	100-200	250-990	250-990	250-990	250-990	100-200	100-200	100-200	100-200	250-990
State										
AR					450					
CA						171 passing, 163 min. (a)		160 passing, 150 min. (a)		
CT				470		148	157	130		
DE										
DC										
FL										
GA		530				150	161			
HI							166	135		
IN					510					
KS										
KY		530				154	139			
LA										
ME										
MD					510					510
MN										
MO		490					153			
MS					530					
MT										
NC						(b)	(b)	(b)		550
NE										*
NH										

APPENDIX A: LIST OF PRAXIS TESTS

Appendix A: Complete List of Praxis Tests, Scores, and State Cut Scores: 1998-99, cont'd.

SUBJECT AREA KNOWLEDGE, cont'd.

	Accounting (PA Version)	Agriculture	Agriculture (CA Version)	Agriculture (PA Version)	Art Education	Art Making	Art Content Knowledge	Art: Content, Traditions, Criticism & Aesthetics	Athletic Trainer (WV Version)	Biology
NJ							136			
NM										
NV						154	156			
NY										
OH					510					
OR			620		610					
PA	*			*			161			
RI										
SC					500		150			480
TN		530						*		
TX					500					
VA		430					160			
WV									158	
WI										
DoDEA										
USVI										

MORE ON APPENDIX A ...

Appendix A: Complete List of Praxis Tests, Scores, and State Cut Scores: 1998-99, cont'd.

SUBJECT AREA KNOWLEDGE, cont'd.

State	Biology & General Science	Biology: Content Essays	Biology: Content Knowledge, Part 1	Biology: Content Knowledge, Part 2	Biology: Content Knowledge	Biology: Pedagogy	Business Education	Chemistry	Chemistry: Content Essays	Chemistry: Content Knowledge	Chemistry: Content Knowledge
Test Number	030	233	231	232	235	234	100	240	242	241	245
Score Range	250-990	100-200	100-200	100-200	100-200	100-200	250-990	250-990	100-200	100-200	100-200
AR	540						550				
CA		157 passing, 150 min. (c)							155 passing, 145 min. (c)		
CT				144	152		620		140		
DE											
DC			152							147	
FL						*					
GA		143**			152**		590		140**		
HI			161			139	550			144	
IN	560						480	460			
KS											
KY	550	139	139				570			144	
LA	580						540				
ME											
MD	570						540	*			151
MN											
MO			156				550				
MS	570						550	510		142	154**
MT											
NC		(d)	(d)			(d)			(f)	(f)	
NE							580				
NH											

Appendix A: Complete List of Praxis Tests, Scores, and State Cut Scores: 1998-99, cont'd.

SUBJECT AREA KNOWLEDGE, cont'd.

	Biology & General Science	Biology: Content Essays	Biology: Content Knowledge, Part 1	Biology: Content Knowledge, Part 2	Biology: Content Knowledge	Biology: Pedagogy	Business Education	Chemistry	Chemistry: Content Essays	Chemistry: Content Knowledge	Chemistry: Content Knowledge
NJ				142			580				
NM										119	
NV			154			146,150**	560		*,**		
NY											
OH	560						540	430			
OR		154	161	156			620		140	144	
PA	*		144	135							
RI											*,**
SC	590						540				
TN		*	146			*	570		*	136	
TX								*			
VA	580						550				
WV			140		152		570				
WI											
DoDEA											
USVI											154

APPENDIX A: LIST OF PRAXIS TESTS

MORE ON APPENDIX A ...

Appendix A: Complete List of Praxis Tests, Scores, and State Cut Scores: 1998-99, cont'd.

SUBJECT AREA KNOWLEDGE, cont'd.

State	Chemistry, Physics & General Science	Communication	Computer Literacy Data Processing	Cooperative Education	Data Processing (DA Version)	Driver Education (WV Version)	Early Childhood Education	Earth/ Space Science	Earth Science Content Knowledge	Economics	Ed. Leadership: Admin. & Supervision
Test Number	070	800	650	810	792	867	020	570	571	910	410
Score Range	250-990	250-990	250-990	250-990	100-200	100-200	250-990	250-990	100-200	250-990	250-990
AR	520						500				
CA											*
CT									157		
DE											
DC							520				
FL							600				
GA											590
HI											
IN							510	420		460	
KS											
KY	510						510				540
LA	530										620
ME											
MD	520						600		152		
MN			*								
MO	510						500		147		
MS											590
MT											
NC							530	530			
NE											
NH											

APPENDIX A: LIST OF PRAXIS TESTS

Appendix A: Complete List of Praxis Tests, Scores, and State Cut Scores: 1998-99, cont'd.

SUBJECT AREA KNOWLEDGE, cont'd.

	Chemistry, Physics & General Science	Communication	Computer Literacy/ Data Processing	Cooperative Education	Data Processing (PA Version)	Driver Education (WV Version)	Early Childhood Education	Earth/ Space Science	Earth Science Content Knowledge	Economics	Ed. Leadership: Admin. & Supervision
NJ									134		540
NM											
NV											590
NY											
OH	520						480				500
OR	570	*		770	*		600				630
PA	*						530	570			
RI											
SC	570						520				590
TN							570		144	560	530
TX											
VA	560					141	490				
WV							530				570
WI											
DoDEA											
USVI											

MORE ON APPENDIX A ...

APPENDIX A: LIST OF PRAXIS TESTS

Appendix A: Complete List of Praxis Tests, Scores, and State Cut Scores: 1998-99, cont'd.

SUBJECT AREA KNOWLEDGE, cont'd.

	Education in the Elementary School	Education of Deaf & Hard of Hearing Students	Education of Students with Mental Retardation	Elem. Ed: Content Area Exercises	Elem. Ed: Curriculum, Instruction & Assessment	Elem. Ed: Curriculum, Instruction & Assess. (K-5)	Engl. Lang., Lit., & Comp.: Cont. Knowledge	Engl. Lang., Lit., & Comp.: Essays	English Lang., Lit., & Comp.: Pedagogy	English Language & Literature	Environmental Education
Test Number	010	271	320	012	011	016	041	042	043	040	830
Score Range	250-990	100-200	250-990	100-200	100-200	100-200	100-200	100-200	100-200	250-990	250-990
State											
AR	500									490	
CA								160			
CT				148	163		172	160			
DE											
DC				*	146		142		*		
FL	560		580	137	151		165				
GA		168		135		154	163	135			
HI				135	164		164		150		
IN	520		560							500	
KS											
KY		156			143			135		550	
LA	550										
ME											
MD	550									500	
MN											
MO					164		158				
MS	540		540							530	
MT											
NC	540		580	(h)	(h)		(i, k)	(i)	(i, k)		
NE											
NH									155, 150**		

APPENDIX A: LIST OF PRAXIS TESTS

Appendix A: Complete List of Praxis Tests, Scores, and State Cut Scores: 1998-99, cont'd.

SUBJECT AREA KNOWLEDGE, cont'd.

	Education in the Elementary School	Education of Deaf & Hard of Hearing Students	Education of Students with Mental Retardation	Elem. Ed: Content Area Exercises	Elem. Ed: Curriculum, Instruction & Assessment	Elem. Ed: Curriculum, Instruction & Instruction & Assess. (K-5)	Engl. Lang., Lit., & Comp.: Cont. Knowledge	Engl. Lang., Lit., & Comp.: Essays	English Lang. Lit., & Comp.: Pedagogy	English Language & Literature	Environmental Education
NJ											
NM							155				
NV				135	158			155			
NY											
OH	510		490								
OR		*	670				164	145			
PA		*			164		153				
RI											*
SC	540		590							500	
TN		*		*	159		157	*	*		
TX											
VA	520		520							520	
WV					155		155				
WI											
DoDEA											
USVI											

MORE ON APPENDIX A ...

APPENDIX A: LIST OF PRAXIS TESTS

Appendix A: Complete List of Praxis Tests, Scores, and State Cut Scores: 1998-99, cont'd.

SUBJECT AREA KNOWLEDGE, cont'd.

State	Foreign Language Pedagogy	French	French: Content Knowledge	French: Linguistic, Literary, & Cult. Analy.	French: Productive Language Skills	General Mathematics (WV Version)	General Science	General Science: Content Essays	General Science: Content Knowledge 1	General Science: Content Knowledge 2	General Science: Content Knowledge
Test Number	840	170	173	172	171	067	430	433	431	432	435
Score Range	100-200	250-990	100-200	100-200	100-200	100-200	250-990	100-200	100-200	100-200	100-200
AR		490									
CA				171	172			150 passing, 140 min. (c.e.l.m)			157
CT			165		163			145			
DE											
DC		520							136	143	
FL											
GA			156		155			120			
HI			158		164				157		145
IN		520									
KS											
KY			144		151					150	
LA		520									
ME											
MD		510									
MN											
MO		500									
MS		510									
MT											
NC			(j)		(j)			(n.o)	(o)	(o)	
NE											
NH											

Appendix A: Complete List of Praxis Tests, Scores, and State Cut Scores: 1998-99, cont'd.

SUBJECT AREA KNOWLEDGE, cont'd.

	Foreign Language Pedagogy	French	French: Content Knowledge	French: Linguistic, Literary, & Cult. Analy.	French: Productive Language Skills	General Mathematics (WV Version)	General Science	General Science: Content Essays	General Science: Content Knowledge 1	General Science: Content Knowledge 2	General Science: Content Knowledge
NJ			146						148	133	
NM											
NV			152		162			140, 135**	150		
NY											
OH		520					370				
OR		620						135	152	150	
PA	*		170								
RI											
SC		520									
TN			160		*			*	138	136	
TX											
VA		570									
WV			131			160				149	
WI											
DoDEA											
USVI											

MORE ON APPENDIX A ...

APPENDIX A: LIST OF PRAXIS TESTS

Appendix A: Complete List of Praxis Tests, Scores, and State Cut Scores: 1998-99, cont'd.

SUBJECT AREA KNOWLEDGE, cont'd.

	Geography	German	German: Content Knowledge	German: Productive Language Skills	Gifted Education (W/V Version)	Government/ Political Science	Health & Physical Education	Health Education	Health & Phys. Ed: Content Knowledge	Home Economics Education	Intro to the Teaching of Reading
Test Number	920	180	181	182	357	930	850	550	856	120	200
Score Range	250-990	250-990	100-200	100-200	100-200	250-990	250-990	250-990	100-200	250-990	250-990
State											
AR								520		520	510
CA			162								680
CT								680		630	
DE											
DC											
FL											
GA			156	166**				650	154	550	
HI	520	490								560	
IN		490				390		420		540	510
KS											
KY			143					550		540	
LA		500								510	
ME											
MD		510								520	
MN											
MO			161					480		560	
MS		550								560	
MT											
NC		540						640		540	540
NE											
NH											
NJ			146							550	560

MORE ON APPENDIX A ...

APPENDIX A: LIST OF PRAXIS TESTS

Appendix A: Complete List of Praxis Tests, Scores, and State Cut Scores: 1998-99, cont'd.

SUBJECT AREA KNOWLEDGE, cont'd.

	Geography	German	German: Content Knowledge	German: Productive Language Skills	Gifted Education (WV Version)	Government/ Political Science	Health & Physical Education	Health Education	Health & Phys. Ed. Content Knowledge	Home Economics Education	Intro to the Teaching of Reading
NM											
NV								600	***	610	560
NY											
OH								480		540	540
OR		620						720		650	
PA							500	500		600	
RI											
SC	520							710		540	500
TN			139			560		570		580	
TX											
VA		560						*		570	
WV			132		161			530		530	
WI											
DoDEA											
USVI											

MORE ON APPENDIX A ...

APPENDIX A: LIST OF PRAXIS TESTS

Appendix A: Complete List of Praxis Tests, Scores, and State Cut Scores: 1998-99, cont'd.

SUBJECT AREA KNOWLEDGE, cont'd.

	Italian	Latin	Library Media Specialist	Marketing Education	Marketing (PA Version)	Mathematics	Mathematics: Content Knowledge	Mathematics: Pedagogy	Mathematics: Proofs, Models & Problems 1	Mathematics: Proofs, Models & Problems 2	Middle School: Content Knowledge
Test Number	620	600	310	560	793	060	061	065	063	064	146
Score Range	250-990	250-990	250-990	250-990	100-200	250-990	100-200	100-200	100-200	100-200	100-200
State											
AR				520		*					
CA			540	520					170 passing, 165 min. (q)	159 passing, 152 min. (q)	
CT	670	770					141				
DE											
DC							141	*	*		
FL						+					
GA		700	620	590			124		139		
HI			610				136	135			
IN			530			530					
KS											
KY		530	590			500	141		141		
LA			560			550					
ME											154
MD			540			520					
MN											
MO				500			137				
MS			610	590		520					
MT											
NC			610	690		530	(p)	(p)			
NE											
NH											

MORE ON APPENDIX A ...

APPENDIX A: LIST OF PRAXIS TESTS

Appendix A: Complete List of Praxis Tests, Scores, and State Cut Scores: 1998-99, cont'd.

SUBJECT AREA KNOWLEDGE, cont'd.

	Italian	Latin	Library Media Specialist	Marketing Education	Marketing (PA Version)	Mathematics	Mathematics: Content Knowledge	Mathematics: Pedagogy	Mathematics: Proofs, Models & Problems 1	Mathematics: Proofs, Models & Problems 2	Middle School: Content Knowledge
NJ				580			130				
NM											
NV							+	135	152		
NY											
OH			520	440		530					
OR			630	690			147	140	144	140	
PA			620	550	*		127				
RI											
SC			590	640		560	136				
TN		540	550	560				*			
TX						580					
VA				*		580					
WV		480	520	600			133				
WI											
DoDEA											
USVI											

MORE ON APPENDIX A ...

Appendix A: Complete List of Praxis Tests, Scores, and State Cut Scores: 1998-99, cont'd.

SUBJECT AREA KNOWLEDGE, cont'd.

	Middle School English Language	Middle School Mathematics	Middle School Mathematics: Cont. Know.	Middle School Science	Middle School Social Studies	Music Analysis	Music Concepts and Processes	Music Content Knowledge	Music Education	Office Technology (PA)	Physical Education
Test Number	049	069	066	439	089	112	111	113	110	794	090
Score Range	100-200	100-200	100-200	100-200	100-200	100-200	100-200	100-200	250-990	100-200	250-990
State											
AR									510		
CA						169 passing, 164 min. (s)	165 passing, 155 min. (s)				
CT	*	*		*	*		150	153			540
DE											
DC											
FL											
GA							145	154			
HI							145	139			610
IN									510		
KS											
KY	*	*		*	*		140	137			540
LA									530		
ME											
MD									530		580
MN											
MO								151	530		
MS											580
MT											
NC						(t)	(t)	*			
NE											550
NH											

Appendix A: Complete List of Praxis Tests, Scores, and State Cut Scores: 1998-99, cont'd.

SUBJECT AREA KNOWLEDGE, cont'd.

	Middle School English Language	Middle School Mathematics	Middle School Mathematics: Cont. Know.	Middle School Science	Middle School Social Studies	Music Analysis	Music Concepts and Processes	Music Content Knowledge	Music Education	Office Technology (PA)	Physical Education
NJ								143			
NM											
NV							*, 150**	*,149**			
NY											
OH											
OR			167			167	170	167			540
PA								158		157	
RI											
SC									480		
TN							*	150			
TX											590
VA									510		
WV								155			
WI											560
DoDEA											
USVI											

MORE ON APPENDIX A ...

APPENDIX A: LIST OF PRAXIS TESTS

Appendix A: Complete List of Praxis Tests, Scores, and State Cut Scores: 1998-99, cont'd.

SUBJECT AREA KNOWLEDGE, cont'd.

	Phys. Ed. Content Knowledge	Phys. Ed.: Movement Forms–Analy./Des.	Phys. Ed.: Movement Forms–Video	Phys. Science Content Knowledge	Phys. Science: Pedagogy	Physics	Physics: Content Essays	Physics: Content Knowledge	Physics: Content Knowledge	Pre-K Education	Psychology
Test Number	091	092	093	481	483	260	262	261	265	530	390
Score Range	100-200	100-200	100-200	100-200	100-200	250-990	100-200	100-200	100-200	250-990	250-990
State											
AR											
CA		158 passing, 152 min., (v)	170 passing, 150 min., (v)				160 passing, 150 min., (m)			250-990	250-990
CT	154	154					135		141		
DE				155							
DC					*						
FL											
GA		148		141**			140**	150**			
HI	160	145		164	151			144			
IN						400				390	480
KS											
KY	152	135						141			
LA											
ME											
MD						*					
MN											
MO	153							133			
MS						520					
MT											
NC	(u)	(u)			(f,n)						
NE						510					
NH											

MORE ON APPENDIX A ...

Appendix A: Complete List of Praxis Tests, Scores, and State Cut Scores: 1998-99, cont'd.

SUBJECT AREA KNOWLEDGE, cont'd.

	Phys. Ed.: Content Knowledge	Phys. Ed.: Movement Forms-Analy./Des.	Phys. Ed.: Movement Forms-Video	Phys. Science: Content Knowledge	Phys. Science Pedagogy	Physics	Physics: Content Essays	Physics: Content Knowledge	Physics: Content Knowledge	Pre-K Education	Psychology
NJ	139							113			
NM											
NV	154	149			142, 147**						550
NY											
OH											
OR	160	141	145				145	147			
PA						440					
RI											
SC											720
TN	152	*			*		*	124			560
TX											
VA						*					
WV	150			142					126	590	
WI											
DoDEA											
USVI											

APPENDIX A: LIST OF PRAXIS TESTS

Appendix A: Complete List of Praxis Tests, Scores, and State Cut Scores: 1998-99, cont'd.

SUBJECT AREA KNOWLEDGE, cont'd.

State	Reading Specialist	Safety/Driver Education	Social Studies	Social Studies: Analytical Essays	Social Studies: Content Knowledge	Social Studies: Interpretation of Materials	Social Studies: Pedagogy	Sociology	Spanish	Spanish: Content Knowledge
Test Number	300	860	080	082	081	083	084	950	190	191
Score Range	250-990	250-990	250-990	100-200	100-200	100-200	100-200	250-990	250-990	100-200
AR	550		500						470	
CA				160 passing, 150 min., (w)		169 passing, 161 min., (w)				170
CT					162					
DE							*			
DC					145					153
FL			560		158					
GA	580				151	156				167
HI					154		144			171
IN			520					440	500	
KS										
KY					146	150				145
LA			550						540	
ME										
MD			530						500	
MN										
MO					152					158
MS			520						530	
MT										
NC	570			(x,y)	(x,y)	(y)				(z)
NE										
NH										

Appendix A: Complete List of Praxis Tests, Scores, and State Cut Scores: 1998-99, cont'd.

SUBJECT AREA KNOWLEDGE, cont'd.

	Reading Specialist	Safety/ Driver Education	Social Studies	Social Studies: Analytical Essays	Social Studies: Content Knowledge	Social Studies: Interpretation of Materials	Social Studies: Pedagogy	Sociology	Spanish	Spanish: Content Knowledge
NJ					153					149
NM										
NV				150	152					(aa,ab)
NY										
OH			520						520	
OR	640			155	158	167				166
PA	570	*			157					166
RI										
SC			550						520	
TN								540		152
TX			540							
VA									540	
WV	520				148					143
WI										
DoDEA										
USVI										

MORE ON APPENDIX A ...

APPENDIX A: LIST OF PRAXIS TESTS

Appendix A: Complete List of Praxis Tests, Scores, and State Cut Scores: 1998-99, cont'd.

SUBJECT AREA KNOWLEDGE, cont'd.

	Spanish: Linguistic, Literary & Cult. Analy.	Spanish: Pedagogy	Spanish: Productive Language Skills	Special Education	Special Education: Application of Core Princ.	Special Ed.: Knowledge Based Core Principles	Special Ed.: Preschool/ Early Childhood	Special Ed.: Teaching Students w/ Beh. Disab.	Special Ed.: Teaching Students w/ Learn. Disab.	Special Ed.: Teaching Students w/ Mental Ret.	Speech Communication
Test Number	193	194	192	350	352	351	690	371	381	321	220
Score Range	100-200	100-200	100-200	250-990	100-200	100-200	250-990	100-200	100-200	100-200	250-990
State											
AR				510							550
CA	171		172								
CT			163		150	155					
DE		*									
DC			*	510							
FL				590							
GA			159		130	152		153	156	153	660
HI		150			141	136					
IN											490
KS											
KY			156		127			147		139	
LA											
ME											
MD				500							500
MN											
MO				490							530
MS				550							510
MT											
NC			(z)	510							560
NE											
NH											
NJ											560

APPENDIX A: LIST OF PRAXIS TESTS

Appendix A: Complete List of Praxis Tests, Scores, and State Cut Scores: 1998-99, cont'd.

SUBJECT AREA KNOWLEDGE, cont'd.

	Spanish: Linguistic, Literary & Cult. Analy.	Spanish: Pedagogy	Spanish: Productive Language Skills	Special Education	Special Education: Application of Core Princ.	Special Ed.: Knowledge Based Core Principles	Special Ed.: Preschool/ Early Childhood	Special Ed.: Teaching Students w/ Beh. Disab.	Special Ed.: Teaching Students w/ Learn. Disab.	Special Ed.: Teaching Students w/ Mental Ret.	Speech Communic- ation
NM											
NV			(aa,ab)			145					580
NY											
OH											640
OR			165		156	155	560				
PA					144	152					
RI											
SC				600							
TN			*	490	*	*	560				570
TX											
VA											470
WV						136	550	156	144	136	600
WI											
DoDEA											
USVI											

MORE ON APPENDIX A ...

APPENDIX A: LIST OF PRAXIS TESTS

Appendix A: Complete List of Praxis Tests, Scores, and State Cut Scores: 1998-99, cont'd.

SUBJECT AREA KNOWLEDGE, cont'd.

	Teaching English as a Second Lang.	Teaching Speech to Stud. w/ Lang. Imp.	Teaching Stud. w/ Emotional Disturbance	Teaching Stud. w/ Learning Disabilities
Test Number	360	880	370	380
Score Range	250-990	250-990	250-990	250-990
AR				
CA				
CT				
DE	520			
DC				
FL			600	590
GA				
HI	510			
IN			540	430
KS				
KY	550			
LA				
ME				
MD				
MN				
MO				
MS			610	

SUBJECT AREA KNOWLEDGE, cont'd.

	Teaching English as a Second Lang.	Teaching Speech to Stud. w/ Lang. Imp.	Teaching Stud. w/ Emotional Disturbance	Teaching Stud. w/ Learning Disabilities
MT				
NC	520		680	610
NE				
NH				
NJ				
NM				
NV		500		
NY				
OH	420		510	390
OR				
PA		*		
RI				
SC			680	670
TN	*			
TX				
VA			*	*
WV				
WI				
DoDEA				
USVI				

Appendix A - Endnotes

a = CA certification in Art requires achieving a combined total score of 331 for both tests by either (1) meeting the passing score of 171 on Art Making (0131) and meeting the passing score of 160 on Art: Content, Traditions, Criticism, & Aesthetics (0132) OR (2) meeting/exceeding the minimum score of 163 on Art Making and meeting/exceeding the minimum score of 150 on Art: Content, Traditions, Criticism, & Aesthetics.

b = NC license for Art K-12 requires a combined score of 479 from Art Making (0131), minimum score 150; Art Content, Traditions, Criticism, & Aesthetics (0132), minimum score 130; and Art: Content Knowledge (0133), minimum score 144.

c = CA certification in Science: Biological Sciences requires achieving a combined total score of 307 for both tests by either (1) meeting the passing score of 157 on Biology: Content Essays (0233) and meeting the passing score of 150 on General Science: Content Essays (043) OR (2) meeting/exceeding the minimum score of 150 on Biology: Content Essays and meeting/exceeding the minimum score of 148 on General Science: Content Essays.

d = NC license for Chemistry 9-12 requires a combined score of 465 from Biology: Content Knowledge; Part 1 (0231); minimum score 154; Biology: Content Essays (0233), minimum score 139; and Biology: Pedagogy (0294), minimum score 135.

e = CA certification in Science: Chemistry requires achieving a combined total score of 305 for both tests by either (1) meeting the passing score of 155 on Chemistry: Content Essays (0242) and meeting the passing score of 150 on General Science: Content Essays (0433) OR (2) meeting/exceeding the minimum score of 145 on Chemistry: Content Essays and meeting/exceeding the minimum score of 140 on General Science: Content Essays.

f = NC license for English 9-12 requires a combined score of 473 from Chemistry: Content Knowledge Part 1 (0241), minimum score of 150; Chemistry: Content Essays (0242), minimum score 135; and Physical Science: Pedagogy (0483), minimum score 139.

g = RI initial teaching license requires passing all three Core Battery tests by either (1) passing each test separately OR (2) achieving a combined score for all three Core Battery tests of 1954, with individual scores not more than four points below the passing score for each test as listed in the table.

h = NC license for Elementary Education K-6 requires a combined score of 310 from Elementary Education: Curriculum, Instruction, and Assessment (0011), minimum score 153; and Elementary Education: Content Area Exercises (0012), minimum score 127.

i = NC license for English 9-12 requires a combined score of 475 from English Language, Literature, and Composition: Content Knowledge (0041), minimum score 154; English Language, Literature and Composition: Content Essays (0042), minimum score 135; and English Language, Literature, and Composition: Pedagogy (0043), minimum score 139.

j = NC license for French K-12 requires a combined score of 322 from French: Content Knowledge (0173), minimum score 137; and French: Productive Language Skills (0171), minimum score 159.

k = NC license for Language Arts 6-8 requires a combined score of 319 from English Language, Literature, and Composition: Content Knowledge (0041), minimum score 152; and English Language, Literature and Composition: Pedagogy (0043), minimum score 135.

l = NC license for Comprehensive Science 6-8 requires meeting the passing score of 150 on the General Science: Content Essays (0433). Additional required examinations are given through the SSAT test series.

m = CA certification in Science: Physics requires achieving a combined total score of 310 for both tests by either (1) meeting the passing score of 160 on Physics: Content Essays (0262) and meeting the passing score of 150 on General Science: Content Essays (0433) OR (2) meeting/exceeding the minimum score of 150 on Physics: Content Essays and meeting/exceeding the minimum score of 140 on General Science: Content Essays.

n = NC license for Comprehensive Science 6-8 requires a combined score of 296 from General Science: Content Essays (0433), minimum score 130; and Physical Science: Pedagogy (0483), minimum score 139.

o = NC license for Science 9-12 requires a combined score of 467 from General Science: Content Essays

(0433), minimum score 130; General Science: Content Knowledge Part 1 (0431), minimum score 143 and General Science: Content Knowledge Part 2 (0432), minimum score 145.

p = NC license for Mathematics 9-12 requires a combined score of 288 from Mathematics: Content Knowledge (0061), minimum score 133; and Mathematics: Pedagogy (0065), minimum score 135.

q = CA certification in Mathematics requires achieving a combined total score of 329 for both tests by either (1) meeting the passing score of 170 on Mathematics: Proofs, Models and Problems Part 1 (0063) and meeting the passing score of 159 on Mathematics: Proofs, Models and Problems Part 2 (0064) OR (2) meeting/exceeding the minimum score of 165 on Mathematics: Proofs, Models and Problems Part 1 and meeting/exceeding the minimum score of 152 on Mathematics: Proofs, Models and Problems Part 2.

r = CA certification in Multiple Subjects requires achieving a combined total score of 311 for both tests by either (1) meeting the passing score of 156 on MSAT: Content Knowledge (0140) and meeting the passing score of 155 on MSAT: Content Area Exercises (0151) OR (2) meeting/exceeding the score of 148 on Content Knowledge and meeting/exceeding the score of 147 on Content Area Exercises.

s = CA certification in Music requires achieving a combined total score of 334 for both tests by either (1) meeting the passing score of 165 on Music: Concepts and Processes (0111) and meeting the passing score of 169 on Music: Analysis (0112) OR meeting/exceeding the minimum score of 155 on Music: Concepts and Processes and meeting/exceeding the minimum score of 164 on Music: Analysis.

t = NC license for Music K-12 requires a combined score of 448 from Music: Analysis (0112), minimum score 131: Music: Concepts and Processes (0111), minimum score 135; and Music: Content Knowledge (0113), minimum score 136.

u = NC license for Physical Education K-12 requires a combined score of 318 from Physical Education: Content Knowledge (0091), minimum score 155; and Physical Education: Movement Forms--Analysis/ Design (0092), minimum score 144.

v = CA certification in Physical Education requires achieving a combined total score of 328 for both tests by either (1) meeting the passing score of 170 on PE: Movement Forms--Video Evaluation (0093) and meeting the passing score of 158 on PE: Movement Forms--Analysis/Design OR (2) meeting/exceeding the minimum score of 152 on PE: Movement Forms--Analysis/Design and meeting/exceeding the minimum score of 152 on PE: Movement Forms--Analysis/Design.

w = CA certification in Social Studies requires achieving a combined total score of 329 for both tests by either (1) meeting the passing score of 160 on Social Studies: Analytical Essays (0082) and meeting the passing score of 169 on Social Studies: Interpretation of Materials (0083) OR (2) meeting/exceeding the minimum score of 150 on Social Studies: Analytical Essays and meeting/exceeding the minimum score or 161 on Social Studies: Interpretation of Materials.

x = NC license for Social Studies 6-8 requires a combined score of 314 from Social Studies: Content Knowledge (0081), minimum score 158, and Social Studies: Analytical Essays (0082), minimum score 135

y = NC license for Social Studies 9-12 requires a combined score of 491 from Social Studies: Content Knowledge (0081), minimum score 158; Social Studies: Interpretation of Materials (0083), minimum score 167; and Social Studies: Analytical Essays (0082), minimum score 145.

z = NC license for Spanish K-12 requires a combined score of 327 from Spanish: Content Knowledge (0191), minimum score 148; and Spanish: Productive Language Skills (0192), minimum score 156.

aa = NV license for Bilingual requires scores from Spanish: Content Knowledge (0191) and Spanish: Productive Language Skills (0192). No minimum qualifying scores in effect until January 1999.

ab = NV license for Spanish requires passing both Spanish: Content Knowledge (0191), minimum score 160, and Spanish: Productive Language Skills (0192), minimum score 156.

ac = OR license for Elementary Education requires achieving a combined total score of 310 for both tests by either (1) meeting the passing score of 155 on MSAT: Content Knowledge (0140) and meeting the passing score of 155 on MSAT: Content Area Exercises (0151) OR (2) meeting/exceeding the minimum score of 147 on Content Knowledge and meeting/exceeding the score of 147 on Content Area Exercises.

APPENDIX A: LIST OF PRAXIS TESTS

Appendix B: List of NES-Developed State Tests: 1998

This appendix contains a listing of the assessments administered by the National Evaluation Systems, Inc., for the teacher certification and licensure process. NES developed individual assessments series for 10 states, including Arizona, California, Colorado, Illinois, Massachusetts, Michigan, New Mexico, New York, Oklahoma, and Texas. Oregon uses the basic skills portion of the California assessments in their teacher certification and licensure process. NES assessments evaluate basic skills, professional knowledge, and subject matter knowledge. States set their own cut score or minimum passing rate for their test takers.

ARIZONA	ARIZONA TEACHER PROFICIENCY ASSESSMENT (ATPA)	PASSING SCORE	SCALE
Basic Skills	Proficiency Examination in Reading, Grammar, and Mathematics	*	*
Professional Knowledge	Professional Knowledge Test	*	*
Subject Matter Knowledge	Elementary Education Subject Knowledge	*	*
	Agriculture	*	*
	Art	*	*
	Biology	*	*
	Business	*	*
	Chemistry	*	*
	Computers	*	*
	Dance	*	*
	Drama	*	*
	Economics	*	*
	English	*	*
	Family and Consumer Science	*	*
	French	*	*
	General Science	*	*
	Geography	*	*
	German	*	*
	Health	*	*
	Health Occupations	*	*
	History	*	*
	Industrial Technology	*	*
	Journalism	*	*
	Marketing	*	*

MORE ON APPENDIX B ...

APPENDIX B: LIST OF NES-DEVELOPED STATE TESTS

Appendix B: List of NES-Developed State Tests: 1998, cont'd.

Mathematics	*
Music	*
Physical Education	*
Physics	*
Political Science	*
Social Studies	*
Spanish	*
Speech	*
Cross-Categorical Special Education	*

*Arizona has not yet established a passing score for the Arizona Teacher Proficiency Assessment.
**Arizona has not yet established a scoring scale for the Arizona Teacher Proficiency Assessment.

CALIFORNIA	PROFESSIONAL ASSESSMENTS FOR CALIFORNIA TEACHERS	PASSING SCORE	SCALE
Basic Skills	California Basic Educational Skills Test (CBEST): Reading	41	20-80
	CBEST: Writing	41	20-80
	CBEST: Mathematics	41	20-80
	Reading Instruction Competence Assessment (RICA)[2]	81	0-120
Subject Matter Knowledge	14 Secondary Subject Assessment for Teachers (SSAT): Agriculture	220	100-300
	12 SSAT: Art	220	100-300
	05 SSAT: Biology	220 passing/208 minimum	100-300
	15 SSAT: Business	220	100-300
	06 SSAT: Chemistry	220 passing/208 minimum	100-300
	11 SSAT: French	220	100-300
	04 SSAT: General Science	220 passing/208 minimum	100-300
	07 SSAT: Geoscience	220 passing/208 minimum	100-300
	20 SSAT: German	220	100-300
	16 SSAT: Health Science	220	100-300
	17 SSAT: Home Economics	220	100-300
	18 SSAT: Industrial and Technology Education	220	100-300
	21 SSAT: Japanese	220	100-300

MORE ON APPENDIX B ...

Appendix B: List of NES-Developed State Tests: 1998, cont'd.

		PASSING SCORE	SCALE
	01 SSAT: Literature and English Language	220	100-300
	19 SSAT: Mandarin	220	100-300
	02 SSAT: Mathematics	220	100-300
	13 SSAT: Music	220	100-300
	09 SSAT: Physical Education	220	100-300
	08 SSAT: Physics	220	100-300
	23 SSAT: Punjabi	220	100-300
	22 SSAT: Russian	220	100-300
	03 SSAT: Social Science	220	100-300
	10 SSAT: Spanish	220	100-300
	24 SSAT: Vietnamese	220	100-300
COLORADO	PROGRAM FOR LICENSING ASSESSMENTS FOR COLORADO EDUCATORS (PLACE)	PASSING SCORE	SCALE
Basic Skills	90 Basic Skills	220	100-300
	91 Liberal Arts and Sciences	220	100-300
Professional Knowledge	92 Professional Knowledge: Elementary	220	100-300
	93 Professional Knowledge: Secondary	220	100-300
	94 Professional Knowledge: Middle School	220	100-300
Subject Matter Knowledge	01 Elementary Education	220	100-300
	04 Mathematics	220	100-300
	05 Science	220	100-300
	06 Social Studies	220	100-300
	07 English	220	100-300
	08 French	220	100-300
	09 Spanish	220	100-300
	10 German	220	100-300
	11 Italian	220	100-300
	12 Latin	220	100-300
	14 Russian	220	100-300

MORE ON APPENDIX B ...

Appendix B: List of NES-Developed State Tests: 1998, cont'd.

		PASSING SCORE	SCALE
	15 Japanese	220	100-300
	17 English as a Second Language	220	100-300
	23 Special Education: Severe Needs - Vision	220	100-300
	28 Art	220	100-300
	29 Music	220	100-300
	32 Physical Education	220	100-300
	02 Early Childhood Education	220	100-300
	16 Bilingual Education	220	100-300
	18 Reading Teacher	220	100-300
	19 Speech	220	100-300
	20 Special Education: Moderate Needs	220	100-300
	21 Special Education: Severe Needs-Cognitive	220	100-300
	22 Special Education: Severe Needs - Affective	220	100-300
	24 Special Education: Severe Needs- Hearing	220	100-300
	25 Special Education: Severe Needs - Communication	220	100-300
	26 Special Education - Profound Needs	220	100-300
	27 Early Childhood Special Education	220	100-300
	30 Drama	220	100-300
	31 Health	220	100-300
	33 Driver Education	220	100-300
	34 Business Education	220	100-300
	35 Distributive Education	220	100-300
	36 Home Economics	220	100-300
	37 Industrial Arts	220	100-300
	40 Agriculture	220	100-300
	42 School Library Media	220	100-300
	43 Media Specialist	220	100-300
ILLINOIS	ILLINOIS CERTIFICATION TESTING SYSTEM (ICTS)	PASSING SCORE	SCALE
Basic Skills	96 ICTS Basic Skills Test: Mathematics	70	0-100

MORE ON APPENDIX B ...

APPENDIX B: LIST OF NES-DEVELOPED STATE TESTS

Appendix B: List of NES-Developed State Tests: 1998, cont'd.

Subject Matter Knowledge	96 ICTS Basic Skills Test: Grammar	70	0-100
	96 ICTS Basic Skills Test: Reading	70	0-100
	96 ICTS Basic Skills Test: Writing	70	0-100
	02 Early Childhood	70	0-100
	03 Elementary	70	0-100
	23 History	70	0-100
	24 Social Science	70	0-100
	25 English	70	0-100
	26 Spanish	70	0-100
	27 French	70	0-100
	28 German	70	0-100
	29 Hebrew	70	0-100
	30 Italian	70	0-100
	31 Latin	70	0-100
	32 Russian	70	0-100
	33 Dance	70	0-100
	34 Speech	70	0-100
	35 Biological Science	70	0-100
	36 Mathematics	70	0-100
	37 Chemistry	70	0-100
	38 Computer Sciences	70	0-100
	39 General Sciences	70	0-100
	40 Physical Science	70	0-100
	41 Physics	70	0-100
	42 Health	70	0-100
	43 Health Occupations	70	0-100
	44 Family and Consumer Sciences	70	0-100
	45 Industrial Technology Education	70	0-100
	46 Agriculture	70	0-100

MORE ON APPENDIX B ...

Appendix B: List of NES-Developed State Tests: 1998, cont'd.

	47 Business/Marketing/Management	70	0-100
	51 Art (6-12)	70	0-100
	52 Music (6-12)	70	0-100
	53 Physical Education (6-12)	70	0-100
	54 Theater Arts	70	0-100
	04 Educable Mentally Handicapped	70	0-100
	05 Trainable Mentally Handicapped	70	0-100
	06 Learning Disabilities	70	0-100
	07 Social/Emotional Disorders	70	0-100
	08 Deaf and Hard of Hearing	70	0-100
	09 Speech and Language Impaired	70	0-100
	10 Blind and Partially Sighted	70	0-100
	11 Physically Handicapped	70	0-100
	12 Media	70	0-100
	13 Reading	70	0-100
	14 English as a Second Language	70	0-100
	48 Art (K-12)	70	0-100
	49 Music (K-12)	70	0-100
	50 Physical Education (K-12)	70	0-100
MASSACHUSETTS	MASSACHUSETTS TEACHER TESTS (MTT)	PASSING SCORE	SCALE
Basic Skills	01 Communication and Literacy Skills Test	70	0-100
Subject Matter Knowledge	02 Early Childhood Education	70	0-100
	03 Elementary Teacher	70	0-100
	04 Middle School Teacher	70	0-100
	05 Social Studies	70	0-100
	06 History	70	0-100
	07 English	70	0-100
	08 Reading	70	0-100
	09 Mathematics	70	0-100

MORE ON APPENDIX B ...

APPENDIX B: LIST OF NES-DEVELOPED STATE TESTS

Appendix B: List of NES-Developed State Tests: 1998, cont'd.

	10 General Science	70	0-100
	11 Physics	70	0-100
	12 Chemistry	70	0-100
	13 Biology	70	0-100
	14 Earth Science	70	0-100
	15 Latin & Classical Humanities	70	0-100
	16 Music	70	0-100
	17 Visual Art	70	0-100
	19 Business	70	0-100
	20 Home Economics	70	0-100
	21 Health Education	70	0-100
	22 Physical Education	70	0-100
	24 English as a Second Language	70	0-100
	25 Special Needs	70	0-100
	26 French	70	0-100
	27 German	70	0-100
	28 Spanish	70	0-100
	29 Chinese	70	0-100
	30 Italian	70	0-100
	33 Technology Education	70	0-100
MICHIGAN	MICHIGAN TEST FOR TEACHER CERTIFICATION (MTTC)	PASSING SCORE	SCALE
Basic Skills	96 Basic Skills	220	100-300
Subject Matter Knowledge	01 Language Arts	220	100-300
	02 English	220	100-300
	03 Journalism	220	100-300
	04 Speech	220	100-300
	05 Reading	220	100-300
	84 Social Studies	220	100-300
	07 Economics	220	100-300

Appendix B: List of NES-Developed State Tests: 1998, cont'd.

08 Geography	220	100-300
09 History	220	100-300
10 Political Science	220	100-300
11 Psychology	220	100-300
12 Sociology	220	100-300
13 Anthropology	220	100-300
14 Cultural Studies	220	100-300
15 Behavioral Studies	220	100-300
16 Science	220	100-300
17 Biology	220	100-300
18 Chemistry	220	100-300
19 Physics	220	100-300
20 Geology/Earth Sciences	220	100-300
21 Astronomy	220	100-300
22 Mathematics	220	100-300
23 French	220	100-300
24 German	220	100-300
26 Latin	220	100-300
27 Russian	220	100-300
28 Spanish	220	100-300
29 Italian	220	100-300
30 Polish	220	100-300
32 Business Education	220	100-300
33 Accounting	220	100-300
34 Business Administration	220	100-300
35 Secretarial Sciences	220	100-300
36 Marketing (Distributive Education)	220	100-300
37 Agricultural Education	220	100-300
38 Industrial Arts	220	100-300

MORE ON APPENDIX B ...

APPENDIX B: LIST OF NES-DEVELOPED STATE TESTS

Appendix B: List of NES-Developed State Tests: 1998, cont'd.

39 Music Education	220	100-300
40 Home Economics	220	100-300
41 Art Education	220	100-300
42 Health, Physical Education, and Recreation	220	100-300
43 Health	220	100-300
44 Physical Education	220	100-300
46 Dance	220	100-300
47 Driver Education	220	100-300
48 Library Science	220	100-300
49 Environmental Studies	220	100-300
50 Computer Science	220	100-300
51 Guidance Counselor	220	100-300
53 Fine Arts	220	100-300
54 Humanities	220	100-300
56 Mentally Impaired	220	100-300
57 Speech and Language Impaired	220	100-300
58 Physically or Otherwise Health Impaired	220	100-300
59 Emotionally Impaired	220	100-300
61 Visually Impaired	220	100-300
62 Hearing Impaired	220	100-300
63 Learning Disabled	220	100-300
64 Autistic	220	100-300
65 Bilingual French	220	100-300
66 Bilingual German	220	100-300
67 Bilingual Greek	220	100-300
68 Bilingual Latin	220	100-300
69 Bilingual Russian	220	100-300
70 Bilingual Spanish	220	100-300
71 Bilingual Italian	220	100-300

MORE ON APPENDIX B ...

APPENDIX B: LIST OF NES-DEVELOPED STATE TESTS

Appendix B: List of NES-Developed State Tests: 1998, cont'd.

		Passing Score	Scale
	72 Bilingual Polish	220	100-300
	73 Bilingual Hebrew	220	100-300
	74 Bilingual Arabic	220	100-300
	75 Bilingual Other	220	100-300
	76 Bilingual Vietnamese	220	100-300
	77 Bilingual Korean	220	100-300
	78 Bilingual Yugoslavian	220	100-300
	79 Bilingual Chaldean	220	100-300
	80 Bilingual Chinese	220	100-300
	81 Bilingual Japanese	220	100-300
	82 Early Childhood Education	220	100-300
	83 Elementary Education	220	100-300
NEW MEXICO	NEW MEXICO TEACHER ASSESSMENTS (NMTA)	PASSING SCORE	SCALE
Basic Skills	New Mexico Assessment of Teacher Basic Skills	*	**
	New Mexico Assessment of Teacher General Knowledge	*	**
Professional Knowledge	New Mexico Assessment of Teacher Competency	*	**

*New Mexico has not yet established a cut score for the New Mexico Teacher Assessments.
**New Mexico has not yet established a scoring scale for the New Mexico Teacher Assessments.

NEW YORK	NEW YORK STATE TEACHER CERTIFICATION EXAMINATIONS (NYSTCE)	PASSING SCORE	SCALE
Basic Skills	90 Elementary Assessment of Teaching Skills, Written (ATS-W)	220	100-300
	91 Secondary Assessment of Teaching Skills, Written (ATS-W)	220	100-300
	01 Liberal Arts and Sciences (LAST)	220	100-300
	023 English Language Proficiency Assessment for Classroom Personnel (ELPA-C)	220	100-300
	024 Target Language Proficiency Assessment (TLPA) - Spanish	220	100-300
	026 Target Language Proficiency Assessment (TLPA) - Haitian Creole	220	100-300
	027 Target Language Proficiency Assessment (TLPA) - Cantonese	220	100-300
	028 Target Language Proficiency Assessment (TLPA) - Mandarin	220	100-300
	029 Target Language Proficiency Assessment (TLPA) - Russian	220	100-300
	030 Target Language Proficiency Assessment (TLPA) - Arabic	220	100-300

MORE ON APPENDIX B ...

APPENDIX B: LIST OF NES-DEVELOPED STATE TESTS

Appendix B: List of NES-Developed State Tests; 1998, cont'd.

		PASSING SCORE	SCALE
	031 Target Language Proficiency Assessment (TLPA) - French	220	100-300
	032 Target Language Proficiency Assessment (TLPA) - Korean	220	100-300
	034 Target Language Proficiency Assessment (TLPA) - Urdu	220	100-300
	037 Target Language Proficiency Assessment (TLPA) - Polish	220	100-300
	043 Target Language Proficiency Assessment (TLPA) - Bengali	220	100-300
	049 Target Language Proficiency Assessment (TLPA) - Vietnamese	220	100-300
Subject Matter Knowledge	02 Elementary Education	220	100-300
	03 English	220	100-300
	04 Mathematics	220	100-300
	05 Social Studies	220	100-300
	06 Biology	220	100-300
	07 Chemistry	220	100-300
	08 Earth Sciences	220	100-300
	09 Physics	220	100-300
	21 Early Childhood Education	220	100-300
	22 English to Speakers of Other Languages	220	100-300
	10 Latin	220	100-300
	11 Cantonese	220	100-300
	12 French	220	100-300
	13 German	220	100-300
	14 Greek	220	100-300
	15 Hebrew	220	100-300
	16 Italian	220	100-300
	17 Japanese	220	100-300
	18 Mandarin	220	100-300
	19 Russian	220	100-300
	20 Spanish	220	100-300
OKLAHOMA	CERTIFICATION EXAMINATIONS FOR OKLAHOMA EDUCATORS (CEOE)	PASSING SCORE	SCALE
Basic Skills	74 Oklahoma General Education Test (OGET)	240	100-300

MORE ON APPENDIX B …

APPENDIX B: LIST OF NES-DEVELOPED STATE TESTS

Appendix B: List of NES-Developed State Tests: 1998, cont'd.

Professional Knowledge		70 OPTE: Early Childhood Education (PK-3)	240	100-300
		71 OPTE: Elementary/ Middle Level (1-8 or 5-9)	240	100-300
		72 OPTE: Middle Level/Secondary (6-12 or 5-9)	240	100-300
		73 OPTE: Multi-Level (PK-12)	240	100-300
Subject Matter Knowledge		11 OSAT: Advanced Mathematics	240	100-300
		42 OSAT: Agricultural Education	240	100-300
		02 OSAT: Art	240	100-300
		10 OSAT: Biological Sciences	240	100-300
		28 OSAT: Blind/Visual Impairment	240	100-300
		40 OSAT: Business Education	240	100-300
		04 OSAT: Chemistry	240	100-300
		30 OSAT: Deaf/Hard of Hearing	240	100-300
		36 OSAT: Driver Safety Education	240	100-300
		05 OSAT: Early Childhood Education	240	100-300
		08 OSAT: Earth Science	240	100-300
		06 OSAT: Elementary Education	240	100-300
		07 OSAT: English	240	100-300
		09 OSAT: Family and Consumer Sciences	240	100-300
		20 OSAT: French	240	100-300
		21 OSAT: German	240	100-300
		01 OSAT: Instrumental/General Music	240	100-300
		37 OSAT: Journalism	240	100-300
		23 OSAT: Latin	240	100-300
		41 OSAT: Marketing Education	240	100-300
		24 OSAT: Middle Level English	240	100-300
		25 OSAT: Middle Level/Intermediate Mathematics	240	100-300
		26 OSAT: Middle Level Science	240	100-300
		27 OSAT: Middle Level Social Studies	240	100-300
		29 OSAT: Mild/Moderate Disabilities	240	100-300

MORE ON APPENDIX B ...

APPENDIX B: LIST OF NES-DEVELOPED STATE TESTS

Appendix B: List of NES-Developed State Tests: 1998, cont'd.

	TEST	PASSING SCORE	SCALE
	12 OSAT: Physical Education/Health/Safety	240	100-300
	13 OSAT: Physical Science	240	100-300
	14 OSAT: Physics	240	100-300
	32 OSAT: Psychology/Sociology	240	100-300
	22 OSAT: Russian	240	100-300
	31 OSAT: Severe/Profound/Multiple Disabilities	240	100-300
	19 OSAT: Spanish	240	100-300
	16 OSAT: Speech/Drama/Debate	240	100-300
	43 OSAT: Technology Education	240	100-300
	17 OSAT: U.S. History/OK History/Government/Economics	240	100-300
	03 OSAT: Vocal/General Music	240	100-300
	18 OSAT: World History/Geography	240	100-300
OREGON	TEST	PASSING SCORE	SCALE
Basic Skills	California Basic Educational Skills Test (CBEST): Reading	41	20-80
	California Basic Educational Skills Test (CBEST): Writing	41	20-80
	California Basic Educational Skills Test (CBEST): Mathematics	41	20-80
TEXAS	EXAMINATION FOR THE CERTIFICATION OF EDUCATORS IN TEXAS (ExCET)	PASSING SCORE	SCALE
Professional Knowledge	03 Secondary Professional Development	70	0-100
	02 Elementary Professional Development	70	0-100
Subject Matter	04 Elementary Comprehensive	70	0-100
	06 Art	70	0-100
	71 American Sign Language	70	0-100
	73 TASC-American Sign Language	70	0-100
	53 Basic Business	70	0-100
	23 Biology	70	0-100
	54 Business Administration	70	0-100
	52 Business Composite	70	0-100
	20 Chemistry	70	0-100

MORE ON APPENDIX B ...

APPENDIX B: LIST OF NES-DEVELOPED STATE TESTS

Appendix B: List of NES-Developed State Tests: 1998, cont'd.

18 Composite Science	70	0-100
24 Composite Social Studies	70	0-100
51 Computer Information Systems	70	0-100
44 Dance	70	0-100
21 Earth Science	70	0-100
27 Economics	70	0-100
16 English	70	0-100
48 French	70	0-100
26 Geography	70	0-100
49 German	70	0-100
25 Government	70	0-100
29 Health Education	70	0-100
28 History	70	0-100
30 Industrial Technology	70	0-100
46 Journalism	70	0-100
50 Latin	70	0-100
19 Life/Earth Science	70	0-100
65 Middle School Science	70	0-100
56 Marketing Education	70	0-100
17 Mathematics	70	0-100
08 Music	70	0-100
10 Physical Education	70	0-100
22 Physical Science	70	0-100
34 Physics	70	0-100
57 Psychology	70	0-100
45 Reading	70	0-100
55 Secretarial Business	70	0-100
58 Sociology	70	0-100
47 Spanish	70	0-100

MORE ON APPENDIX B ...

APPENDIX B: LIST OF NES-DEVELOPED STATE TESTS

Appendix B: List of NES-Developed State Tests: 1998, cont'd.

42 Speech Communication		70	0-100
41 Theater Arts		70	0-100
31 Vocational Home Economics		70	0-100
33 Vocational Agriculture: Horticulture		70	0-100
32 Vocation Agriculture: Production		70	0-100
05 All-Level Art		70	0-100
07 All-Level Music		70	0-100
09 All-Level Physical Education		70	0-100
40 Special Education-Hearing Impaired		70	0-100
72 TASC		70	0-100
66 Bilingual Elementary Comprehensive		70	0-100
67 Bilingual Endorsement		70	0-100
14 Early Childhood Education		70	0-100
12 English as a Second Language		70	0-100
11 Generic Special Education		70	0-100
41 Information Processing Technologies		70	0-100
35 Learning Resources		70	0-100
38 Severely Emotionally Disturbed and Autistic		70	0-100
37 Severely and Profoundly Handicapped		70	0-100
36 Visually Impaired		70	0-100
75 Braille		70	0-100
80 TOPT French		70	0-100
81 TOPT Spanish		70	0-100

Appendix D

Teacher Requirements in Six States

IDAHO'S TEACHER LICENSURE SYSTEM

The state of Idaho is in the midst of adopting a standards-based accountability system for students. The state board of education approved, and the legislature recently adopted, achievement standards in five content areas for students in grades 9-12. The state board is currently drafting achievement standards for students in K-8 that will be phased in over the next several years. There is also a movement under way to adopt new standards for teachers that are linked to the student standards. At this time, the standards for teachers seeking initial license are based on the standards of the National Council for Accreditation of Teacher Education (NCATE). The curriculum at teacher education programs in Idaho higher-education institutions is aligned with the NCATE standards.

Presently, the state requires teacher candidates to have graduated from an approved teacher education program and to have met the state's coursework requirements for initial teacher certification. There are no state-mandated testing requirements. The course requirements for elementary teachers include a minimum of 24 semester hours of professional education preparation and a minimum of 44 semester hours of general basic education classes. The course requirements for a secondary certificate include a minimum of 20 semester hours of professional education preparation and a minimum of a 30-semester-hour major and a 20-semester-hour minor, or a 45-semester-hour composite major for a secondary certificate. The state specifies that secondary education teachers must show competence to teach in two content areas for an initial teacher credential.

Based on an institutional recommendation from an Idaho college or university verifying that the teacher candidate has met the state's course requirements for either elementary or secondary teachers, the candidate is granted an initial teacher credential. Idaho's policy for granting initial teacher certification does not require candidates to demonstrate their knowledge, skills, or abilities to teach through any formal testing program (Educational Testing Service or National Evaluation Systems). However, because the state has spent a large amount of money in recent years equipping all schools with modern technology to advance student learning, the state, in 1999, instituted a requirement that initial teachers demonstrate computer competency. Teacher candidates can demonstrate computer competency through a passing score on the Idaho Technology Competency Examination, the Idaho Technology Portfolio Assessment, or the Idaho Performance Assessment.

Idaho Teacher Preparation Programs

In Idaho there are six higher-education institutions with state-approved teacher education programs (five of which are also NCATE accredited). The state grants liberty to the higher-education institution in structuring its teacher education program as long as the course requirements are fulfilled. For this reason the teacher education programs at the higher-education institutions in the state are not uniform in either their entry requirements or program design. Several of the teacher programs in the state are highlighted below.

Teacher Education at Boise State University

At Boise State, students apply for admittance into the teacher education program during their sophomore year. Entry into the teacher education program is based on several criteria, including a student's professional documentation, academic standards, and professional standards. The first criterion—professional documentation—substantiates the student's ability and desire to work with children. Students are asked to provide written evidence of prior work with children or young people in a formal setting, to write an essay describing the significance of the experience as it relates to the student's professional goals, and to provide letters of recommendation from professionals familiar with the student's work with children.

To fulfill the second criterion—academic standards—students are required to have a minimum grade point average (GPA) of 2.5. Students are also required to have at least a C on each teacher education prerequisite class. Students applying for entry into the elementary education program are required to complete classes in English composition, math, and science as well as seven teacher education classes. They are also required to earn a set passing score on the math (175) and writing (172) portions of Praxis I. Students interested in becoming secondary education teachers have less specific course requirements for entry into the teacher education program but must major in a content area (biology, math, Spanish, etc.). Students applying for entry into the secondary education program must receive a set passing score (172) on only the writing component of Praxis I.

The final criterion for admittance into the teacher education program—professional standards—is based on faculty's judgment of a student's skills, behavioral characteristics, and disposition for being a teacher. The Teacher Education Professional Standards Committee reviews and approves each student's application for admittance into the program by weighing his or her performance on each criterion.

During their junior year, students must apply to student teach. For an elementary education major to be eligible for student teaching, the student must have a GPA of at least 3.0 in all teacher education classes and a 2.75 overall. The student must also have successfully completed a microteaching assignment in one of four elementary education curriculum and instruction courses and must have a recommendation from a faculty member.

After the student has completed the bachelor's degree in either elementary or secondary education and completed all teacher education requirements, the student provides the College of Education with all necessary paperwork, including the application for an Idaho Professional Education Credential. The dean of the College of Education will then recommend the candidate to the Idaho board of education for a teaching credential.

Teacher Education at Albertson College

The foundation of the teacher education program at Albertson College is the liberal arts, with students required to major in a content area. The teacher education program is a five-year program built around the Interstate New Teacher Assessment and Support Consortium (INTASC) standards. These teaching standards include subject matter knowledge, adapting instruction to individual needs, classroom motivation/management, and assessment of student learning. Students who are interested in being teachers are placed in a cohort as freshmen and remain with the same cohort for the duration of the program. Students interested in becoming teachers also have a team of mentors, including an academic adviser, an education professor, and a K-12 teacher, who guide their development throughout the program.

Students apply for formal admittance into the teacher education program during their sophomore year. To be considered for admission into the program, students must have a cumulative GPA of 2.75. Students must also submit the portfolio they maintain throughout the program for consideration. The portfolio must show evidence of a reflective attitude toward teaching, an understanding of how children learn, and an involvement in the education community. The final factor is a successful interview with the student's mentors.

After elementary and secondary education students have graduated, the students must complete a fifth-year internship in the schools in order to be recommended for an Idaho teacher certificate. A formal review of the student's portfolio must also occur prior to approval for entry into the internship program. At this time, the student's portfolio must show some evidence of each teaching standard. The portfolio should also emphasize the student's knowledge of the subject matter and ability to plan instruction. Specifically, the portfolio should highlight the student's ability to integrate technology into instruction and to use multiple instructional strategies.

The portfolio is formally reviewed for a final time at completion of the internship program, prior to the student receiving an institutional recommendation for an Idaho teacher certificate. During this final review, the portfolio should show evidence of mastery of all teaching standards and should include the candidate's philosophy of teaching, a resume, and other items helpful in obtaining a teaching position. With an institutional recommendation to the state by the college, students are granted an Idaho teaching credential.

Teacher Education at Lewis-Clark State College

The faculty in the education division at Lewis-Clark believe that a qualified teacher must demonstrate knowledge, skills, and disposition related to seven main areas or qualities of professional competence—appropriate professional conduct; knowledge of the foundations of the profession; content mastery; skills as an educational designer, facilitator and evaluator; and capacity for reflective practice. As such, the faculty has designed a comprehensive evaluation process for deciding which students are admitted into the program.

The criteria for admission to the teacher education program include satisfactory completion of prerequisite coursework with a grade of B or better in each course, a minimum cumulative GPA of 2.75 (secondary education teacher candidates must have at least a 3.0 in their major teaching field), professional experience working with children, three faculty references, a passing score on all four sections (writing, interview, technology, and math and science) of the education division's entrance examination (an institution-developed test), and an application to the program. There is a systematic weighting of the criteria, with greater weight assigned to scholarship. After submitting an application with all relevant information, a student is formally interviewed and required to write an extemporaneous essay. The interview and essay are given numerical weights by the interview panel, which makes the final recommendation for admission. Students lose points during the admission process for paracompetencies and moral turpitude.

The elementary and secondary teacher education programs have three phases. Students complete phase I, Pre-Professional Studies, prior to admission to the program. Phase II, Professional Studies, begins once students are admitted into the program and includes evaluation strategies and theoretical foundations.

The final phase, Professional Internship, lasts a year and includes student teaching and seminars.

At the completion of the teacher education program and prior to being recommended for state certification, students must pass a final review of their work. Each student must complete a formal oral evaluation by at least three faculty members at which time the candidate's teaching portfolio is evaluated. After the candidate passes the final oral review, he or she submits the requisite paperwork to the college's education division. The college will then endorse the student with an institutional recommendation and forward all paperwork to the state's education agency for the graduate's teaching credential.

Changes In Initial Teacher Licensure System

Idaho is in the process of adopting new teaching standards based on the INTASC model: knowledge, disposition, and performance. The standards will be aligned with the newly adopted K-12 achievement standards and will reflect a move to performance-based standards. The new teaching standards were adopted by the state's board of education in the fall of 2000. The state's MOST (Maximizing Opportunities for Students and Teachers) program, which is overseeing the revision and adoption of new teaching standards, is focusing on four components: teacher preparation, certification, professional development, and the teaching environment.

In August 2000 the MOST program received a Title II grant from the U.S. Department of Education to further the state's process in implementing aspects of the program, specifically to assist the state in revising initial teacher certification and certification renewal requirements, to hold institutions with teacher education programs accountable for preparing quality teachers, and to improve alternate routes to teacher certification for highly qualified individuals from other fields and professions.

WYOMING'S TEACHER PREPARATION SYSTEM

Wyoming is one of the latest states to adopt a statewide standards-based student testing program—the Wyoming Comprehensive Assessment System. WyCAS was designed to measure how well students in grades 4, 8, and 11 are mastering the recently developed state standards in reading/language arts and mathematics, with student performance on the WyCAS reported at the state, district/school, and individual student levels. The results of WyCAS are used not only to assess student performance but also to provide information to the schools and districts for evaluating their teaching and curriculum.

Yet Wyoming is one of the few states that has not adopted teacher testing requirements for candidates seeking an initial teaching license. To receive an initial license in the state, a teacher candidate must complete an approved teacher preparation program at a regionally or nationally accredited institution or complete a successful portfolio verifying competence of the Professional Teaching Standards Board (PTSB) standards. A teacher candidate must also complete either a course or test on the U.S. Constitution and the Wyoming Constitution. There are no state-specified testing requirements.

The state has established program approval standards for teacher education programs. The PTSB oversees program approval in the state. It also delineates teaching standards that must be included in an approved teacher education program pertaining to both coursework and field practice. Currently, there are only three higher-education institutions (four-year colleges/universities) with state-approved programs, with only one program—the University of Wyoming—residing in the state. The other two institutions with approved and accredited teacher education programs are in neighboring states—Black Hills State University in South Dakota and Regis University in Colorado.

All teacher candidates trained in the state matriculate through the University of Wyoming at some point in their teacher preparation program. Students can either attend the University of Wyoming for their entire degree or start the teacher preparation program at one of the state's seven community colleges, graduate with an associates degree in elementary or secondary education, and then attend the University of Wyoming at Laramie, the Casper College Center, Powell College Center, or one of five professional development schools to complete their degree.

Teacher Preparation Program

The University of Wyoming's teacher education program has four levels. Students in the first level take an introductory course on teaching and spend supervised time in a school setting working with a mentor teacher while fulfilling general education requirements. The first level of the program (called "Becoming a Teacher") can be fulfilled at either a community college or the university. At the end of the sophomore or second year after completing the two introductory education courses and obtaining a first aid certificate, all students in the state must apply for admittance into the university's teacher education program.

To be admitted into the program a student must have at least a 2.5 cumulative GPA in the first two years of school. Though the state does not have testing requirements for teacher licensure, the University of Wyoming requires teacher education students to have an ACT-composite score of 21 (if the composite score is 18 to 20, a minimum 3.0 cumulative GPA is required). Similarly, though neither Wyoming nor South Dakota requires testing for initial licensure, Black Hills State requires students to have successfully completed Praxis I (formerly the Pre-Professional Skills Test) with set passing scores in all three areas (mathematics, writing, and reading) for admittance into the teacher education program.

After a student has been admitted to the University of Wyoming's teacher education program, he or she is considered to be at the second level of the program, called "Teacher as a Decision Maker." At this level students take more coursework on the principles of teaching and learning and gain additional educational experience in the classroom at their grade of choice. Students also fulfill requirements for coursework in their majors at this time. The elementary education program requires majors to select a concentration (21 credit hours) in cultural diversity, environmental studies, creative arts, interdisciplinary early childhood, and special education, while the secondary education majors have content requirements to fulfill.

All students must then apply for admittance at the end of their junior year to the third level called "Methods in Humanities, Literacy, and Math/Science." To be admitted to the third level, students must have at least a 2.5 GPA and have completed all specified prerequisite coursework for enrolling in the level three methods courses. During level three, students spend approximately 11 weeks attending classes and 4 weeks in the schools applying what they are learning. In the final level, called "Residency in Teaching," students spend a full semester in residency at a school setting completing a student teaching experience.

Initial Certification

Upon graduation, a teacher candidate applies to the PTSB for a Standard Teaching Certificate (one type of certificate for all teachers). Each candidate provides the PTSB with a transcript verifying completion of the teacher education program. The PTSB reviews the transcript (for a fee of $175) along with a form signed by university personnel documenting that the candidate graduated from a state-approved program and endorsing the candidate as possessing the requisite knowledge and competencies to be a teacher.

There is one alternative route to certification in Wyoming for those students who have not completed a teacher education program but who have completed a bachelor's degree and have experience working with school-age children (in lieu of student teaching experience). Certification decisions in such cases are made based on a portfolio the candidate submits to the PTSB.

ALASKA INITIAL TEACHER LICENSURE SYSTEM

The state of Alaska adopted a statewide educational reform effort, the Quality Schools Initiative (QSI), in 1998. The four key components of the QSI are high academic standards for all students; quality standards for educators; family, school, business, and community partnerships; and excellent schools. The QSI established new performance standards in reading, writing, and mathematics as well as content standards in history, science, geography, citizenship, the arts, world languages, and healthy life skills.

The standards for educators adopted by the Alaska Board of Education in 1994 outline the skills and abilities that Alaskan teachers should possess for effective teaching. The standards are for all teachers, including beginning teachers, and include content knowledge, knowledge of how students learn, and knowledge of how to facilitate, monitor, and assess student learning. The goal is for teaching to be directly linked to student achievement in a results-based accountability system.

Another aspect of the state accountability system involves setting high standards for candidates seeking an initial teacher license in the state. The state added a requirement that all candidates must take Praxis I (Reading, 175; Writing, 174; and Math, 173) prior to receiving a license. Candidates must also complete an approved teacher education program and have earned a bachelor's degree. Candidates must submit an institutional recommendation prior to being granted an initial license and must fulfill a recency requirement. Candidates must also complete a course in Alaska studies and multicultural or cross-cultural education. Candidates apply directly to the state for initial license ($165 application fee).

As part of the accountability system, the state has recently adopted NCATE standards for program review of all teacher education programs. Hence, all programs (public and private) are required to obtain NCATE accreditation. There are five higher-education institutions in the state with approved teacher education programs. A major redesign of the teacher education program offered at the state's universities is now under way. A brief description of the redesign follows.

Redesign of Teacher Education

The University of Alaska offers three of the five teacher education programs in the state in Anchorage, Fairbanks, and Southeast (in Juneau), respectively. In 1999, the president of the University of Alaska statewide-system designated teacher education as one of his top priorities for the university system, and this has resulted in increased funding for the schools of education. One result of the focus on the teacher education programs has been to strengthen the subject matter preparation of prospective teachers. Accordingly, both the president and the university regents have supported the development of postbaccalaureate teacher education programs. All students who apply for admission to postbaccalaureate programs must have completed a four-year content degree. All campuses currently have postbaccalaureate programs for elementary and secondary teacher education. Additionally, new undergraduate degree programs for future elementary teachers are being designed. The new four-year degrees in education include liberal studies components that provide future elementary teachers with a breadth of coursework across the disciplines.

The Alaska Partnership for Teacher Enhancement (APTE) was formed to guide and oversee redesign of the teacher education programs at the University of Alaska, Anchorage (UAA). Two of the goals are to assure that the teacher education components are aligned with both the Alaska student and educator standards and to assure that graduates of the programs are effectively prepared to meet the unique needs of students in the state. The APTE is a partnership involving urban and rural school districts (three of the poorest in the state), the Alaska Board of Education and Early Development, private business, and the university. University partners include the College of Arts and Sciences, the School of Education, the UAA Provost's Office, the UA Office of the President, and the Institute of Social and Economic Research. The inclusion of multiple partners within the university is a demonstration of the understanding that the preparation of teachers is an integral part of the entire university community.

Under APTE vision, the postbaccalaureate teacher education curriculum is based on strong content preparation. Also, teaching candidates will complete a year-long internship in the schools, and a supervision team for each prospective teacher will include a K-12 mentor, a UAA College of Arts and Sciences tutor, and a faculty member from the UAA School of Education. Several new institutional structures will be put in place to monitor and guide changes in the teacher education program. For example, the Teacher Education Council will be an advisory body that will evaluate the progress of the UAA in making appropriate program modifications and assuring the involvement of all relevant parties. Multiple teams will develop teacher education courses and plan the clinical experiences and internships. There will also be a curriculum coordinating committee that will be responsible for development of the curriculum in a manner that assures maximum curricular coherence.

Post Baccalaureate Teacher Preparation at the University of Alaska

In July 2000 the UAA began a new postbaccalaureate program for future elementary and secondary education teachers. It is a one-year integrated program that combines 36 credit hours of coursework and field experience. Admission requirements include completion of a bachelor's degree with a minimum GPA of 3.0; GRE minimum scores of 400 in the verbal, mathematics, and analytical sections; Praxis I scores that meet Alaska state requirements; and appropriate Praxis II scores. Applicants must also provide evidence of experience with school-aged children and three letters of recommendation that highlight the applicant's qualifications to teach. After applications have been screened, strong candidates are interviewed and final admission decisions are made.

The program follows a cohort model and students begin the program in June. Summer coursework includes nine credit hours of education foundation content and an introduction to educational technology. During the fall and spring semesters, students take six credit hours of methods coursework and receive six credits for school internships. Students complete the certification program the following June with a three-credit course entitled "Internship Capstone Seminar:

Analysis of Teaching and Learning." Upon completion of the teacher certifica-tion program, candidates can apply to the state for an initial teacher's license. To complete the master's of education degree, students must complete an addi-tional 12 credits of coursework.

The other two University of Alaska campuses, Fairbanks and Southeast, also have suspended admission into their bachelor's teacher education programs and have adopted similar fifth-year teacher certification and master's of teaching programs. Admission into the programs on both campuses is contingent on an applicant completing a bachelor's degree (3.0 GPA), obtaining Alaska passing scores on Praxis I, and providing three letters of recommendation. At the Univer-sity of Alaska, Southeast, applicants also must submit a portfolio of written materials. At the University of Alaska, Fairbanks, applicants must submit a vitae/resume, a four– to five-page statement of goals highlighting why the appli-cant wishes to study in the education program, and their qualifications and edu-cational experience. Applicants must also submit GRE scores for the secondary program, while GRE scores are required for admission to the elementary pro-gram only if a candidate's GPA is less than 3.0. Finally, applicants must com-plete an extemporaneous writing sample in person on campus.

Teacher Education at Alaska's Private Schools

Sheldon-Jackson College is one of two private higher-education institutions in Alaska that offer an undergraduate teacher education program. Sheldon-Jack-son has an open admissions policy and largely serves native Alaskans. All students are required to meet competencies in reading, writing, and mathematics and to fulfill general course requirements. To be admitted to the four-year tradi-tional teacher education program, students must have a minimum cumulative GPA of 2.5. To remain in the program, students must maintain a 2.5 GPA in all education courses and obtain a first aid/CPR certificate. Students must also take Praxis I, with student teaching contingent on passing at the 50th percentile or higher on all subtests.

Alaska Pacific University is a small private institution located in Anchorage that also has a Rural Alaska Native Adult (RANA) program. The university offers an undergraduate major in K-8 education at its home campus and through RANA. Students apply for admission into the teacher education program during their sophomore year after meeting the general university course requirements. Students must have a cumulative GPA of 2.75 or better to be admitted. Several field experiences are built into the program, and students complete the teacher education program with a 15-week practicum in the schools.

NEBRASKA'S TEACHER LICENSURE SYSTEM

The Nebraska Board of Education establishes the state's standards for teacher education program approval and initial teacher licensure. There are four rules that guide the approval of teacher education programs and licensure of teachers in the state. The four rules describe the regulations that govern the approval of teacher education programs in the state (Rule 20), outline the general guidelines for granting teaching licenses in the state (Rule 21), refer to the basic skills test requirement for all teacher education majors and include the passing scores that have been in effect since 1989 (Rule 23), and outline the specifications for content majors or endorsements for teachers (Rule 24).

The rules are generally reviewed and revised every five years with guidance from the Nebraska Council on Teacher Education, an advisory group established by the board to monitor and make recommendations to it about issues pertaining to teacher education and teaching standards. The members of the council are appointed by the state board and represent teachers, the higher-education community, administrators, school board members, and the state department of education.

To be granted an initial teacher license in Nebraska, a teacher candidate must fulfill certain criteria. The teaching candidate must be a graduate of an approved teacher education program, with institutional verification provided for each candidate. All prospective teacher education majors must meet the basic skills requirement in reading, writing, and mathematics by passing either the Content Mastery Examination for Educators or Praxis I. Nebraska legislative statute requires students to pass the basic skills exam prior to being admitted into a teacher education program; hence, all candidates from state-approved teacher education programs have previously met this certification criterion.

Legislative statute also mandates that candidates complete a special education course requirement as well as a requirement for human relations training prior to being granted an initial teacher license. In 1967 the Nebraska legislature authorized development of standards of conduct and ethics that all teachers, including initial teachers, must adhere to as well. Nebraska's certification rule also has a recency requirement that can be met through two consecutive years of teaching experience in the same school system in the previous five years or by taking at least six semester hours of approved credit within the past three years of the candidate's application date.

The Nebraska Board of Education requires all students seeking admission to teacher education programs (and those seeking licensure in the state) to provide evidence that they have no felony convictions or misdemeanor convictions involving abuse, neglect, or sexual misconduct. Students/licensure applicants with such convictions are automatically rejected and can only be approved for admission to the program or licensure following a successful appeal to the commissioner of education and the Nebraska Board of Education.

Teacher Preparation Programs

In Nebraska there are 16 higher-education institutions with approved teacher education programs, the majority (13) of which are NCATE accredited. Nebraska's higher-education institutions have freedom in designing their teacher education programs as long as the coursework requirements required by the state and the standards in Rule 20 are fulfilled. Several of the state's teacher education programs are highlighted below.

Teacher Education at the University of Nebraska, Lincoln

The University of Nebraska, Lincoln, has the largest education school in the state, serving some 2,000 undergraduates and 750 graduate students each year. A student interested in becoming a teacher can apply for admission into the teachers college directly from high school as long as the student is in the upper half of his or her high school graduating class or has met minimum scores on the ACT or SAT (Step I). All other interested students apply for admission into the teacher education program during their sophomore year.

To be considered for admission into the teacher education program (Step II), a student must meet the following criteria: completion of at least 42 credit hours with a minimum GPA of 2.5, specific coursework requirements, she or he must have passed the basic skills exam required by the state, faculty recommendations, and she or he must have successfully completed the first phase of the college technology requirement. In deciding which students to admit into the program, the faculty selection committee considers the academic achievement of each student; accomplishments in areas such as second-language acquisition, math, and computer skills; a student's ability to work in cross-cultural settings with members of diverse groups; and the student's commitment to the profession and his or her ability to meet the state's professional standards.

The scholar-practitioner model serves as a framework for student learning in the teacher education program at the University of Nebraska. With this model there is a greater emphasis on active learning, inquiry, and reflection for the students, with more school-based methods and practicum experiences provided. In the teacher education program, there are over 40 teaching endorsements available across the three tracks of elementary, middle, and secondary education.

To be eligible for the student teaching experience (Step III), a student must have senior standing with a minimum cumulative GPA of 2.5. Specific course requirements also must be fulfilled to be eligible for the full-day, 16-week student teaching experience. After a student has completed the student teaching experience, has completed a minimum of 125 credit hours with at least a 2.5 cumulative GPA, and has earned a 2.5 GPA in the endorsement (no grade lower than a C in endorsement and professional courses), the student applies to the

College of Education for both a degree and a recommendation for a state teacher's certificate.

Teacher Education at Wayne State College

The history of Wayne State College documents the institution's allegiance to the preparation of teachers. The institution began in 1891 as the Nebraska Normal School. It was purchased by the state in 1910 and renamed the State Teachers College at Wayne, with a bachelor's degree in education the only degree available from 1910 to 1949. The institution was given its present name in 1963, with a school of education established several years later.

There has always been an open admissions policy at Wayne State College, with the institution committed to a multicultural education for its students. All students who have graduated from an accredited high school are admitted into the institution. Students who are interested in becoming teachers must apply to the teacher education program, which has four gateways or stages. The benchmark criteria for admittance into the program (Gateway 1) include completion of at least 15 credit hours at Wayne State College, with a cumulative GPA of 2.5 or higher in all coursework and a C or better in coursework in endorsement areas and professional education classes. Students must also have passed Praxis I at the state-specified scores and have a field experience recommendation from a classroom teacher.

Gateways 2 and 3 are specific to each student's program area—elementary, secondary, or special education. The benchmark criterion for Gateway 2 involves obtaining three faculty recommendations, with slightly different requirements depending on the student's program area. The benchmark criterion for Gateway 3 pertains to fulfilling coursework requirements. Gateway 4 is initiated by applying for student teaching and is passed through by successfully completing the semester-long student teaching experience.

Teacher Education at Creighton University

Creighton University is a private Jesuit college with a strong liberal arts core curriculum. All students must fulfill coursework requirements in five categories: theology, philosophy and ethics, cultures, ideas and civilizations, natural science, social science, and skills (math, writing, foreign language). Students apply for entry into the teacher education program during their sophomore year. Students must have achieved the state's passing scores on Praxis I, fulfilled several course requirements, and have an overall GPA of at least 2.5 to be considered for admission into the program. A selection-and-retention committee reviews the applications and determines who is eligible for admission into the program. During the junior year, students in both the elementary and secondary programs acquire field experience in both public and parochial school settings. Student teaching occurs during the senior year.

Title II State Grant

Nebraska is exploring different methods to assess the strength of its teacher education programs and was awarded a Title II grant by the U.S. Department of Education to support this endeavor. The grant will be used to pilot the use of teacher tests as a possible accountability measure of teacher education programs. The state will pay the testing costs for students who will be student teaching in elementary, middle, and high schools during the 2000-2001 and 2001-2002 academic years. All students will take the Principles of Teaching and Learning test, an Educational Testing Service product. Students seeking an endorsement in elementary education will also be required to take the ETS's Elementary Education: Curriculum, Instruction, and Assessment. There is no plan to incorporate the use of these tests as additional requirements for an initial teaching license. The state intends to explore the use of student's scores on these tests as one measure of the strength of its teacher education programs.

CALIFORNIA'S TEACHER PREPARATION SYSTEM

The state of California is currently experiencing a significant shortage of teachers, with a predicted need for an additional 250,000 to 300,000 teachers in the next decade. The demand for new teachers is fueled by changes in state policy regarding class size reduction, a high number of teachers seeking retirement, and significant growth in the student population. The state anticipates that 1 million more students will be attending California schools by 2005 than did in 1998-1999. The greatest need for teachers is, and will be in the near future, in elementary education, special education, language acquisition and development, mathematics, and science. Urban and rural areas are experiencing the most significant teacher shortages. To address the demand for new teachers, a variety of teacher preparation programs have been developed in the state to provide multiple opportunities for individuals to seek teacher licensure and accelerate the time line for certification.

There are three general pathways to gaining preliminary teacher licensure in California: traditional teacher preparation programs, district internship programs, and university internship programs. California has also established a preinternship program that assists emergency teachers in meeting prerequisites for entry into one of the three formal teacher preparation programs. Each program is highlighted below.

Traditional Teacher Preparation Programs

Traditional teacher preparation programs are part of higher-education institutions. Currently, there are over 70 higher-education institutions offering teacher education and certification programs in California. During the 1997-1998 academic year, 19,156 teacher candidates were prepared by higher-education institutions in the state and received initial licensure. Among the teachers earning initial licensure, 4,654 obtained their first credentials. Over 14,500 had previously held certification such as a long-term emergency permit or substitute certification that authorized them to serve in classrooms. In the 1997-1998 school year, California state universities prepared 55 percent of the teachers, private or independent institutions prepared roughly 40 percent, and University of California institutions prepared 4 percent (California Commission on Teacher Credentialing, 2000).

There are several basic requirements for enrollment in California teacher preparation programs. To enroll, an individual must take the California Basic Educational Skills Test (CBEST) for diagnostic purposes. Some institutions require individuals to pass the test prior to formal enrollment. All individuals must pass it in order to earn the teaching credential.

CBEST assesses a candidate's proficiency in reading, writing, and mathematics in the English language. Separate scores are provided for each of the three sections. All three sections must be passed, and a test taker may take one, two, or three sections at a given administration. There is no limit to the number of times a candidate may sit for the test. CBEST is offered six times a year and costs $40 each time. The testing time is approximately four hours for the entire test (50 questions each for reading and math and two writing sections). An individual taking only one or two sections of the test may use the entire four-hour period to complete the section(s) taken.

In most cases an individual must hold a bachelor's degree from a regionally accredited university prior to formal enrollment in a teacher preparation program. Many institutions allow individuals to complete some of the teacher preparation courses in their undergraduate program but do not allow them to formally enroll in the program until they have earned a degree.

California has begun to allow universities to develop "blended" programs that integrate a bachelor's degree program with a teacher preparation program. Candidates in these programs earn a preliminary credential at the time they earn their degree in an academic area. Currently there are 31 institutions of higher education with such approved programs.

State standards do not specify a GPA requirement for admittance to a teacher preparation program. However, a GPA requirement may be established within the program developed by a particular institution. For admittance into most California State University programs, a GPA at the median for the candidate's major is typically required. To enter programs at University of California schools, a GPA of at least a 3.0 is required. Some private institutions permit conditional admittance into their teacher preparation programs with a GPA lower than 2.5.

There are additional requirements that must be met for a candidate to be granted a California teaching license, including completion of either a course or an examination on the U.S. Constitution, completion of a "teaching of reading" course, and passage of a test on reading instruction—the Reading Instruction Competence Assessment (RICA). Candidates who seek a Multiple Subject Teaching Credential (elementary school teachers) or an Education Specialist Instruction Credential must take the RICA, which assesses a candidate's knowledge and skills of effective reading instruction. A candidate can pass RICA by taking either the written examination (paper-and-pencil assessment, including a constructed-response section and a 70-item multiple-choice section) or the video performance assessment (candidate-created videotapes of the candidate teaching reading). The written examination is offered six times a year, at a cost of $122 per administration. There are three times in the year that a candidate can submit a video performance assessment for review, at a cost of $220 per administration.

The requirements also include demonstration of subject matter competence by one of two options: (1) completion of a program of subject matter coursework at a commission-approved institution or (2) passage of the commission-approved examination(s) for the credential area. Elementary teachers must pass the Multiple Subjects Assessment for Teachers (MSAT), which measures knowledge in seven content areas: literature and language studies, mathematics, history/social sciences, science, visual and performing arts, human development, and physical education. There are two sections to the MSAT: a multiple-choice content knowledge section (testing time is two hours, 120 items) and constructed-response content area exercises section (testing time is three hours, 18 questions). A candidate can sit for either or both sections at one of the eight test administrations. If both sections are taken at one time, the cost is $215 ($70 for the content knowledge section, $110 for the content area exercises, and $35 for registration). If the sections are taken separately, the cost is $105 for the content knowledge section and $145 for the content area exercises.

Depending on the subject matter, secondary school teachers choosing the examination option to meet the subject matter requirement must pass either the Single Subject Assessment for Teaching (SSAT) exams or a combination of SSAT and Praxis content tests. For example, teacher candidates seeking licensure in health science must pass only the SSAT, while a teacher candidate seeking licensure in mathematics must pass the SSAT in general mathematics content as well as two Praxis tests—Proofs, Models, and Problems (Parts I and II). There are six testing dates for Praxis; the cost is $105 to $120 ($70 to $85 plus $35 for registration), depending on the tests taken. There are four testing dates for the SSAT; the cost ranges from $100 to $145 depending on the test taken.

The majority of higher-education institutions seek candidates who have completed their baccalaureate and meet the other stated requirements prior to admittance to the teacher preparation program. Several of the state's universities do allow undergraduates to enroll in teacher education programs with the provision that these requirements be met prior to formal enrollment in a program and student teaching. Upon completion of most teacher preparation programs, candidates are awarded a preliminary license that is valid for five years.

There are several different kinds of preliminary teacher licenses in California, and most institutions offer preparation for several of the licenses. The most common licenses granted by the state are the Multiple Subject Teaching Credential and the Single Subject Teaching Credential. The Multiple Subject Teaching Credential authorizes public school teaching in a self-contained classroom in preschool, kindergarten, grades 1 through 12, and classes organized primarily for adults. Secondary school teachers are granted a Single Subject Teaching Credential, which authorizes teaching in a departmentalized classroom. Single subject credentials are issued in 13 different subject-areas, and the holder is authorized to teach only in the subject area(s) listed. Due to the diversity of student enrollment in California, the state has also instituted a multiple- and single-subject certification with either a cross-cultural, language, and academic development emphasis (CLAD) or bilingual, cross-cultural, language, and academic development emphasis (BCLAD).

Although the higher-education institutions have enhanced/added to their teacher preparation programs, there continues to be a shortage of teachers. To assuage the need for licensed teachers, the state of California granted initial licensure to some 5,000 teachers from out of state in the 1997-1998 school year. The same year the California legislature passed a number of provisions that eased the transition of teachers from other states into California. The state also granted 31,061 emergency permits and 4,791 waivers in the 1997-1998 school year (out of the total 63,418 initial licensures granted by the state). Teachers must be working toward receiving initial licensure while on internships, emergency permits, or waivers. Several programs have been developed to support teachers with emergency or internship certification while they seek initial licensure. Each type of program is highlighted below.

University Internship Programs

Many higher-education institutions in the state have entered into a partnership with local school districts and established university internship programs. The programs are designed to provide participants with classroom experience while they are enrolled in the academic teacher preparation program. A candidate is issued a "university internship credential" once enrolled in a California Commission on Teacher Credentialing-approved internship program, with verification of employment from the relevant school district. University internship credentials are offered in several areas, including Multiple Subject Teaching,

Single Subject Teaching, Multiple Subject Teaching with CLAD and BCLAD emphases, and Single Subject Teaching with CLAD and BCLAD emphases.

Enrollment requirements for university internship programs vary depending on the type of credential sought and the requirements established by the respective college or university in tandem with the respective school district. All require possession of a bachelor's degree, passage of the CBEST, and completion of at least 80 percent of the subject matter competence requirement. Currently, there are 20 California state universities, 7 Universities of California, and 22 private institutions with approved internship programs. In the 1997-1998 academic year, 2,306 individuals were issued internship credentials to teach through university partnership programs across the state.

The university internship can be based on several different models depending on the needs of the districts that the universities are serving. Institutions such as California State University, Hayward, determine in partnership with the respective school districts (Alameda and Contra Costa counties and Oakland, Concord, and Hayward school districts) whether a student participates in the program as a student teacher or a full-paid intern. Depending on the partnership and the needs of the district, the program might be community based with the intern teaching all day and enrolled in classes at night. Under this kind of program, such as with the Oakland Unified School District, interns seeking a single-subject credential complete the program in seven quarters. In other partnerships, students may spend considerable time in the schools gaining student teaching experience prior to taking full leadership of a classroom. For example, students enrolled in the School-University Partnership Internship Program at San Jose State attend school for two summers, with a full paid internship for two academic years, though the student remains in the role of a student teacher throughout the program.

District Internship Programs

During the 1997-1998 school year, there were 103 districts with 20 percent or more of the teacher staff on emergency permits or waivers. The majority of the districts with high numbers of teachers on emergency permits or waivers are in urban areas. For example, in the Los Angeles area, some districts report that 30 to 50 percent of the teachers in their schools have emergency permits or waivers, with three out of four new hires uncredentialed in the Los Angeles Unified School District as of August 2000 (www.lausd.k12.ca.us/).

To decrease the number of teachers with emergency permits and waivers, six large urban districts have established district intern programs taught by school district employees. The teachers participating in this program are granted a "district intern certificate," valid for two years, from the state. To qualify for a district intern certificate, an individual must have completed a baccalaureate or higher degree from a regionally accredited college or university. To receive the single-subject authorization, the intern must have a major or minor in the subject to be taught or have passed the appropriate subject matter assessment. For the multiple-subject (self-contained classroom) authorization, the intern must have at least 40 semester units of coursework in language studies, literature, mathematics, science, social science, history, humanities, the arts, physical education, and human development and must have passed the MSAT. Additionally, the interns must pass the CBEST and possess a certificate of clearance verifying the personal identification and good moral character of the intern. This clearance process is required for the issuance of all California credentials, certificates, and permits.

In the Los Angeles Unified School District, the tuition-free program is available in elementary education, elementary bilingual (Spanish), secondary English, secondary science, and secondary mathematics. Interns receive 120 hours of preservice prior to classroom assignment, with subsequent classes held once a week during the school year (in English or Spanish). The interns also work with a mentor teacher during the program. An additional training component of at least 64 hours is held the second summer. District interns qualify for benefits and a salary during the two-year contractual period. Approximately 700 interns participated in the program as of August, 2000 <www.lausd.k12.ca.us/>. The Los Angeles Unified School District also has a district intern program for special education teachers.

Preinternship Program

The preintern certificate, an alternative to the emergency permit, is available only to individuals in approved preintern programs conducted by school districts and county offices of education that have received state grants to fund these programs. The preintern certificate program was designed to improve the effectiveness and retention of teachers with emergency certification. The goal of the program is to offer emergency licensed teachers support and training to meet the requirements of teaching intern and credential programs. To qualify for a preintern certificate, an individual must have a baccalaureate degree and must have passed the CBEST.

Additionally, to be eligible for a preinternship certificate for elementary teaching, an individual must show intent to complete the MSAT and show verification of successful completion of coursework (at least 40 semester units with a C grade) in four of the following areas: language studies, history, literature, humanities, mathematics, the arts, science, physical education, social science, and human development. To be eligible for a single-subject teaching preintern certificate, the candidate must show intent to complete the appropriate content assessment (Praxis and/or SSAT) and have completed 18 semester units in the subject to be listed on the certificate. At this time, the single-subject teaching preintern certificate is available in mathematics, science, and English. Individuals who have completed the subject matter requirement or student teaching and/ or a credential program are not eligible for this program.

There are currently 58 approved preintern programs, funded with state grants. These programs serve approximately 300 California school districts. In the San Francisco Unified School District, the preintern program provides up to two years of support for teachers with emergency licensure. Teachers with preintern certificates attend MSAT preparation workshops along with workshops on classroom management and instructional strategies. Teachers with preintern certificates also receive classroom support and coaching from a mentor teacher.

Title II State Grant

California is planning to reform its licensure and certification requirements and has been awarded a Title II grant from the U.S. Department of Education to support this endeavor. The grant funding is being used to develop and implement standards-based teaching performance assessments for teaching credential candidates, to reduce the number of teachers working with emergency permits by expanding alternative preparation programs, to reduce teacher shortages in math by funding the preparation of math teachers, and to assist colleges and universities to align teacher preparation standards with standards for student performance.

MARYLAND'S LICENSURE SYSTEM

Over the past decade the state of Maryland has implemented an innovative and challenging educational reform program—the Maryland School Performance Program. The reform platform has dramatically altered the state's student assessment program. Maryland has adopted a multifaceted assessment program that holds both schools and students accountable. The Maryland School Performance Assessment Program (MSPAP), adopted in 1990 and launched in 1991, is an assessment program whose primary goal is to provide information that can be used to improve instruction in the schools. MSPAP is administered annually to third, fifth, and eighth graders and assesses how well students solve problems cooperatively and individually, apply what they have learned to real-world problems, and relate and use knowledge from different subject areas. MSPAP results are provided at the school level in five content areas and are a high-stakes accountability tool for the state. Currently, nearly 100 of Maryland's 1,298 schools have failed to improve their academic performance and are eligible for reconstitution by the state.

For individual students there are academic benchmarks that must be met in the third, fifth, eighth, and twelfth grades. The benchmarks are established in reading, writing, mathematics, science, and social studies. Additionally, new high-stakes standards-based tests are being phased in as a requirement for high school graduation. By 2005 students must pass exams in government, English, and either geometry or algebra to graduate. By 2012 students will be required to pass 10 exams to graduate. The exams will include algebra, geometry, U.S. history, world history, government, English (1, 2, and 3), and science (passage on two tests—earth and space science, physics, chemistry, biology).

As the state seeks greater accountability from its K-12 schools and students, it also now requires greater accountability from its colleges of education. In the late 1980s the Maryland Higher Education Commission established the improvement of teacher education programs in the state as a major objective. A teacher education task force was formed by the commission and charged with the redesign of teacher education programs in the state. The final report of the task force was released in 1995 and contained many principles and recommendations. The main components of the report call for a strong academic background for all teacher candidates; preparation of teacher candidates based on extensive clinical experience in the schools, especially professional development schools; a comprehensive monitoring and performance assessment of candidates; and linkage with K-12 priorities and standards. The work of the task force has been, and continues to be, the driving state policy for teacher education reform in the state.

The desire for increased accountability is evident in changes in the approval and accreditation process for colleges of education in Maryland. The changes in approval and accreditation requirements for colleges of education are rooted in *What Matters Most: Teaching for America's Future* (1996). After release of the report, 12 states, including Maryland, volunteered to evaluate the level of alignment between their current systems and the recommendations of the report. The work of a state task force during the summer of 1997 caught the attention of state representative Howard "Pete" Rawlings of Baltimore (District 40), who sponsored a bill before the Maryland General Assembly calling for national accreditation of teacher education programs in the state. House Bill 733 was passed by the Maryland General Assembly in 1998 requiring institutions in the state that offer teacher education programs to seek national accreditation, and Governor Glendenning signed it into law.

The statute requires all colleges and universities that offer undergraduate or graduate teacher education programs to be accredited by a national accreditation agency recognized by the U.S. Department of Education and endorsed by the Maryland State Department of Education (MSDE). For Maryland the national accrediting body that meets the state's criteria is the NCATE. The Accreditation and Eligibility Determination Division of the U.S. Department of Education verified that NCATE is the only teacher education accreditation agency it currently recognizes.

The statute required that by July 1, 2000, each college or university must either file its intent to seek national accreditation or certify to the state (MSDE) that it already had achieved national accreditation. An institution can be waived from meeting the NCATE requirement if its enrollment is less than 2,000 full-time equivalent or it is a nationally recognized professional school of fine arts specializing in music or art. The institutions affected by the statute have until July 2004, to receive NCATE certification. The statute also specifies that the state will assume payment of fees incurred in conjunction with the accreditation process and provide partial coverage of costs incurred by the on-site review. At the time of the law's enactment requiring NCATE accreditation, four of Maryland's 22 colleges of education were already NCATE accredited.

Initial teacher licensure in Maryland is contingent on candidates completing an approved teacher education program. The state also requires teacher candidates to meet the qualifying scores on Praxis I and II prior to being granted an initial license, although it does not specify when candidates must take the tests during their preparation for initial licensure. The Maryland State Board of Education recently adopted high qualifying scores on the Praxis assessments as part of the state's school reform initiative. Passing scores for Praxis I are 177 for mathematics, 177 for reading, and 173 for writing. As state superintendent Nancy Grasmick said, "Our qualifying scores [on Praxis I] are among the highest required for certification among the states. Our plan includes both high qualifying scores and periodic reviews of those scores so that we maintain the level of quality instruction in our schools" (news release from MSDE, Feb. 23, 1999). The state also selected new Praxis II content and pedagogy tests and set the qualifying scores at high levels.

Traditional Undergraduate Teacher Preparation Programs

For undergraduates, admission to most Maryland teacher education programs occurs at the end of the sophomore year. Requirements for entry into the programs are similar across institutions and include a minimum GPA of 2.5 (Coppin, Frostburg) to 2.75 (Salisbury State). Students must have completed several prerequisites, including coursework in English and math. Many institutions also require students to meet the state's qualifying scores on Praxis I prior to admittance into the program. Some programs have additional requirements such as completing a speech course or test, 20 documented hours of working with diverse populations in different settings, and completion of an entrance portfolio.

Programs in the state require students to complete 120 credits (University of Maryland) to 128 (Frostburg) credits. The coursework is similar across programs, is guided by state-recognized national standards, and currently meets the MSDE reading course requirements. Most programs either require or strongly advise that elementary education candidates have either a specialization or a minor in a content area to fulfill the department's requirements. In addition to the requirements of most education majors, the Maryland State Board of Education recently regulated additional courses in reading instruction for licensure. Poor performance on the state assessment (MSPAP) in eighth grade and on the

National Assessment of Educational Progress led the board to establish the new regulations that require regular and special education teachers at the early childhood and elementary levels to complete 12 semester hours (four courses) in specific reading content, such as language development, phonics, and reading assessment. Regular and special education teachers at the secondary level must complete six semester hours (two courses) in reading instruction.

Maryland has also sought to improve the quality of its teacher candidates through the establishment of a network of professional development schools (PDS) throughout the state. PDSs are a collaborative effort between a school system and a higher-education institution and are formed to increase the amount of time teacher candidates spend in the school and to intensify their training prior to licensure. In several models teacher candidates arrive in August and have a full-time internship in a school for the academic year. Being in the school for the entire academic year provides teacher candidates with the opportunity to participate in all aspects of a teacher's life at school. Each school may have a unique emphasis, such as technology, career preparation, or reading. Classes for teacher candidates are taught in the school by resident teachers and faculty members (much like university teaching hospitals). PDSs are mostly sponsored by the state, with additional funding from school systems and higher education institutions. As of July 2000, there were 150 PDSs in Maryland, some of which are multisite. As a part of the state's teacher incentive program, the state announced that an additional $1.2 million will be used to increase the number of PDSs in 1999-2000. The state's goal is to have all preservice programs be performance based and include an extensive internship in a professional development school by the end of 2004.

Along with the required field experience, candidates have to also complete Praxis II before graduation. Some institutions require students in teacher education programs to only take Praxis II prior to graduation (Morgan State University), while others specify that graduation is contingent on passage of Praxis II (Coppin State University). Upon graduation from an approved teacher education program, students apply directly to the state for an initial license.

Alternative Certification Program

Most teachers in Maryland receive initial certification after completing undergraduate programs, but the state has encouraged all higher-education institutions to also establish programs for initial teacher certification at the postbaccalaureate level for career changers. The master's program is typically a one-year full-time program. Numerous programs include two summer school sessions and two academic semesters, while others are part time and may take two to three years. Candidates entering the program must have a baccalaureate degree and appropriate content coursework in the area in which they are seeking licensure.

Maryland has also established a resident teacher program in two school systems—Baltimore City and Prince George's County. These two systems have the highest percentage of teachers with emergency/provisional certification. The resident teacher program is an alternative route into teaching and was designed for arts and science college graduates and individuals seeking a career change. To enter the program, candidates must possess a baccalaureate degree from an accredited institution in the area of the classroom assignment, have received a B or better in courses related to the area of assignment, submit qualifying scores on Praxis I and II, and completed 135 hours of study (aligned with the Essential Dimensions of Teaching—Maryland's standards for teacher candidates). Once the requirements are met, the teacher candidate receives a resident teacher certificate and may be employed by a state school system as a resident teacher. During employment, a resident teacher must complete an additional 45 hours of study (for secondary teachers) or an additional 135 hours of study (for elementary teachers) and receive mentoring for each year employed as a resident teacher (four-year limit to employment with this certificate) and provide verification of satisfactory teaching performance (for every year spent teaching). Pending budget approval, the state will allocate additional funds ($1 million per year for three years) to establish resident programs statewide.

Title II State Grant

Maryland is strengthening its school-based preservice and continuing professional development programs and was awarded a Title II grant by the U.S. Department of Education to support this initiative. Funds from the grant are also being used to strengthen teacher education programs through a focus on state and national K-12 student standards and high-level teacher certification requirements and to increase the state's accountability system for teacher preparation programs.

Appendix E

An Economic Model of Supply and Demand for Teachers

Teacher licensure testing affects the quantity and quality of teachers through its effect on the supply of and demand for teachers. An analysis of the costs and benefits associated with teacher licensure testing, therefore, requires an understanding of the determinants of supply and demand.

THE SUPPLY OF TEACHERS

To fix ideas, we first present an analysis of teacher supply in the case where there is no licensure testing. In both cases, with and without licensure testing, it is assumed that in the general population of potential teachers the proportion who would be competent as teachers is given by q_c (and the proportion who would not by $q_I = 1 - q_c$). This assumption is in keeping with the notion that licensure tests are designed to distinguish only among the two groups: those who are competent (with respect to the skills that are measured by the test) and those who are not. In what follows, we refer to the two types of individuals, would be competent teachers and would be incompetent teachers, as belonging to group C and group I, respectively.

No Licensure Testing

A simple model of occupational choice is adopted here in which an individual chooses among occupations according to which provides the greater compensation (wage).[1] The wage offered to teachers in a given labor market is

---

[1]Allowing for other forms of monetary compensation, for forms of nonmonetary compensation such as working conditions, as well as for psychic aspects of employment, although important components of the overall value attached to working in an occupation, would not change the conclusions of the analysis.

denoted by w and, because competency is assumed to be indeterminate without a test or for institutional reasons, the wage offer is assumed to be the same regardless of whether the teacher is competent or not.[2] However, the wages of individuals outside of teaching do differ. In particular, individuals who would be competent teachers have a wage distribution in alternative occupations with a given mean of $w_C{}^a$ and individuals who would be incompetent teachers have a distribution with mean wage $w_I{}^a$.

Individuals choose teaching versus an alternative occupation depending on which provides the higher wage. Thus, an individual k in group C who would command a wage of $w_{Ck}{}^a$ in a nonteaching occupation chooses teaching if and only if $w > w_{Ck}{}^a = w_C{}^a + \varepsilon_{Ck}{}^a$, where $\varepsilon_{Ck}{}^a$ reflects the deviation of the individual's wage from the mean wage of group C. Analogously, an individual j in group I would choose teaching if and only if $w > w_{Ij}{}^a = w_I{}^a + \varepsilon_{Ij}{}^a$, where $\varepsilon_{Ij}{}^a$ reflects the deviation of the individual's wage from the mean wage of group I. Given these rules for choosing an occupation, the probability that an individual in group C chooses teaching is given by $\alpha_C = \Pr(\varepsilon_{Ck}{}^a < w - w_C{}^a)$. Likewise, the probability that an individual in group I chooses teaching is $\alpha_I = \Pr(\varepsilon_{Ij}{}^a < w - w_I{}^a)$. From these definitions it is easy to see that the proportion of individuals who choose to be teachers at any given wage is $q_C \alpha_C + (1 - q_C) \alpha_I$, and the proportion of them who would be competent teachers is $\Pi_C = q_C \alpha_C / [q_C \alpha_C + (1 - q_C) \alpha_I]$.

As the wage paid to teachers increases, teaching becomes more attractive to both groups (both α_C and α_I are increasing in the wage, w). However, it is not possible to determine whether the proportion of teachers who are competent increases or decreases as the wage paid to teachers increases. The effect of the wage on the relative supply of competent teachers, that is, on Π_C, depends on the level of the wage paid to teachers and on how the distribution of wage offers in alternative occupations differs between the two groups. In the analysis that follows, it is assumed that the wage paid to teachers is in a range such that the proportion of competent teachers does not change with the wage, that is, Π_C is independent of w.

Figure E-1 shows the supply of teachers as a function of the wage paid to teachers. The number of teachers, denoted by T, is increasing with the teachers' wage. The proportion of competent teachers (at wage w_0 and, by assumption, at any wage) is given by E_0 / T_0.

Licensure Testing

Assume now that all potential teachers must take a licensure test. The purpose and design of the test are to distinguish between the two groups, which it

---

[2]The assumption that competency cannot be determined absent a test and that, even if it could be, school districts would not use competency as a necessary condition of employment, is a crucial rationale for adopting a state licensure test. The analysis takes this as given.

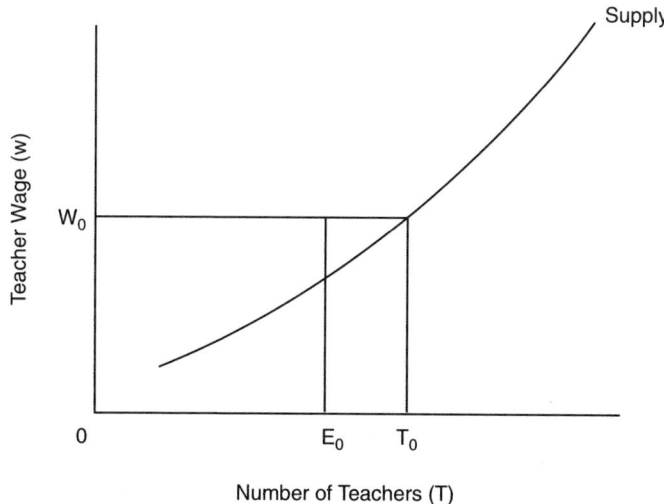

FIGURE E-1 The supply of teachers: no licensing test.

NOTES:

T_0 = number of individuals who would choose the teaching occupation at wage W_0;

E_0 = number of individuals in group C who would choose the teaching occupation at wage W_0.

may do with varying success. To capture the imperfect nature of tests, let m_I and m_C be the proportions of incompetent and competent individuals, respectively, who are classified as incompetent.[3] Thus, if the test could discriminate perfectly, m_I would be one (all those from group I would be determined to be incompetent) and m_C would be zero (none of those from group C would be determined to be incompetent). It is reasonable to assume that m_I exceeds m_C for current licensing tests, although the extent to which this is true is unknown and may differ among both the type of skills that are tested (basic skills, subject matter knowledge, pedagogical content knowledge) and among different tests of the same skills.

Further, assume that a cost must be incurred to take the test, including both a monetary cost, which is the same for both groups, and a cost in terms of the effort involved in preparing for the test, which may differ between the two groups.[4] These costs are denoted by t_I and t_C. Although stronger than necessary,

---

[3]The proportion of those who are not competent but who are classified as competent, $1 - m_I$, is the type 1 error of the test and m_C is the type 2 error.

[4]The monetary cost may, in fact, be higher for group I if those individuals take the test more times (in order to pass it) than group C. In addition, the cost of failure is increased by specialized course-work required for licensure in teaching. To the extent that these education courses have a lower

it is also assumed that individuals know to which group they belong (but the licensing authority does not, which is the rationale for the test).

When there is a licensure test, an individual can choose only whether or not to take the test. Becoming a teacher depends on whether one passes the test, that is, whether one is classified as competent or not. Given this framework, an individual k from group C chooses to take the licensure test if and only if $w - t_C / [1 - m_C] > w_C^a + \varepsilon_{Ck}^a$.[5] Similarly, an individual j from group I chooses to take the test if and only if $w - t_I / [1 - m_I] > w_I^a + \varepsilon_{Ij}^a$. As in the case of no licensure testing, define $\alpha_C = \Pr(w - t_C / [1 - m_C] - w_C^a > \varepsilon_{Ck}^a)$ and $\alpha_I = \Pr(w - t_I / [1 - m_I] - w_I^a > \varepsilon_{Ik}^a)$ to be the probabilities that the group C and group I individuals choose to take the test, respectively.

Note that the relevant (effective) cost of the test in making this decision is the actual cost divided by the probability of being determined to be competent. Thus, for example, if the test were perfect ($m_I = 1$ and $m_C = 0$), only individuals from group C would decide to take it (group I individuals essentially face an infinite cost) and all of them would pass and become teachers. In general, increasing the probability that individuals will be found to be incompetent, regardless of the group, reduces the number of individuals who choose to take the test, which reduces the supply of teachers.

With an imperfect licensure test, the supply of both types, those who would be as well as those who would not be competent teachers, is lower than if there were no licensure test. There are two reasons for this result. The first is mechanical. Individuals who fail the test are simply precluded from choosing to be a teacher. To the extent that some group C individuals are misclassified by the test ($m_C > 0$), the supply of competent teachers will be reduced. The second reason is due to behavior. The cost of the test makes the teaching occupation relatively less attractive than alternative occupations, and, as in the first reason, misclassifying competent people ($m_C > 0$) increases that cost and reduces their supply.

Formally, the supply of competent teachers is $q_C (1 - m_C) \alpha_C$ and the supply of incompetent teachers is $q_I (1 - m_I) \alpha_I$, with the total supply of teachers given by their sum. The proportion of teachers who are competent at some given wage is, therefore, $\Pi_C = q_C (1 - m_C) \alpha_C / [q_C (1 - m_C) \alpha_C + q_I (1 - m_I) \alpha_I]$. As in the

---

market payoff outside teaching than would alternative courses the individual might have completed had the teaching occupation not been chosen, an opportunity cost is incurred. Individuals who fail licensure tests, and thus do not get a teaching job, will receive lower wages in an alternative job compared to the wage they would have received had they taken courses in pursuit of an alternative occupation.

[5] An individual k who chooses to take the licensure test expects to earn a wage net of the cost of the test of $(1 - m_C)w + m_C w_{kC}^a - t_C$ and compares that to w_{kC}^a in making the decision about whether to take the test. This comparison reduces to the expression in the text. With a positive opportunity cost of failure associated with specialized coursework, the net wage outside teaching is $w_{kC}^a - m_C$ times the difference in the teaching and nonteaching wages due to the specialized education coursework.

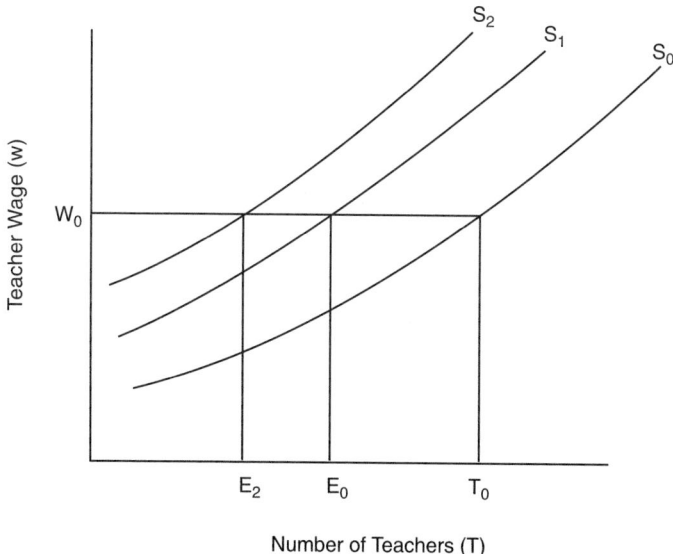

Number of Teachers (T)

FIGURE E-2 The supply of teachers: perfect licensing test.
NOTES:
S_0 = supply of teachers when there is no licensure tests;
S_1 = supply of teachers when tests are not costly;
S_2 = supply of teachers when tests are costly;
T_0 = number of individuals who would choose the teaching occupation at wage W_0;
E_0 = number of individuals in group C who would choose the teaching occupation at wage W_0;
E_2 = number of individuals in group C who would choose the teaching occupation at wage W_0 when tests are costly.

no-licensure case, it is assumed that Π_C is independent of the wage. However, the proportion of competent teachers is directly related to the efficiency of the test in distinguishing between the two types and to the cost of the test for the two reasons given above.

Figure E-2 depicts the supply of teachers in the case of a perfect test as compared to the no-test case shown in Figure E-1. The supply curve labeled S_0 corresponds to the no-test case. Recall that E_0 is the number of individuals in group *C* who would choose the teaching occupation. The supply curve corresponding to S_1 shows the supply of teachers when there is a license test but when its cost is zero. In that case, at each wage all of the teachers are competent. S_2 shows the supply of teachers when the test is costly. In that case, as when the test is not costly, all of the teachers are competent, but there are fewer at any wage

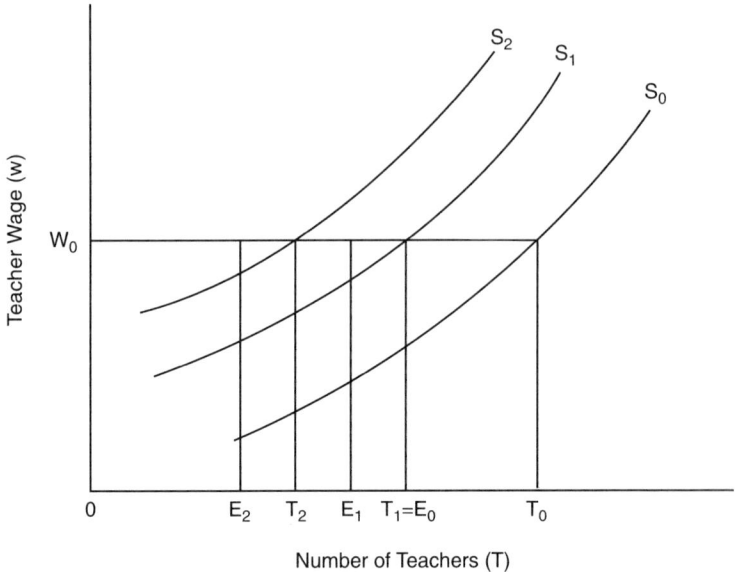

FIGURE E-3 The supply of teachers: imperfect licensure test.
NOTES:
S_0 = supply of teachers when there is no licensure test; S_1 = supply of teachers when tests are not costly;
S_2 = supply of teachers when tests are costly;
T_0 = number of individuals who would choose the teaching occupation at wage W_0;
T_1 = number of individuals who would choose the teaching occupation at wage W_0 when tests are not costly, and who pass the test;
T_2 = number of individuals who choose the teaching occupation at wage W_0 when tests are costly and who pass the test;
E_1 = number of individuals in group C who choose the teaching occupation at wage W_0 when tests are not costly and who pass the test;
E_2 = number of individuals in group C who choose the teaching occupation at wage W_0 when tests are costly and who pass the test.

who choose to be teachers. Thus, even a perfect licensure test will lead to a reduction in the supply of competent teachers if the test is costly.[6]

Figure E-3 shows the intermediate case, where the test is imperfect, that is, where there are type 1 and type 2 errors. The original no-test supply is again

---

[6]One of the costs of the test that is ignored here, by assuming that individuals consider only their expected wage and are therefore not risk averse, is the cost associated with the uncertainty that the test creates.

shown as the baseline case. S_1, as before, shows the supply of teachers when there is a test, but the test is not costly. In that case the number of teachers at wage w_0 is assumed to be T_1 (which, for illustrative purposes, is depicted as being equal to E_0, the number of competent teachers when there is no test). Note that the only reason for this reduction in supply is due to the mechanical feature of the test. However, because an imperfect test does not correctly identify all of the incompetent teachers from group I, only E_1 of the T_1 teachers are competent. However, under the maintained assumption that m_1 exceeds m_C, the fraction of teachers who are competent is increased through the use of the test, that is $E_1/T_1 > E_0/T_0$. With a costly test, the number of teachers falls further to T_2 at the wage w_0. In addition, if the (effective) cost of the test is higher for the incompetent, there will be a tendency for the proportion of teacher who are competent among the T_2 teachers to rise further. Thus, an imperfect licensure test will reduce the number of competent teachers but by less than the overall supply of teachers.

Raising Passing Scores

The same analysis would apply to raising passing scores on existing licensure tests. In Figure E-3, let S_0 be the supply curve associated with an existing (imperfect) licensure test, say one with a low passing score. A test with a low passing score will tend to have only a small supply effect (relative to a no-licensure test regime) as the proportion of individuals in both groups taking the test who are determined to be incompetent will be small (m_I and m_C are both small). Increasing the passing score will tend to increase both m_I and m_C. To the extent that m_I increases faster than m_C, the relative number of competent teachers will tend to increase, although the supply (at a given wage) of both competent and incompetent teachers will fall. As passing scores are continually raised, however, it becomes more and more likely that the supply of competent teachers falls by more than does the supply of incompetent teachers. When potential teachers are mostly competent, increasing passing scores will eliminate mostly competent teachers.

If nothing else changes when licensure tests are used or passing scores are raised, in particular, if the wage to teachers is not affected by the reduction in supply, class size will rise. Whether overall student learning increases or decreases would depend on whether students are better off with competent teachers in larger classes or with a mix of competent and incompetent teachers in smaller classes. But wages are unlikely to be unchanged. To see that, the demand for teachers must be modeled.

THE DEMAND FOR TEACHERS

The model of demand, like that of supply, is illustrative. Only an outline of the model is presented here, and the basic conclusions are stated. Consider a school district in a municipality that supplies not only educational services but other local public goods. The municipality, for given tax revenues, decides on the amount to spend on education, whose only variable input is the number of teachers, and spends the residual amount on the other local public goods.[7]

Student learning is assumed to depend only on the number of competent teachers; incompetent teachers produce no learning.[8] It is thus assumed that reducing the number of teachers if they come solely from the set of incompetent teachers will not reduce student learning even though the number of students per competent teacher (class size) rises.[9] The school district (or equivalently the municipality) takes teachers' wages as given; that is, it must compete with other municipalities for teachers in the same labor market. Like the wage, the municipality also takes as given the fraction of teachers who are competent. The municipality maximizes a community welfare function that depends on student learning and on the amount of other local public goods that it purchases for the community.

Maximizing community welfare leads to a demand function for teachers (derived from the demand for student learning) that depends on the competitively determined market wage and on the fraction of competent teachers (which we assumed above to be independent of the wage offered to teachers) in the total supply. As usual, it can be shown that the demand for teachers is declining with the teacher wage. In addition, the demand for teachers can either rise or fall at any given wage as the proportion of competent teachers in the total supply of teachers increases. However, the demand for competent teachers at any give wage must rise with an increase in the proportion of competent teacher in the total supply. The importance of this last result will become clear below. The market demand for teachers is the (horizontal) sum of the demand across municipalities in the same teacher labor market.

THE EQUILIBRIUM TEACHER WAGE AND NUMBER OF COMPETENT TEACHERS

The equilibration of market demand and supply determines the teacher wage and the number of teachers who are employed. Given the proportion of teachers

---

[7]In a more complete model, one would not take as given the level of tax revenues collected by the municipality.

[8]Again, this is in keeping with the intended purpose of licensure tests, which are not designed to determine teacher quality beyond competency.

[9]A more complete model would also allow for separate class size effects. Allowing for class size effects would provide a rationale for employing additional teachers independent of the proportion of teachers in the total supply who are competent. The essential qualitative implications of the model are not sensitive to this extension.

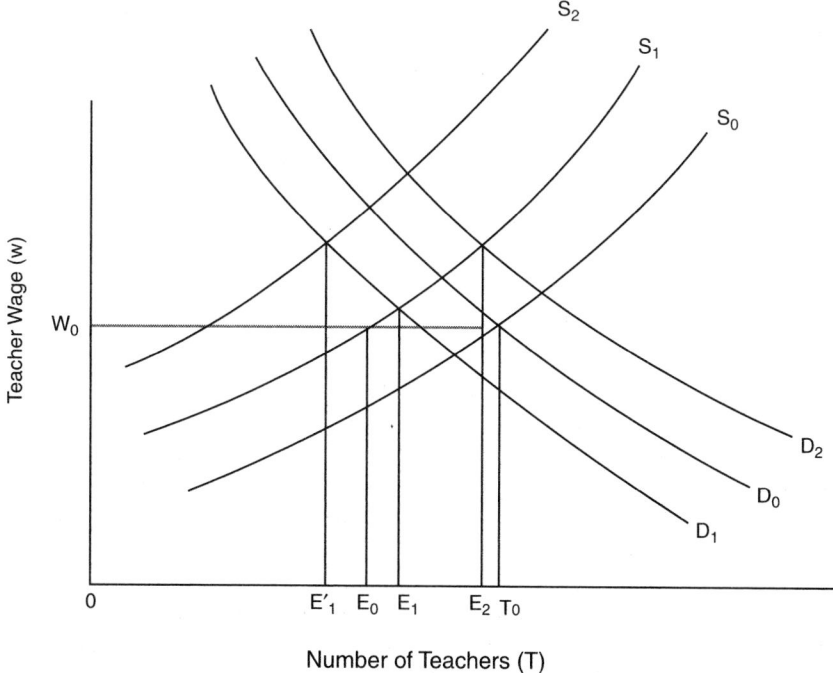

FIGURE E-4 Equilibrium in the market for teachers: perfect licensure test.
NOTES:
S_0 = supply of teachers when there is no licensure test;
S_1= supply of teachers when tests are not costly;
S_2 = supply of teachers when tests are costly;
D_0 = market demand for teachers when there is no licensure test;
D_1 = market demand for teachers when all individuals who pass the test are competent
Case I;
D_2 = market demand for teachers when all individuals who pass the test are competent
Case 2;
T_0 = Number of individuals who choose the teaching occupation at wage W_0;
E_0 = Number of individuals who choose the teaching occupation at wage W_0;
E_1 = Number of individuals in group C employed as teachers when tests are not costly
and when demand is given by D_1;
E_2 = Number of individuals in group C employed as teachers when tests are not costly
and when demand is given by D_2;
E'_1 = Number of individuals in group C employed as teachers when tests are costly and
when demand is given by D_1.

who are competent, that is, given the properties of the licensing test, the number of teachers who are competent is also determined.[10]

Figure E-4 considers the case of a perfect licensure test, incorporating market demand into Figure E-2. Recall that a perfect test has the property that all those who pass it are competent and all those who do not pass are not competent. D_0 represents market demand for teachers when there is no licensure test. The equilibrium wage is w_0, the equilibrium number of teachers is T_0, and the number of competent teachers is E_0. S_1 represents the supply when the test is costless. As seen, if the wage remained at its original equilibrium, the number of teachers would be E_0 and the fraction of competent teachers would be one (all teachers are competent with a perfect test). However, given that the fraction of competent teachers is one, independent of the wage, the demand curve may shift either up or down. The model tells us only that the demand will not shift down so much that the number of competent teachers falls below what it was in the baseline no-licensure case. Regardless of the direction in which demand shifts, the wage paid to teachers will rise, but this new wage simply reflects the appropriate scarcity of competent teachers. Because the number of competent teachers rises, student achievement also rises.

With a costly test, the supply of teachers shifts further to S_2. There is no further shift in the demand for teachers (the proportion of competent teachers is still one). In this case it is possible that if the test is costly enough the number of competent teachers will actually fall, for example, from E_0 to $E_{1?}$. Even in a less extreme case in which the number of competent teachers rises and thus so does student learning, it is possible that the municipality would be better off without the test given the higher wage that must be paid to teachers.[11] However, recall that in the case of a perfect test, only group C individuals take the test and the effective cost is the same as the actual cost. If the cost of the test to the competent group can be considered small, a perfect test would not contain this inefficiency. The more imperfect the test, the more likely the test is to reduce community welfare.

Setting Passing Scores

The same analysis also applies to the case where the test classifies all group I individuals correctly but some of those from group C are mistakenly classified

---

[10]Formally, the supply function is given by $S = S(w, m_C, m_I, q_C, t_C, t_I)$, the demand function by $D = D(w, P_C)$, and the proportion of competent teachers by $P_C = P_C(m_C, m_I, q_C, t_C, t_I)$. m_C and m_I are given by the testing technology.

[11]In an extended version of the model in which there are additional inputs to student learning, the point would be that there might be potentially less costly methods of increasing student learning than through use of licensure test.

as not competent (type 2 error). This outcome could arise if the test is inherently imperfect in the sense that there does not exist a passing score for which there are no classification errors or because the test would be perfect at a specific passing score but the passing score is set at too high a level. As with a perfect test, only group C individuals take the test, but unlike the perfect test some of them fail. In this case, the shift (fall) in supply is larger than that depicted in Figure E-4 by the movement from S_0 to S_1, even when the test is costless. Depending on how big this type 2 error is, the number of competent teachers may fall below the number when there is no licensure test. Even if the result is not that extreme, this restriction on supply leads to an artificially high wage that might not be the most efficient way to spend community resources.

The analysis of passing scores is more complicated when the test is imperfect in the sense of having both type 1 and type 2 errors. Setting a low passing score may increase the proportion of competent teachers only slightly relative to the situation without a test, but it protects against artificially restricting the supply of competent teachers. Setting a high passing score may increase the proportion of competent teachers a great deal but risks reducing significantly the number of competent teachers and artificially increasing the wage. As the prior discussion makes clear, quantitatively assessing the efficacy of licensure testing requires a great deal of information, about not only the accuracy of the test but also the perceived costs to the test takers, alternative market opportunities of potential teachers, and constraints on the tax revenues of municipalities.

Appendix F

Alternative Assessment Case Studies

PERFORMANCE ASSESSMENT OF EXPERIENCED TEACHERS BY THE NATIONAL BOARD FOR PROFESSIONAL TEACHING STANDARDS

The National Board for Professional Teaching Standards (NBPTS) provides an example of a large-scale, high-stakes performance assessment of teaching that draws on portfolio and assessment center exercises. While NBPTS assessments are intended for voluntary certification of experienced teachers (teachers who have been practicing in their subject areas for at least three years), this case is relevant to the committee's focus on assessment of beginning teaching in at least two ways. First, it provides an example of a model that states may choose or have chosen to emulate. Second, states may decide to grant licenses to candidates certified by the NBPTS. Finally, NBPTS certification is viewed by its proponents as an integral phase in a teacher's career development that can and should be consonant with earlier phases of assessment and development.

The NBPTS is an independent organization governed by a 63-member board of directors, most of whom are classroom teachers. Its mission is to "establish high and rigorous standards for what accomplished teachers should know and be able to do, to develop and operate a national voluntary system to assess and certify teachers who meet these standards, and to advance related education reforms for improving student learning in American schools" <www.nbpts.org>. In addition, NBPTS seeks to forge "a national professional consensus, to reliably identify teachers who meet [these] standards," and to communicate what accomplished teaching looks like" (Moss and Schutz, 1999:681). The NBPTS is in the process of developing standards and assessments for more than 30 certification fields identified by the subject or subjects taught and by the developmental level of the students.

For each certificate, development work starts by articulating a set of content standards, based on the five core propositions set forth in the NBPTS central policy statement (National Board for Professional Teaching Standards, 1996:2-3; see Box F-1). The drafting of the content standards for each certificate based on these core propositions is handled by a committee comprised primarily of teachers experienced in the relevant subject area along with experts in child development, teacher education, and the relevant academic discipline. Public review and comment are obtained for the content standards, and the feedback received is used in the final revision of the standards (Moss and Schutz, 1999).

The final version of a content standards document states that the standards "represent a professional consensus on the critical aspects of practice that distinguish exemplary teachers in the field from novice or journeymen teachers. Cast in terms of actions that teachers take to advance student outcomes, these standards also incorporate the essential knowledge, skills, dispositions, and commitments that allow teachers to practice at a high level" (e.g., National Board for Professional Teaching Standards, 1996:1). Moss and Schutz (1999:682-683) describe the Early Adolescence/English Language Arts Standards:

[T]here are 14 distinct Early Adolescence/English Language Arts (EA/ELA) Standards. . . . Standard II states that:

"Accomplished EA/ELA teachers set attainable and worthwhile learning goals for students and develop meaningful learning opportunities while extending to students an increasing measure of control over how those goals are pursued." . .

This standard is then elaborated into a full-page description that includes statements such as, "Educational goal-setting is an interactive process in the middle-grades English teacher's classroom. . . . These activities often include a strong mixture of student involvement and direction"; "in carrying out learning direction activities, accomplished teachers adjust their practice, as appropriate, based on student feedback and provide many alternative avenues to the same learning destinations"; or "the planning process is inclusive, no one is allowed to disappear."

Box F-2 provides an overview of the standards for EA/ELA. These content standards are then used to guide all aspects of assessment development for that certification assessment.

Once the content standards are created for any given certificate, the assessment developers (now primarily at Educational Testing Services, or ETS) are joined by a second committee of approximately eight experienced teachers in the development and pilot testing of assessment tasks and the accompanying rubrics that will be used to score candidates' performances. Although each assessment

BOX F-1
Five Propositions of Accomplished Teaching

The National Board for Professional Teaching Standards seeks to identify and recognize teachers who effectively enhance student learning and demonstrate the high level of knowledge, skills, abilities and commitments reflected in the following five core propositions.

1. **Teachers are committed to students and their learning.**
   Accomplished teachers are dedicated to making knowledge accessible to all students. They act on the belief that all students can learn. They treat students equitably, recognizing the individual differences that distinguish one student from another and taking account of these differences in their practice. They adjust their practice based on observation and knowledge of their students' interests, abilities, skills, knowledge, family circumstances and peer relationships.

   Accomplished teachers understand how students develop and learn. They incorporate the prevailing theories of cognition and intelligence in their practice. They are aware of the influence of context and culture on behavior. They develop students' cognitive capacity and their respect for learning. Equally important, they foster students' self-esteem, motivation, character, civic responsibility and their respect for individual, cultural, religious and racial differences.

2. **Teachers know the subjects they teach and how to teach those subjects to students.**
   Accomplished teachers have a rich understanding of the subject(s) they teach and appreciate how knowledge in their subject is created, organized, linked to other disciplines and applied to real-world settings. While faithfully representing the collective wisdom of our culture and upholding the value of disciplinary knowledge, they also develop the critical and analytical capacities of their students.

   Accomplished teachers command specialized knowledge of how to convey and reveal subject matter to students. They are aware of the preconceptions and background knowledge that students typically bring to each subject and of strategies and instructional materials that can be of assistance. They understand where difficulties are likely to arise and modify their practice accordingly. Their instructional repertoire allows them to create multiple paths to the subjects they teach, and they are adept at teaching students how to pose and solve their own problems.

3. **Teachers are responsible for managing and monitoring student learning.**
   Accomplished teachers create, enrich, maintain and alter instructional settings to capture and sustain the interest of their students and to make the most effective use of time. They also are adept at engaging students and adults to assist their teaching and at enlisting their colleagues' knowledge and expertise to complement their own.

Accomplished teachers command a range of generic instructional techniques, know when each is appropriate and can implement them as needed. They are as aware of ineffectual or damaging practice as they are devoted to elegant practice. They know how to engage groups of students to ensure a disciplined learning environment, and how to organize instruction to allow the schools' goals for students to be met. They are adept at setting norms for social interaction among students and between students and teachers. They understand how to motivate students to learn and how to maintain their interest even in the face of temporary failure. Accomplished teachers can assess the progress of individual students as well as that of the class as a whole. They employ multiple methods for measuring student growth and understanding and can clearly explain student performance to parents.

4. **Teachers think systematically about their practice and learn from experience.**
   Accomplished teachers are models of educated persons, exemplifying the virtues they seek to inspire in students—curiosity, tolerance, honesty, fairness, respect for diversity and appreciation of cultural differences—and the capacities that are prerequisites for intellectual growth: the ability to reason and take multiple perspectives, to be creative and take risks, and to adopt an experimental and problem-solving orientation.

   Accomplished teachers draw on their knowledge of human development, subject matter and instruction, and their understanding of their students to make principled judgments about sound practice. Their decisions are not only grounded in the literature, but also in their experience. They engage in lifelong learning, which they seek to encourage in their students.

   Striving to strengthen their teaching, accomplished teachers critically examine their practice, seek to expand their repertoire, deepen their knowledge, sharpen their judgment and adapt their teaching to new findings, ideas, and theories.

5. **Teachers are members of learning communities.**
   Accomplished teachers contribute to the effectiveness of the school by working collaboratively with other professionals on instructional policy, curriculum development, and staff development. They can evaluate school progress and the allocation of school resources in light of their understanding of state and local educational objectives. They are knowledgeable about specialized school and community resources that can be engaged for their students' benefit, and are skilled at employing such resources as needed.

   Accomplished teachers find ways to work collaboratively and creatively with parents, engaging them productively in the work of the school.

SOURCE: National Board for Professional Teaching Standards, 1996.

BOX F-2
Standards Overview: Early Adolescence/
English Language Arts (EA/ELA)

The following standards are presented as facets of the art and science of teaching English language arts to young adolescents. They are an analytical construct, created to provide a closer accounting of the critical aspects of accomplished practice. However, in real time these segments of teaching occur concurrently because teaching is a seamless activity with many disparate purposes being served in the classroom at any given moment.

Preparing the Way for Productive Student Learning
   I. Knowledge of Students
       Accomplished EA/ELA teachers systematically acquire a sense of their students as individual language learners.
  II. Curricular Choices
       Accomplished EA/ELA teachers set attainable and worthwhile learning goals for students and develop meaningful learning opportunities while extending to students an increasing measure of control over how those goals are pursued.
 III. Engagement
       Accomplished EA/ELA teachers elicit a concerted effort in language learning from each of their students.
  IV. Learning Environment
       Accomplished EA/ELA teachers create a caring, inclusive and challenging environment in which students actively learn.
   V. Instructional Resources
       Accomplished EA/ELA teachers select, adapt and create curricular resources that support active student exploration of literature and language processes.

Advancing Student Learning in the Classroom
  VI. Reading
       Accomplished EA/ELA teachers engage their students in reading and responding to literature, and in interpreting and thinking deeply about literature and other texts.
 VII. Writing
       Accomplished EA/ELA teachers immerse their students in the art of writing.
VIII. Discourse
       Accomplished EA/ELA teachers foster thoughtful classroom discourse that provides opportunities for students to listen and speak in many ways and for many purposes.
  IX. Language Study
       Accomplished EA/ELA teachers strengthen student sensitivity to and proficiency in the appropriate uses of language.
   X. Integrated Instruction
       Accomplished EA/ELA teachers integrate reading, writing, speaking and listening opportunities in the creation and interpretation of meaningful texts.
  XI. Assessment
       Accomplished EA/ELA teachers use a range of formal and informal assessment methods to monitor student progress, encourage student self-assessment, plan instruction and report to various audiences.

Supporting Student Learning through Long-Range Initiatives
XII. Self-reflection
    Accomplished EA/ELA teachers constantly analyze and strengthen the effectiveness and quality of their teaching.
XIII. Professional Community
    Accomplished EA/ELA teachers contribute to the improvement of instructional programs, advancement of knowledge, and practice of colleagues.
XIV. Family Outreach
    Accomplished EA/ELA teachers work with families to serve the best interests of their children.

SOURCE: National Board for Professional Teaching Standards, 1996.

task is designed in light of the standards specific to a given certificate, NBPTS has adopted a framework that generalizes across certificates to guide the work of all development teams.

Each assessment consists of two major parts: a portfolio to be completed by candidates in their home schools and a half-day of testing at an assessment center. The school-based portfolio consists of (1) three entries that are classroom based and include two videos that document the candidate's teaching practice through student work and (2) one entry that combines the candidate's work with students' families, the community, and collaboration with other professionals. The six assessment center exercises require candidates to demonstrate their knowledge of subject matter content.

Box F-3 provides a detailed overview of the EA/ELA assessment tasks. A formal multistate pilot test is administered before the assessments are released for the first operational use.

Each assessment task is scored in accordance with a rubric prepared during the task development phase. NBPTS scoring rubrics encompass four levels of performance on a particular task, with the second-highest level designated as meeting the standards of accomplishment.[1] Further, the terminology used in each scoring rubric closely mirrors the language of the relevant content standards.

Following initial use of the assessment, at least three extensively trained assessors and other teaching experts select a sample of responses to be used in training and certifying the scorers. The small group charged with selecting the

---

[1]The rubrics for each exercise describe four different performance levels representing score "families" of 1 (low), 2, 3, and 4 (high). Within each score family, an assessor can choose to assign a "+" or a "–" .25 indicating somewhat higher and lower levels of performance. The passing score for each exercise is designated as the lower end of the 3 family, "3–," or 2.75.

BOX F-3
Early Adolescence/English Language Arts

The NBPTS has developed standards for what accomplished Early Adolescence/ English Language Arts teachers should know and be able to do. This certificate is designed for teachers of students ages 11-15. The assessment is performance-based and designed to evaluate the complex knowledge and skills of teaching described in the standards. The assessment process consists of two components: the portfolio entries and the half-day assessment center exercises. The certification decision is based on candidate performance as judged against the NBPTS standards for accomplished practice.

The Portfolio

The portfolio for the Early Adolescence/English Language Arts assessment provides teachers with the opportunity to present a sample of their actual classroom practice over a specified time period. The portfolio consists of four entries*:

- **Analysis of Student Growth in Reading and Writing**—Through written commentary and samples of students' responses, teachers provide evidence of their ability to engage students in the study of literature and writing. Two writing samples from each of two students provide evidence of how the teacher uses the writing process to improve the students' abilities in written expression. The teacher analyzes each of the work samples in relation to specified goals and to identify the students' growth as a reader and a writer. The analysis includes assessment and evaluation of the impact of feedback on the students' growth. The reflection includes consideration of how the teacher can improve his/her practice and implications for future instruction.
- **Instructional Analysis—Whole Class Discussion**—Through written commentary and a 15-minute videotape, teachers demonstrate the strategies that they use to engage students in whole-class discussion. The commentary includes analysis of the goals and strategies for instruction. The video provides evidence of instruction, the learning environment, and engagement of the students. Teachers demonstrate how they engage all the students in meaningful discourse about a topic, concept, or text important to their English Language Arts curriculum. The commentary also includes reflection on the teacher's practice, analysis of successes and ways of improving, and implications for future instruction.
- **Instructional Analysis—Small Groups**—Through written commentary and a 15-minute videotape, teachers demonstrate their practice of small group instruction about a significant English language arts concept. Students may be discussing their reading, sharing writing, collaborating on projects, or participating in other learning activities which are appropriate for small groups. The videotape should show the teacher circulating among the groups and interacting with the students. The commentary includes discussion of the teacher's knowledge about the students as well as an analysis of the goals for the instruction. The reflection addresses implications for future instruction.
- **Documented Accomplishments: Contributions to Student Learning**—Teachers demonstrate their commitment to student learning through their work with students' families and the community and their development as

learners, leaders, and collaborators. This entry is designed to capture evidence of the ways in which a teacher's role is broader than what the teacher does in the classroom. Teachers submit descriptions and analyses of their activities and accomplishments. The commentary includes discussion of why the activities and accomplishments are significant in the particular teaching context and what impact they had on student learning. In addition, teachers are asked to compose a brief interpretive summary related to these accomplishments.

The Assessment Center

The half-day of assessment center exercises examine subject matter content. There are six written exercises, and teachers are given 30 minutes to complete each. One score is reported for each exercise. The exercises measure knowledge in the following areas:

- Literary analysis and structure, including literary devices
- Universal literary themes and literary works
- Reading strategies
- Knowledge of language study
- Analysis of writing conventions and components of effective writing

* exercises are currently undergoing revision; these descriptions are subject to change

SOURCE: *NBPTS Next Generation Certificate Overviews*, April 2001.

benchmarks is instructed to choose them so that assessors see that there are different ways to achieve a score. Those who select benchmarks and score portfolios are subjected to a series of training exercises designed to assist them in identifying and controlling any personal biases that might influence their selection.

Most exercises are scored independently by two assessors with a third, more experienced assessor used to adjudicate scores that differ by more than a prespecified amount. For some exercises, where interrater reliability is deemed sufficient, only a sample of exercises is double scored. A weighting strategy is employed to combine scores on the exercises and to form the total scores on the assessment. This weighting strategy is selected by another committee of teachers who must choose from among four predetermined weighting strategies. To make certification decisions (accomplished/not accomplished), the total score is compared to a predetermined passing score that is uniform across certificates. This performance standard is equivalent to receiving a just-passing score on each of the exercises, although high scores on one exercise can compensate for low scores on others.

The uniform performance standard set by the NBPTS was based on a series of empirical standard-setting studies. These studies explored a number of different standard-setting methods (see Jaeger, 1998; Educational Testing Service, 1998). In all of the investigations, panels of experienced teachers were asked to make decisions based on profiles of scores across exercises. The process was "typically iterative, in which individual panelists—thoroughly familiar with the tasks, rubrics, and standards—were given an opportunity to discuss and revise their individual decisions about score profiles in light of feedback on other panelists' decisions and on the practical implications of their own decisions. From this set of revised individual decisions, the assessment developers computed the 'recommended' performance standard" (Moss and Schutz, 1999:685). The NBPTS adopted the uniform performance standard for all certificates based on the results of these early studies along with consideration of the practical implications of setting the standard at different levels (e.g., minimizing adverse impact for groups of candidates, minimizing the anticipated proportion of candidates who are misclassified as failing the exam due to measurement error).

In addition to documentation of the development process, five other kinds of validity evidence are routinely gathered and examined for each assessment:

1. Content-related evidence of validity is examined by convening a panel of experienced teachers in the subject area to independently rate (a) the extent to which each of the content standards describes a critical aspect of highly accomplished teaching and (b) the importance and relevance of each exercise and rubric to each content standard and to the overall domain of accomplished teaching.

2. "Scoring validation," as defined by the assessment developers, is evaluated by assembling another panel of experienced teachers in the subject area to rank randomly selected pairs of exercise responses. These rankings are then compared to the rankings obtained from the official scoring.

3. Information regarding reliability and errors of measurement is reported as (a) error associated with scores given by different assessors, (b) error associated with the sampling of exercises, and (c) misclassification estimates (i.e., estimates of the proportion of candidates incorrectly passing and failing) due to both of these sources of error.

4. Confirmation of the predetermined passing standard is obtained by convening a panel of experienced teachers, who have also served as assessors. The panel examines different possible profiles of exercise scores, rank ordered by total score, and draws lines where they believe the passing standard should be.

5. Evidence regarding bias and adverse impact is provided by (a) reporting certification rates by gender, ethnicity (where sample sizes permit), and teaching

context and (b) investigating the influence of having exercises scored by assessors of the same and different ethnicity as the candidate.

The test developer, ETS, publishes a technical manual (Educational Testing Service, 1998) that describes the methodology for these studies, provides annual updates of technical information for each certificate, and publishes outcomes for each administration. The technical manual is available to the public. The annual updates are available only to NBPTS members, staff, consultants, and advisory panel members. Special studies are frequently presented at national conferences. The NBPTS's validity research agenda, technical reports, and reports of special studies are routinely reviewed and commented on by the Measurement Research Advisory Panel, a panel of independent scholars whose backgrounds are primarily in educational measurement.

In addition to these routine studies, NBPTS has undertaken a number of special validity/impact studies, many of which are still in progress. These include (1) an external review of complete portfolios by a diverse panel exploring differences in performance between African American and white candidates (Bond, 1998); (2) a study of rater severity and the effects of different scoring designs (Englehard, et al., 2000); (3) a survey of how teachers prepare for the exam (Lynch et al., 2000); (4) a survey of assessors' impressions about the impact of training and scoring on their professional development (Howell and Gitomer, 2000); and (5) a comparison of NBPTS evaluations with others based on classroom observations and interviews (Wylie et al., 2000). A recently released study compared the teaching practices of NBPTS certified teachers with other teachers and compared samples of student work from classrooms of the two groups of teachers (Bond et al., 2000).

NBPTS assessments are voluntary; passing the assessment results in a certification of accomplishment. To be eligible for NBPTS certification, a teacher must have completed a baccalaureate degree; must have a minimum of three years of teaching experience at the early childhood, elementary, middle, or secondary levels; and must have a valid state teaching license for each of those years or, where a license is not required, the teacher must be teaching in a school recognized and approved to operate by the state.

For the 2000-2001 testing year, the examination fee was $2,300. A number of states and other education agencies have programs in place to subsidize this cost, and NBPTS publicizes that information on its website. Candidates are given approximately 10 months to complete the portfolio tasks and attend the assessment centers. Since each exercise is scored independently, a candidate who does not pass the assessment may bank scores on the exercises passed and retake exercises on which a failing score was received (below a 3 on a four-point scale) for a period of two years after being notified of his or her initial scores. NBPTS publishes a list of newly certified teachers each year. States and local education agencies have their own policies about how the scores are used, including how teachers are recognized and rewarded for receiving NBPTS certification. These include the granting of a state license for teachers transferring into the state, salary increases and bonuses, and opportunities to assume new roles. (See <www.nbpts.org> for a summary of state incentives.)

The NBPTS's direct involvement in professional development and support activities is limited. For instance, the board offers short-term institutes for "facilitators" who plan to support candidates for certification and a series of "Teacher Development Exercises" that can be purchased and used in local workshops. NBPTS does, however, work informally with state and local education agencies and with teacher education institutions to support and publicize local initiatives (see Box F-4). For instance, NBPTS provides a list of ways that state and local education agencies and institutions might support its work and offers contact information for local agencies to interested teachers. In addition, NBPTS's web page contains information about the activities of its affiliates and provides examples of the variety of professional roles that board-certified teachers have assumed. It should be noted that while NBPTS supplies information on local contacts and activities, it does not monitor the quality, relevance, or usefulness of this information.

Through its certification assessments and related activities, NBPTS hopes to "leverage change" in the contexts and culture of teaching. The board hopes to (1) make "it possible for teachers to advance in responsibility, status, and compensation without having to leave the classroom" and (2) encourage "among teachers the search for new knowledge and better practice through a study regimen of collaboration and reflection with peers and others" (National Board for Professional Teaching Standards, 1996:7).

CONNECTICUT'S TEACHER PREPARATION AND INDUCTION PROGRAM

Overview

Connecticut, working in collaboration with the Interstate New Teacher Assessment and Support Consortium (INTASC), provides an example of a state that has implemented a licensing system that relies on performance assessments. Connecticut's Beginning Educator Support and Training program is a comprehensive three-year induction program that involves both mentoring and support for beginning teachers as well as a portfolio assessment. The philosophy behind Connecticut's teacher preparation and induction program is that effective teaching involves more than demonstration of a particular set of technical skills. The program is based on the fundamental principle that all students must have the opportunity to be taught by a caring, competent teacher and that, in addition to command of subject matter, effective teaching requires a deep concern about students and their success, a strong commitment to student achievement, and the

BOX F-4
Support for Teachers Seeking NBPTS Certification

Teachers who seek—and those who achieve—NBPTS Certification deserve recognition for their efforts and accomplishments. More and more school districts, state legislatures, state boards of education and colleges of education are supporting and encouraging teachers in their quests for NBPTS Certification. There are many ways policymakers can help.

School Districts
BEFORE a teacher seeks NBPTS Certification
* Schools and districts can organize seminars to introduce teachers to NBPTS Certification and help them determine if they are ready to seek certification.
* Schools and districts can pay the assessment fee in full or in part.

DURING a teacher's participation
* Schools and districts can offer professional development days for teachers to prepare portfolio entries.
* Schools and districts can help organize study and support groups for teacher candidates.
* Schools and districts can offer technical support, such as the use of computers and video cameras, to help candidates prepare portfolios.

AFTER a teacher achieves NBPTS Certification
* Schools and districts can offer salary supplements.
* Schools and districts can publicly recognize teachers' accomplishment.
* Schools and districts can recognize NBPTS Certification as qualification for teachers to serve as mentors or lead teachers.

States and State Departments of Education
AFTER a teacher achieves NBPTS Certification, states can . . .
* Offer salary supplements and bonuses.
* Offer license renewal exemptions.
* Offer license portability to NBPTS Certified Teachers who relocate.
* Recognize NBPTS Certification as qualification for teachers to serve on special committees or task forces.

Undergraduate Colleges of Education
BEFORE a teacher achieves NBPTS Certification . . .
Colleges of education can base program curriculum on the propositions of the NBPTS for Professional Teaching Standards.

AFTER a teacher achieves NBPTS Certification . . .
Colleges of education can recognize certification as criterion for adjunct faculty.

SOURCE: National Board for Professional Teaching Standards, 1996.

conviction that all students can attain high levels of achievement (Connecticut Department of Education, 2000). This philosophy is reflected in Connecticut's Common Core of Teaching (CCT), which is intended to present a comprehensive view of the accomplished teacher, detailing the subject-specific knowledge, skills, and competencies the state believes teachers need in order to ensure that students learn and perform at high levels. The CCT encompasses: (1) foundational skills and competencies common to all teachers from prekindergarten through grade 12 and (2) discipline-based professional standards that represent the necessary knowledge, skills, and competencies (Connecticut Department of Education, 1999). The specific components of the CCT appear in Box F-5.

Connecticut's program covers three aspects of teachers' development: preservice training, beginning teacher induction, and teacher evaluation and continuing professional growth. The CCT guides state policies related to each of these phases, which are described below.

Preservice Training

At the preservice phase, teacher education programs are expected to demonstrate that teacher candidates are knowledgeable about the CCT as well as the state's achievement test batteries, the Connecticut Mastery Tests, and the Connecticut Academic Performance Test (Connecticut State Department of Education, 1999). The training requirements for prospective teachers are specified in terms of a set of standards, as distinct from a list of required courses. The standards encompass the body of knowledge and skills the state believes individuals should develop as they progress through the teacher education programs. The approval process for teacher education programs is based on these standards, and teacher education programs are expected to demonstrate that students achieve them. Prospective teachers in Connecticut must pass Praxis I, have a minimum B minus average to enter a teacher preparation program, and must pass Praxis II to be recommended for initial licensure (Connecticut State Board of Education, 2000).

Beginning Educator Support and Training (BEST) Program

BEST is a comprehensive three-year induction program that is required for all beginning teachers. The program has two components: (1) support and instructional assistance through mentorship, seminars, distance learning, and support teams over a two-year period and (2) assessment of teaching performance through a discipline-specific portfolio assessment (Connecticut State Board of Education, 2000). The goals of the BEST program include:

- ensuring that all students have high-quality, committed, and caring teachers;
- promoting effective teaching practice leading to increased student learning;

BOX F-5
Components of Connecticut's Common Core of Teaching

Connecticut's Common Core of Teaching:
Foundational Skills and Competencies

I. Teachers have knowledge of:
   A. Students
      1. Teachers understand how students learn and develop.
      2. Teachers understand how students differ in their approaches to learning.
   B. Content
      1. Teachers are proficient in reading, writing, and mathematics.
      2. Teachers understand the central concepts and skills, tools of inquiry and structures of the discipline(s) they teach.
   C. Pedagogy
      1. Teachers know how to design and deliver instruction.
      2. Teachers recognize the need to vary their instructional methods.

II. Teachers apply this knowledge by:
   A. Planning
      1. Teachers plan instruction based upon knowledge of subject matter, students, the curriculum, and the community.
      2. Teachers select and/or create learning tasks that make subject matter meaningful to students.
   B. Instructing
      1. Teachers establish and maintain appropriate standards of behavior and create a positive learning environment that shows a commitment to students and their success.
      2. Teachers create instructional opportunities that support students' academic, social, and personal development.
      3. Teachers use effective verbal, nonverbal, and media communications techniques which foster individual and collaborative inquiry.
      4. Teachers employ a variety of instructional strategies that enable students to think critically, solve problems, and demonstrate skills.
   C. Assessing and adjusting
      1. Teachers use various assessment techniques to evaluate student learning and modify instruction as appropriate.

III. Teachers demonstrate professional responsibility through:
   A. Professional and ethical practice
      1. Teachers conduct themselves as professionals in accordance with the Code of Professional Responsibility for Teachers (Section 10-145d-400a of the Certification Regulations).
      2. Teachers share responsibility for student achievement and well-being.
   B. Reflection and continuous learning
      1. Teachers continually engage in self-evaluation of the effects of their choices and actions on students and the school community.
      2. Teachers seek out opportunities to grow professionally.
   C. Leadership and collaboration
      1. Teachers serve as leaders in the school community.
      2. Teachers demonstrate a commitment to their students and passion for improving their profession.

SOURCE: Connecticut Department of Education [May 7, 2001].

- providing effective support and feedback to new teachers so that they continue to develop their knowledge base and skills and choose to remain in the profession;
- providing standards-based professional development for both novice and experienced teachers; and
- developing teacher leaders by recognizing and relying on experienced teachers to support, assess, and train beginning teachers.

As part of the program, school administrators assign new teachers to mentors, provide opportunities for new teachers to work collaboratively with more senior teachers, provide time for professional development, ensure that new teachers have access to resources and support structures, evaluate teachers and offer constructive feedback, and provide an ongoing orientation program <www.state.ct.us/sde>.

During their first year, beginning teachers are evaluated at the district level through live and video observations. They learn how to systematically document their teaching practices and to use student work to demonstrate student learning, and they develop a long-term plan for professional growth. During year two, teachers use feedback from year one to improve their teaching techniques, and they begin to plan for portfolio development. With guidance from their principal, teachers design a professional development plan that supports the BEST portfolio process and that uses the portfolio components as an avenue to support growth in planning, instructing, student work analysis, and reflecting. The portfolio is submitted in the spring of the second year. During the third year of the induction phase, teachers continue to work on the portfolio, as needed, and share their portfolio experience with other beginning teachers. Third-year teachers begin to expand their goals to focus on district and school improvement goals. They also begin to document their professional responsibilities in preparation for professional growth and tenure <www.state.ct.us/sde>.

The Portfolio Assessment

The portfolio assessment is intended to provide a thorough representation of a teacher's performance through documentation of teaching over time and by focusing on a specific content/discipline area. In the portfolio, teachers document their methods of lesson planning, teaching and facilitation of student learning, assessment of student work, and self-reflection within a unit of instruction. The portfolio includes evidence from multiple sources, such as lesson plans, videotapes of teaching, teacher commentaries, examples of student work, and formal and informal assessments (Connecticut Department of Education, 1999). Portfolio assessment requirements vary depending on the beginning teacher's teaching assignment and license endorsement. Content-focused seminars, run by trained teachers, help beginning teachers learn about ways to meet subject specific standards so as to demonstrate content-specific teaching practices (Connecticut State Department of Education, 1999:4).

Scorers are trained to evaluate the portfolios using criteria based on content-focused professional teaching standards. Each portfolio is evaluated by at least two experienced educators with extensive teaching experience in the same disciplinary areas as the beginning teacher. Scorers receive up to 70 hours of training and must meet a proficiency standard in order to be eligible to score a portfolio. In scoring the portfolio, scorers first review the included materials to make notes about the evidence provided. Scorers then organize the evidence around a series of guiding questions derived from the discipline-based standards. The two scorers independently evaluate the quality of the teaching documented in the portfolio according to scoring rubrics and benchmarks and then convene and decide on a final portfolio score. Any portfolio that does not meet the standard of "Competent" is rescored by another pair of assessors. If the second evaluation results in a different score, a "Lead" assessor adjudicates the final score. Teachers whose portfolios do not meet the competency standards are eligible for a personal conference with a portfolio assessor during which they receive individualized feedback about the evaluation (Connecticut State Board of Education, 2000). Such teachers may submit another portfolio during the third year of teaching. If a teacher fails to meet the standard by the third year, the teacher is ineligible to apply for a provisional certificate and cannot teach in Connecticut public schools. To regain certification, an individual needs to successfully complete a formal program of study as approved by the state.

Support for Mentors

School districts are responsible for appointing mentors to beginning teachers. Mentors must have at least three years of teaching experience and must be willing to make the time commitment involved in mentorship activities. Mentors are required to attend a series of training workshops designed to help them prepare for their role in offering guidance to the beginning teacher and in preparing for the portfolio assessment. Mentors and support team leaders receive 20 hours of training focused on the CCT and 10 hours of annual update training.

Professional Development

Throughout the continuous professional growth phase, the components of the CCT are used to establish standards for the evaluation of teachers (according to the Guidelines for Comprehensive Professional Development and Teacher Evaluation) and to guide teachers in selecting appropriate professional development to meet individual as well as local district goals (Connecticut Department of Education, 1999). Teachers who hold either a provisional or professional license must also complete 90 hours of professional development every five years to maintain their licenses. Professional development activities should be directly related to improving teaching and learning.

Role of Other Staff

A number of staff play a role in Connecticut's induction and evaluation program. The school principal is responsible for ensuring that beginning teachers are aware of the BEST program's requirements. Principals facilitate opportunities for mentors and beginning teachers to meet (and to observe each other's classrooms); assist with arranging classroom coverage; and provide resources for portfolio preparation (e.g., videotaping equipment). District facilitators are responsible for providing BEST program orientation sessions, ensuring that beginning teachers receive adequate support from mentors, and arranging for release time so that the mentor and beginning teacher can meet. Release time is acquired by using substitute teachers for the beginning teacher and the mentor(s). The state department of education (through six regional educational service centers) provides distance learning seminars to train mentors and portfolio assessors on the portfolio assessment. The department manages the program; sets policies, standards, and procedures; and assures that the assessment portfolios are reliable and valid.

Studies of Technical Characteristics

The state has conducted numerous studies associated with developing the portfolio assessment, evaluating its psychometric characteristics, and assessing its overall impact on teacher competence in the state. For all subject areas, the discipline-specific standards were developed by committees of experts in the particular subject area, including teachers, curriculum specialists, administrators, and higher-education representatives. As part of the development process, job analysis studies were conducted. Representative samples of teachers, administrators, and higher-education faculty participated in surveys in which they rated the standards in terms of their importance for beginning and experienced teachers, their relevance to the job of teaching, and their importance for advancing student achievement. The standards were further validated by having teachers complete journals to document the degree to which the standards were represented in their actual teaching.

Experts' judgments and portfolio performance data are used in setting the standards for the portfolio assessment and determining the cutpoints. Bias and sensitivity reviews are conducted for the portfolio handbook (the guidelines given to beginning teachers for constructing their portfolios and all related scoring materials), and portfolio performance is broken down by race, gender, type of community, and socioeconomic status to examine disparate impact. Generalizability studies are implemented to estimate reliability of portfolio scores.

A number of studies have been conducted to collect construct-related evidence of validity. These studies have examined the relationships between teachers' performance on the portfolio and (1) other quantitative measures, such as their grade point averages, SAT scores, and Praxis I and II scores; (2) case studies of teachers' performance in the classroom; and (3) student achievement test results in English/language arts, reading, and mathematics.

Additional studies have examined the consequences associated with program implementation. Program effectiveness is evaluated through surveys of mentors, portfolio assessors, school administrators, principals, central office personnel, beginning teachers, and higher-education faculty. In addition, portfolio scorers evaluate their own teaching skills before and after participating in scorer training activities. This information is used qualitatively to judge the impact of scorer training on actual classroom teaching practices.

OHIO'S TEACHER INDUCTION PROGRAM

Overview

Ohio provides an example of a state that plans to incorporate a commercially available program into its licensing system. Ohio is in the process of redesigning its licensing system. The new system, which will be implemented in 2002, includes a comprehensive induction program for beginning teachers, requirements for performance assessment during the induction year administered by the Ohio Department of Education, and procedures to ensure continued professional development for experienced teachers. The new system will eliminate procedures through which teachers were awarded permanent "lifetime" licenses and instead will implement a two-stage system. During the first stage, individuals who complete an approved teacher preparation program and pass required tests (Praxis II, Principles of Teaching and Learning, and the appropriate Praxis II subject matter examination) receive a provisional license. The provisional license is good for two years, is renewable, and entitles individuals to work as full-time or substitute teachers. Teachers who successfully complete Ohio's new Entry Year Program and pass a performance assessment (Praxis III) will receive a professional license (the second stage). The professional license is good for five years, and renewal requires completion of an approved professional development plan and a master's degree or the equivalent after 10 years of teaching.

The Entry Year Program

The new system will require beginning teachers to participate in the Entry Year Program, an induction program designed to provide mentorship, support, and additional learning experiences for new teachers. Ohio has spent the past seven years piloting the Praxis III Classroom Performance Assessment for beginning teachers and approaches for teacher induction programs and is in the process of standardizing approaches to its Entry Year Program. Development and implementation of an Entry Year Program will be the responsibility of individual school districts, but the state will provide guidelines and financial support for development activities. Districts are required to develop an implementation plan, provide orientation sessions, identify and train mentors, arrange for release time for mentors to work with entry-year teachers, conduct assessment activities, and coordinate with higher-education institutions.

As part of the Entry Year Program, experienced teachers serve as mentors to beginning teachers. Whenever possible, mentors teach the same subject or grade level and are located in the same building as the beginning teacher. Serving as a mentor can be incorporated into a veteran teacher's professional development plan and can count toward licensure renewal. Mentor teachers work on an ongoing basis with beginning teachers. They engage in activities designed to help beginning teachers develop their skills in instructional planning and preparation, presentation of various learning activities, and assessment of students' learning.

According to state guidelines, individuals selected to be mentors should be experienced teachers and should demonstrate an awareness of instructional methods and professional responsibilities needed to improve teaching skills and increase student learning. Districts are required to operate an in-depth training program for mentors on ways to conduct observations, provide feedback, and offer professional guidance and support to beginning teachers.

Ohio is focusing on using ETS's PATHWISE Induction Program-Praxis III Version as the basis for its Entry-Year Program. In Ohio this program is called the Ohio FIRST (Formative Induction Results in Stronger Teaching) Year Program.

The PATHWISE Induction Program-Praxis III Version

The PATHWISE Induction Program-Praxis III Version grew from a need for mentors to assist new teachers to focus on successful teaching under the Praxis III framework (D. Gitomer, ETS, personal correspondence, July 1999). The two pieces of the program—the observation/induction system (provided by the district) and the performance assessment (administered by the Ohio department of education)—are built on the same domain of teaching skills. These domains are:

• *Organizing content knowledge for student learning*—how teachers use their understanding of students and subject matter to establish learning goals, design or select appropriate activities and instructional materials, sequence instruction, and design or select evaluation strategies.
• *Creating an environment for student learning*—the social and emotional

components of learning as prerequisites to and context for academic achievement, including classroom interactions between teachers and students and among students.

• *Teaching for student learning*—making learning goals and instructional procedures clear to students, making content comprehensible to students, encouraging students to extend their thinking, monitoring students' understanding of content, and using instructional time effectively.

• *Teacher professionalism*—reflecting on the extent to which the learning goals were met, demonstrating a sense of efficacy, building professional relationships with colleagues, and communicating with parents or guardians about student learning.

Each domain consists of a set of four or five assessment criteria (for a total of 19) that represent critical aspects of teaching (see Box F-6). These criteria were developed over a six-year period based on information collected from job analyses, reviews of empirical and theoretical research, and examinations of states' licensing requirements for teachers (Wesley et al., 1993).

The job analyses involved asking teachers and others familiar with teaching about the importance of the various tasks beginning teachers perform. The job analyses were conducted separately for elementary (Rosenfeld et al., 1992b), middle (Rosenfeld et al., 1992c), and secondary school teachers (Rosenfeld et al., 1992a). A series of literature reviews were also conducted to document what is known both empirically and theoretically about good practice for teachers in general and for beginning teachers in particular (Dwyer, 1994). Finally, information on the teacher licensing requirements of all 50 states and the District of Columbia was compiled. A nationwide content analysis of state performance assessment requirements also was carried out to determine the content overlap among the systems and to highlight distinctive differences (Dwyer, 1994).

Based on the findings of these studies, the test developers drafted an initial set of assessment criteria which were presented to a national advisory committee for comment. Committee comments led to revisions in the criteria, followed by a pilot test of the criteria in two states (Minnesota and Delaware). The results of this field testing formed the basis for finalizing the assessments made available for inspection and initial use by states in the fall of 1992.

According to the ETS developers, the criteria were developed so as to "infuse a multicultural perspective throughout the system" (Dwyer, 1994:4). This perspective is based on the premise that "effective teaching requires familiarity with students' background knowledge and experiences (including their cultural resources), and effective teachers use this familiarity to devise appropriate instruction" (p. 4). The criteria are intended not to prescribe a particular way of teaching but to allow for flexibility in how they can be demonstrated in various classroom contexts.

BOX F-6
PATHWISE Induction Program-Praxis III Version
Assessment Criteria

Domain A: Organizing Content Knowledge for Student Learning
  A1: Becoming familiar with relevant aspects of students' background knowledge and experiences.
  A2: Articulating clear learning goals for the lesson that are appropriate to the students
  A3: Demonstrating an understanding of the connections between the content that was learned previously, the current content, and the content that remains to be learned in the future.
  A4: Creating or selecting teaching methods, learning activities, and instructional materials or other resources that are appropriate to the students and that are aligned with the goals for the lesson.
  A5: Creating or selecting evaluation strategies that are appropriate for the students and that are aligned with the goals of the lesson.

Domain B: Creating an Environment for Student Learning
  B1: Creating a climate that promotes fairness
  B2: Establishing and maintaining rapport with students
  B3: Communicating challenging learning expectations to each student
  B4: Establishing and maintaining consistent standards of classroom behavior
  B5: Making the physical environment as safe and conducive to learning as possible

Domain C: Teaching for Student Learning
  C1: Making learning goals and instructional procedures clear to students
  C2: Making content comprehensible to students
  C3: Encouraging students to extend their thinking
  C4: Monitoring students' understanding of content through a variety of means, providing feedback to students to assist learning, and adjusting learning activities as the situation demands.
  C5: Using instructional time effectively

Domain D: Teacher Professionalism
  D1: Reflecting on the extent to which the learning goals were met
  D2: Demonstrating a sense of efficacy
  D3: Building professional relationship with colleagues to share teaching insights and to coordinate learning activities for students
  D4: Communicating with parents or guardians about student learning

SOURCE: Educational Testing Service, 1995c. Used by permission of the author.

Praxis III: Classroom Performance Assessment

Praxis III is a performance assessment designed to measure beginning teachers' skills in relation to 19 criteria (see Box F-6). The Praxis III assessment uses three data collection methods: (1) direct observation of classroom practice, (2) written descriptions of students and lesson plans, and (3) interviews structured around the classroom observation. Prior to being observed, the beginning teacher provides the trained assessor with written documentation about the general classroom context and the students in the class, as well as specific information about the lesson to be observed. The observation allows assessors to gain a first-hand understanding of the teacher's practices and decisions. The written documentation provides a sense of the general classroom context and the students in the class as well as specific information about the lesson to be observed. Semistructured interviews with the teacher before and after the observation provide an opportunity to explore and reflect on decisions and teaching practices. The interviews also allow assessors to evaluate the teacher's skill in relating instructional decisions to contextual factors, such as student characteristics and prior knowledge (Dwyer, 1994:2-3).

The design of Praxis III was based on the premise that "effective teaching requires both action and decision making and that learning is a process of the active construction of knowledge." This guiding conception makes explicit the belief that "because good teaching is dependent on the subject matter and the students, assessments should not attempt to dictate a teaching method or style that is to be applied in all contexts" (Dwyer, 1994).

PATHWISE Induction Program

The PATHWISE Induction Program is designed to prepare beginning teachers for the Praxis III assessment and to provide opportunities for professional development growth. The PATHWISE system is intended to be a "flexible system responsive to an individual's personal teaching style," incorporating "constructive assessment that fosters growth and professional development in students and first-year teachers by recognizing their strengths as well as their weaknesses" (Educational Testing Service, 1995b:3). The system provides opportunities for beginning teachers to interact with mentors to (1) identify their strengths and weaknesses, (2) develop a plan for improving their teaching skills, and (3) improve their skill in reflecting on their teaching practices.

The program consists of a series of structured interactions between beginning teachers and their mentors. The interactions are referred to as "events," and the activities associated with each event are designed to encourage collaboration between beginning teachers and their mentors. A brief description of the types of events follows:

- The initial interaction is called the Teaching Environment Profile. This event requires beginning teachers to examine the context of their teaching by collecting information about their students and about the environment (including the district and the community) within which the school is located.

• The next interaction is called Profiles of Practice—Observation of Classroom Practice. Two observation events take place in which the mentor teacher observes the beginning teacher leading an instructional lesson. The mentor then provides feedback based on the observation and on review of planning materials, oral and written reflections, and examples of student work.

• Three inquiry tasks are also scheduled for beginning teachers. These tasks require beginning teachers to explore specific aspects of their teaching practice. To complete each event, beginning teachers must gather information about a selected aspect of teaching using a variety of resources, including their colleagues, research journals, and texts. Together with the mentor, the beginning teacher develops a plan of action to try out in the classroom, implements the plan, and reflects on the experience. The inquiry events focus on ways to establish a positive classroom environment, design an instructional experience, and analyze student work.

• Teachers also participate in two events called Individual Growth Plans. The individual growth plans are designed to help beginning teachers determine how best to focus their efforts throughout the entire induction process. To complete these events, beginning teachers must prepare a plan for professional learning that takes into account their teaching practices, school or district initiatives, and other challenges they may face.

• The final induction activities are referred to as Closure Events: Assessment and Colloquium. These interactions help bring closure to the year by engaging beginning teachers in self-assessment, encouraging a final evaluation of professional learning, and promoting the sharing of professional knowledge with other beginning teachers.

A total of 10 events occur over the course of the school year. All of the inquires and observations make use of planning, teaching, reflecting, and applying what is learned. The activities encourage beginning teachers to participate in reflective writing, conversations with experienced colleagues, and ongoing examination of teaching in relation to student learning (Educational Testing Services, 1995a).

Training of Mentors and Assessors

Since the PATHWISE Induction Program-Praxis III Version relies on effective use of observational data, extensive training is required. ETS offers three levels of training for the program. An initial two-day training in the PATHWISE Classroom Observation system acquaints individuals with the 19 criteria that form the basis for the program and is a prerequisite for other levels of training. Participants receive instruction in recording observational data, analyzing written contextual information, using written and observational information to evaluate performance, writing summaries of teacher performance, and providing feedback to beginning teachers. Training relies on simulations, case studies, sample evaluation forms, and videotapes.

A four-day training session familiarizes individuals with the PATHWISE Induction Program-Praxis III Version. This seminar focuses on training mentors in the uses and purposes of 10 ten events and in developing their mentoring and coaching skills.

The seminar for Praxis III assessors is the final level of training and is five days in duration. The training consists of a series of structured activities during which participants learn to recognize the presence of each of the 19 Praxis III criteria. Participants learn to evaluate written information provided by the teacher, take notes during classroom observations, and conduct semistructured interviews. The training process utilizes a variety of stimuli, including worksheets, sample records of evidence, simulations, case studies, and videotapes. Trainees receive feedback from instructor and fellow participants. They also engage in professional reflection through journal writing.

Implementation of Pathwise Induction Program-Praxis III Version in Ohio

ETS offers training for mentors and assessors but also provides instructional modules for individuals to learn how to conduct the training sessions. Individuals in Ohio have learned the ETS procedures, and the state now offers its own training sessions.

Training in the PATHWISE Classroom Observation System has been incorporated into Ohio's preservice program to introduce students to the 19 criteria. Many state institutions have incorporated the domains into their preservice education programs, and their focus will be on using the PATHWISE rubrics to evaluate students' progress. PATHWISE Classroom Observation System training is also available for teachers who plan to become mentors. Approximately 15,000 teachers have completed this training (John Nickelson, Ohio Department of Education, personal communication, March 19, 2001).

Implementation of the Praxis III Performance Assessment

Beginning teachers in Ohio will be required to pass Praxis III starting in 2002. Ohio teachers who do not pass it after their first year may try again during the second year. Failure to complete the Entry-Year Program's requirements successfully after the second attempt will result in loss of the provisional license until such time as the candidate completes additional coursework, supervised field experiences, and/or clinical experiences as designated by a college or university approved for teacher preparation and is recommended by such college or university.

ABILITY-BASED TEACHER EDUCATION AT
ALVERNO COLLEGE

Overview

In this case study the committee provides a description of teacher education and assessment as practiced at Alverno College, in Milwaukee, Wisconsin. Alverno College undertook development of a performance-based baccalaureate degree over 20 years ago (Diez, et al., 1998). This change resulted in an overhaul of the college's curriculum and its approach to teaching. The approach is characterized by publicly articulated learning outcomes, realistic classroom activities and field experiences, and ongoing performance assessments of learning progress. Alverno's program is of interest because it provides an example of a system in which a party other than a state or district could warrant teacher competence. The focus here is on Alverno as a working program that can expand the debate about other models for warranting teacher competence.

Alverno College has an enrollment of approximately 1,900 students in 66 fields of study, 300 of whom are education majors. With the exception of a postbaccalaureate teacher certification program and the master of arts in education program, all programs admit only female students. Two-thirds of Alverno's students are from the Milwaukee area, and about 30 percent are members of minority groups. There are about 100 faculty members, and the average class size is 25. The next section provides a brief overview of Alverno's philosophy and practices.[2]

Abilities and Learning Outcomes for the Baccalaureate Degree

At Alverno College an ability is defined as "a complex integration of knowledge, behaviors, skills, values, attitudes, and self-perceptions" (Diez et al., 1994:9). The general education courses provide students with the opportunity to expand and demonstrate each of eight abilities:

• *Communication*—an ability to communicate effectively by integrating a variety of communication abilities (speaking, writing, listening, reading, quantitative, media literacy) to meet the demands of increasingly complex communication situations.

• *Analysis*—an ability to be a clear thinker, fusing experience, reasoning, and training into considered judgment.

---

[2]Mentkowski and Associates (2000) gives a comprehensive picture of Alverno's practices and philosophy, and Zeichner (2000) provides an independent description of Alverno's teacher education practices.

• *Problem solving*—an ability to define problems and integrate a range of abilities and resources to reach decisions, make recommendations, or implement action plans.

• *Values within decision making*—an ability to reflect and to habitually seek to understand the moral dimensions of decisions and to accept responsibility for the consequences of actions.

• *Social interaction*—an understanding of how to get things done in committees, task forces, team projects, and other group efforts.

• *Global perspective*—an ability to articulate interconnections between and among diverse opinions, ideas, and beliefs about global issues.

• *Effective citizenship*—an ability to make informed choices and develop strategies for collaborative involvement in community issues.

• *Aesthetic responsiveness*—an ability to make informed responses to artistic works that are grounded in knowledge of the theoretical, historical, and cultural contexts.

The abilities cut across disciplines and are subdivided into six developmental levels. The six levels represent a developmental sequence that begins with objective awareness of one's own performance process for a given ability and specifies increasingly complex knowledge, skills, and dispositions. Students must demonstrate consistent performance at level 4 for each of the eight abilities prior to graduation. An example of the development levels for problem solving appears in Box F-7.

Each of Alverno's educational programs also defines a set of abilities distinctive to each major and minor area. These outcomes, identified by faculty as essen-

---

BOX F-7
Levels of Learning Outcomes for Problem Solving

Level	Benchmark
1	Articulate own problem-solving process, making explicit the steps taken to approach the problem(s)
2	Analyze the stucture of discipline- or profession-based problem-solving frameworks
3	Use discipline- of profession-based problem-solving frameworks and strategies
4	Independently examine, select, use, and evaluate various approaches to develop solutions

In majors and areas of specialization:

5	Collaborate in designing and implementing a problem-solving process
6	Solve problems in a variety of professional settings and advanced disciplinary applications

SOURCE: Alverno College Faculty, 1973/2000.

tial learning outcomes, relate to and extend the general education abilities (Loacker and Mentkowski, 1993). Within the major area of study, students are expected to achieve at least a level 5 for each of the program's abilities (Zeichner, 2000).

Abilities and Learning Outcomes in Teacher Education

Alverno's Department of Education offers degree programs in elementary, early childhood, secondary, bilingual, music, art, and adult education. All education programs are designed to foster the same set of teaching abilities. These teaching abilities define professional levels of proficiency that are required for graduation with a major in any of the teacher education programs. The teaching abilities refine and extend the general education abilities into the professional teaching context. While the professional teaching abilities are introduced in the first year, they receive heavy emphasis during the junior and senior years. The teaching abilities include:

- *Conceptualization*—integrating content knowledge with educational frameworks and a broadly based understanding of the liberal arts in order to plan and implement instruction.
- *Diagnosis*—relating observed behavior to relevant frameworks in order to determine and implement learning prescriptions.
- *Coordination*—managing resources effectively to support learning goals.
- *Communication*—using verbal, nonverbal, and media modes of communication to establish the environment of the classroom and to structure and reinforce learning.
- *Integrative interaction*—acting with professional values as a situational decision maker, adapting to the changing needs of the environment in order to develop students as learners.

Each of the above education abilities is further described for faculty and candidates through maps (Diez et al., 1998). In the maps, development of the ability is defined in terms of what teachers would be expected to do with their knowledge and skills at various stages of their development. An example based on skill in integrative interaction follows: the *beginning* teacher would demonstrate ability in integrative interaction by showing respect for varied learner perspectives; the *experienced* teacher would provide structures within which learners create their own perspectives; and the *master* teacher would assist learners in the habit of taking on multiple perspectives. This type of mapping is intended to "capture the interactions between knowing and doing" (Diez et al., 1998:43).

Alverno's Program for Education Majors

Alverno's program for education majors is designed to address the developmental needs of learners. Concepts are addressed in an integrated fashion, across multiple courses and settings to enable a "deepened understanding" that comes with repetition of concepts (Diez, 1999:233). The program is characterized by extensive opportunities for field experiences that require candidates to apply what they have learned. Coursework and field experiences are sequenced to build developmentally across the years of the program. For example, candidates begin with coursework and field experiences that require them to apply the frameworks they are learning with individual students or small groups in tutorial settings. They progress to more complex tasks with larger groups and whole-class instruction. The assignments gradually increase in complexity, requiring candidates to attend to multiple factors in their planning, their analysis of the classroom, and their implementation of learning experiences (Diez, 1999:233).

Self-reflection and self-assessment skills are emphasized at Alverno. Faculty have developed a set of reflective logs that guide students in each of four semester-long field experiences prior to student teaching. These logs are intended to help students develop their skills in the five education abilities. According to Diez (1999), the logs direct students to make links between theoretical knowledge and practical application (which develops skill in conceptualization and diagnosis), to observe processes and environments of learning (coordination skills), to translate content knowledge into suitable short presentations or learning experiences (communication skills), and to begin to translate their philosophy of education into decisions regarding all aspects of teaching environments and processes (integrative interaction).

The first stage of the education program is the preprofessional level. To apply to the preprofessional level, students must have completed one year of coursework, a required one-credit human relations workshop, and a portion of the math content requirements (Zeichner, 2000). The preprofessional stage lasts two semesters. During this time, education students begin to integrate the knowledge bases of the liberal arts disciplines with the process for applying the material from these disciplines (Alverno College Institute, 1996). The subject area methods courses are taught during this stage. These courses connect teaching methods with material learned in liberal arts general education courses. Performance assessments during this stage may consist of such activities as requiring teacher candidates to create a lesson for a given grade that incorporates knowledge about developmental psychology. Other performance assessments involve simulations in which prospective teachers take on the various roles that teachers play, such as conducting a parent-teacher conference, being part of a multidisciplinary evaluation team, or working with district planning activities. This period includes two pre-student teaching experiences.

After two semesters in the preprofessional stage and completion of two of the pre-student teaching experiences, teacher candidates can apply for admission to the professional level. To be admitted, they must successfully complete the first two field experiences (and provide letters of recommendation), demonstrate a specific ability, meet the statewide minimum cutoff scores on the required

Praxis exams, and pass several standard assessment exercises that are spread throughout the program (Zeichner, 2000). An example of one these standard assessments is the Behavioral Event Interview and Self-Assessment described by Zeichner (2000:10):

> [This assessment is] an hour-long interview conducted in the second semester of field experiences. Each education department member interviews two students each semester. The aim of the interview is to give students a chance to talk about their actions and thinking in relation to working with pupils. It focuses on stories elicited by questions (e.g., Can you tell me about the time you came to a realization about children's development through an experience with a child or children?). The students then are asked to use their stories as data for a self-assessment process focusing on the five advanced education abilities (e.g., Where do you see yourself drawing upon x ability? Where do you see a need to strengthen this ability?). The interview is audiotaped and students take the tape with them to complete a written self-assessment. They set goals for their next stage of development in the teacher education program and then meet for a second session with the faculty interviewer.

The final two semesters are considered the beginning of professional practice, during which student teaching occurs. To be accepted for student teaching, students must demonstrate communication ability at level 4, successfully complete all four pre-student teaching experiences, and pass another standard assessment exercise—the Professional Group Discussion Assessment. Zeichner (2000:11) also describes this assessment:

> Students compile a portfolio that includes a videotape of their teaching together with a written analysis of that teaching in relation to the five advanced education abilities, cooperating teacher evaluations, etc. The student then participates in a half-day interview with principals and teachers from area schools who are part of a pool of over 400 educators helping to assess students' readiness for student teaching.

Assessment as Learning

The philosophy behind Alverno's program is based on the premise that only through integrating knowledge, skills, and dispositions in observable performances can evidence of learning be shown. Assessment is treated as integral to learning. It is used both to document the development of the abilities and to contribute to candidates' development. Alverno's faculty describe their approach as assessment as learning (Diez et al., 1998). As practiced at Alverno, assessment as learning has the following features:

- Expected learning outcomes or abilities are stated, and candidates are aware of the goals toward which they are working.
- Explicit criteria for performance are outlined to guide candidates' work and to provide structure for self-assessment.

- Evaluations are based on expert judgments using evidence of candidates' performance and weighing it against established criteria.
- Feedback is intended to be productive; it is not aimed at judgment alone but on ongoing development.
- All assessments include the experience of reflective self-assessment.
- Assessment is a process involving multiple performances. Candidates experience many assessments using multiple modes, methods, and times to provide a cumulative picture of their development.

Assessment begins during orientation and continues through graduation. For instance, all new students complete an initial communications assessment that includes writing and presenting. The presentation is recorded on videotape, and each student evaluates her own performance before receiving diagnostic and prescriptive feedback from expert assessors.

Alverno faculty believe that performance assessments should be as realistic as possible and should closely mimic the experiences of practicing teachers. In developing the curriculum, they have identified the variety of roles that teachers play. Performance assessments include simulations of parent-teacher interactions, multidisciplinary team evaluation, the teacher's work with district or building planning, and the teacher's citizenship role, as well as actual classroom teaching (Diez et al., 1998:2).

Each course is structured around the assessments and learning outcomes that must be demonstrated to claim mastery of the course material. Box F-8 contains two examples: the learning outcomes for a course at Alverno and a course assessment designed to evaluate mastery of one of the outcomes.

Coursework is intentionally sequenced to reflect developmental growth and to provide for cross-course application of concepts. For example, a mathematics methods course assessment might ask students to (1) create a mathematics lesson plan for first graders that incorporates concepts from developmental psychology, (2) teach the lesson, and (3) describe the responses of the learners and the adaptations made.

Alverno requires that student teachers perform all of the duties of a teacher effectively, assuming full responsibility for the classroom for a minimum of four weeks in each placement. They start and end each day of teaching on the same schedule as the cooperating teacher. Their performance is assessed on the five professional teaching abilities by the cooperating teacher, the college supervisor(s), and the student teacher herself.

Research and Program Evaluation

Alverno has documented in detail the ways in which its program abilities were developed. The eight general education abilities were identified during discussions with faculty members about "what it means to say that a student has

---

BOX F-8
Learning Outcomes for Integrated Reading 3

- Analyze and apply learning theory in designing and implementing literacy instruction.
- Assess literacy development of intermediate students and prescribe appropriate teaching strategies.
- Use knowledge of writing workshop and reading workshop strategies and implement workshops in the intermediate classroom.
- Evaluate text and trade books for use with intermediate learners.
- Integrate technology to enhance the writing process in the classroom.
- Show refined communication skills to support professional growth.
- Demonstrate knowledge of classroom research with understanding of the dynamics of the classroom and of how to improve practice.

Assessment of Learning Outcome 2:

Assess literacy development of intermediate students and prescribe appropriate teaching strategies.

To assess mastery of the second outcome, students are asked to develop and use a rubric to assess actual intermediate-grade writing samples. Students analyze writing samples for strengths and weaknesses, and plan appropriate teaching strategies based on that analysis. Students then collaborate in formulating a teaching plan. Finally, they evaluate their own efforts on each component of the task.

Successful performance in this assessment depends on satisfying four criteria: (1) assessing the developmental level of the learner's performance and providing sufficient evidence to support the judgment, (2) diagnosing areas requiring attention/instruction and providing an appropriate teaching plan, (3) contributing to the group discussion of the process, and (4) assessing one's own performance on all components of the task.

Each of these four criteria is mapped to one or more of the education abilities at a specified level of performance (e.g., *Diagnosis* at level 5, *Coordination* at level 5) and noted as such in the course syllabus. Hence, assessment criteria are always publicized, and the paths connecting particular concrete activity and general abstract ability can be easily traced. Assessments and their links are reviewed on an ongoing basis by interdisciplinary teams. Similar assessments and sets of criteria exist for each level of outcome for each of the abilities.

SOURCE: Adapted from Alverno College Institute (1996:7).

---

completed a liberal arts baccalaureate degree" (Diez, 1999:41). The abilities emerged from faculty discussions focused on such questions as: What should a woman educated in liberal arts be able to *do* with her knowledge? How does the curriculum provide coherent and developmental support to her learning? What counts as evidence that a student has achieved the expectations of the degree, the major, and the professional preparation? Once the abilities were defined, the discussions centered on pedagogical, developmental, and measurement questions. Descriptions of the abilities and corresponding performance levels have evolved over the years as a result of many factors. There is ongoing interdisciplinary consultation and review. Each faculty member is expected to serve on a program evaluation and development committee.

Alverno's performance-based assessments are designed to reflect the actual work of beginning professional teachers. They cover the content and skills considered relevant to the tasks that teachers are expected to perform. In addition, the context for assessments is intended to reflect real-life teaching situations, representing a broad sample of performance situations (broader than would be expected for assessments that focus on basic skills and subject matter knowledge). Committees of faculty members routinely audit the contents of the assessments (during regularly scheduled departmental meetings) to verify that they are appropriate and that they reflect current thinking about what teachers should know and be able to do.

Multiple judgments are obtained of each student's skills and knowledge. Each student is observed and assessed hundreds of times as they participate in classroom and field activities. Evaluations utilize multiple contexts, multiple modes, and multiple evaluators. There are formal, "milestone" assessments staged at relevant points in the curriculum, such as the Behavioral Event Interview and Self-Assessment and the Professional Group Discussion Assessment described above, as well as less formal, ongoing, in-class assessments. The institution has processes in place for refining and updating criteria for judging students' performance.

There have been both internal and external reviews of the program. The institution has maintained an Office of Research and Evaluation since 1976 (Mentokowksi, 1991). Through this office, a comprehensive longitudinal study of 750 students was conducted that tracked students from entry into the program through two years after graduation. For this study, researchers collected information on (1) student performance in the curriculum on college-designed ability measures; (2) student perceptions of reasons for learning, the process of learning, and its value for their own career and life goals; and (3) students' personal growth after graduation (Mentkowski and Doherty, 1984).

Another piece of the longitudinal study involved collecting data from a group of alumnae five years after graduation. This research focused on how abilities learned in college transferred to the work setting, the extent to which alumnae continued to grow and develop after college, and how graduates were doing in their careers and further learning in the long term. This study used multiple research instruments (17) to collect data, including questionnaires, tests, essays, and interviews (Alverno College, 1992-1993).

In addition, surveys have collected data from Alverno graduates on their perceptions about the college's program and the extent to which they felt prepared to teach upon graduation (Zeichner, 2000). Surveys and focus groups with principals have examined employers' perceptions of the preparedness of Alverno graduates (Zeichner, 2000). Surveys have also compared longevity in the teaching field for Alverno alumnae with graduates of other programs.

Licensing Practices in Wisconsin

Wisconsin currently requires that students admitted into its teacher education programs pass a basic skills test. Alverno also has developed its own assessments for reading, listening, writing, speaking, and quantitative literacy through four levels, and these are required for graduation. Entering the classroom requires endorsement from the institution from which one graduates. Alverno uses successful completion of field experiences and course requisites and its many formal and informal assessments of students as the basis for warranting readiness to teach.

In 2004 the state of Wisconsin will require candidates for teaching positions to present portfolios demonstrating their performance in relation to several professional teaching standards. Candidates who pass the portfolio review will be granted provisional licenses to teach for three to five years while pursuing professional development goals related to the standards. The portfolios are meant to comprise performance assessments compiled near the time of graduation. In addition, the state's standards make provision for a yet-to-be-specified content examination.

Appendix G

Biographical Sketches of Committee Members

David Z. Robinson (*Chair*) is a former executive vice president and treasurer of the Carnegie Corporation of New York. He also served as executive director of the Carnegie Commission on Science, Technology, and Government, which recommended improvements in the mechanisms by which the federal and state governments incorporate scientific and technological knowledge into decision making. Prior to joining the Carnegie Corporation, Dr. Robinson worked in the White House as a staff scientist in the Office of the President's Science Advisor and as vice president for academic affairs at New York University. He was a member of the Panel on Alternatives for the National Research Council's Committees for a Study of the Structure of the NIH, the Committee on Minorities in Science, and the Committee on Women in Science. Dr. Robinson received his Ph.D. in chemical physics from Harvard University.

Linda Darling-Hammond is the Charles E. Ducommun professor of teaching and teacher education at Stanford University, where her research focuses on school restructuring, teacher education, and educational equity. She also is executive director of the National Commission on Teaching and America's Future, a blue-ribbon panel that has studied policy changes aimed at improving teaching and schooling. She served as chair of both New York State's Council on Curriculum and Assessment and the Model Standards Committee for the Interstate New Teacher Assessment and Support Consortium. She is coauthor of *A License to Teach: Raising Standards for Teaching* (Jossey-Bass Inc., 1999). Dr. Darling-Hammond received her Ed.D. in urban education from Temple University.

Carl A. Grant is the Hoefs-Bascom professor of teacher education and a professor of Afro-American studies at the University of Wisconsin, Madison. His research focuses on multicultural education and teacher education, and he is president of the National Association for Multicultural Education. Dr. Grant received his Ph.D. in education, curriculum, and instruction from the University of Wisconsin.

Milton D. Hakel is a professor and the Ohio Board of Regents eminent scholar in psychology at Bowling Green State University. His research focuses on leadership development, performance appraisal, job analysis and compensation, and employee selection. He also is president of Organizational Research and Development, Inc., a firm that provides human resources research consultation. Dr. Hakel serves on the National Research Council's Board on Testing and Assessment. He received his Ph.D. in psychology from the University of Minnesota.

Abigail L. Hughes is associate commissioner of the Division of Evaluation and Research, Connecticut State Department of Education and is responsible for the state's student assessment program, beginning teacher induction program, and statewide data collection, evaluation, and research. Prior to joining the Connecticut agency, she served as director of instructional services for a regional service agency in New York state, as a teacher in Maryland and Florida, and as a curriculum coordinator in Ohio. Dr. Hughes received her Ph.D. in educational administration and an M.B.A. from Ohio State University.

Mary M. Kennedy is a professor in the College of Education at Michigan State University, where her research focuses on teacher education and learning. From 1986 through 1993, she directed the National Center for Research on Teacher Learning, a federally funded research center based at Michigan State University. Dr. Kennedy received her Ph.D. in educational psychology from Michigan State University.

Stephen P. Klein is a senior research scientist at the RAND Corporation, where he conducts studies on educational testing policies and practices. He also provides consulting services for various certification and licensing examinations. Dr. Klein served on the National Research Council's Committee on Appropriate Test Use and the Committee on Education Finance. He is also coauthor of *A License to Teach: Raising Standards for Teaching* (Jossey-Bass Inc., 1999), Dr. Klein received his Ph.D. in industrial psychology from Purdue University.

Catherine Manski is a lecturer and field instructor for English student teachers in the Department of English, University of Illinois, Chicago. Previously, she was a social studies and English-as-a-second-language teacher at West High

School in Madison, Wisconsin. Ms. Manski received her M.S. in curriculum and instruction from the University of Wisconsin, Madison.

C. Ford Morishita is a biology teacher at Clackamas High School in Milwaukie, Oregon, and was the 1997 Oregon State Teacher of the Year. He also teaches in the School of Education at Portland State University. He received his M.A.T. in biological science from Lewis and Clark College.

Pamela A. Moss is an associate professor in the School of Education at the University of Michigan. Her research focuses on the validity of educational assessments, particularly the assessment of teachers. Dr. Moss serves on the joint committee revising the Standards for Educational and Psychological Testing of the American Educational Research Association, the American Psychological Association, and the National Council of Measurement in Education. She also cochairs the technical advisory committee for the Interstate New Teacher Assessment and Support Consortium and serves on the Measurement Research Advisory Panel of the National Board for Professional Teaching Standards. Dr. Moss received her Ph.D. in educational research methodology from the University of Pittsburgh.

Barbara S. Plake is director of the Oscar and Luella Buros Center for Testing and the W.C. Meierhenry distinguished university professor at the University of Nebraska, Lincoln. She is coeditor of the *Mental Measurements Yearbook* and *Applied Measurement in Education*. Dr. Plake serves on the American Psychological Association's Committee on Psychological Tests and Assessments. She received her Ph.D. in educational statistics and measurement from the University of Iowa.

David L. Rose is an attorney in private practice in Washington, D.C., specializing in equal employment opportunity issues and other employment-related matters. From 1969 through 1987, he was chief of the Employment Litigation Section, Civil Rights Division, U.S. Department of Justice, which is responsible for enforcement of laws requiring nondiscrimination in employment and equal employment opportunity. Mr. Rose received his L.L.B. from Harvard Law School.

Portia Holmes Shields is president of Albany State University. A former teacher and reading specialist, she has also served as the dean of the School of Education at Howard University. Dr. Shields received her Ph.D. in early childhood and elementary education from the University of Maryland, College Park.

James W. Stigler is a professor of psychology at the University of California, Los Angeles. His research focuses on comparative studies of mathematics and science teaching and learning among elementary and middle school children in different countries, including Japan, China, the Czech Republic, Netherlands, Switzerland, Australia, and the United States. Dr. Stigler is coauthor of *The Teaching Gap: Best Ideas from the World's Teachers for Improving Education in the Classroom* (The Free Press, 1999). He received his Ph.D. in developmental psychology from the University of Michigan.

Kenneth I. Wolpin is a professor of economics at the University of Pennsylvania. His research focuses on life-cycle decision making. Dr. Wolpin serves on the National Research Council's Board on Testing and Assessment. He received his Ph.D. in economics from the Graduate School of the City University of New York.

Index

A

Ability-based teacher education at Alverno College, 322-330
  abilities and learning outcomes for the baccalaureate degree, 322-324
  abilities and learning outcomes in teacher education, 324
  Alverno's program for education majors, 324-326
  assessment as learning, 326-327
  research and program evaluation, 327-330

Accountability
  and evaluation, 196-198
  of higher education institutions for quality of teacher preparation, 8-9, 170-171
  for holding states and higher education institutions, 138-145
  improving with teacher licensure tests, 136-146
  for programs that prepare teachers, 198-201

Accreditation of teacher education programs, 42-43

ACT, 132

Administration of teacher licensure tests, 77-78

Administrative provisions, under Public Law 105-244, 194-196

Admission requirements, for teacher education, state-specified, 43

Alaska's initial teacher licensure system, 57-58, 269-272
  post baccalaureate teacher preparation at the University of Alaska, 271-272
  redesign of teacher education, 270-272
  teacher education at Alaska's private schools, 272

Alternative assessment strategies
  ability-based teacher education at Alverno College, 322-330
  analysis of, 158-162
  case studies, 298-330
  Connecticut's teacher preparation and induction program, 308-315
  Ohio's teacher induction program, 315-321
  performance assessment of experienced teachers by the NBPTS, 298-308

Alternative preparation programs for teachers, 44
  in Maryland's licensure system, 285-286

Alverno College, 149, 156-158
  ability-based teacher education at, 322-330
  assessment as learning, 326-327
  outcomes for the baccalaureate degree, 322-324
  outcomes in teacher education, 324
  program for education majors, 324-326
  research and program evaluation, 327-330

Angoff. *See* Modified Angoff method

U

V